JESUS:

WHO IS HE?

JESUS

Who Is He?

by

Flor Hofmans

Translated by

Mary Foran

NEWMAN PRESS

Glen Rock, N.J.   New York, N.Y.

Amsterdam   Toronto   London

A Newman Press Edition, originally published under the title *Het licht van de wereld*, © 1966 by Patmos-Antwerpen, Belgium.

NIHIL OBSTAT:
Rev. Robert E. Hunt, S.T.D.
Censor Librorum

IMPRIMATUR:
✠ Thomas A. Boland, S.T.D.
Archbishop of Newark

April 4, 1968

The Nihil Obstat and Imprimatur are official declarations that a book or pamphlet is free of doctrinal or moral error. No implication is contained therein that those who have granted the Nihil Obstat and Imprimatur agree with the contents, opinions or statements expressed.

Library of Congress
Catalog Card Number: 68-31260

Published by Newman Press
Editorial Office: 304 W. 58th St., N.Y., N.Y. 10019
Business Office: Glen Rock, New Jersey 07452
Printed and bound in the
United States of America

Contents

Foreword

"That I may know him" (Phil. 3, 10).

There are brilliant books about Christ, some a bit too brilliant. I have not read many of them and am not trying to emulate them. Fortunately there are also scholarly books about Christ and they cannot by their nature be scholarly enough. However, they are often too difficult for nonspecialists. There are also books of a meditative nature that have consciously chosen Christ as their main theme. In the final analysis these are indispensable.

The following pages extend in both these directions and are intended as a modest preparation for further study and deeper reflection. For this reason there are sufficient footnotes to give an idea of the full extent of the field but not too many for those who are not scripture scholars. There has likewise not been an attempt to achieve the introspective atmosphere of a meditation or the somewhat elevated style of a dissertation—more objective data are necessary, i.e., a knowledge that enlightens, which is perhaps a little dry, but solid, varied and critical.

Our sole purpose is to get to know Christ personally. What did he say? What did he do? Who is he? In my opinion these three questions contain Christ's whole message in the gospels, and the answer—although sketched all too imperfectly in this book—is so very beautiful and sheds so much brightness over our whole existence that we do not hesitate to summarize it in one forceful sentence from John: "Jesus is the light of the world."

I have written this book with mixed feelings of satisfaction and dissatisfaction. The natural fear of any author that others would produce a better result than he is in this case transformed into joy. This or that introduction to the gospels will disappear, but the gospels will remain. The hope of the introducer is to make himself dispensable in the best manner: "He must increase, but I must decrease" (Jn. 3, 30).

Santiago
April 19, 1964

F. HOFMANS

Introduction

With Modern Eyes

We can see only with our own eyes, and our view is necessarily that of our own day. We have only modern eyes for making the acquaintance of Christ. Our eyes see sharply, somewhat skeptically; they desire to fathom the cosmos, cling to what is concrete, become blurred when faced with wide syntheses, and feel the need to look, observe, examine and enjoy along with others, that is, as a community.

Those who wish to speak about Christ today must bear this in mind. It is a condition for being understood and equally one for understanding. Whole books can be compiled with impeccably developed biblical subjects without ever touching the bottom. Understanding is reaching the bottom and standing on it. And this happens only when there is a living bond, an essential relationship between the foundation and the person, between what is spoken and who is understanding it—in our case, between the Gospel and modern man.

Consequently, the Word of God, which we refer to as the Gospel, has to be *translated* not only into English but also into the post-atomic age or, if we wish to express it more modestly to future generations, into the penultimate technological age. This will present a serious problem for the *method* of this book. Yet before considering this, we must question the very purpose of a study of Christ.

Modern man looks forward. The past is in general too infirm to be dwelt upon for long. Moreover, when all is said and done, it is over and irretrievably lost. The future alone is important, and we are in a position to guide it. Together with spaceships we are also steering the ship of time. Man has just now become both the subject and author of his own history. Our first question is therefore: What is the meaning of Christ for the future of mankind?

3

CHRIST AND OUR FUTURE

Is Christ written in the future of our continent and of that other continent which is our innermost self? What will become of religions and, in particular, of Christianity in the next few centuries? If it is merely a matter of surviving the next thirty or forty years and then dying out, it is not worthwhile, even if I can (which certainly seems incredible) in the meantime manage to acquire my own "eternal salvation." If God exists—and without God there is no heaven—then he cannot desert the world. He is the creator of heaven and earth. Consequently . . .

In my opinion, the future of religions is seen by many people wearing rose-colored glasses. It is clear that the phenomenon of religion is passing through a crisis such as has never existed before. For the first time in history, millions of human beings are declaring that they do not believe in God. Many more are in practice living without need of him, while a very great number of people consider it a useful and urgent task to radically exterminate religion.

The new ideal—and consequently the new religion if religion is what one considers to be the most important thing in life, the absolute—seems to consist in meeting quite different needs than those of a religious nature.[1] The trends that really determine world opinion and the "prevailing" mentality are in most cases not religious; they have become so powerful that they have in many cases already destroyed religion. For a religion that is no longer the most important thing in life is no longer absolute. It is consequently no longer a religion, even if "it lives on" in thousands of customs and formulae.

What Are Modern Needs?

What the modern needs are, we find strikingly typified in the following conversation between the famous mayor La Pira of Florence and the ambassador of a Communist country:

"What are the essential problems of your city?" asked the ambassador.

"The same," answered La Pira, "as those of your capital and of all cities, great and small, in all countries of the world. That is to say, we have to provide people with an assured entry to everything that is necessary for meeting their direct needs."

"And what are those direct needs?"

"The following: a house for living, a factory (or a shop or a field or an office) for working, a school for learning, a hospital for recovering from illness, finally, at the end of this list, but occupying first place in the scale of values and in the order of aims, a church (or a temple or a mosque or a pagoda, etc.) for praying." [2]

La Pira's list with its five items is of course incomplete, but it does have the correct symbolism and suggestive power. The needs will differ in their concrete form and also depend on the stage of development. In the first four forms of emancipation, of freedom, we see a house, that is to say, a place no longer on the premises of a large landowner, but apart, with one's wife and children, something of one's own, a home where you can speak freely and eat. We see a factory or work that provides a salary; men no longer being paid in kind, and if need be, fleeing from the dying countryside and having no elbowroom in a city, but at least doing what you want with your own money. And your children will go to school and emancipate themselves even more there, free with regard to customs, traditions, prejudices; school renders one critical and emancipates thinking itself. And the hospitals liberate you from the tyranny of superstition, charlatans, and even to a certain extent from the pallid ghosts called sickness and death. To work for these four fundamental needs of the modern city is to emancipate man, and this is a "deliverance" which is felt by all. Is this to be the religion of the future?

La Pira mentioned a fifth major need, i.e., a place, or perhaps more appropriately expressed, the conditions for *praying*. Agreement on this is not so unanimous. In its stead, many would place another fifth category alongside a home, factory, school and hospital, e.g., culture, beauty, science, play. These, too, are higher things. Even in Communist countries people write about something in the nature of a sixth sense that emits signals: "Not from bread alone . . ."

The question is, however, whether this exalted experience, which has its houses of stillness and its festive halls and which seeks to impart the highest emotions to its members, is really of a genuinely religious nature. Must we also not place alongside the temple and

---

[1] It seems impossible to me in Dutch to use the name, "service of God," for such religion; a religion without God is, after all, too silly. A godless religion is at least linguistically not so silly.

[2] Related by La Pira himself during a lecture in Brussels on March 11, 1958, and published in *Esquisses pour une politique chrétienne* (Paris, Plon, 1958), p. 31. The conversation itself took place in 1955.

mosque, the pagoda and chapel, the theaters and festive palaces, the stadiums and museums, or more simply, the poetic spots on roaring coasts or between the white-capped mountains? The problem is, in fact, to know whether our mystic function is going to operate with or without God. And here the task of Christianity is—and this will appear from what follows—decisive.

Christianity and Progress

An important element in predicting the future of religions is their power to be reconciled with modern progress. It is, after all, impossible to live with two ideals or, according to the words of Jesus, to serve two masters. Whoever is carried along by the universal urge to cover the "usual" needs as quickly and as completely as possible —points one to four in La Pira's list—will eventually have to choose a form of "mysticism"—point five of La Pira—which is to be brought into harmony with it. Well then, can religion be reconciled with the progress which completely characterizes "normal" life in our century of technical revolutions?

The Marxists answer this question in the negative and launch themselves with a somewhat naïve optimism into creating an earthly paradise that cannot even be visited by angels. Many others influenced by existentialism say, "No," just as clearly but with the lucid pessimism of experience proper to the better-off classes: God does not exist, nor does progress have a purpose. Others choose mystical unity with God, but flee from the world of "progress," which they consider irreconcilable with their religious ideals. Think of the innumerable sects in all parts of the world in whose mysterious and sometimes wretchedly hysterical atmosphere both the very poorest and the refined seek their refuge (for the most part temporarily).

Attempts also occur here and there to make religion coincide completely with progress. What God asks, it is said, is the total placing of our capabilities, both active and contemplative, in the service of our fellowmen. For God is a creator and man is his fellow-creator. We must use all our material and mental gifts to transform the world with our reason and heart into the most perfect planet, at the same time into a magnificent factory and center for journeys into space, one great garden in which art, love among men and world peace live together. The love of God is consequently nothing but the cult of the personality and a sense of human brotherhood.

Such a religion, which does not, in fact, consist of a clearly visible organized group, is not without greatness and attraction. The Deists, the Freemasons, and philanthropic movements sought something of this kind. Certain circles of humanists also move in this direction and unconsciously not a few who call themselves Christians. For one cannot of course *be* a Christian and reduce one's relationship to God to what is intrahuman; this is, among other things, a Christianity without Christ.

Christianity certainly promotes the reconciliation of progress and religion, but separates both carefully in origin and nature. It is fairly generally accepted that the past has confirmed this partnership. The Church has been the heir, bearer and discoverer of a large amount of culture. Yet, has it that task or even that possibility for the future as well?

Without expressing an opinion about the cultural-historical and social role that Christians have to fulfill in the future—it is possible that this will not be anything at all specific—we should contend that no other religion is to such an extent in agreement with the aspirations and with the structure itself of the modern world. It can perhaps be stated in one word: the modern world and Christianity are essentially *historical*, i.e., their whole spirituality is based on facts and realities and, in particular, they look upon history as moving in a straight line, progressive and advancing in a certain direction.

This involves a basic modification in the view of our existence. The Greek idea of history, for example, was cyclic and indeterminate, being an eternal return to the same starting points.[3] The pre-Christian *religions* were, and are, cyclic, i.e., intimately connected with nature—the seasons, the festivals of newly born light and creative summers, the sacrifice of the firstborn, the initiation of adolescents, the singing of dirges around the dead, and then again an imploring for the mysterious blessing of the child. Generations come and go; religions confer more solemnity to their entry and some consolation to their exit, but basically all is vanity. Modern man would like best to forget such religion; he sinks into the intoxicating oblivion of a progress that can throw into ecstacies at least a

[3] We still find the same view today about the world event as a history without purpose in civilizations which were influenced but little by Christianity, e.g., in Rwanda. Cf. D. Nothomb, "Une conception africaine de l'Histoire et du Temps," in *Lumen Vitae* 18 (1963), pp. 278-288, in particular pp. 282-286.

good part of his nature. Other religions, less bound to nature, more refined in their psychology, and more tragic in the nobility of their nirvana or the sensuality of their initiating eroticism likewise cannot maintain themselves in the slippery basis of that modern torrent of progress; they are static and can at most be second-rate elements in the dynamics of present-day society.

Yet, Christianity is different. It is, in fact, a main feature of God's revelation in ancient and modern Israel that it leads us into a history with its forward-propelling force and its aim.[4] For those people life was always an adventure and the fortunes of a race, a positive "story of suffering."

It is almost four thousand years ago that Abraham was the first to believe in Yahweh and in the future; he became the father of a people on the march. The expectation of a messiah slowly began to surge in their hearts. It increased to a squall and did not abate after the first coming of Jesus, but broke forth as if with tongues of fire and spread over the whole world.[5] In addition to the faith of Abraham, *hope* is one of the three pillars in the Christian's view of life; hope is of course directed toward the future, i.e., is progressive. And love, as understood by Christianity, renders that hope universal through the medium of a winning generosity.

The three divine virtues—the expression of the most intimate element in our manner of reaching God—consequently contain an essential element of progress. It is not a question here of opportunism, a tactical move by the Church to absorb the rough thrusts of the progressives. Listen to our two-thousand-year-old Credo to perceive at the source that we are living toward Christ's return, building on the final "communion of saints."

Christianity is the only religion which is by its nature so related to the modern urge for progress. We cannot expect from any other religion such a profound reconciliation and synthesis, even if the positive attempts at synthesis do come limping along somewhat in the rear. The success, the contradiction and the imperfections of the visionary harmonizations of Teilhard de Chardin may suffice as a hint here. The conclusion is this: If the stream of evolution becomes even more violent, perhaps all natural religions can be washed away. Since Christianity can follow and by its nature, already goes on ahead of the stream, it can become its task to keep awake single-handedly the sense of God in mankind. For this reason, the religions of the bible remain up to date.[6]

CHRIST AND OUR PRESENT

What we have said, though important in itself, does not express the deepest meaning of Christianity, for Christianity is not a constantly adapted theory any more than an appropriate plan of action for determining the course of the world. It is a new way of thinking, a mutation of our deepest nature. Christianity is our hope not so much because it extends its living arm into the future but principally because it has roots in the space of the present, which reach what is everlasting and divine. The area of experience of the Christian is even more fascinating than that of technical and cultural progress.

Of what does this experience consist? It is nothing but the participation—in community with the apostles and Christians of all centuries, with the mystical and hierarchical Church—in *the experiencing of Christ,* i.e., in the most intimate nature of our being where (in spite of all the literature about irrevocable seclusion) we have in a mysterious way an extremely sensitive and receptive point of contact with our creator and share with our co-created brothers and sisters in the life of Christ.

He who is truly a human being and a personal God had a unique experience among us. What his hands did, his words said and his heart loved, introduced a totally non-existent dimension into the whole of human activity. And just as the heart of the child can beat in its mother's womb with the blood that comes from the larger heart, just as love allows us to enter and causes us to move, full of happiness or sorrow, in the garden of the deepest longings and finest emotions of another person, we also share in the God-incarnate experience of Christ. We do share, but differently, less tangibly and more really.

---

[4] There are also cyclic elements in Christianity, e.g., the weekly and annual rhythm of the liturgy, but they are accidental. Thus, Christmas and Easter could be celebrated in two different hemispheres at the same time without losing their meaning.

[5] Justinus, the first great Christian publicist (ca. 165 B.C.) uses this expression remarkably often. One lives in a sphere of expectation, yearning for the "second coming."

[6] Cf. Mario Zanartu, *Roman Catholic Ethic and Economic Development* (Microfilm University of Columbia, Ann Arbor, 1962); Desarollo económico y moral católica," in *Cuadernos de Economia* 2 (1964), pp. 47-91 (discussion of the theses of F. Night, *The Economic Order and Religion* (London, 1947); M. Weber, *The Protestant Ethic and the Spirit of Capitalism* (New York, 1958).

The clearest expression of this contact is found among the mystics—from John and Paul, via Augustine, Palamas, Bernard, Francis, Thomas à Kempis, Teresa, John of the Cross, to the so greatly beloved Carmelites of Lisieux and to Charles de Foucauld who evermore radiates a presence, and to the many who walk beside us in the street today and eat from the same plates as we, but whose names we do not yet know. We sometimes perceive upon reading their writings or upon hearing their voices an "echo" of their experience, to use the expression of William James.

These people, who were sometimes highly talented, as was Augustine, or already had a rich range of experiences behind them in the aesthetic, sentimental, or even morally religious field, and on the other hand, led, and continued to lead, the simplest of lives, declare to all that it was an experiencing of Christ which determined their lives. It was an experience that was something completely new for them, something that they had never expected to exist, a certainty with which to defy all courts of law, forcing them to fall to the ground and shout with joy, and so powerful, in effect, that one of such moments of unity seemed sufficient to live with the cross to the end of the world. Prior to the meeting they had perhaps been honest people, now they are people in love; previously perhaps diligent and persevering, now adventurers: previously full of a realization of responsibility, now apostles, servants, martyrs; previously well-instructed and informed, now, however, prophets. The prophets of the Old Testament already had a certain intuition about Christ and renewed their people. According to the Gospel, Christians should also be prophets; [7] they are to renew the appearance of the world and suffer persecution, and their deepest experience which is safe through the Holy Spirit will cause them to say: "Jesus is Lord." [8]

This mystical experience is nothing but the result in the psychological sphere, somewhat susceptible of observation, of what is essential for every Christian. It is a conscious and magnificently serious play with the great realities of birth from God, one's own frailty, forgiveness, the ever-recurring Word of God as a double-edged sword, so wounding and so curative, and the climaxes of presence in the celebration of the eucharist and the experiencing of "caritas." To assent to all this and to surrender to it with confidence is to believe. These are all forms of contact with Christ.

To us, just as for the person born blind at the pool of Siloam, belief is a meeting with a person.[9] The essence of our Christianity is not that we are unimpeachable, enterprising and sympathetic. No, but that soon we shall meet Jesus face-to-face. And one glimpse of the risen Lord will make clear to us what his presence has been in our lives. There is no assessment of good and bad deeds; but solely a becoming aware of rejected or accepted encounters. Both for modern and ancient eyes this is the nucleus of Christianity: to be linked with Christ himself in the most direct way.[10]

Listen for a moment to someone with ancient eyes? It is someone who can compare, who was well-endowed with natural talents, of noble blood and carefully educated: "But whatever gain I had, I counted as loss for the sake of Christ. Indeed I count everything as loss because of the surpassing worth of knowing Christ Jesus my Lord. For his sake I have suffered the loss of all things, and count them as refuse, in order that I may gain Christ . . . that I may know him and the power of his resurrection, and may share his sufferings" (Phil. 3, 7-11).

These words of Paul alone would perhaps have been sufficient to warrant a lengthy and thorough study of Christ for our time.

FIVE PHASES IN OUR KNOWLEDGE OF CHRIST

In order to understand properly the meaning of this book and its method, it is useful to pause for a moment and consider the successive phases through which our knowledge of Christ normally passes.

[7] Cf. Mt. 5, 11-12; 10, 41.
[8] Cf. 1 Cor. 12, 3.
[9] Jn. 9, 35-38.
[10] The characteristic feature of Christianity is that it is a revealed religion. Other religions are attempts by man to ascend toward God; Christianity is the result of a divine initiative. It is a coming of God toward us. This way of putting things is correct, at least if it is properly understood, and then it coincides with what has been said above. For revelation is, in fact, much more than the communica-

tion of a number of truths. It is a delivering intervention, an event that is concrete in Jesus and that develops further in concrete human beings who become involved in Christ's life through faith, the sacraments and a life of love. We have called this involvement an "experience of Christ" and viewed the whole matter somewhat more stuntedly from our point of view, not from the metaphysical heights of the planning God. That is the only difference.

1. *Searching*

During this period, which is sometimes prolonged and can assume a thousand forms, we proceed from our experiences. We circle around our dark ego in our effort to find a glimmer of light. Even those baptized as children have to pass through this period. There is no conscious belief without questioning. Blondel set out this essential character of this process magnificently in *L'Action:*

"Man questions himself about his final destination. This way of reasoning leads toward the mystery, and from there all things acquire their significance and meaning. Suddenly, the whole world appears as a mystery, or at least as the sign of a mystery because of its connection with man's final destination. Men are the bearers of the mystery in an infinitely deeper sense, since they all possess a mystery that can be objectivized, but which first has to be revealed. They cannot however execute that revelation or disclosure perfectly themselves. They are searching for what they are without being able to explain it completely. I am too large for myself; there is in me something more than I myself, and I feel very well that, if I cannot realize myself completely, this is not to be imputed solely to my weakness but also to the excess of my riches. In this way, the mind becomes spontaneously receptive to the Christian mystery for which it longs without being able to lay claim to it and, in particular, without being able to realize it by its own power." [11]

2. *The Meeting*

If the meeting with Christ does, in fact, take place, it will happen in three "places": in the Gospel, in the eucharist, and in contact with people. It is, however, possible to have such contacts for a considerable period without receiving the grace of encounter. For a grace is necessary: a conversion, a change in mentality, a theological mutation, something in the nature of what the famous Father Nadal observed in the case of outstanding theologians who, once they had *experienced* the *Exercises*, confessed, greatly moved, that they had only then become theologians, that now they understood for the first time what they lacked after so much study, lessons, books, and discussion." [12]

"That theological *mutation* about which Father Nadal speaks, is a conversion of our whole nature, of our wills and, consequently also, of our minds. It is the conversion of St. Ignatius at Manresa which still goes on today. Expressed more accurately, it is Jesus who, together with St. Teresa, gives a new shape to all those who, thanks to her, allow themselves to be 'attracted' by him. It is Jesus who, together with Charles de Foucauld, perfects the conversion of all those who study this latter with an integral, critical mind and enter into his 'spiritual itinerarium,' which is he himself, the new and living path of the Church today. It is Jesus who, together with Thomas Aquinas, converts all who are, through a conscientious and complete study (both noetic and pneumatic) of his theology, today initiated into the maturing process of his theology from the editing of the *Prima Pave* to the discussions of his *De Malo*." [13]

That meeting effects a real conversion. Man is snatched away from his narrow anthropocentric circle. He experiences the gratuity, the "excess" [14] of the love of God who not merely loves us first,[15] but did this precisely "when we were yet without strength." [16] The result is a real dispossession. Whoever meets Christ loves someone else more than himself. He no longer wishes to be autonomous, but wishes to disappear so that Christ might appear.[17]

We must honestly dare to say this, particularly to the humanists, just as Blondel did in a magnificent letter to Edouard Le Roy: "I think that the initial autonomy of our will has to declare itself in agreement with and long for the real and irreducible heteronomy of divine love. We experience temporary destruction, subjection, mortification, all the momentarily cruel capabilities of the will which supremely establish love's realm in us. Upon thorough reflection we see and feel that it is here a matter of the insertion, the installation in us of the infinite that broadens us until we cry with pain. And this is the true goodness, for God shapes us in this way according to his shape in place of adapting himself to our own. It is God who causes us to seek our salvation in that happiness of BEING-FOR-HIM (and that is the immutable truth), and not in the ambition to HAVE-HIM-FOR-US, which is the excess, so much more pleasant, since the reciprocity exists by virtue of direct affirmation. 'Oh, it is not something to laugh about that I have loved you!' Angela of Foligno heard the inner voice of the bridegroom say. No, the super-

---

[11] J. Lacroix, *Histoire et Mystère* (Tournai, 1962), p. 132.

[12] Letters of P. Nadal (in Latin), Part 4, p. 667.

[13] A. Hayen, "Science sacrée et Vie théologale," in *Sciences ecclésiastiques* 15 (1963), pp. 21-38; the quotation is on p. 24, No. 4.

[14] Cf. Eph. 2, 4.

[15] Cf. 1 Jn. 4, 10.

[16] Rom. 5, 6-8.

[17] Cf. the testimony of John the Baptist (Jn. 3, 30).

natural is not only a grace we assimilate while we remain ourselves, it is a consuming fire and basically a heteronomy, not a slavish one as if it were a command from a master who imposes his iron yoke upon us, but a law of infinite love which in the first place addresses our legitimate autonomy and enables us with the aid of the first gift of which she is the bearer to receive the new gift, namely, acceptance, deification."

"And if that is so, then may we not let Christianity be degenerated radically by excluding all heteronomy as far as possible, by making an appeal—in a singular return to intellectualism—to the 'God of the philosophers,' against the God of the gospels, against that Jesus concerning whom St. Teresa said that it is the most ghastly mistake of the spiritual life to imagine that one shall achieve a deeper inspection of the deity by leaving aside his humanity?" [18] In a word the meeting places us forever under the sanctifying lordship of the God-man.

3. The Testimony, or in Biblical Language, the Prophecy

It is, after all, impossible to keep such a radical meeting to oneself, however much it may have taken place in secret. Not to proclaim the great fact would be being unfaithful to the meeting, as Paul declares to Agrippa.[19] Testimony is something quite different from a lesson. A prophet is not a professor, but literally someone who speaks in the place of another. He is a person inspired, the mouth of another. For the meeting is characterized, as we have seen, by a taking possession. It is no longer Paul who lives, but Christ in him. The proclamation of the Gospel is consequently no longer a duty, but a necessity. Christ does not leave us in peace; his love constrains us.[20]

Ours is obviously an imperfect preaching. And there are many who either cannot or will not speak and proclaim the Gospel from the housetops *through their lives*. The consequences are in any case not commensurate with the objective content of the words, and the testimony of life does not obey completely the laws of sociology. For there is here a presence. Prophecy is a charisma, the most important charisma after the "apostolate" (in the strict sense: the apostles, the hierarchy).[21] This charisma or, in general, the testimony, follows *directly* upon the meeting, before systematic study and at the same time as contemplation. Whoever wishes to study theology must first have testified alone or in an organized group. Novices must, after having been together with Jesus intensely for months, go to the vineyard and the fields which are lying fallow before returning to the desks of the seminary, just as Paul immediately began to bear witness in Damascus itself, going only thereafter to the desert of meditation and contemplation.[22]

4. *Study and Contemplation*

In the course of the compelling, or perhaps even burdensome witnessing, the obvious fact obtrudes that one meeting is not adequate for knowing Jesus thoroughly. A new searching is needed, more intense than previously, but with a new mentality and new methods. It is now no longer a search for my ego, in order to realize myself, but a listening to him. We now know that everything proceeds from him, we expect nothing from ourselves. Protestants, Orthodox, and Catholics agree that it is here a question of listening to the *present-day* Christ. The resurrected one speaks *today*. The reading and consideration of the Scriptures are means for hearing him now.

The ensign bearer of *Formgeschichte*, Martin Dibelius, expressed it graphically in a lecture given in 1935, when he pointed to a painting in the university library at Heidelberg where the artist, Fritz Mackenzen, have depicted the Sermon on the Mount with Jesus "not on a Palestinian eminence, but in the milieu in which he himself was painting," surrounded by Mackenzen's contemporaries. "The conviction hiding itself behind this painting is clearly recognizable. In the Sermon on the Mount Jesus is speaking *to us today*. His exhortations and promises are directed less to the people of a past age and a far distant country than to us. And thus an event from the life of Jesus is related to belief in Christ, the Savior . . . The master of Nazareth appears as the Lord of the Christian Church." [23]

This attitude, through which we become contemporaries of Jesus, not by "transporting" ourselves in our imagination to "his time," but as a result of an awareness of the present activity of the resurrected one, is the basis of Christian theology. For the theological

---

[18] Maurice Blondel, *Lettres philosphiques* (Paris, 1961), pp. 258-259.
[19] Acts 26, 19-20.
[20] 2 Cor. 5, 14.
[21] 1 Cor. 14, 1.39; Eph. 4, 11.

[22] Acts, 9, 20-23; Gal. 1, 17-18.
[23] Martin Dibelius, "Evangelienkritik und Christologie," in *Botschaft und Geschichte*, Vol. I (Tubingen, 1953), p. 293.

attitude is the desire to understand from God himself *what* he does around the center Christ, and *who* he is, together with Christ and the Spirit. Theology is belief which seeks to understand, according to the maxim of Anselm. It seeks to understand not because of doubt, not in order to prove, but in order to understand from inside and in a certain sense, from on high, in order to read the epic of God's deeds under the lamp of God's Word, and at the same time to see him in the light and to attain the tangibility of his deeds through his love which is never extinguished.

Theology is necessarily a dialogue, for the light shines in the darkness. We live in two or more worlds, and compelled by the Spirit, we look for unity. Everything must be brought into confrontation: the earthly realities with the most spiritual values, the opinions of others with our own suppositions, theory, which seems to be so perfect, with practice, which is so very different. Theology has to integrate everything and will consequently often come to grief. We must have patience and, above all, we must enter into conversation with the world, our friends, the emptily gesticulating masses in red buses and gaping into shop windows, the singing community, the saints, our own weaknesses and dreams.

In its most beautiful moments, listening to and pondering on God's Word can pass into contemplation, a quiet looking in the often barren morning clearness of belief for the Lord. That is the highest theology and also the most perfect knowledge of Christ that is possible before final contemplation, although we must immediately add here that the *experiencing* of love, which we have left out of consideration in the process of the knowledge of Christ, is of chief importance also for its value as knowledge.

5. *Explanation and Discussion*

Once again, we must now return to the others, but with a wider vision and greater peace. Where contemplative calm is lacking, discussion can degenerate into fanaticism and create dissention instead of acceptance, and the instruction of fellow believers becomes a demonstration of arrogance. Before personal study and reflection, one must certainly bear witness, but not discuss or teach. Only after the fourth phase can one indulge in apologetics in a Christian manner, i.e., render on account of the hope which lives in us, full of reverence and certain of Jesus' inestimable value, in order in this way to serve our fellowmen genuinely in the search for their mission in life.[24]

The same must be said of instruction, contacts with friends in the faith, conversation groups, the whole of education. It cannot be anything but a communication arising from contemplation of the contemplated one. It is the explanation not of a series of religious problems which *we* have mastered, but of the great, secret ordinance, the decision which God took in Christ and realized in the fullness of time; the emergence, in modest but firm and matured loyalty, not in favor of a series of virtuous principles, but for a Person in whom one believes.[25]

Whoever wishes to instruct without meeting Christ again and again anew in contemplation and reflection, will invoke belief where he no longer sees, while belief is, after all, that which discovers in the still twilight phase of the glorious light the meaning of all things, and shines in the dark corners of our existence.

With these five phases of the knowledge of Christ before our eyes we are in a position to follow more accurately the method adopted in this book.

THE METHOD

The first aspect of our method will perhaps not arouse so much resistance. The reader may even find it obvious that we have directed our intention entirely to the fourth phase in the growing knowledge of Christ which has just been analyzed. We shall consequently not help in the search for the meaning of life out of our own unrest; rather do we already assume a fundamental meeting with Christ and a personal championing of him through witness. Whoever still feels very hesitant toward Christ or whoever has still definitely not yet said, "Yes," and has rather by chance started to read, should recall that the author *has to choose* his intention sometimes and consequently to renounce other possibilities.

We assume an already lively interest in Christ. A listening attitude, a theological focus; in a word, the desire to know Christ as thoroughly as possible and from himself.

[24] Cf. 1 Pet. 3, 15. [25] Cf. Eph. 1, 8-10.

This attitude implies chiefly a reflection, an effort to integrate everything into that knowledge of Christ which exceeds all things, but which excludes nothing. And it consequently implies, as we saw, conversation with the world and particularly with all who reflect on the same Christ. Whereas ample and grateful use was made in the previous volumes of this *Introduction to the Gospels* of the contribution of Christians of other confessions—it is, after all, no secret that in the study of the bible Protestant scholars had a great lead (and still have in many respects) on the Catholic—must the conversation have to be terminated now that it is a matter of what undoubtedly concerns us all very much more, namely, the meaning of the gospels, the Person of Jesus himself?

This is why we have adopted an eucumenical method, even an ecumenical *intention* which, after all, coincides with my being a Catholic. For being a Catholic and being ecumenical is, after all, the same thing. Do not both words mean "to be universal?"

Just as it would be poor ecumenism to conceal that I am a Catholic, so it would also be poor Catholicism not to listen with sympathy (in the deepest sense of the word having the same feeling together) to all that is good and true, from whatever side it may come. I have never seen in this a conflict with obedience to the decisions—sometimes infallible, sometimes obligatory without therefore being infallible or incapable of revision—of the authority of the Church. I admit here that I have been willing to learn much from Protestants, that I quote freely from their books and feel myself closely related to them. Yet I declare myself just as solidly with the Church which people identify (in not such a happy way) as the "Roman," Church and solidly also with its errors which I neither deny nor defend, any more, however, than I cast them off from myself as if I had no single fault in them nor duty to revise them. The method followed here is also Catholic in the sense that the writer knows that he cannot understand Christ on his own according to his own taste. In order to know Christ, one has to possess the Spirit of Christ, and this was promised in a very special way to the college of the apostles and to all who were to believe in him through their word.

It follows from this for me that I have to remain in the Church for knowledge of Christ, in community and under the direction of the successors to the apostles united with the successor of Peter. I admit that this has consciously and more often even unconsciously inspired and shaped my interpretations without, however, having forced me to even one insincerity or uncritical postulate.

Three Loyalties

When we try to set down in greater detail how we are to listen to the message of the gospels, how we are to view the Person of Jesus, things become more complicated. It is not likely that the method chosen will meet with the approval of everyone. Consequently, we should just like to explain the principles on which it is based, not with the intention of protecting it with the sword of polemics and even less of presenting it as the only one offering salvation. We do, however, consider that these principles will help the reader's understanding of the present work and, to be perfectly frank, that they contain an implicit criticism of a considerable part of our christological literature. To the degree that he finds these principles valid, each person will draw concrete inferences, preferably make the necessary distinctions, not forget charity, and, I hope, also apply criticism together with charity to the shortcomings of this book.

As principles we set up a threefold loyalty:

1. *Loyalty to the Original Wording*. In order to know Jesus, we must penetrate to the roots, into the mentality of the gospels. We must know the geographical and historical framework. We must feel the stylistic forms, know how our texts have evolved, what the characteristic feature of each gospel is, etc. According to the rules of historical knowledge and, in a special way because of the dogma of the inspiration of the Scriptures, it is absolutely necessary that our knowledge of Christ be in close contact with the gospels as the original source in this field. Not vaguely, by remote allusions and poorly understood proof-texts, but directly with wording and everything.

It is for this reason that this volume was preceded by two other volumes in which the framework and the origin, growth and form of the four gospels were studied in a way which, we hoped, initiated the reader himself into the *text*. We then presuppose in this part familiarity with the data and consistency of the text. This must allow us, in constant touch with the inspired words, to penetrate now to the core of God's message.

We shall, for the same reason, also not always choose the "clearest" of the basic texts for our considerations. In order, for example, to examine the divinity of Jesus, we shall not start from John, where it is expressed on every page, but first struggle through the less clear but more original information of the synoptics. Basing oneself solely on later, even if more expressive wordings, leads inevitably to a distortion of the truth and to a devaluation of those texts themselves, for they lose their function as a result, namely, to present the grace of the light deepened by contemplation and experience.

2. *Loyalty to Tradition.* The religious person adopts a somewhat suspicious attitude toward the gospels. So much is written and it is often so difficult to read. Does my relationship to God depend on my grammatical grounding and my literary taste? Many people who really hunger and thirst for Christ, who would satisfy themselves from the water of the living Word which is full of the name of Jesus in the sermon, the retreat, the conversation, find their emotions checked if people speak to them too much about books, even if they are the gospels.

That is perhaps a mistrust of the impersonal: one cannot ever completely feel through letters. Contact with people, separately and in communion, is always more personal. One feels whether it is genuine or not; it is not so difficult to sift the sparkle from the word and external appearance and to keep only the golden core of reality. Don't you hear how Jesus, "the inspirer from whom we so oft take the Word," says to you, "Don't treat me as an object of study?" [26]

One essential element is really missing even from the best literary-historical study of the gospels, namely, the sounding board of life. And this sounding board is precisely tradition. For tradition is, after all, something very different from the oral transmission of "truths" which are not "contained" in the Holy Scriptures. Before anything had been written down about him, Jesus had revealed himself to the whole small Church. Knowledge of Christ already flourished in songs, celebrations of the eucharist, and in a reforming of life. When the gospels appeared, everyone understood them in the light of that living tradition of which they were the fruit, the crowning and henceforth also the basis.

And that tradition continues, under the leadership of the authority intended by Christ, although the molding phase was already "finished" at the death of the last apostle. There are in a family things which one understands well only when one has *lived* in the *sphere* of the family, has seen the gestures, knows the habits, has felt the meaning of the seven hundred sounds that are to be heard at the table on Christmas Eve. There are things which the best chronicle cannot record at all. The Church Fathers, the councils, the saints, the hierarchy, one's colleagues are an indispensable commentary on the life of Jesus.

3. *Loyalty to Our Time*. It is our task to ensure the translation, yes, the incarnation of the Gospel into words and even more, into the life of our time. The Bible movement should not become a school of archaeology in which highly gifted pupils calmly discuss magnificent Hebrew terms and Roman procurators or coins. Jesus wanted to be understood by a group of Galilean peasants who had no idea at all that the world is round and that it is conceivable to visit the moon. Undoubtedly, he now, too, wants to speak to us today. We are drawn and offended, blessed and analyzed by the press, radio, technology, civilization and economy. The Gospel has to be interpreted into this language just as it was translated by Paul from the Palestinian rural tongue into the Greek language of the cities in a way that was to have been somewhat closer to Luke than in his epistles, but which in any case contained a thorough renovation. For our contemporaries, the ascension of Jesus cannot be the same as in the 1st century. We even know through direct observation that there is a space around the earth in which cosmonauts can circle, but certainly no temple with God's throne. What then does "ascension" mean? We must certainly not obscure anything here. It is precisely for this reason that we must speak in the language that everyone speaks today.

Another new problem arises from psychology. A modern person cannot imagine that we should know another person without having access to his psychology. If Christ became a *human being*, his psychological personality must, at least to a certain extent, be accessible to us. The ancients in general and consequently, also the evangelists, did not have this trouble. This is a further reason for a necessary adaptation in the way of speaking, to be preceded by study.

Can the three loyalties just mentioned be reconciled in one work? Must we not distinguish from case to case, according to author, subject, public? To what genre does this present book really belong? Is it exegesis, bible theology or dogma, or, in another jargon, positive or systematic theology? A somewhat further developed application of the above mentioned principles must allow us to give a more or less satisfactory answer to these questions.

[26] Written in the diary of M. Blondel, on April 7, 1889; cf. M. Blondel, *Carnets intimes* (Paris, 1961), p. 196.

Attitude

Of the questions just asked, one can be answered clearly: this book is *not an exegesis*. Exegesis is a systematic explanation of continuous texts. If is found in (complete or partial) commentaries; it is assumed here, but not developed. Is this book then either biblical theology or simply theology?

Before answering, let us repeat once again what we wish to do, namely, to hunt down as well as possible the real *message* of the gospels which we assume still applies in our time. That takes us away from biblical theology as it is understood today. Biblical theology after all lacks the link with tradition and, in particular, with the present-day manner of speaking and thinking. The best biblical theologies naturally try as well as possible to make use of our linguistic instruments, but their real task is nevertheless to offer a synthesis which to a certain extent remains within the limits of biblical thought and expression. In other words, they try to know a biblical author as well as possible from *his* point of view or they try, if it is a question of several authors (for example, the authors of the gospels), to indicate the evolution of thought, but always to experience the matter in such a way as if they went step by step with them and reproduced their ideas systematically.

That also really is theology, i.e., a synthesis of ever-valid revelation with contemporary philosophy, but a theology of an earlier period and of a given milieu, for example, the theology of Mark or of John [27] or, as Cullmann developed it in a masterly way in its application to our subject, a Christology of the whole of the New Testament.[28] On the one hand, our intention is much more limited: it is directly a matter of the message of the *gospels*. On the other hand, we wish to integrate that message thoroughly into *our* time, not merely to know how Mark experienced Christ with his own picture of the world and limited information, but to go even further than the profound, primeval Jewish and sometimes also neo-Greek contemplations of John.[29] We are seeking what *Jesus* himself meant, what he did in reality, who he *is* at root, and that extends beyond Mark and John, although it is the essence of their message. Because it is *we* who want to understand and say it *for ourselves*, we necessarily come into another (and just as restricted) world of thought, namely, the contemporary one.

It therefore seems as if we have arrived at a theology pure and simple. Naturally, it is not a theology—in this case a Christology—

which has hardly any further contact with the gospels, or which seems to direct the whole of its enthusiasm and energy on Scholastic distinctions which seek to reduce everything to one basic principle, such as the hypostatic union, and does not give one minute's attention to preaching and the psychological personality of Jesus, or loses itself in a series of minor questions, inherited from a late medieval series of intellectual problems.[30] Theology is necessarily contemporary, and that is what we wish to be. Well then?

And it is not this either, for theology must not leave one single essential factor out of consideration, while in this book merely incidental appeal is made to the excellent information of Paul and the other New Testament writings beyond the gospels. Our contact with the Fathers is all too thin, the richness of tradition is not systematically utilized. Moreover, the reader may often miss a more developed philosophical analysis or a higher power of synthesis. That is, after all, beyond me and the length of a single book.

We really find ourselves in an intermediate phase. We are proceeding from the fact that the message of the gospels can be summarized in one word, namely, Jesus. Now, in order to know Christ,

[27] Notice the plural in R. P. Casey, "The Earliest Christologies," in *Journal of Theological Studies*, 9 (1958), pp. 253-277.

[28] O. Cullmann, *Christologie du Nouveau Testament* (Neuchatel, 1958); English translation: *Christology of the New Testament* (Westminster, 1964); cf. a number of explanations in "Dialogue sur le Christ," in *Choisir* (Fribourg in Switzerland), I, 9-10, (1959-1960), pp. 17-23. Cf. also G. Sevenster, *De Christologie van het Nieuwe Testament* (Amsterdam, 1948); V. Taylor, *The Person of Christ in New Testament Teaching* (London, 1958); F. Hahn, *Christologische Hoheitstitel, Ihre Geschichte im frühen Christentum* (Göttigen, 1963).

[29] A very good survey of the problem, the literature and a personal point of view (all unfortunately solely from a Protestant standpoint) is found in W. Kunneth, *Glauben an Jesus? Die Begegnung*
der Christologie mit der modernen Existenz, 2nd ed. (Hamburg, 1963). We shall, however, adhere much more closely to the texts themselves, and consequently scarcely touch upon many modern disputes. An excellent bibliographical guide to all our problems, as well as first acquaintance with the solutions will be found in R. Schnackenburg, *The Theology of the New Testament* (New York, 1962).

[30] We hope we will not scandalize anyone by saying that the theology of the incarnate Word is, as yet, not in very good shape. All Catholic theology is suffering, according to the judgment of many, from a lack of integration and even of confrontation (this being a condition for integration) with the acquisitions of the knowledge of man and the world in recent centuries. Think, for example of the chapter on the theological training of future priests in *Sendung und Gnade* by K. Rahner.

three things are required and are sufficient for a contemporary mentality, namely, knowledge of his ideas, a sketch of his personality and, since both things in *this* case point to something deeper, an approach to his mystery. The fact that the first two points are usually not treated in contemporary theological tracts about Christ and are not named even in the Credo does not dissuade us from our view.

In order to know someone, we must know what thoughts inspire him, certainly if he proclaims them in public. After all, the evangelists, too, looked upon the content of Jesus' message as belonging essentially to "the Gospel of Jesus"; [31] and moreover, they offer abundant information for drawing substantiated conclusions concerning Jesus' personality and mystery, aspects which they, in most cases implicitly, certainly wanted to communicate reliably. Our procedure itself will have to indicate that we really find ourselves with this threefold plan in a homogeneous line with the gospels.

In our development of each part, we try to arrive at a synthesis for our age. Yet, not at a fully developed synthesis and at a complete contemporary philosophy of life based on Christ. That would become a complete system of dogma and morals, in twenty-three volumes. We remain halfway, with approximately the following criterion. We are trying to make a present-day synthesis, insofar as this has an *express* basis in the gospels and only in the gospels. That is logical, bearing in mind that it is here a question of an introduction to the *gospels*. It will then become an unfinished work, but not necessarily a mutilated one, since we shall in any case call upon *all* New Testament material (and later penetration of tradition), but then only insofar as is necessary in order to pass from the explicit evangelical data to our time.

A few examples will illustrate this further. The kingdom of God is, according to the gospels, the main subject of Jesus' preaching. We consequently take it as the starting point, but in order to analyze it, we ask *our* questions. What is the concrete (visible) content, the dimensions, the active elements, the principle of realization of that kingdom? In order to understand love fully, likewise a subject of Jesus, we resort to a modern, phenomenological penetration of the nature of love and of its degrees. We illustrate the facets of the personality of Jesus not from the summaries of the gospels, but with the help of modern psychological categories, yet naturally, at every turn; at least that is the way we wanted it. Everything is genuinely based on the texts themselves. When one passes from the one world of thought to the other, the danger of forcing and consequently of distorted conclusions is far from imaginary.

Consequently, the method used in the last part seems somewhat easier in which the mystery of Jesus is seen in its successive phases: the incarnate one, the pilgrim, the messenger, the redeemer, the transfigured one, the returning one. This modern or, if you like, evolutionary view, links up closely with that of the gospels and of the ancient Church, although we stand here before a new difficulty, namely, the incomprehensibility of the mystery itself.

We have now covered the main elements. We have summoned ourselves to appear before the court and already find ourselves, as they say in Spanish, between the sword and the wall. "That book is neither exegesis, nor biblical theology, nor theology!" It can perhaps best be regarded as a modest contribution to a Christology in embryo. Yet, that would be too great an honor for what has arisen and grown from the simple desire to *introduce* the reader to the personal reading of the gospels.

Neither an Anthology nor Exercises

In the preceding volumes of this *Introduction* there were inserted in each case in separate chapters an anthology of modern and ancient authors. They have been omitted here. On the other hand, we have made a fairly comprehensive selection from recent literature relating to the most important subjects touched upon. In our choice we aimed at *technical* value, so that one really can expect a further exploration of the subject and also more effort in reading. A confessional distinction was not made here, since we considered that at this level of our subject we were concerned only with confirmed, personally thinking readers.

For similar reasons this book has no "exercises." Whoever set to work in the two previous parts will certainly have gained enough insight to look for himself and find and carry out interesting exercises, which remains a duty and pleasure even for the most advanced

[31] Cf. the opening words of Mark 1, 1.

exegete. This gradation was intended. In the first volumes we did not assume per se that the reader was skilled in biblical detective work. That must now and again have offended those who did possess this proficiency. Now too, it will certainly be true that many a reader will have a deeper and more complete insight than is offered here, so that this book may be useless to him. This would increase my joy: if only the Lord becomes known.

Part One

The Message of Jesus

We are confronted by two dangers at the beginning of this first part. On the one hand, the message of Christ calls for such drastic and up-to-date reforms that we might want to begin hastily to "adapt" his "doctrine," and tend to forget, as it were, that it is *someone's* doctrine. And yet, was it not the intention of the gospels to help us to know *Christ*?

On the other hand, there is also a danger in limiting ourselves to a systematic analysis of the utterances of Christ. We need dictionaries, concordances, commentaries, scholarly works and articles to look up what his favorite terms were, how he developed his subjects, what the *background* and historical effects were, etc. That work is indispensable, but only leads us halfway, for it could also have been done at the beginning of the 2nd century, and we want to know *in our terminology* how Jesus thought and what he wanted.

It is clear that the attempt to escape from this second danger catches us in the snares of a third, namely, the net of the famous *Hineininterpretierung*, in which someone's words are merely the screen onto which we project our own thoughts. Yet, a real obstacle does not prohibit an attempt that is indispensable.

We hope to get to know Christ by way of his message. For someone *is* to a large extent what he *says*. It is impossible to know the resurrected Christ or Christ the worker of miracles without having listened to Christ the prophet. The demands of conciseness will oblige us to omit many aspects; there are, however, two questions which are inseparable as well as irreducible:

1. What is the destiny he assigns to mankind as a whole?
2. How does he regard the individual person?

Here we have the two chapters which make up this part of our study. These two headings presuppose that the religion of Christ does not simply amount to "saving one's own soul" and yet, that it is, on the other hand, completely personalistic. If it is true that

27

"only Christianity assures the human person a transcendent destiny
in an inseparable unity, and humanity a destiny that is communal"
(H. de Lubac)—people usually say the direct opposite: individuals,
good or bad, have the same destiny, and only the community will be
transcendent and live on I know not how long—then we owe this to
the great plan of God revealed in Christ. But let us first remind
ourselves of the historical development of the preaching of Jesus.[1]

PROBABLE EVOLUTION OF THE APPEARANCE OF JESUS

"In many and various ways God spoke of old to our fathers by
the prophets; but in these last days he has spoken to us by a Son"
(Heb. 1–2). We no longer know precisely when this great historical phenomenon began, nor how it developed from year to year.
There is, in my opinion, still no single genuinely safe chronology.[2]
The opinions of the best exegetes, historians and even astronomers
contradict one another.[3] Discussions flared up again through the
discoveries near the Dead Sea, but without an apparent result. The
calendar of the sect does not provide us with any certainty about
the date of Jesus' death. Let us therefore assume that Jesus, born in
about 7 B.C.—"the apocalyptic year"—began to appear in public at
the age of about thirty-five.[4] His preaching, to be placed between
A.D. 26 and 33, lasted between one and a half and four years and was
brutally broken off on the eve of a Passover.

The development of that preaching is known to us in broad outline. We distinguish five phases:

1. *He began to preach* in the footsteps of John, the preacher of
penitence, in his vicinity and with the same message about an approaching intervention of God: the kingdom is at hand.[5]

2. *He continued preaching with success in Galilee*, for a period of
two years, on Saturdays in the synagogues, but often also in the
open air with a prophetic accent. The features of the kingdom
appear; people hear the conditions for entering into it. The Sermon
on the Mount (Mt. 5–7) presents a synthesis, though very incomplete, of that program. In the meantime, Jesus takes a group of
disciples into his work; there is much advice for novice missionaries
in the Sermon on Missions (Mt. 10).

3. *A crisis*, the open resistance of the religious leaders of the
people, resulting in constant disputes—various collections are to be

found in Mark—and the internal resistance encountered by Jesus also among the masses dampen the original enthusiasm. Jesus changes his method and reveals in apocalyptic parables the mysterious destiny of the kingdom.[6] The kingdom has to pass through a phase of growth, full of shame and disgrace; a cross is outlined on the horizon, while the crowd returns home and to business as usual.

4. *The consecration of the twelve* takes place for the most part after the crisis. Jesus avoids large meetings and even withdraws from the country for a time.[7] He dedicates himself with special care to the twelve who go with him, explains the coming time of the passion and takes steps for the future life of his community.[8]

5. *A prophetic announcement* of the coming intervention of God is the last thing Jesus has to say in words. It is in Jerusalem itself that he makes in menacing, prophetic parables a pathetic appeal to his people, and that his mission begins to fail; the withering of the fig tree and the urgent warnings to vigilance move in this tragic atmosphere.[9] There then follows the plot and death.

[1] We refer to the many studies in this area cited in our previous works.

[2] Check the articles under this and similar headings in any good dictionary of the bible.

[3] It is the task of the astronomer to determine the years in which the new moon in Palestine fell on a Friday or Saturday.

[4] Cf. the description given by E. Stauffer, *Jesus, Gestalt und Geschichte* (Bern, 1957), p. 41.

[5] Cf. Mt. 3, 2; 4, 17; Jn. 1, 19-43.

[6] Mt. 13; Mk. 4.

[7] Cf. Mt. 15, 21; 16, 13.

[8] Cf. pp. 87-90.

[9] Mt. 20, 1-16; 21, 28-46; 22, 1-13 = Mt. 21, 18-21; cf. Mk. 13, 6-9 = Mt. 24-25. See also footnote 6 above.

I
The Fate
of Mankind

"Soon afterward he went on through cities
and villages, preaching and bringing the
good news of the kingdom of God"

(Lk. 8, 1).

It is often possible to summarize the life's work of the great
people in history in one word. For Mohammed, it was Islam, i.e.,
surrender to the Word of God; for Columbus, the discovery of
the Indies (what was to become America); Luther's ideal was the
reformation of the Church; that of Marx was communism. Without
publishing a manifesto, Jesus, too, championed one great aim. Those
who had heard him a few times in the synagogue or who left their
homes to hear him speak again on a mountain slope or by a lake, all
knew beforehand what it would be about. They knew his subject:
malkoet ha-sjammaim, the kingdom of heaven.[1]

Matthew describes the beginning of his appearance as follows:
"From that time Jesus began to preach, and to say, 'Repent, for the
kingdom of heaven is at hand.' "[2] To a certain extent, that is his only
topic; whenever people want him to remain longer than is necessary
at a certain place, his answer is: "I must preach the good news of
the kingdom of God to the other cities also, for I was sent for this
purpose."[3] It became a strong, broad, impetuous movement which
swept rapidly through the country. The intense activity is summarized by Luke in one sentence: "Soon afterward he went on
through cities and villages preaching . . . the good news of the
kingdom of God."[4] We may say that the good news, that is,
the essential feature of Jesus' preaching (so essential that it became

30

the title of the four gospels) amounts to the kingdom of God.[5] And that too will have to be the message of the disciples: "And preach as ye go, saying, 'The kingdom of heaven is at hand.' " [6]

By this one word Jesus takes a stand with regard to the fate of mankind. To realize that, is a first requirement for understanding the message of Jesus; and nevertheless, misunderstandings on this point are not uncommon.

Contemporary Opinions about the "Kingdom of Heaven"

Many of our contemporaries—Marxists and others—imagine the kingdom of God of the Christians as a (hypothetical) reality in the hereafter. The expression, "kingdom of heaven" promoted that opinion. Heaven is, after all, for after death. At the most, one could also consider it as an internal attitude. In any case, it has nothing to do with the fate of mankind and the future of the nations as we know them. On the contrary, though Christians may be virtuous and sympathetic people, they are negative elements within the framework of progress: consciously or unconsciously they are "counterrevolutionaries." The reason is not far to seek: "True Christians are made to be slaves, and they are not disturbed by this; this short life has all too little significance for them" (J. J. Rousseau). According to this view, the kingdom of God is consequently, at most, inner peace, the acceptance of suffering and injustices, something that is not of this world. It is blessed by conformists and cursed by Communists.

Even Christians themselves have conflicting opinions. If we consider practicing Catholics, they can be classified into two groups. "The one group views with anxiety the exertions of the Church in the field of the temporal; the other welcomes them with cries of jubilation and views them as her most proper good, beyond any question . . . The problem is this. Can we reduce the function of the cosmos and of human labor, of civilization and history to a mere training ground on which people drill and acquire merits for a merely spiritual kingdom of God? If this is so, then the greatest

---

[1] "Kingdom of heaven" is absolutely the same as "kingdom of God."
[2] Mt. 4, 17.
[3] Lk. 4, 43.
[4] Lk. 8, 1.
[5] Gospel and kingdom of God are literally coupled in Mt. 4, 23; 9, 35; 24, 14; cf. also 13, 19: "the *word* of the kingdom."
[6] Mt. 10, 7.

acquisitions of human effort in the field of art, civilization, science, society and technology are merely aids for practicing the inner life and are not of the least importance for the final result of the play being nothing more than a lengthy and fascinating scenario of trial performances which will never reach the stage . . . What is realized by the talent, dedication and effort of human beings would merely be an "opportunity" to amass merits for the other life." [7] Or is the kingdom perhaps of this world, in spite of Jesus' declaration to Pilate? [8]

Let us not ask the question in the terms "of this world" or "not of this world," which are difficult for our time to appreciate. Let us also not drive ourselves back into the already specialized problem of the meaning of earthly realities, the problem of an incarnated versus a spiritualistic Christianity. Our question is then: Does this kingdom have a significance for the fate of *mankind* and if so, what is it?

The Disciples Knew It

No single disciple of Jesus would have doubted it. They knew it even before they made the acquaintance of Jesus, for the "kingdom of heaven" was a subject with a past.[9] God, who was Lord of heaven and earth, had ruled over his people since Abraham. He had made a covenant with them and would, at the decisive moment, make a new and eternal covenant.

God intervenes in this world. He comes in power into the history of mankind. That is the basic teaching of the prophets, in other words, of the whole Jewish religion. Formerly, the decisive intervention was looked forward to as "the day of Yahweh." In the last few centuries prior to Christ, the term, "kingdom of heaven," had become the customary designation for the approaching reign of God.

It was particularly the publication of the apocalyptic visions in the Book of Daniel which gave great relief to that kingdom of God. The unknown author placed himself in the position of the ancient prophet Daniel, and in a mighty *flashback* he described the great empires of the past—the Babylonians, Medes, Persians, Greeks, Syrians. Then came his message: soon a new and indestructible empire was to appear which the prophet would announce with these words: "I saw in the night, visions, and, behold . . . one like the son of man . . . came to the Ancient of Days, and was presented before him. And to him was given dominion and glory and kingdom, that all peoples, nations, and languages, should serve him; his dominion is an everlasting dominion, which shall not pass away, and his kingdom one that shall not be destroyed." [10]

Could one reduce such a kingdom of God, placed in evident contrast to the great kingdoms of history, to a purely individual matter and then preferably after death? Jesus' contemporaries did not think so. On the contrary, they had given it a strongly nationalistic color: the kingdom of God would, among other things, settle with the Romans. If Jesus then also calls himself the son of man in a clear and repeated allusion to the vision of Daniel, then however much he may refuse to allow himself to be proclaimed king or make political statements, nobody could possibly think of equating the kingdom of heaven with the castle of the soul.

What Jesus says about the kingdom is never a description of what awaits the soul after its death and even less of the process of growth of grace in our innermost selves. To equate those matters is to narrow the highway to an alley, for to Jesus, the kingdom of God is really that which pours into the world like an army. The enemy is strongly armed, but now at last a stronger Person has come who throws him out of it: "But if it is by the Spirit of God that I cast out demons, then the kingdom of God has come unto you." [11]

The comparison with a highway is really still much too narrow. In the Lord's prayer, the prayer for the coming of the kingdom of God stands, according to Matthew, between that for the hallowing of God's name, who fulfills heaven and earth, and the fulfillment of his will, on earth as in heaven. [12] Whenever the apostles said this prayer in two's on their exploratory journeys in between two annunciations of the kingdom, then their souls glowed with longing, but no one thought of his innermost self.

Whenever they did think of themselves, then it was to vie for the places of vice-president and chairman of the chamber at the right and left hand. [13] And, according to Luke, who is careful to avoid

[7] J. Ochagavia, "De qué mundo es su Reino?" a remarkable article in *Mensaje*, 118 (May, 1963), pp.147-154. This question is very topical in countries with development problems.

[8] Cf. Jn. 18, 36.

[9] For the historical background, cf. Vol. I, Hofmans, *De achtergrond. Palestina, toen Jezus daar leefde.* Hereafter reference to this volume will be cited simply as Vol. I.

[10] Dan. 7, 13-14.

[11] Mt. 12, 28.

[12] Mt. 8, 9-10.

[13] Mt. 20, 20-28.

criticizing,[14] they make use of the last conversation with Christ to ask about the moment when the kingdom of Israel is to be restored.[15] Jesus never answers: "But friends, that comes only after death," or "It is in your own soul." He merely says that the kingdom of God has other laws of growth, that no one knows the phases and that, in any case, blood will be spilled for it.[16] Who would think of *persecuting* anyone because he wants to love God in his innermost self and believes in a hereafter?

It is consequently abundantly clear that the kingdom of God is concerned with human *community*. To know the secrets of the kingdom of God—a privilege which neither the prophets, nor the righteous, nor the kings possessed [17]—is to understand the fate of mankind. For the field in which the children of the kingdom are the good seed, is the *world*.[18]

Characteristics of the Kingdom of God Brought by Jesus

Is it possible to discover the characteristics of a kingdom of God which was proclaimed by a wandering prophet who never developed his idea in a systematic way? The exegetes hesitate.[19] It is mainly the question of its immediate or delayed initiation that the opinions differ considerably. There will always be disagreements, particularly since a merely historical study is here impossible and inadequate: "A synthesis of all texts is, when all is said and done, a matter of theological attitude." [20] Study, contemplation and conversation will, however, always serve to increase our insight.

Though what now follows is not intended as a complete synthesis, I believe that a review and somewhat deeper look at the consciousness of Jesus as described in the gospels allows us to discover the salient aspects of the kingdom of God:

1. According to its concrete content: a kingdom of righteousness and peace.

2. According to its dimensions: universal and transcendent.

3. Its true countenance: the family of the Father.

4. The active elements: God who does everything; people who give themselves totally.

5. The principle of realization: mediation.

We shall limit ourselves to a concise development of these points.

A KINGDOM OF RIGHTEOUSNESS

Was our ideal of justice expressed by Jesus in its present-day meaning of the intransigent demand of equality in the personal and social sphere? Upon reading most exegetical studies we gain the impression that it was not.[21] The social side of Jesus' preaching is, in any case, so lightly covered that we experience great encyclicals like *Rerum Novarum* and *Pacem in Terris* as *foreign bodies* in revelation; they are certainly beautiful and even necessary at this time, but not organically linked with the Gospel. We are indeed struck by the point that practically no scriptural basis is indicated in these Encyclicals, this being extremely rare in such documents.

Could it be true that someone who reads the gospels regularly and without prejudice does not continually receive blows which startle him out of his social contentment? Is it reasonable and defensible that the Christian community, in its loyalty to the gospels, can stand aloof from the mighty battle for justice, merely intervening in order to

[14] Cf. Vol. I Hofmans, *Omstaan, groli en gestalte van de vier evangeliën.* Hereafter reference to this volume will be cited simply as Vol. I.

[15] Acts 1, 6; cf. Lk. 17, 20; 19, 11.

[16] The baptism and the chalice mentioned to the sons of Zebedee refer to martyrdom (Mt. 20, 20-28).

[17] Mt. 13, 17; Lk. 10, 23.

[18] Mt. 13, 38.

[19] Some important books: J. Bright, *The Kingdom of God* (New York, 1953); J. Bonsirven, *Le Regne de Dieu* (Paris, 1957); F. Gils, *Jésus Prophète dans les Evangiles synoptiques* (Louvain, 1957); R. Schnackenburg, *Gottesherrschaft und Reich. Eine biblisch-theologische Studie* (Freiburg im Br., 1959); *De Kerk in het Nieuwe Testament* (Antwerp, Patmos, 1964); A Feuillet, "Le Regne de Dieu et la personne de Jésus d'apres les évangiles synoptiques," in, *Introduction à la Bible* (Robert-Feuillet) (Tournai, 1959), II, pp. 771-818; N. Perrin, *The Kingdom of God in the teaching of Jesus* (Philadelphia,

1963).

[20] R. Schnackenburg, *op. cit.*, p. 79; in this connection he lists seven different theories.

[21] The most broadly conceived study is that of I. Giordani, *Il messagio sociale di Gesú* 4 vols., (Milan, 1954). Interesting comments on the social aspect of Jesus' preaching in L. Lallemand, *Histoire de la charité*, 5 vols., (Paris, 1902-1912); F. Meffert, *Der Kommunismus Jesus und der Kirchenväter* (M-Gladbach, 1922); A. M. Brouvier, *Jesus en de sociale vragen* (Zutphen, 1933); L. Ragaz, *Die Bergpredigt* (Bern, 1945); E. Percy, *Die Bottschaft Jesu. Eine traditionskritische und exegetische Untersuchung,* (Lund, 1953), pp. 45-81; J. Ratzinger, *Die christliche Brüderlichkeit,* (Munich, 1960); R. Völkl, *Christ und Welt nach dem Neumen Testament,* (Wurzburg, 1961); V. Van Baelen, *Het problem van de ontwikkelingslanden,* (Antwerp, Patmos, 1963), pp. 53-77.

preserve the *status quo,* and thus continuing to enjoy the help of the powerful or to preserve its *own* interests? [22]

This would be surprising, for Jesus was, after all, a prophet. Was it not characteristic of the prophets, from the first great one called Amos, who was a shepherd, to oppose with a booming voice all those who accumulated treasures through injustice and violence, who trampled down the weak and extorted the tribute of corn to build for themselves houses of stone, who accepted bribes and forced aside the poor in the gateway (the court of justice), who held themselves aloof from all misery, installed themselves firmly on the seat of violence, and stretched themselves out lazily on ivory couches to drink the very best wine? "And the revelry of those who stretch themselves shall pass away." [23] When Amos defends the poor man who is sold for a pair of shoes,[24] and Jesus states that the poor are blessed and that the kingdom of God is for them,[25] does not that place us in contact with concrete needs and demand tangible acts?

Jesus must also know that the *messiah* is in a special way to be the herald and restorer of justice, such as a long prophetic tradition demanded.[26] It was especially said of the "Suffering Servant of Yahweh," with whom Christ was to identify himself, that he was to proclaim justice to the peoples, was not to extinguish the smouldering hearth, and not falter until he had established justice throughout the whole earth. He was to open the eyes of the blind and to release the prisoners from the dungeon.[27] No one looked upon these words purely spiritually. Matthew finds the prediction fulfilled in the cures that Jesus performed.[28]

We must go even further. If we hear the gospels with an open mind and do not hide behind all manner of theories about hyperboles, then we must admit that Jesus' condemnation of injustice is even more thorough and terrible than that of the prophets. Nowhere is the *choice* stated so clearly: "No one can serve two masters . . . you cannot serve God and mammon." [29] "It is easier for a camel to go through the eye of a needle than for a rich man to enter into the kingdom of God." [30] Jesus is moreover more positive and annoyingly practical: "Go, sell what you possess, and give to the poor." [31]

If we wish to discover wherein that justice consists, we must beware not to appeal too much to the term, "justice," which had in the time of Jesus a more general meaning and often indicated simply piety and holiness.[32] Nevertheless, even in Jesus' time there still comes through something of the original, prophetic significance. If the beatitudes proclaim blessedness to those who hunger and thirst after justice [33] and suffer persecution as a result, then certainly not only personal piety can be intended here.[34] Who would think of pursuing his neighbor simply because he leads an inner life? Violent persecutions assume even among the victims a certain perseverance, a public opinion which has to be reckoned with. However this may be, we shall *not* in the following analysis rely on the term, "rights."

If we wish to analyze to some extent the program of justice from Jesus' point of view, then we can make a distinction between three aspects: the struggle against injustice, constructive principles and practical execution.

As far as the struggle against injustice is concerned, Jesus differs from most social champions of today through what we could call an ultraconfessional point of view. He says directly that he has come to fight. Against whom? In the first place, against sin, against the devil. Most plans for reformation put metaphysical evil in parenthese and are applied solely to better laws and structural reforms.

We are not thinking of condemning those a-confessional movements or of holding ourselves aloof from them. It must merely be stated here clearly that Jesus should not personally be called a social

---

22 We quote the accusation of a noted philosopher: "In fact the Church has never been seen to take a stand against a lawful government simply and solely because it acted unjustly, nor to back a revolution simply because it was just. On the contrary, she has been seen to favor rebels because they protected her tabernacles, her ministers and goods. God can never dwell perfectly on earth so long as the Church feels more obligation toward her ministers than toward other people, is more concerned about her own temples than about the houses of Guernica. A Christian revolt does indeed exist, but it is localized and only emerges when the Church is threatened" (M. Merleau-Ponty, *Sens et non-sens,* Paris 1948, p. 363).

23 We quote Amos 3, 9-15; 5, 7-15; 6, 3-7.

24 Amos 2, 6.

25 Mt, 5, 3.

26 Cf. Is. 9, 6; 11, 4-5; Jer. 23, 5-6; 2 Sam. 23, 3; Zech. 3, 8; Rev. 19, 11.

27 Is. 42, 1-4.

28 Mt. 12, 15-21.

29 Mt. 6, 24.

30 Mt. 19, 24.

31 Mt. 19, 21.

32 A few examples may suffice here: the "just" are the good (Mt. 5, 43; 9, 13; Lk. 14, 14), the innocent (Mt. 23, 35; 27, 29), the holy people (Mt. 1, 19; Lk. 2, 25; 23, 50; Acts 10, 22). Justice is the same as sanctity, perfection (Mt. 5, 20; Lk. 20, 20; 23, 47; Acts 3, 14). Cf. A. Descamps, L. Cerfaux, "Justice et Justification," in *Dict. Bibl. Suppl.* Vol. 4, (1949). col. 1417-1510.

33 Mt. 5, 6.

34 Mt. 5, 10.

leader in the present-day pluralistic sense. What he did is not for this reason less important, for injustice does have a cause; it is not due merely to clumsy organization or backward economy. The kingdom of justice has a great enemy,[35] who is none other than the "ruler of this world," [36] i.e., there is someone who weaves together the threads of evil into a giant rope, a dignified orchestra leader dressed in black, a leader of the cacophony of sin performed in the world theater, someone who has an influence everywhere, who seduces, monopolizes and, to a certain extent, can feel himself lord and master of the rich of the world and their glory.[37] It is this powerful one who is cast out now that the kingdom of God has to begin.[38]

The first Christians knew that they had to join in a battle not merely against "flesh and blood" but against the powers, the spirits in the air.[39] It would be a great mistake to look upon the devil as a sort of personification of their inner struggles and temptations.

What now are the constructive principles of that gigantic battle which sets out to cause justice to triumph in the world? All the standards of the gospels really apply here, but four of them—two negative and two positive—occupy a special place:

1. *Against hypocrisy.* The attacks of the prophet of Nazareth against hypocrites must have been appalling. Even in the version of the phlegmatic Matthew they cause shivers to pass down our spines.[40] Completely in the line of the ancient prophets who proclaimed justice, and who also denounced all formalism, Jesus takes up the struggle against the world of pretence. Yet, he is more practical, sober, dangerous. He directly attacks certain traditions, from the almost innocent cleaning of dishes to the pompous Korban practices for the benefit of the temple.[41] He dares to place a pharisee below a publican, solely on the basis of that hypocrisy! [42] Whoever dares to be so sharp—and we know of many other statements, just as biting and more imaginative [43]—has to pay for it dearly. Nothing is, however, more just than the rejection of hypocrisy. It seems a simple principle of sound reason. And yet, how rare! Who shall count the centuries in which mankind lived in the accepted lie as if nature demanded the existence of free men and slaves, enslaved races and nations of rulers? Who could pay for even a millionth part of the propaganda of the deliberately spread lie which favors the egoism of a person, a business, or a country? [44] Hypocrisy is a form of lie through which one refuses to count oneself as the equal of

others. And that lie has a leader, namely, the great liar and the father of the lie.[45] By this we know enemy number one of the kingdom and, at the same time, the weapon of the prince of injustice.

2. *Against respect of persons.* This is merely one form of hypocrisy, but a particularly malicious and virtually ineradicable one. People give privileges for their own interests or for reasons of servility and thus perpetuate injustice in the world. Even the enemies of Jesus admitted that he was upright, did not care for any man, and did not regard the person of man.[46] Few explicit sayings have been preserved, but the whole of the behavior of Jesus withstands the test. He could not flatter. And the apostles followed his example. Who will forget the painfully concrete and alarmingly up-to-date attack of James against the place of honor for the rich woman with the ring? [47]

3. *The golden rule* expresses, as it were, the basic principle of the kingdom. It is perfect justice, and moreover has a psychological effectiveness. Do unto others as you would they should do unto you. That is nothing new. It is, according to Jesus, merely the summary of the law and the prophets.[48] There are contained in this one rule the greatest possible reforms and we see in advance what mutual relations will be like in eternal salvation.

4. *The final judgment* over our lives will be formed according to the degree to which we have contributed to the realization of human brotherhood, for the hungry, the naked, the sick, the displaced persons are brothers of the judge himself.[49] If this is, according to Jesus, the standard of the highest court of justice, then we must expect of his followers, of those who take him seriously, that they will actually work toward "a better world."

These four points, the importance of which can scarcely be over-

---

[35] Mt. 13, 27: one should note that the parables of this chapter deal with the kingdom of God.

[36] Jn. 12, 31; 14, 30; 16, 11.

[37] Mt. 4, 8-9.

[38] Mt. 12, 28.

[39] Eph. 6, 11-12; cf. 2, 2; 1 Cor. 2, 8.

[40] Mt. 23.

[41] Mt. 15, 1-20.

[42] Lk. 18, 9-14.

[43] Cf. Mt. 6, 1-18.

[44] One need only think of the reportage and propaganda from the Kremlin during Stalin's time, according to Trotsky "the greatest lie factory in the history of mankind," and of the brand of "official truth" in numerous Western countries.

[45] Jn. 8, 42-46. When heaven finally begins, the cry will be this: "Outside is everyone who loves and practices falsehood" (Rev. 22, 15).

[46] Mt. 22, 16.

[47] Jas. 2, 1-9.

[48] Mt. 7, 12.

[49] Mt. 25, 31-46.

estimated, are merely different applications or aspects of one basic principle, namely, that of the *fundamental equality of all persons.* It is with this that justice in the world stands or falls.

If our intuition were correct, namely, that Jesus really aimed at giving an impulse by concrete principles to the reforming of society, then we understand why he helped so many people. Those people expected something concrete. People do not come into the street with women and children merely to hear spiritual dissertations. People would never think of appointing their retreat master as king.[50] And they were only partly wrong.

There must then be traces of *practical realization.* And there are. A striking refrain occurs in the gospels, namely, "Give to the poor." [51] That was not obvious at that time! It is possible that in this point Jesus worked hand in hand with the Qumran sect; and in any case, he took part in the baptizer's movement, in which bread and clothes were distributed.[52] His small group also had a common purse intended for helping the poor.[53]

A typical case is Zaccheus who spontaneously renounces half his possessions and still retains enough to give fourfold to those whom he had squeezed.[54] "The meaning of this story is clear: if Jesus enters a man's house, two things automatically penetrate the consciousness of the host—the need of the poor and the doubtful origin of his own prosperity." [55] So intense is this helping activity in the circle of the disciples that a polemic can arise which concludes with the words: "For you always have the poor with you." [56] That is a sober and sobering statement through which all hot-tempered future dreams of a socio-political nature are renounced. Yet, it is no proof of social indifference. On the contrary, precisely because Jesus considered poverty to be an actually ineradicable evil, he did not leave the solution of the problem of the poor to a future project of an organizational nature, but fought in his time and in his surroundings untiringly for those who suffered from poverty.[57]

The first Christians must indeed have heard and seen certain things. How otherwise would they have had the idea of selling their possessions in great numbers, of distributing the yield and of having everything in common? [58] Luke, who tells of this with enthusiasm, was competent to record the action, but not to inspire it. This certainly came from Jesus himself.

Paul, who had never heard Jesus preach and had not participated in his messianic activity, was requested by his colleagues to organize a large collection. The idea certainly came from somewhere. A simple caprice was incapable of moving a person such as Paul to a task which would require the maximum use of diplomacy, an art in which he had not been greatly endowed by nature.[59] When he writes to the Galatians: ". . . only they would have us remember the poor, which . . . I was eager to do," [60] then he introduces us to the great and new offensives launched by Christianity.

The efforts of the first Christians are reflected even more clearly in the Epistle of James. Faith must be consistent; in other words, lead to deeds: "If a brother is ill-clad and in lack of daily food, and one of you says to him, 'Go in peace, be warmed and filled,' without giving him the things needed for the body, what does it profit?" [61] He quotes the commandment of loving one's neighbor as oneself as "the royal law," [62] demands a just reward for the workers,[63] the end of mutual wars and battles,[64] a more democratic spirit in liturgical meetings [65] and utters scathing words against the fire which causes a world of injustice to arise, namely, the evil tongue.[66] In a word, we find here all the great principles of Jesus' kingdom of justice. If we now consider that this man was Jesus' cousin, who became bishop of Jerusalem and exerted a very great influence on expanding Christianity,[67] then the message of Jesus certainly seems to have unleashed something.

A KINGDOM OF PEACE

We have always thought that the kingdom of Christ was one of peace. We were touched by the song of the angels about a warm Christmas Eve during a cold winter. There was in our hearts a great nostalgia for deep, interior peace. Yet, did we ever associate this

[50] Jn. 6, 15.
[51] Mk. 10, 21; Lk. 12, 33; Mt. 25, 35.
[52] Lk. 3, 10-14.
[53] Mk. 14, 5; Jn. 12, 5; 13, 29.
[54] Lk. 19, 8.
[55] E. Stauffer, *Die Botschaft Jesu damals und heute* (Bern, 1959), p. 89.
[56] Mk. 14, 7.
[57] E. Stauffer *op. cit.*, p. 88.
[58] Acts 2, 44-45.
[59] On this collection and Paul's cautious behavior cf. Acts 11, 29-30;

12, 25; Rom. 15-28; 1 Cor. 16, 1-4; 2 Cor. 8-9.
[60] Gal. 2, 10.
[61] Jas. 2, 15-16.
[62] Jas. 2, 8.
[63] Jas. 5, 4.
[64] Jas. 4, 1-2.
[65] Jas. 2, 1-9.
[66] Jas. 3, 5.
[67] On the important role he played, cf. Acts 12, 17; 15, 13; 21, 18; **Gal.** 1, 19; 2, 9.12.

with "justice"? Were peace *and* justice working together to build
our ideal world? Did Jesus' words about peace acquire their *true*
perspective?

When Jesus sent out his disciples, it was in order to proclaim the
kingdom. But what did they have to say about it? The evangelists
tell us scarcely anything about this, and what they do say—and
what we must consequently normally regard as being essential—is in
most cases usually played down. They had to bring their goodness
to the homes of men, such an intense goodness that it would effect
miracles and peace.[68] Is it really possible that an ordinary greeting
was meant by Jesus when he said: "Go, and upon entering, say:
'Good day!'" And in a similar way the final words of Jesus would
be an equivalent of "Good-bye for now, keep well!" [69] if he wished
peace for the sick woman, the sinner, and the disciples.[70]

In common with justice, Jesus' peace must be seen against a
prophetic background. These two things are connected throughout
the Old Testament in a very concrete sense. "Justice and peace are
the messianic commodities par excellence," say G. Spicq, alluding
to Revelation 7, 3, where Jesus is represented as the genuine Melchizedek, whose name means: "king of justice" and also "king of
peace." [71]

We cannot consequently deal lightly with the two or three
beatitudes in which, alongside the just, precisely the peacemakers,
the meek and the merciful are blessed.[72] We are confronted here
with something essential, and something *positive*. It is not a matter
of weakness or resignation. The peacemakers will be called *children
of God*, i.e., they shall resemble God in a special way, belong to the
same family. Now, particularly for the Semite, God is par excellence the active one, the creator, the reconciler. The God of peace
is he who crushes Satan under the feet of the faithful [73] and who
caused the great shepherd of the sheep to rise from the dead.[74] God
is not a God of disorder, but of peace, i.e., of concord.[75] The
peacemakers are consequently the bringers of peace, the reconcilers;
they literally *create* unity where there was estrangement or
hatred.

Seen with modern eyes, two things in particular seem striking to
me for the content and quality of that peace:

1. *The principle of forgiveness*. A kingdom of mere justice
would still be inhuman. People are imperfect, and their relations
cannot be regulated on the basis of faultless lives. The only solution

in the case of mistakes both in the family and in the State is forgiveness, although this does not of course exclude punitive measures. Jesus laid such great stress on this that it seems for some people the most characteristic point of Christian morals. He makes forgiveness a condition of prayer, *his* prayer in fact! Matthew and Luke stress this even further, each in his own way.[76] Just as the prophets demand justice before acts of cult, Jesus forbids coming to the altar with an offering without first having granted forgiveness.[77] Our readiness to forgive must be unlimited: it must recur seventy times seven, i.e., eternally.[78] The reason is perfectly clear from the parable: Whoever is forgiven a debt of ten thousand heavy mortgages, may not send his neighbor into prison for a hundred small notes.[79]

It is striking how all the apostles, irrespective of their temperaments, have stressed this demand for forgiveness, even of the rewarding of evil with good.[80] This will be one of the foundations of a new community.

2. *The principle of non-violence.* Whoever says non-violence thinks of Ghandi and consequently, of conflict. The principle of non-violence presumes that people know what they want to obtain, are not afraid, wish to make great sacrifices, but will not resort to the use of weapons other than those of a moral nature. And that is just what Jesus wants. He sends his disciples as sheep among wolves.[81] He rides into Jerusalem, as a king, as the founder of a kingdom, but not seated on a warlike horse. "Fear not, daughter of Zion; behold, your King is coming, sitting on an ass's colt." [82] He does not wish to be defended either by the swords of his disciples or by the legions of his Father.[83] And it is precisely here that his

[68] Mt. 10, 8; 11, 5; Lk. 10, 5-7; 9, 1-2.

[69] Mk. 5, 3; Lk. 7, 50; 8, 48; Jn. 20, 19.21.26.

[70] Cf. J. Comblin, *Theologie de la Paix*, Vol. I: *Principes* (Paris, 1960), pp. 181-201.

[71] C. Spicq, *L'Epitre aux Hébreux* (*Bibl. Jerus.*), 1957[2], p. 37.

[72] Mt. 5, 5.7.9. The authenticity of v.5 (meek) is disputed.

[73] Rom. 16, 20.

[74] Heb. 13, 20.

[75] 1 Cor. 14, 33.

[76] Matthew says: "As we also have forgiven our debtors." (Mt. 6, 12; cf. v. 14-15); Lk. 10, 4 speaks of forgiving all who are indebted to us.

[77] Mt. 5, 24; cf. 38-47.

[78] Mt. 18, 22.

[79] Mt. 18, 22-35. A single talent is in itself a fabulous sum, a heavy charge. A denarius represents the daily wage of a worker in an underdeveloped country.

[80] Cf. 1. Thess. 5, 15; Rom. 12, 14; 1. Pet. 3, 9; cf. 2, 15-24; 1 Jn. 4, 10-11; Jas. 3, 17.

[81] Mt. 10, 16.

[82] Jn. 12, 14-16; at that actual moment the disciples did not realize the significance of what they were witnessing.

[83] Mt. 26, 51-54.

victory over the prince of darkness lies, who thought he had already won the victory.[84]

Such readiness for martyrdom, even for the cross, demands heroic courage. It also implies the courage for an open point of view, for opposition and (momentary) separation. To restore justice is a labor involving struggle and tears. Jesus foresaw painful divisions,[85] and in that sense, he declared that he was not coming to bring peace, but the sword.[86]

It is precisely to that seemingly powerless devotion to peace that Jesus ascribes a special efficacy. The kingdom will be established since it is a kingdom of peace. Why is Jesus himself so irresistible? Why does *everyone* wish to be taught by him? Because he is *meek and lowly in heart*.[87] And the same thing will happen for those who are genuinely his disciples. They will be persecuted, for a servant does not stand above his master, but people will also live by their words! [88]

Not long ago we experienced a touching illustration of this. On the day of his coronation, on November 4, 1958, while the Catholic world cast an unsympathetic glance at the heavily bent man who had to follow the great Pius XII, Pope John XXIII expressed a conviction which seemed a bit too simple: "It is a fact that the physiognomy of all popes reflects the face of Christ, or rather should reflect it . . . Yet the core of divine instructions and the lesson which summarize and support everything is this word of the gospels: 'Learn from me; for I am gentle and lowly in heart.' I beseech you, that you should henceforth always pray on behalf of your high priest that he may obtain the favor of being able daily to progress in that evangelical mildness and lowliness. We are, in fact, certain that the greatest progress and most favorable developments will spring from the practice of this virtue, and that thanks to this way of acting, as father of all who believe, events of great importance will take place, even as far as the social and earthly aspects of human necessities are concerned."

One can hardly say that the way in which Pope John understood the peace of Christ did not cause something to stir in the world. Just to give an example, he placed groups of Protestants and those of Orthodox beliefs in the best positions in St. Peter's for the largest Council in history, and received from Khrushchev more than congratulations and telegrams of sympathy. His testament, *Pacem in*

Terris, just as the peace of the Lord, was not given from the world, but certainly for the world in which it is effective as a seed of the kingdom.[89]

Peace is a germinating seed; James reminds us of this in a sentence which summarizes magnificently the preceding pages: "And the harvest of righteousness is sown in peace, for the benefit of those who make peace." [90] To discuss how that peace has *now* to be created, or sown, falls outside our framework and competence. Christianity has achieved good results, although negative points still stand on our balance sheet: religious wars, the inquisition, the world record in annihilation practices.[91] The apostles crossed Palestine and sailed over the sea as bearers of peace to the homes of men. They reconciled masters and slaves, held their agapes and gave the kiss of peace. They established peace on the scale of the society at that time: the *family*, the small circle, the association. If we wish to imitate them, then we have to be the first in the definitive regulation of colonialism, effectiveness of the United Nations, solidarity with the underdeveloped peoples, elimination of atomic and hydrogen bombs, eradication of racism and the furtherance of the ecumenical movement.

Yet, this whole spirit of "Pax Christi" must continue to be built upon the everyday practice of forgiveness and upon the renunciation of violence in *all* relationships, and that will have to begin, just as for the apostles, by bringing peace *into our homes*. And here too it will be important, just as in the matter of justice, not to restrict ourselves to surface appearances. There is an enemy of peace, the specialist in the use of violence and torture, the "murderer from the beginning." [92] Only those can cope with him in the final analysis who can be fully called children of God, that is, those who have become related by nature to the "God of peace." [93]

[84] Jn. 14, 30; 16, 11; cf. 12, 32.
[85] Mt. 10, 34.
[86] Mt. 10, 37-39; Lk. 12, 51-53; 14, 26-27.
[87] Mt. 11, 28-30.
[88] Jn. 15, 20.
[89] Jn. 14, 27; 16, 33; cf. J. Comblin, *op. cit.*, pp. 202-210.
[90] Jas. 3, 18; see also the previous context, where love of peace is ranked high among the qualities of "heavenly wisdom."

[91] A survey of cases of extermination in world history noted between A.D. 325 and 1912, about 24,321,000 people murdered by non-Christians and 17,390,000 by Christians. Cf. E. Stauffer, *op. cit.*, p. 20.
[92] Jn. 8, 44.
[93] Rom. 15, 33; cf. 16, 20; 1 Cor. 14, 33; 2 Cor. 13, 11; Phil. 4, 9; 1 Thess. 5, 23; 2 Thess. 3, 15; cf. Heb. 7, 2; 13, 20.

UNIVERSALITY

It seems to us today so obvious that the kingdom of God must have universal dimensions that we almost no longer see how original this feature is.[94] For the Jews, to a certain extent the most universalistic people in the world never succeeded in bringing their ideals into harmony with the practical nationalism of daily life and even of religion.[95] Jesus himself could be placed on the same level by a superficial observer, for he never appeared beyond the limits of his own country. He seems to have kept far away from the large Hellenistic cities in Palestine itself,[96] refusing to give the bread of the children to dogs—a term of abuse which must certainly go back to him[97]—and forbidding his disciples formally to enter the path of the heathens or to proclaim the message in Samaria.[68]

For us, nevertheless, it is an already established fact that he did, after all, proclaim a universal kingdom. All we have said points to this. How can a kingdom which is not directed to *all* men be just?

Upon closer inspection, we discover an antinomy. To start with, there is the absence of a mysticism of Israel. Throughout the whole Old Testament we hear that the men of God are involved with the present and future of the house of Israel. Their oracles, even the most universal of them, always remain within the perspective of their own race. We do not find that atmosphere in the gospels. We see, on the contrary, heathen examples cited with obvious intent: the widows of Sarepta and the Syrian Naaman,[99] the conversion of Niniveh, the queen of Sheba,[100] the centurion of Capernaum[101] and a whole caravan of Samaritans.[102]

These were still only slight cracks in the wall surrounding the chosen people. What indignation must then have been caused by the clear declaration that God's people enjoy no exclusive privilege. The workers of the eleventh hour, the heathens, will receive just as much as they who toiled from the break of day.[103] This openness will have its effect: "I tell you, many will come from east and west, and sit at table with Abraham, and Isaac, and Jacob in the kingdom of heaven, while the sons of the kingdom will be thrown into the outer darkness."[104]

The positive step toward the heathens was taken by the synoptic evangelists, each in his own way, after the resurrection.[105] And John reveals to us in a characteristic anecdote the reason for this action and this mystery. A few Greeks wish to see Jesus, but he retorts that contact at that moment would be unprofitable. The grain of corn has first to die and ripen in the soil.[106] Only the cross opened the furrows for this harvest: this was the ransom for the "many," [107] or to hear it from Jesus himself through the words of John: "And I, when I am lifted up from the earth, will draw all men to myself." [108]

This is a totally new principle of universality. Previously, a few people had admittedly arrived at the *idea* of a universal community, such as Plato's *Republic*, "for reasons of symmetry," according to the somewhat cruel, but true remark of Bergson. Yet they did not touch the foundations of human nature, and were consequently powerless in the face of ancient privileges, the spirit of caste and nationalism. It is very probable that even Jesus' principle of complete equality and the rejection of any respect of persons would not have been in a position to change matters really even if Peter expressly invokes that principle in order to include the heathens in the Christian community.[109]

It was in fact Paul who first gave the decisive turn, not as if *he* were more inclined to universality—perhaps the contrary—but he understood the import of the *Person* of Jesus as the principle of the new community. It is not the law, it is not idealistic principles that make us one. Paul's discussion with Peter exposes the new basis in one sentence, indicating why the heathens have equal rights: ". . . a man is not justified by works of the law, but through faith in Jesus Christ." [110] It is the mystical connection with the crucified and

[94] Cf. W. Gallus, *The Universality of the Kingdom of God in the Gospels and the Acts of the Apostles* (Washington, 1945); A. Fridrichsen, "Contribution a l'étude de la pensée missionnaire dans le Nouveau Testament," in *Conjectanea Neotestamentica*, Vol. 6, (Uppsala 1937); M. Meinertz, "Jesus und die Heidenmission," in *Neutest. Abhandl.* (1935).

[95] In a certain sense, the broad-thinking Romans and Hellenists were, after all, more narrowminded; it is easy to declare oneself universal if one rules over everyone.

[96] Cf. Hofmans, *De achtergrond. Palestina, toen Jezus daar leefde.*

[97] Mt. 15, 26; Mk. 7, 27; omitted by Luke.

[98] Mt. 10, 5-6.

[99] Lk. 4, 25-27.

[100] Mt. 12, 38-42; Lk. 11, 29-32.

[101] Mt. 8, 5-10.

[102] Lk. 10, 33-37; 17, 15-19. Jn. 4.

[103] Mt. 20, 1-16; cf. A. Feuillet, "Les ouvriers de la vigne et la théolgie de l'alliance," in *Recherches sciences relig.* 34. (1947), pp. 303-327.

[104] Mt. 8, 11.

[105] Mt. 28, 16-20; Mk. 16, 15-18 (by Mark or by an editor); Lk. 24, 47.

[106] Jn. 12, 20-24.

[107] Mk. 10, 45.

[108] Jn. 12, 32.

[109] Acts 10, 34.

[110] Gal. 2, 16.

resurrected Christ which is the principle of actual universality. Only through the cross of Jesus did two worlds become one. He pulled down the separating wall by destroying the emnity *in his flesh*.[111] This gave rise to the boldest affirmation of antiquity: "Here there cannot be Greek and Jew, circumcised and uncircumcised, barbarian, Scythian, slave, free man, but Christ is all, and in all." [112]

This confirms and completes the information in the gospels, according to which Jesus founded a universal kingdom of God, not by *saying* that he was tolerant in his thinking, but by *giving his life* (as the God-man and servant of the Father) for the benefit of all.

The real origin of Christian universalism consequently lies in the cross and only partly in Jesus' preaching. Even the disciples were not in a position to understand such a thing prior to the coming of the Spirit. A great deal of deepening and enlightenment was necessary before Peter penetrated to the "mystery." Universality is for him the mysterious aspect of the plan for salvation: [113] Through faith *all people* have free access to God, whom it had pleased to allow his whole fullness to dwell in the man, Jesus, "and through him to reconcile to himself all things, whether on earth, or in heaven." [114] Consequently, the celebration of the eucharist is the universal moment of our time, on condition that the eating of his body and the drinking of his blood take place in a spirit of receptivity to him who shed that blood for the saving of the many.

TRANSCENDENCE

Among the contemporaries of Jesus, only the Sadducees rejected the resurrection. They believed that God's kingdom could have meaning for man only in a temporal context, as it once did for centuries-long according to the Old Testament. In the gospels, it is crystal clear that Jesus speaks of a kingdom that is final and eternal. It has even become usual to regard Christianity as a religion of "heaven," though it is doubtful if this is exactly what Jesus meant and established. We have to go into this a bit deeper.

Not a few commentators on the Gospel texts about the kingdom of God distinguish between two kinds of statements. There are those which point to a kingdom beyond this life, and others which indicate the beginnings of the kingdom here on earth. The very ambiguity of the term is held to account for its various uses, but this is hardly a good explanation. On the contrary, Jesus always spoke of one and the same kingdom.

The difficulty lies with ourselves. We look upon death as such a violent break that our notion of time is limited to the duration of our own lives. What comes after is either a kind of long, dark interim or else a direct flight upwards to a wholly spiritual world. We place the eschatological feast [115] in a place completely cut off from the world as we know it, and this seems to contradict what is said about the kingdom of God being already within us.[116] In fact, the gospels even establish the time of the kingdom: John the Baptist marks the end of a period,[117] and the casting out of devils announces the arrival of the kingdom.[118]

The apparent contradiction disappears only when we view the total picture: God's kingdom *is* eternal, but it has *already* begun.[119] In one sense there is nothing more to expect, for the last days are here. And because the eschatological period is underway, we long for its perfect realization, much as our excitement grows when a movie finally begins to appear on the screen.

The first Christians, knowing that this was to be the final phase of human history, did not tie themselves down. As the last sprint began, they stretched their legs and craned their necks and called out to the victor who had gone before them. For Paul's friends, the resurrection was the starting shot and the small communities along the Mediterranean echoed with the cry, "Lord, come!" [120] If Jesus

[111] Eph. 2, 14-17.

[112] Col. 3, 11.

[113] Eph. 1, 9; 3, 9-10; Col. 1, 26-27.

[114] Col. 1, 20.

[115] Mt. 8, 11; 22, 1-14; cf. Is. 25, 6; Rev. 19, 9.

[116] Lk. 17, 20-21.

[117] Lk. 16, 16.

[118] Mt. 12, 28.

[119] There is already an extensive literature on the problem of the "consequent," or "realized," eschatology. See among others: W. G. Kummel, *Das Neue Testament, Geschichte der Erforschung seiner Probleme* (Freiburg, 1958), pp. 286-309; R. Schnackenburg, "Eschatologie im Neuen Testament," in *Ex. Theol. Kirche,* (1952²), pp. 1088-1093; A. Feuillet, "Parousie," in *Dict. Bibl. Suppl.,* Vol. 6, (1960),

cols. 1331-1419. Among the most important of recent studies, besides Feuillet's article just mentioned, we quote: O. Cullmann, *Christus und die Zeit* (Zurich, 1946) (1962³); C. H. Dodd, *The Parables of the Kingdom* (London, 1946); R. Bultmann, *Geschichte und Eschatologie* (Tübingen, 1957); Eng. trans: *History and Eschatology* (New York, Harper, 1962); J. A. T. Robinson, *Jesus and His Coming* (London, 1957); W. Kreck, *Die Zukunft des Gekommenen, Grundprobleme der Eschatologie,* (Munich, 1961); St. S. Smalley, "The Delay of the Parousia," in *Journ. Bibl. Lit.* 83 (1964), pp. 41-54.

[120] 1 Cor. 16, 22; cf. 11, 26; Rev. 22, 20; cf. v. 17.

comes, all darkness will be dispelled, the disciples will see him and be with him, and the whole of creation, even the animals and the trees, will celebrate the definitive redemption.[121] But this will be on earth, in a renewed universe during the last phase.[122]

The reality was sobering. Christians died and Christ had not yet returned! Entire generations passed away and nothing unusual happened! Violent persecutions stilled the initial enthusiasm and the Christians became restless and anxious.[123] Yet, Christ had predicted that though the kingdom had come, difficult times were ahead. The disciples should have understood this when they heard the apocalyptic parables, especially the one retold in small gatherings far from the excitable masses. The kingdom of God is incredibly small, tiny as a mustard seed; weeds will grow with the grain, more weeds than one could imagine; fishes in the net are not all healthy, and it would be an impossible task to purify the Church of her less-than-ideal members.[124]

Are there two phases to the kingdom after all? In one sense Yes, but essentially No. The transcendent is now present. Whoever burns with desire to be with Christ[125] will toil day and night, travel, teach, spread the principles of social justice,[126] and judge positively all human values.[127] The first Christians didn't choose between transcendence and incarnation; they knew that all things created had acquired absolute value through the incarnation. The transmaterial was now present in matter. The *eternal* kingdom *was* begun.

And where then is the stress, on the *now* or on the *eternal?* On both, but much more on the eternal. In the spirit of late-Jewish spirituality, Jesus spoke often of the contradiction between "the present time" and "the age to come,"[128] and between "treasures on earth" and "treasures in heaven."[129] It may appear on the surface that this way of speaking is not consonant with the idea of kingdom, almost as if death and judgment are the determining events and not the coming of the kingdom. But, in fact, the transcendent and eternal notes of the kingdom are so strongly emphasized here that "eternal life" and the "kingdom of God" have become interchangeable.[130]

The most forceful expressions in this direction are doubtlessly the words: "What does it profit a man . . ."[131] and the parables of the wealthy farmer[132] and the rich man.[133] These passages reject any purely inner-worldly ideal. To be rich, cultured and famous is worthless if one's "soul" has to suffer. Jesus was no Platonist for whom the soul rejoiced in its liberation from the body and who felt that the soul must be carefully protected during its time on earth. As the parallel text from Luke shows, "soul" is simply another term for "person" when this latter is considered in the perspective of eternity and of preparedness for the judgment.[134] Jesus regards eternity very concretely: it is better to go into heaven with one eye than into hell with two.[135] To lose one's soul is to lose one's whole self.

To escape the temptation of obscuring what is clear or of deceiving oneself in this matter, perhaps one has to have had some experience of death—a sense of the relativity of all things which we feel as death threatens a loved one, for example—or one has to have encountered the risen Christ in whom eternity is *today*. Paul knew the shortness of time: he who marries must be as if he were not married.[136] This doesn't mean that he must live as a celibate,[137] but rather that he must be guided by a higher ideal than that of the rich man or of the successful businessman.[138] What else can we expect when we compare the temporal with the eternal?

THE TRUE VISAGE: THE FAMILY OF THE FATHER [139]

The reader may have the impression that this heading is far from our point. After dealing with the concrete characteristics of the kingdom of God, it would appear that "the family of the Father" is too vague. Though Jesus surely called God his Father, can this

[121] Cf. Rom. 8, 19-22.
[122] See below the last chapter.
[123] Cf. 2 Pet. 3, 8-11; also 1 Thess. 4, 13-18; 2 Thess. 2, 1-12.
[124] Mt. 13, 24-33; Mk. 4, 26-29; 1 Cor. 15, 24.
[125] Phil. 1, 23.
[126] 1 Thess. 4, 11; 2 Thess. 3, 8-12.
[127] Cf. Phil. 4, 8-9.
[128] Mt. 12, 31; Mk. 10, 30; Lk. 20, 34-35.
[129] Mt. 6, 19-21.
[130] Mk. 9, 45-47.
[131] Mk. 7, 36-37.
[132] Lk. 12, 13-21.
[133] Lk. 16, 19-31.

[134] Lk. 9, 25; see also pp. 77-78.
[135] Mk. 9, 43-48.
[136] 1 Cor. 7, 29-31.
[137] 1 Cor. 7, 5.
[138] 1 Cor. 7, 30.
[139] Cf. G. Schrenk, G. Quell, "Pater" in *TWNT*, 5, pp. 946-1024; H. W. Montefiore, "God as Father in the Synoptic Gospels," in *New Test. Studies*, Vol. 3, (1956), pp. 31-46; P. Schreurs, "La paternité divine dans Mt. 5, 45 et 6, 26-32," in *Ephem. Theol. Lov.*, 36 (1960), pp. 593-624, with an excellent exposition of the problem and bibliography (pp. 594-599).

have been more than the expression of an ardent and poetic sentiment?

It is true that the gospels offer little explanation and less speculation on the meaning of divine fatherhood. A definitive explanation requires a specific theological viewpoint which, in turn, demands that certain preliminary questions be answered about, for example, Christ's divinity, his incarnation, and so on. This matter is of such vital importance, however (Christ even relates it with the theme of kingdom), that we have to go a little deeper into it here. What we are looking for is none other than the already present, trans-material reality, that is to say, the true but not yet visible visage of redeemed humanity.

Our point of departure is the remarkable fact that from the very beginning the most varied groups of Christians have lived in the conviction that they were all brothers and in a very special way, children of God. "See what kind of love the Father has bestowed upon us, that we should be called children of God, and such we are," says John.[140] St. Peter claims that we are as newborn children who call Father him who judges without respect of persons and who has made us a holy, priestly people.[141] According to St. Paul, we have gone through an incredible revolution: we are new creatures! [142] He never tires of repeating that this new life, received in baptism, is poured into our hearts by the Holy Spirit who allows us to pray, "Abba, Father!" [143] Another Christian says that we have "become partakers of the divine nature." [144]

It is impossible to explain all these texts as "strongly metaphorical"; we are dealing with something real. Nor is it purely individual, in the sense of a private intimacy with God. The new birth is, in fact, necessary in order to enter the kingdom.[145] When James invites us to live constantly before the face of God the Father, he is reminding us of the election which made us heirs of the kingdom.[146]

The priesthood of the faithful is communal as a matter of course, not because it is common to all, but because all exercise their priestly function as a community, that is, they have free access to God. The name, "brothers," which they have in common with various other circles, has a distinctive meaning: "So then you are no longer strangers and sojourners, but you are fellow citizens with the saints and members of the household of God." [147] "Members of the household of God" means that our expression, "the kingdom of God," also implies "the family of God."

What we must examine now is whether this fact was proclaimed by Jesus. The diversity of the sources already provides an argument in favor of such an assumption. Besides, how would, they have dared to make such a claim and what reasoning could they have employed in support of it? Brilliant though Paul may be, the simple fact of the resurrection does not prove, logically speaking, that we have become children of God. And how could Paul know it, since a risen figure brings to pass, but does not speak?

Two facts provide us with valuable pointers. In the first place, it is established that in his *personal prayer* Jesus always addresses his "Father." This is clear from all the texts.[148] Since *we* know it, the apostles must have known it. For that matter, the prayer which he taught them at their own request also beings with "Father." [149] It is important to note that we are not dealing here with a purely individual prayer, but with the ardent prayer of the entire Christian community, which desires that God's name shall be glorified over the entire world, that his plan of salvation shall be accomplished "on earth as it is in heaven" and expressly—in both Luke and Matthew —that his *kingdom* shall come.[150] This already strongly suggests that the Christians, those who belong to the kingdom, as such feel themselves members of a family of which God is the Father.

We find the second pointer in a number of cases in which Jesus does not speak of the kingdom of heaven, but of the kingdom *of the Father*. These occasions are always closely connected with the disciples. They are the "little flock" who have been granted the kingdom by *their* Father.[151] It is they, too, who are told, intimately in an otherwise objective Matthew: "So it is not the will of my Father who is in heaven that one of these little ones should perish," [152] This

---

140 1 Jn. 3, 1; cf. Jn. 1, 12-13; 14, 19-24.
141 1 Pet. 1, 17; 2, 2. 9-10.
142 2 Cor. 5, 14-17; Gal. 6, 15.
143 Rom. 8, 15; Gal. 4, 5-6.
144 2 Pet. 1, 3-4.
145 Jn. 3, 5.
146 Jas. 1, 25; 2, 5.
147 Eph. 2, 19; cf. 3, 5-6; Heb. 3, 6; 12, 22-23; "the assembly of the firstborn."
148 Cf. Mt. 11, 25; 26, 29-32; Mk. 14,

36; Lk. 10, 21; 22, 42; 23, 34-46; Jn. 11, 41; 12, 27-28; 17, 1.
149 Mt. 6, 10; Lk. 11, 2. The short formula of Luke ("Father") is here undoubtedly more original than that of Matthew's" Our Father who art in heaven."
150 Mt. 6, 10; Lk. 11, 2.
151 Lk. 12, 32.
152 Mt. 18, 14.

is evidently not purely poetic, a fitting name for the Father because he has created a nature so overwhelmingly beautiful, with
birds and flowers, or because his providence safeguards man, although these texts also seem to refer to a saving, creative, and thus
specifically fatherly activity.[153] The remarkable thing indeed is that
the reference here is not to a God-man relationship, since the words
are addressed to a particular, well-defined group: "your Father." It
is he too who has given the group the special gift of the kingdom,
the Spirit,[154] with the result that they will shine like the sun in the
kingdom of their Father.[155] From all this the apostles could conclude: the kingdom belongs to the Father; he who enters the kingdom, therefore, has God as his Father.

Relying upon these weighty arguments we may then also assume
a metaphysical depth in other cases, as when Jesus speaks of the
infinite mercy of God who seeks the lost sheep, grants forgiveness
to the prodigal son and certainly the most typical case, exposes the
entire mutual relationship to the elder son: "You are always with
me, and all that is mine is yours." [156] Is this then no longer metaphorical, but a direct rendering of the actual state of affairs? If this
is so, we must come to the same conclusion regarding the demand
for forgiveness, in imitation of the Father, who makes his sun to rise
on the evil and the good.[157] This would be not so much a philosophical principle of equality as a consequence of God's fatherhood.
And the same may also be said of the truly limitless confidence
which we may place in him.[158]

There is possibly one last text that puts us on the track of the leap
in the apostles' train of thought. It concerns Jesus' cry of jubilation
when he asserts that no one knows him except the Father, and that
only he himself knows the Father (and those to whom he chooses to
reveal him).[159] The reference here is naturally to a *vital* knowledge
of the Father that presupposes a certain identity. If it is certain that
Jesus is uniquely the "son" of the Father in his devotional life and in
ordinary everyday life, and if, then, that son has chosen to reveal his
own experience to them in a truly brotherly manner—for have we
not, in fact, discerned this complete equality, even in weakness and
suffering, with sin alone excluded,[160] and had they not seen him
with their eyes, felt him with their hands [161]—then they were en-
titled to assume that together with Jesus, and thanks to him, they
became members of one family, with God as their Father.

We have already seen that the apostles did indeed arrive at this conclusion, although the gospels offer us no certainty concerning the manner in which they did so. I believe, however, that the suggestions I have just made are not entirely improbable.

Whatever the exact facts of the matter, the result was overwhelming. The realization that the kingdom of righteousness and peace, having universal dimensions in time and space, was by nature strictly divine—not only in the sense that God is its origin but that it ends in the apotheosis of humanity through a new personal relationship with the "Father,"—unleashed in the world an unparalleled mystical offensive. Jesus, the first and incomparably the greatest of all mystics, sets in motion a wave of contact with God that still continues and that undoubtedly will not end until it is transformed into a clear contemplation and an even more perfect apprehension of the Father's love.

It would not be feasible here to give even a short sketch of this development in which humanity became in a certain measure experimentally aware of the infinitely great *rapprochement* between itself and God. We shall also pass over the question of whether it is not precisely *this* consciousness of God's fatherhood which is called upon to save what is "holy" in a historical development in which nature is becoming increasingly "profane." Has not this humanity, freed from superstition and with head held high, become in a special manner capable of that awesomely glorious calling assigned by the preacher of the kingdom to the king of creation? Let us hope that this may provide a working hypothesis for scholars more adequately equipped to deal with this theme.

We, on our part, wish merely to determine how far in our present times this fatherhood of God provides the answer (still for the greater part unconscious) to the increasingly evident need for brotherhood among the people. It may well be the special task of the evangelists of our time to translate Jesus' message into modern terms, by showing how even after Jesus, who is the embodiment of this *rapprochement*, whole ranges of stirring and deeply sincere movements for brotherhood develop and grow from an intimately

[153] Mt. 6, 26-32. Cf. J. Schreurs, *op. cit.*
[154] Mt. 10, 20.
[155] Mt. 13, 43.
[156] Lk. 15, 31.
[157] Mt. 5, 44-45.
[158] Mt. 7, 11; Lk. 11, 9-13.
[159] Mt. 11, 25-27; Lk. 10, 21-22. This statement is so significant that one is surprised at first to find it in the synoptics; it is, therefore, currently known as the "Johannine logion."
[160] Heb. 2, 11-14; 4, 15; cf. Rom. 8, 28-29.
[161] 1 Jn. 1, 1-2.

warm relationship with him who makes all brothers, since he is the
Father of all. Such movements aspire to promote a sensitive yet
vigorous approach to everything relating to the human community.
Such an aspiration is expressed in the prayer of an important, modern founder of fraternities:

> Father,
> I place my trust in you.
> Do with me what you will.
> I thank you.
> I am prepared for everything,
> I accept everything,
> if only your will be done in me
> and in all your creatures.
> I desire nothing else, my God.
> I lay my soul in your hands,
> I give it to you
> with all the love of my heart,
> because I love you,
> because it is for me a necessity of love
> to give myself,
> to abandon myself to you without reserve,
> with infinite trust
> for you are my Father.[162]

There is one last conclusion to be noted here. The fact that the
"divine humility" goes so far brings a radical renewal to the entire
struggle for the right and even to the passive zeal for peace. This
ardor, which is nowhere greater than among mystics, becomes increasingly disinterested. If God is truly a Father, then everything
belongs to him. This point is so important that we must devote a
separate section to it.

GOD WHO DOES EVERYTHING

Is it necessary to prove that only God can bring forth children of God, that only the Father can form his family? This seems
self-evident, yet, we are constantly tempted to think that it is *we*
who must found the kingdom of God, that it is we who must help it
along, defend it and bring it to completion.

Jesus has always shown most plainly that everything is done by the Father. He invented the plan and is the true organizer of the kingdom. At every hour of the day he is busy seeking laborers for his work [163] or else he lets out his vineyard.[164] He prepares the great feast [165] and sends the invitations [166] to prodigal sons as well as to the excessively servile or self-sufficient firstborn.[167] We are accustomed to consider Jesus as the good shepherd. This perspective is derived from John [168] and is undoubtedly correct and profound, yet, Jesus himself forcefully states that his Father is the true shepherd whose activity lies at the basis of every return to the fold.[169]

God's activity is at once more profound, more fundamental and at the same time more sublime and more encompassing than any similar human effort could be. He alone thus holds the decisive trump cards that the human players would so gladly like to play. He alone knows the *hour*—this is a constant theme of early Christian conviction [170]—and he alone assigns the responsible positions, paying no heed to the ludicrous projects of those who imagine they can render him important services.[171]

Jesus expresses this same idea again in a different, perhaps more paradoxical manner. The kingdom of God is a present, a gift.[172] It is in no way a reward for a good life, but an initiative that comes from God. He loved us first; [173] when we were still sinners and in a state of total helplessness, he sent us his son, and it is precisely thus that he proves his characteristic love for us.[174] This we read in John and Paul, but Jesus puts it even more strongly, for his conclusions are more concrete. It may well be that God's gift comes as a surprise to the grievous sinner and the woman of easy virtue and invites them to total conversion.[175]

In this context one must view the important and ever perplexing pronouncement, that only children will enter the kingdom of God.[176] For indeed, children possess nothing and know that they have nothing to offer; they must receive everything: life, food,

---

[162] This "prayer of submission" of Charles de Foucauld is said every evening by the "fraternities" which have recourse to him.
[163] Mt. 20, 1-16.
[164] Mt. 21, 33-46.
[165] Mt. 22, 1-14.
[166] Lk. 14, 15-24.
[167] Lk. 15, 11-32.
[168] Jn. 10.

[169] Lk. 15, 3-7; Mt. 18, 12-14.
[170] Mk. 13, 32; Mt. 24, 36. 44. 50; 25, 13; Acts 1, 6-7; 1 Thess. 5, 1; 2 Pet. 3, 8-10; Rev. 3, 3.
[171] Mt. 20, 23.
[172] Lk. 12, 32.
[173] 1 Jn. 4, 10.
[174] Rom. 5, 6-8.
[175] Mt. 21, 31-32.

clothing, education, affection . . . It is such as they who possess the right mentality to accept the great gift of God.

These then are the principles. Sometimes the disciples are given an illustration. When, for example, things are going well for the kingdom, as during the disciples' first successful trial trip, Jesus exults and praises . . . the Father who reveals his secrets through such simple instruments.[177] Even more striking is the case of Peter who has discovered who Jesus is and seems sure of his ground. Jesus looks him in the face, congratulates him and immediately points out to him the true underlying cause of the event: "For flesh and blood have not [i.e., nothing human, nothing of yourself] revealed this to you, but my Father . . ." [178] On another occasion it will be at the sight of the yellow-white fields, with their ripe richness waiting for the harvest. The kingdom of God too is a great harvest, therefore, and once again we have the typical and to us, surprising statement, "Pray therefore the Lord of the harvest that *he* may send out laborers . . ." [179]

From this premise, which was self-evident for the apostles—otherwise they would never have begun—we may of course expect extraordinary things. For though God will normally keep to the rules of the human game, as principal actor he will nonetheless often allow himself a special set. For miracles will happen. Jesus promises it.[180] His disciples will not merely speak words of peace or simply be models of righteousness; they will be accompanied by signs. They must, for example, be in no way inferior to the mighty prophets of the Old Testament like Elijah and Elisha of whom Luke chiefly speaks, who performed great miracles of compassion and peace.

One of the results of this constant and reiterated insight is the *confidence* that is so characteristic of true Christianity. Men like John and Paul, who were anything but passive, seem to take a positive delight in emphasizing this dependence. Without Jesus we can do nothing, says John; no one can approach him unless the Father draws him near; still less can anyone snatch us from his hand, for the Father will not desire it.[182] Paul will show his beloved Philippians something even more intimate and more efficient than the ties of apostolic friendship and training: "I am sure that he who began a good work in you will bring it to completion at the day of Jesus Christ . . . for God is at work in you, both to will and to work for his good pleasure." [183]

At the close of the 1st century, the Christians were scourged by bestial persecutions and drew from that trust the certainty that enabled them to contemplate with the visionary of the Apocalypse an immense multitude of victors.[184] God cannot lose.

This dependence bore yet another good fruit. Not only did this love for the working God inspire heroic deeds for God; it also imparted a special quality to that love, as evidenced especially in the mystics. For, as Ruusbroec puts it, the whole of mysticism is based upon this "firstness" of God.

The mystic knows that his own fervor no longer blazes up from a purely human heart. "The love that devours him is not solely the love of a person for God: it is the love of God for all mankind. By way of God, through God, he loves humanity with a divine love. This is no longer the brotherhood preached by the philosphers in the name of reason, stressing that all men share in the same reasonable nature. One may incline respectfully before such a noble ideal, but one does not embrace it with passion. The mystical love for humanity, which is the same as God's love for his work, a love that created everything, would reveal the mystery of creation to anyone who knows the right questions to ask. It is in essence more metaphysical than moral." [185]

He who knows from certain experience that God does everything and that he himself and all mankind are born of love, has access to a deeper zone where, in the midst of sorrow and betrayal, pain can gain no entry, and all is peace as in God. It is this realization that constitutes the irresistible attraction of these people who are in such close contact with sin and supplication. They are often clumsy giants of meekness, gifted with a diamond power not their own.

Is Bergson right when he maintains that Christianity and mysticism are inseparably linked to all eternity and that the facts compel us to seek the explanation and the origin of this "dynamic religiosity" in which mankind may trust? Is he right to say that this origin is in fact the historical figure of Christ and that all great

[176] Mk. 10, 13-16.
[177] Lk. 10, 21.
[178] Mt. 16, 17.
[179] Mt. 9, 37-38.
[180] Mk. 16, 17-18; Lk. 10, 19; cf. Jas. 5, 14-15; Acts *passim*.
[181] Lk. 4, 24-27; 7, 15 (= 3 Kings 17, 23 LXX) etc.; cf. J. Comblin *op. cit.*, pp. 185-192.

[182] Jn. 5, 30; 6, 44; 10, 29.
[183] Phil. 1, 6; 2, 13.
[184] Rev. 7, 4-9.
[185] H. Bergson, *Les deux sources de la morale et de la religion* (Paris, 1948[58]); Eng. trans: *Two Sources of Morality and Religion* (Garden City, Doubleday, 1954).

mystics will be merely imitators and original yet imperfect continuers of what the Christ of the gospels was in perfection: one receptivity to the Father? [186]

The answer is a prayer of thanks.

THE PERSON WHO MUST GIVE THE WHOLE OF HIMSELF

It is not God alone who acts but also man, whose activity will increase precisely in the measure that God makes use of him. Nothing is so mistaken as the idea that God's work hinders or neutralizes human spontaneity, freedom and action. On the contrary, nothing liberates so many and such vital forces as the consciousness of being God's instrument. For the mystic, whose deepest intrinsic nature may be described as "a soul which acts and is used, whose freedom coincides with the divine operation," [187] the consciousness of God's all and of his own nothingness is the source of a most intense activity. And in this he is again literally following the example and the precepts of Jesus.

For to Jesus the kingdom of God is truly the "one thing that is necessary," that which must be "sought" and which relegates all the rest to second place,[188] or to put it metaphorically, the kingdom of God is the hidden treasure—this was intended for the farmer—or the precious pearl (which appealed to the men of that period even more than the women) for which everything else must be sacrificed.[189] These few texts would suffice, if we merely wished to "prove" that nothing more important exists.

Yet, there is more. Jesus is molding a mentality. He teaches his followers to pray, "Thy kingdom *come!* Thy will be done!" This may seem a trump card in the hands of the passive, a premium for the resigned "who take everything as it comes." But no, it is the perfect harmony between the consciousness of God's all-embracing activity and man's cooperation, not only outwardly and mechanically but from the depths of his being, from his desires, his wishes and his heart.

The "will of God" is not a decree that descends upon us ready-made and in the form of trials and afflictions, although these are essential, but is the will to salvation, the saving plans, the great undertaking. It is God's will that not one of these little ones should perish,[190] that all men should be saved.[191] It is his pleasure (literally:

his goodwill) to achieve this by means of the small and insignificant, like shepherds and a group of none too brilliant disciples [192] and in particular by means of the cross, something incomprehensible to human scheming.[193] But for this very reason this will of God entails complete submission and enthusiastic devotion: children and the poor wager everything; only the recklessly involved go to the cross.

The prayer, "Thy will be done," is thus no excuse for those who leave everything in the hands of blind chance or of the crafty enemy. The *engagement* that Jesus requires implies much more than the observance of a few precepts of worship and personal virtue bearing no relation at all to our true motives in life: job, family, friends. It is, in fact, the arrow of our deepest intent with all its sharpness and with all the wounds it will leave behind that must be aimed at the kingdom of God.

It is only too easy to find excuses; readers of Luke are well aware of what can be thought up to avoid accepting the invitation to the banquet of the kingdom.[194] There must be no evasions and more than goodwill alone. Half-work is not good enough for Jesus. His disciples must not resemble the foolish contractor who begins an ambitious edifice and only realizes afterward that he is not capable of finishing it, or the brainless general who has neglected to ascertain the numerical strength of the enemy.[195] All talents must be brought into play [196] and all difficulties courageously and directly tackled, even if it should cost an eye, a hand, or a leg.[197] Is this Jesus himself speaking, or can we detect some echo of the Christian community or of Luke, who complains of the disproportion between the children of light and the children of darkness, who are evidently much more enterprising in their affairs, more astute and more forceful, like the "unjust steward." [198]

Yet, even more than in his darting words, the disciples saw Jesus' standpoint revealed in his deeds. The Father does all, said Jesus, and he meant it, but this divine activity was channelled through his own

[186] H. Bergson, *op. cit.*, p. 254.
[187] H. Bergson, *op. cit.*, p. 246.
[188] Mk. 6, 33.
[189] Mt. 13, 44-46.
[190] Mt. 18, 14.
[191] 1 Tim. 2, 4; cf. the commentary by H. van den Bussche on these prayers in "Het Onze Vader," in *Coll. Brug. Gand.* 5 (1959), pp. 289-335; 467-495.
[192] Lk. 2, 14; Mt. 11, 26; Lk. 12, 32; cf. Gal. 1, 15.
[193] Mt. 16, 21-24.
[194] Lk. 14, 15-24.
[195] Lk. 14, 28-33.
[196] Mt. 25, 14-20; cf. Lk. 19, 12-27.
[197] Mk. 9, 46.
[198] Lk. 10, 4.

hands, his thoughts, his feelings, his contacts, through his weary
legs, his voice hoarse with speaking, his ever-warm smile, and his
tireless devotion to his task. This the disciples witnessed every day.
They knew his high tempo, experienced the freshness, the diversity
and the unfathomable depth of his well-prepared parables, well-
thought-out phrases and that sparkling speech which welled up
from an overfull heart and a tirelessly occupied spirit. They had
never seen anybody with such an active mind, so concerned, so rich
in ideas, and attentive in his friendship, even to the point of working
miracles.

Jesus' manner of acting taught the apostles how they too should
be active. They may well have retained with a mixture of exaspera-
tion and humor the advice he gave them during their training.
"Salute no one on the road." [199] A greeting indeed takes so much
time, and there is so much to be done. An apostle may not fritter
away his life in a series of nights out with the boys or coffee ses-
sions. To sum up in the idiom of our modern life: justice and
peace will not fall into our laps.

Pacem in Terris . . . We must diligently and actively assimilate
this phrase, in memory of an unforgettable pope. His words were
indeed words of peace but we must be cautious! For peace is one of
those words that are frequently used and misused, and any false and
tendentious interpretation would distort the entire meaning which
Christ's representative intended it to have. Take care, for the peace
of John XXIII does not consist of a simple, courteous desire, nor is
it a purely doctrinaire, carefully and well-documented instruction.
It is, however, a view of life and of society. For us it is and must
be a command and a bond, an earnest and solemn warning that
might be translated thus: peace is not something that is absorbed,
but is constructed, created . . . peace, that is, the ideal way of life
for humanity, does not develop spontaneously. Man must desire and
create it.[200]

THE PRINCIPLE OF REALIZATION: MEDIATION

It may seem a departure from the rules of healthy balance to
devote a separate section to an idea that occupies little place in the
Gospel: that the kingdom of God will be realized through mediation. And yet this point deserves our fullest attention, not only

because it is of the utmost importance for our time—there are currently an immense number of misunderstandings in this connection, such as the "fate of the unbaptized" and "no salvation outside the Church"—but because, qualitatively speaking, it occupies a decisive place in Jesus' preaching.

Basically, we are seeking the answer to the question, already posed by Celsus and frequently repeated since: Why was your Savior born so late? Are all those who died before his coming and all who remained outside his circle of contacts afterward to be deprived of what you call your salvation? It is thus no superfluous task to determine exactly how the kingdom of God is realized, the ways, the instruments, the laws of its development.

The principles of all this were latent in Jesus' surroundings. At the very initiation of the history of salvation, it was proclaimed with Abraham: "I will bless those who bless you, and him who curses you I will curse; and by you all the families of the earth will bless themselves." [201] The chosen people will, according to the songs of Deutero-Isaiah, be the instrument through which redemption will be granted to the peoples.[202] The painful purification of the People of God will be to the benefit of the entire world.

When Matthew and Luke began their gospels with a genealogical register, this was not merely to show that Jesus was "truly man" as we moderns conceive it but in order to demonstrate the organic link between him and all his forebears, beginning with Abraham, for the one, or simply with Adam, for the other.[203] Joseph, the son of David, will give to the son of Mary, his betrothed, the name Jesus, for he will be what his name implies, a redeemer, someone who frees others from sins they had committed.[204] All these facts forcefully express the basic principle of mediation: one people is the instrument of salvation for others; one savior redeems many.

This principle, which is constantly being applied in the natural order—one has only to think of the nature of procreation, education, inheritance, the thousand ways of representing and intervening in another's favor—may meet with a certain resistance when applied

[199] Lk. 10, 4; cf. the beautiful commentary by L. Cerfaux in *De Zendingsrede* (Doornik, 1958), pp. 39-48.

[200] Address by the then Cardinal Giovanni Batista Montini, Pentecost, 1963, shortly before the death of Pope John XXIII.

[201] Gen. 12, 2-3.

[202] Cf. Is. 42; 49; 53. Here we leave aside the questions of whether the suffering servant is a person; in any case, he is at least the people, too.

[203] Mt. 1, 1; Lk. 3, 38.

[204] Mt. 1, 21.

to our relationship with God. Is there anything more personal than
my love of God, my sin, my repentance, my forgiveness?

Many people today are so remote from the ties, so tenuously expressed in every birth which bind us together into one human family, that they almost deny any possibility, even for God, of touching the depths, the most personal essence of themselves. It would be
impossible or inadvisable to attempt to treat this problem here. It
must only be said that according to the Gospel, the realization of
the kingdom of God is based upon the possibility of the deepest
kind of communication.

In the first place and above all, let us consider Jesus himself. In his
actions and in his conversations with the most intimate of his disciples, it will become increasingly evident that his task extends much
further than preaching and healing. He does not even desire a powerful organization, but in his person the song of the suffering servant
will be uniquely fulfilled. The content of his life is to serve, to give
his life as ransom for the many.[205] He himself is a grain of wheat
which, dying, bears much fruit.[206] He is, according to the mysterious prophecy of the high priest, the one man who dies for all the
people; this means, clarifies John, that he would die, not for the
people alone but also in order to gather together the children of
God who are scattered abroad.[207]

We shall shortly examine in more detail how this conviction is
one of the most important clues to an understanding of Jesus' personality.[208] For the moment it is sufficient to recall the fact that
the classical doctrine of Christ the mediator is based upon the
express statement by Paul,[209] and even higher and more esssen-
tially, upon Jesus' own actions and words, at least as they were
later understood.

Jesus does not stand alone. The disciples will share the master's
fate, not only in the matter of persecution but also in the matter of
fruitfulness; people will listen to them; they will bear much
fruit.[210] This is said with Johannine clarity, although the synoptic
gospels already suggest it with more literal fidelity: there exists in
the kingdom of God something like the all-permeating salt, the light
that shines for others,[211] the city on the hill,[212] the leaven in the
meal.[213] We are inclined to interpret these texts purely in the sense
of our duty as missionaries. They possess, however, a more than
moral significance, for this last is merely the result and the logical

outcome of a metaphysical quality of the new order introduced with the kingdom of God. "No man is an island"; each is a mediator for others.

This rule holds good in the first place for those who were visibly and deliberately gathered together by Christ. They are the small flock and as such, must form an organic unit, linked in a compact mass with the shepherd. For to them the Father has granted the kingdom, not for them alone but for all who through their intermediary will be gathered into the union that exists between Christ and the Father.[214]

Yet this little flock will not remain small, for it is at the same time a Church, a gathering house, firmly built upon the disciple who had been given the byname "Rock" (*Kefas Petrus*).[215] Yet no matter how big this Church grows, she is never the same as the kingdom; she is the chosen, powerful, instrument of this kingdom, the house where the keys are kept, the doctrine, the living community, the vital entry.

The faith of the Church will be a sign for the whole world, and more than a sign, she will be a mother, a beautiful tender woman who gives life. For is she not the intimate partner, the bride of Christ, virginal (since she wishes only to know her betrothed) and thus normally unfruitful? But precisely on this account, she is the fruitful one who exults because she has so many children.[216] And within the Church, too, the faith of the few will strengthen, enrich and guide the others; this was particularly true of Peter, who was to help his brothers in a way that was then still difficult to define.[217]

The same, in a scarcely less remarkable manner, can be said of all the apostles, for they will judge the twelve tribes of Israel,[218] which not alone gives some indication of their worthiness, but is the result of an inner bond. God does not allow strangers to be judged by strangers. On the contrary, he allows the ignorant and the straying to be helped by those who share in the same weakness, as this is true of the son of man, our high priest.[219]

205 Mk. 10, 45.
206 Jn. 12, 24.
207 Jn. 11, 49-52.
208 Cf. pp. 109ff.
209 1 Tim. 2, 5; cf. Hebr. 8, 6; 9, 15; 12, 24.
210 Jn. 15, 8.16.20.
211 Mt. 5, 13-16.

212 Mt. 5, 14.
213 Mt. 13, 33.
214 Lk. 12, 32; Jn. 17, 20-21.
215 Mt. 16, 18-19.
216 Gal. 4, 25-27.
217 Lk. 22, 32.
218 Mt. 19, 28.
219 Jn. 5, 27; Heb. 4, 15; 5, 1-2.

We have here a point of contact with the age-old idea held by so
many peoples, i.e., that men can act as mediators between ourselves
and God or gods. These are the priests. They are chosen from the
people and "isolated," [220] and they possess more "power" than the
best of the crowd. Jesus does *not* continue in this line. He avoids
the company of the priests and recruits disciples completely outside
any priestly criterion. He will be the only mediator and yet the
apostles will be absorbed in his work. He will be heard in them.[221]
Through them he will grant forgiveness; he will bind and loose.[222]
He is the abiding giver and for this reason they must *freely* communicate what they receive.[223] In this way he remains the sole mediator, and—this is new—there is still other mediation (in him). The
law of creation is thus without any distortion sublimely caught up
in the work of re-creation.

In a special manner this law of mediation also applies to those who
wish to devote the whole of their lives to Jesus himself. The great
instrument of his mediation is the cross; he who takes up his cross
and follows him, he who loses his life for him shall he not also find
everything that was the lot of Jesus? [224] Undoubtedly, for Jesus
himself pointed out the difference in the manner of influencing "in
the world" and among his own people. In the world to have influence is to exert power. "But it shall not be so among you; but
whoever would be great among you must be your servant . . . for
the son of man also came not to be served but to serve and to give
His life as a ransom for many." [225] It is thus no invention of Paul's
generous nature when he desires also to be a servant of Yahweh and
rejoices that he may suffer for others and for his part supplement
what is lacking in the torments of Christ in his flesh, [226] for the sake
of his body so that his life may be manifested in his mortal flesh and
in . . . the others.

Must we go even further and assume that Jesus' principle also
holds good for the material world? Does his redemption also affect
nature? Once again one might be inclined to answer with an em-
phatic "No". For Jesus remarks soberly that the loveliest flowers
bloom for only one day and are then thrown into the fire.[228] Nowhere does he give evidence of a cosmic temperament and yet, just
as the prophets had prophesied in mighty images of the future, just
as his contemporaries were accustomed to do, Jesus spoke of a re-
birth.[229] In an apocalyptic speech, the substance of which may

without doubt be literally attributed to him, he sees signs in the universe.[230] These are portents of the end, but also of the beginning, even for nature itself. Everything will share in the mighty conversion to be brought about by the kingdom of God. Nature will not have to groan too long, for the days will be shortened "for the sake of the elect." [231]

The fate of mankind is indeed significant for the entire universe. At least this is how Jesus' disciples understood it. John expects a new earth and a new heaven, that is, a basic renewal of *everything*,[232] and the new Jerusalem is a shining example of coexistence between definitive humanity, the whole of nature, the Father and the lamb; [233] a truly new and truly earthly paradise that conjures up the image of the first.[234] Another apostle-disciple urges the hastening of the day of God because according to his promise, we wait for new heavens and a new earth where righteousness will dwell.[235] But no one puts it so clearly as Paul: "For the creation waits with eager longing for the revealing of the sons of God . . . the glorious liberty of the children of God. We know that the whole creation has been groaning in travail together until now . . ." [236]

A modern mentality will experience no difficulty in situating this element in the framework of a macroevolution and in viewing Christianity as a new and decisive phase in the "phenomenon of man," a branch which does not die out but on the contrary, allows everything to share in what it has received itself. Let us, however, build upon what Paul tells us concerning the outcome of the kingdom of God. "Then comes the end, when Christ will deliver the kingdom to God the Father, after destroying every rule and every authority and power . . . When all things are subjected to him, then the Son himself will also be subjected to him who put all things under him, so that God may be everything in everyone.[237]

That is the ultimate intention: God who is everything in everyone. Then the mediation principle will have completed its task;

---

220 Ex. 28, 1; Heb. 5, 1.
221 Lk. 10, 16.
222 Mt. 18, 15-18.
223 Mt. 10, 8.
224 Mt. 10, 38-39.
225 Mk. 10, 43-45.
226 Col. 1, 24-25.
227 2 Cor. 4, 10-12; cf. 1, 6-7.
228 Mt. 6, 30.
229 Mt. 19, 28.
230 Mk. 13, 24-25; Lk. 21, 25-28.
231 Mk. 13, 20.
232 Rev. 21, 1.
233 Rev. 21, 9 22, 5.
234 Rev. 22, 1-3.
235 2 Pet. 3, 12-13.
236 Rom. 8, 19-22.
237 1 Cor. 15, 24-28.

priests and substitution sacrifices will no longer be necessary. God is there directly for everyone in a harmoniously created whole. The "economy of salvation" has completed its task, since salvation is now an eternal present, without the problems and pain of an "economy." It is worth the trouble to devote oneself wholeheartedly to this aim just as Jesus did until the end, who "presented himself . . . to them during forty days and speaking *of the kingdom of God*" *(mine)*.[238]

[238] Acts 1, 3.

II
The
Christian

Anyone who has once been caught in the atmosphere of the kingdom of God feels as the bite of an adder any attempt to represent or to experience Christianity as a collection of pious souls. And since the kingdom of God is the work of God, he will also instinctively be on his guard against the attempt to mold "strong personalities." It was not Jesus' intention either to console whining souls or to train a pack of bruisers. Consolation and training will be the *result* of the kingdom.

It will be, however, an inevitable and striking result. Truly new personalities will be in the making. Jesus' message will give rise to a characteristic type of person whom for convenience sake we shall call by the old name, Christian. Even slight acquaintance with the gospels, however, teaches us that such a Christian "type" was by no means a theme of Jesus' preaching. And yet we would ask that the construction of this section should not be dismissed out-of-hand as artificial. It can, it seems to me, be proved that Jesus was intensely concerned with what we in modern terms call the "personality," and considered this as an essential component of his preaching. Since this entire section is constructed upon the basis of this personalism, it will be necessary to clarify our thesis somewhat.

How does the preaching of the kingdom of God begin? With the demand for a conversion, a change of mentality.[1] This is no transient, introductory idea; the apostles interpreted it as a condition to be fulfilled by each new member of God's kingdom. In order to enter the kingdom of God, one must be born again, begin completely anew like a child emerging from its mother's womb.[2] To

---

[1] Mt. 4, 17.
[2] Cf. H. Pohlmann, *Die Metanoia* *als Zentralbegriff der christlichen Frömmigkeit* (Leipzig, 1938); J.

offer oneself for baptism is to be prepared to be buried and to rise
again with Christ [3] not only on the ontological plane, deep under the
surface of our consciousness, but also psychologically, to receive a
fresh conscience and to lead a new life.[4]

A man like Paul, who thought that despite his comparative youth
he was justified in boasting of his unyielding Jewish personality, ". . .
as to righteousness under the Law" [5]—such a man began anew, relin-
quishing all that he had gained (but naturally, faithfully, and gratefully retaining the enormous amount of good), "in order that I may
gain Christ and be found in him." [6] He had, as it were, acquired a
new personality and desired that God should find only this at the
judgment. For this reason, after twenty or thirty years of life as a
Christian,[7] he was still hastening onward: "Not that I have already
obtained this, or am already perfect . . . Brethren, I do not consider
that I have made it my own, but one thing I do: forgetting what lies
behind and straining forward to what lies ahead, I press on toward
the goal for the prize of the upward call of God in Christ Jesus." [8]

Each Christian has been called and has a vocation. It is not sufficient just to patch up a few qualities of character. A radical change
is required. The apostles might be able to make up long lists of
virtues and sometimes they do,[9] but from the time of Paul's first
epistle they always include the unsurpassable trilogy of the divine
virtues: faith, hope and charity.[10]

What is involved thus is really the putting on of a new man.[11]
This penetrating change—which differs sharply from the reaction
of someone who glances into the mirror, sees who he is, then goes
away and forgets what he was like [12]—presumes the existence of
some sort of model. And this is precisely what we are seeking without as yet coming to any decision regarding the necessity of "imitat-
ing" anyone or anything at all.[13] We wish only to determine that
the apostles considered being a Christian as "being changed into his
likeness, from one degree of glory to another, for this comes from
the Lord who is the Spirit." [14] We are therefore justified in seeking
in Jesus himself the principles of this re-creation.

One of Jesus' most personalistic pronouncements was this: "For
what will it profit a man if he gains the whole world and forfeits his
own person. Or what shall a man give in return for himself?" [15]
Here the Greek, *psychè*, is translated first by *person* and then by
himself. Modern commentators are unanimous in rejecting the classical Catholic and Lutheran translation, "in exchange for his *soul*,"

since this introduces the Platonic concept of soul which contrasts a spiritual substance with the body which is considered as good as independent of it. This was certainly not Jesus' intention. Still less, however, can he have intended to say anything so banal as "Of what use is any gain if you lose your (ordinary) life, What is more precious than your (ordinary) life?"

The reference is indeed to life—*psychè* often has this meaning—but in this context, to life in the profoundest sense of the word, to that which is not magnified by external riches or diminished by martyrdom. In modern terminology this is precisely the human *person*. "Nothing on earth equals the person," aptly comments A. Durand.[16] But nineteen centuries earlier Luke had already translated that word for his readers: "What does it profit . . . if he loses . . . himself?" (*heauton*).[17] We thus establish that Jesus was extremely conscious of the incomparable value of the human person.

Jesus employs an image to express the same idea: we are all invited together to the feast of the kingdom of God, but each individually must provide his own *festive garment*.[18] This is not at once sanctifying grace, nor is it purely goodwill; clothing is the symbol of the whole appearance, of the attitude that characterizes the person. "Fine linen is the righteousness of the saints," says John.[19] And in yet a different way the distinctive nature of the Christian's attitude to life is emphasized in a series of contrasts between the Old Law and what Jesus says, concluding with this exhortation: "You, therefore, must be perfect as your heavenly Father is perfect." [20] The reference is not immediately to the "perfection" of which the spiritual writers speak; the context rather suggests mercy and Luke

Schniewind, *Das biblische Wort von der Bekehrung*, (Berlin, 1947).

[3] Jn. 3, 4-5; cf. 1 Pet. 2, 2.

[4] Rom. 6, 4; Col. 2, 12.

[5] Phil. 3, 6.

[6] Phil. 3, 8-9.

[7] The date of Philippians is disputed; the Epistle probably dates from an imprisonment in Ephesus, ca. A.D. 56; otherwise, Rome, ca. A.D. 62.

[8] Phil. 3, 12-15.

[9] Jas. 3, 17-18; Gal 5, 22-23. Lists of sins were much more numerous, e.g., Mk. 7, 20-23; 1 Cor. 6, 9-10; Gal. 5, 19-21; Rom. 1, 29-30; 2 Tim.

3, 2-5.

[10] 1 Thess. 1, 3; cf. 1 Cor. 13, 13.

[11] Eph. 4, 24; Col. 3, 10.

[12] Jas. 1, 23-24.

[13] See also pp. 262-263.

[14] 2 Cor. 3, 18.

[15] Mt. 16, 26.

[16] A. Durand, *Evangile selon Saint Matthieu* (Paris: Verbum Salutis, 1938 24), p. 318.

[17] Lk. 9, 25.

[18] Mt. 22, 11-12; cf. 9, 16.

[19] Rev. 19, 8.

[20] Mt. 5, 48.

indeed employs this term.[21] In any case we are dealing with a pronounced personalistic concept of man, since we must be perfect *as the Father is;* nothing is so personal, so full of distinctive life, as God.

In short, it does not seem such a utopian idea after all to search the gospels for that ideal personal image which Paul had in mind when he confessed that his aim was "to present every man mature in Christ." [22] In all probability Jesus had not much to say about the psychological process of this re-creation. This point, too, we can leave out of consideration. Our foremost aim is to discover the *components* of that Christian type and this task is not without its dangers. A certain degree of subjectivism is perhaps unavoidable, since Jesus himself worked with other categories and left us only random pronouncements. And yet we have a real desire to know what *Jesus* meant and not merely to follow a comfortable little plan of our own making. On the other hand, our aim itself requires a certain psychological coherence: a non-psychological description of a human type is pure nonsense, at least if one accepts that psychology means insight into human nature.

Assuming thus that our task is a possibility, we shall content ourselves, by way of a working hypothesis, with a portrait comprising the following components:

1. The *basis:* integral love of truth.
2. *Two focal points* of attention and love: God and one's neighbor.
3. *Three qualities* of this love: generosity, humility, joy.
4. The intimate *unity factor:* the bond with Jesus.

The very structure of this schema should help us to learn how helpful it is likely to prove in assessing and understanding Jesus' intentions. For the sake of honesty, and in order to reveal the trend of our thought, we give here the five premises upon which we base our argument. A "portrait of the Christian according to Christ" must:

(a) possess the spirit and, if possible the letter of the *Sermon on the Mount;*

(b) be in harmony with the *life* of Jesus himself;

(c) find its echo in the teaching of the *apostles;*

(d) constantly recur in the lives of the *saints;*

(e) possess a degree of *psychological coherence;*

We call these premises, since they are presented without proof for the readers' own judgment, although in my opinion, they are completely demonstrable. We insist only on the urgent necessity of taking some step to reconcile modern man with a strictly reliable exegesis of the Gospel.[23]

THE BASIS: INTEGRAL LOVE OF TRUTH

Blessed are the pure in heart! [24] Everything is contained in this beatitude. We must be completely honest, with all the candor and sincerity that is in us. As the eye is the lamp of the body, so must our heart be bright and luminous, for if the heart is sullied, the darkness is indeed great.[25]

To me, these statements reflect a fundamental aspect of Jesus' mentality. The whole issue goes much deeper than mere candor of speech, although Jesus stressed this too: "Let what you say be simply, 'Yes' or 'No'; anything more than this comes from evil." [26] For this reason a Christian may not swear.[27] And even all this is very little, although it is still rarely possible to take a Christian at his word. What Jesus desires is nothing less than absolute truthfulness in our relationship with God, in our relations to our fellowmen and also to ourselves. Nothing must escape the glare of truth. And so fundamental a veracity can undoubtedly form the basis of an attitude to life which can be sharply reflected in the twentieth-century search for authenticity.

Let us attempt to gauge now if it really is genuine:

[21] Lk. 6, 36. On this entire question, cf. J. Dupont, "Soyez parfaits (Mt. 5, 48). Soyez misericordieux (Lk. 6, 36)," in *Sacra Pagina* 2. (1958), pp. 150-162.

[22] Col. 1, 28.

[23] Anyone interested in a Christian anthropology based on the New Testament has far to seek. In one of the rare theologies of the New Testament of 470 pp., one finds 15 pages on man and principles of Christian life and 20 pages on "duties" toward God and man; (J. Bonsirven, *Theology of the New Testament* [Westminster, 1952], pp. 360-375; 128-148). Entirely different is the method of E. Stauffer, *Die Botschaft Jesu, damals und heute*. There is scarcely a page one can read without protest, but at the same time one is confronted with the vocation of a servant of the Gospel today.

[24] Mt. 5, 8; the reference here is not, in the first place, to sexual purity.

[25] Mt. 6, 22-23.

[26] Mt. 5, 37.

[27] Mt. 5, 34.

1. *Veracity in Relation to God*

This is the central theme of the Sermon on the Mount. Words, rites, fasts, alms—all these mean nothing if the intention is not pure, for as Jesus points out, the Father sees in secret.[28] The examples given—prayer, fasting and alms—are the three typical (Old Testament) pious practices, and thus cover the whole field of our relationship to God.[29] They prove the thesis stated by Matthew at the beginning: beware of practicing your piety before men in order to be seen by them.[30] Jesus applied this principle so vigorously that he was drawn into direct conflict with the specialists of the world of outward appearances, the Pharisees. The struggle was fought so grimly and efficiently that it left its mark in the dictionaries; wherever Christianity had any influence on a language, *pharisaical* meant hypercritical. One must read Mark 23, in order to understand the equation of the two terms, though it must be pointed out that not all pharisees deserved this reproach.

God does not desire sanctimoniousness, but a true worship. It is Jesus' mission to dedicate this worship "in spirit and truth," says St. John, "for such the Father seeks to worship him." [31] Those who either deliberately or unconsciously reject this idea stand forever sculpted and unmasked upon the great temple square, upright, thanking God for the excess of perfection of which their noble hearts are conscious, thankful too for everything of which they cannot be accused, in contrast to that publican there, a little further away, who dares not lift his eyes, and whose presumed or real sins the pseudo holy man gloatingly recites.[32] A cutting parable indeed.

2. *Veracity in Relation to Man*

All the great men of history have desired this to a greater or lesser degree. "Uprightness is the beginning and end of all," says Confucius. Buddha, the enlightened, taught his four truths discovered beneath the famous fig tree, the sacred truths concerning suffering, the origin of suffering, the conquest of suffering and the path to this conquest. According to Zarathustra, sincerity and loyalty form the basis of a harmonious society; truth is the sign of our union with Ahuramazdah, the supreme being. Socrates taught us his "Know thyself." Why then should Jesus not do the same?

But, of course, he did! His teaching, however, goes much deeper.

It is not sufficient to know oneself in order thus to learn control and to make good use of one's talents. Since man is at once earthly and divine, he must endure a blinding light. People are not isolated figures guiltlessly walking, growing and seeking. They are the vineyard of the Father, and this master of the vineyard is carefully, omnisciently busy cutting away the dead growth and pruning what is fresh and untainted.[33]

To put it less picturesquely: Jesus makes man conscious of his sin. He does not dwell with illusions; he has an unrivalled knowledge of man, and as John puts it, "needed no one to bear witness of man; for he himself knew what was in man." [34] For this reason, he began his message with a call to conversion, to a change of heart. For this reason, he continued to reveal the truth about ourselves, razor-sharp and humiliating, so that anyone who did not understand it was not capable of becoming his disciple: "I came not to call the righteous, but sinners." [35] Only he who loves the truth so much that of his own initiative he takes his place among the sinners, can be said to be called. There are no exceptions to this rule, not even the group of the twelve. Is there any other book in the world in which the authors give themselves so unglorious a role as do the apostles in the gospels? [36]

To be truthful does not mean only to confess, "I am a sinner." We must also admit that the origin of the evil lies in ourselves, that sin proceeds from our "evil eyes." [37] Nowhere does Jesus suggest that the devil bears responsibility for our sins, or that everything is all a mistake. He leaves but one way out: repentance.

Such depth of truth places our relationships with others in an entirely different light. From now on we shall no longer seek motes in the eyes of others, without first eliminating the beam that entirely impedes our own sight.[38] We shall under no circumstances feel justified in judging our neighbor.[39] On the contrary, contact with others will help us to review our own lives and to give each other new chances to see.[40]

---

[28] Mt. 6, 4.7.8.18.
[29] Acts 10, 2.4.
[30] Mt. 6, 1.
[31] Jn. 4, 23.
[32] Lk. 18, 9-14.
[33] Jn. 15, 2.
[34] Jn. 2, 24-25.
[35] Mt. 9, 13.
[36] See Vol. 2.

[37] Mk. 7, 20-23; the evil eye can be rendered as "envy" but the entire context stresses that the cause lies *in ourselves.*
[38] Mt. 7, 3.
[39] Mt. 7, 1.
[40] Lk. 17, 3, more universal than Mt. 18, 15-17.

This will be the essential basis for the first Christian community and is even now the prime condition of good work in our gatherings, our ecumenical contacts and every form of apostolate. We humans are accustomed always to talk endlessly about how right we are. Others know this, too, and can only look on with wonder and interest when they see how natural we find it always to be in the wrong in relation to the eternal truth which we wish first and foremost to seek and to accept *for ourselves*. On such a basis great houses of unity can be constructed.

One of the qualities of an integral love of truth is that it does not oppress, but liberates. "The truth will make you free." says Jesus in a significant text of John.[41] The devil, in contrast, the arch liar, who of his very nature speaks falsehood, is always the great tyrant, the oppressor, the murderer.[42] He who loves the truth must fear no one. This is a quality that even Jesus' enemies cannot deny him,[43] and which he himself requires of his disciples. They will have to proclaim from the housetops what he has taught them in private, and suffer the consequences.[44]

This freedom will culminate in the apostolic *parrèsia*, a mixture of candor and confidence and one of the favorite themes of Paul [45] who knows that he is constantly being "tested" by God and for whom the hereafter will bring only a fuller knowledge of God.[45] Then we shall know God as he knows us, now and from the beginning.[46] To know God as he knows me: what a prospect for someone who bases all his aspirations upon a love of truth!

Let us now withdraw into perspective and look back with John's eyes, around the year A.D. 75, at Jesus' life and message. We ask ourselves what can provide the basis for a human life and an attitude to life and think in the first place of Jesus himself. And then we see that from the beginning to the end he was a witness to the truth. Not only is he the light of the world,[47] he is the way and the truth [48] that make us all "children of light." [49]

Solemnly he declares before Pilate that he has come into the world to bear witness to the truth.[50] He is certainly not speaking here of a notional truth, or even of a well-understood but purely human sincerity. In John's vision, Jesus is the supreme revelation, but a revelation incarnate, concrete, fighting with people of flesh and blood, for such is the way of the world; people often prefer darkness to this supreme truth because their works are evil and the truth would bring them to light,[51] because their inspiration is all too often their own vanity and not reality.[52]

These are not the pious musings of a dreamy disciple.[53] A carpenter's intransigent love of truth has had unbelievable results.[54] From the 1st century there were thousands of people, including women, who were willing to suffer a most horrible death to prove their fidelity to this demand for truthfulness: [55] Even during persecution truth must not be denied. The converted philosopher Justin, who was to follow the same bloody way, explains why the Christians do not disavow during interrogation: "We do not wish to live in lies." [56] It leaves a bitter taste in the mouth when we contrast this attitude with the modern speculation on how far one may go in applying the mental reservation.

These applications are infinite in number and diversity. From the Protestant principle of free elucidation which consists primarily of a desire to hear the Word of God integrally and faithfully without any hindrance to Catholic apologetics which, from the 1st century, aspired to examine soberly where God's paths lie.[57] They vary from the painful searching of Newman, who requested the *kindly light* in order to be able to take one step to the fearful doubts proceeding from the liveliness of their faith and their very sincerity, which so many saints had to endure. From the terrible realization of the first converts who, in a world dominated by lies and cunning, burst into tears when they heard Christ's demand for a love of truth ("Never in my whole life, O Lord, have I spoken one true word, but lived always sly among all and allowed my lie to pass for truth among all the people . . .) [58] to the moving cry of John XXIII: "Think, honor, say, do what is true . . . Have clear ideas on the

[41] Jn. 8, 32.
[42] Jn. 8, 44-45.
[43] Mt. 22, 16.
[44] Mt. 10, 27.
[45] 1 Thess. 2, 2; Phil. 1, 20; 2 Cor. 3, 12; 7, 4; Col. 2, 15; Eph. 3, 12; 6, 19-20.
[46] 1 Cor. 13, 12. "As I have been fully understood" is a passive construction to avoid the name of God typically Jewish. Thus it means "as God understands me."
[47] Jn. 8, 12; 9, 5.
[48] Jn. 14, 6.

[49] Jn. 12, 36; cf. Lk. 16, 8.
[50] Jn. 18, 37-38.
[51] Jn. 3, 19-20.
[52] Jn. 5, 44; 12, 43.
[53] Jn. 1, 5.11; cf. 12, 46.
[54] Jn. 14, 17; 15, 20.
[55] Jn. 16, 13.
[56] Rev. 3, 2.
[57] Here, we shall pass over in silence the errors made in the application of both principles.
[58] *The Shepherd of Hermas*, "Commandments," 3, 2.4; cf. Vol. 2.

great realities of God and of man . . . speak the truth readily and sincerely, with the courage of a martyr or a confessor . . . The truth is a light in which each individual must be bathed so that it may give the tone for each action of his life . . . No, beloved sons, never lend yourselves to any violence upon the truth. View such a deed with revulsion . . . Never depart by a hairsbreadth from those glorious gifts of God: light, sound, color and their application in art and technique, painting, journalism; television . . . Never violate man's natural tendency towards truth, upon which foundation the entire structure of his nobility and his greatness is built up." [59]

What a pity it is that many Catholics, including members of the clergy—I cannot say in what measure this applies to myself—have by their behavior contributed to the bad name we have in the world of not being able to listen, of retaining a mass of prejudices, of being blind traditionalists, of condemning without having heard the defense. Let us return to the true wisdom which, in the words of the brother of the Lord, is without uncertainty or insincerity.[60] Let us take care not to allow on this point any deviation from the truth, for in the words of Pope John, any such deviation threatens the nobility and greatness of the entire man. Let us see now how the building can be constructed on this foundation.

FIRST FOCAL POINT: LOVE OF GOD [61]

On a certain day the rabbis, whose lists numbered 365 prohibitions and 248 commandments, inquire which commandment was, in fact, "the first of all" (according to Mark) or "the great commandment" (according to Matthew).[62] They are not so much seeking the one which is relatively the most weighty, but what is qualitatively the most important, in other words, the central commandment that binds all the others together, from which the others may be derived. Just as the high priest may be called the "chief priest," [63] there must also be a chief commandment. Jesus agrees with them and gives without hesitation the central theme: "You shall love the Lord your God with all your heart and with all your soul and with all your mind. This is the greatest and first commandment. And a second is like it: you shall love your neighbor as yourself."

In Matthew's version, Jesus concludes by saying that all the law and the prophets "depend" on these two commandments; in other words, these two commandments are the *focal points* about which everything else is centered. According to Mark, the conclusion is: No other commandment is greater than these—which is not simply a repetition but a conclusion that either elevates these two commandments to a special category (Spicq) or else polemically postulates that in case of conflict, all the other "commandments" (of the rabbinic law) must yield to these (Manson, Stauffer).

Without pausing to inquire how far this "double commandment" can be described as new,[64] we shall now attempt to penetrate more deeply into every part of it in the conviction that according to Jesus' mentality, we are dealing here with the chief content of the Christian act. God and our neighbor are the two focal points of our attention and our will.

In what, according to the Gospel, does the love of God consist? And in the first place can such a love be *commanded*? To answer these questions we must start by avoiding two extremes. On the one hand, "love," for a Semite, is not at all the same as the heart-flutterings of a couple who have just fallen in love. The completely different method of contracting marriages would exclude such a notion. For Jesus love is certainly an act of *will*. Love of God will consist of the complete orientation of our wills toward the will of God. To the eternal question which every encounter with Jesus evokes: "Lord, what do you want me to do?" [65] the answer always reflects in a more or less concrete fashion what constitutes the *will of God*.

But this will is neither arbitrary nor imposed from outside; the other extreme to be avoided is thinking of the love of God as the disinterested and impassive carrying out of a series of orders. To do the will of God is to become a member of Jesus' family [66] not because we thus become more dear to him but because brothers and sisters possess a similar disposition that naturally must either be or become spontaneous. More than this, the love of God may be

---

[59] *Radio message*, Christmas, 1960.

[60] Jas. 3, 17.

[61] Here we must mention especially the three-volume standard work by G. Spicq, *Agapé dans Le Nouveau Testament. Analyse Des Textes* (Paris, 1958). Eng. trans: *Agape in the New Testament* (New York, Herder and Herder, 1963).

[62] Mk. 12, 28; Mt. 22, 36.

[63] Cf. 2 Chron. 24, 11.

[64] Jesus quotes two texts from the Old Testament and even the combination was not new. The commentators consider the novelty to lie either in the radicalism, or in the actual execution, or in the new content.

[65] Cf. Acts 2, 37; 16, 30; 22, 10.

[66] Mk. 3, 35.

compared with the strongest forms of human love and may conflict with it. We must love God more than father, mother, spouse, children, brothers and our own lives.[67] This must surely be the purpose of our entire being, of our passion, and of our spontaneity.

We must therefore not allow ourselves to be misled by a text in which the Christian attitude is depicted as a scrupulous obedience, in which the useless servant gazes in silence at the hands of his master.[68] Jesus uses the term, "love." This must surely have some significance, and what we seek now is a psychological insight into the love that Jesus brought and demanded. For our analysis we chose the simple, easily checked psychological fact, that every form of human love passes through the following three phases or stages: [69]

1. Love is born of attention: forgetting oneself for one moment and desiring to express all that one is.

2. Love thrives on giving, full of the pain of growing desires and sustained by hope.

3. Love is consummated in the permanent forgetfulness of self in the union of *our* happiness.

Naturally we do not intend to reduce Jesus' teaching on love to this pattern. It is merely easier to evaluate the bearing of his demands and recommendations within this typically human framework.

First Phase: Attention

Jesus taught us by word and deed to direct our attention increasingly to the Father. The entire preaching of the kingdom of God is full of the Father, as we have already seen.[70] It was impossible to hear Jesus speak and not to be personally confronted with the Father. He who has been gained for the kingdom of God focuses all his attention on the Father.

Let us now apply this principal more expressly to our own attitude. In this case we must begin by *listening* to God. All the prophets had demanded this, for they were men of hearing and peculiarly sensitive to a message. Jesus makes no distinction between listening to the Word and carrying it out.[71] This listening is of the utmost importance: It creates an opening upward that liberates us from the eternal cycle of our conversations-with-ourselves and from self-preoccupation. For this reason the kingdom of God begins with the sowing of the Word, which must be gathered carefully, persistently, despite the preoccupations of daily life, even during times of persecution. This is the real meaning of the *important* parable of the sower.[72]

He whose attention is fixed on God will also *see* things to which he was blind before: the signs of the times and the "finger of God." [73] He who is prepared to forget himself for a moment and to watch keenly what God does must begin to love. For our eyes see what the prophets and the righteous were not allowed to contemplate.[74] Besides, the revelation of the Father is communicated to us by the Son himself, humbly and meekly.[75]

The Christian thus is somebody with sharp hearing and keen sight, somebody who searches for God and, like all lovers, is curious. It is characteristic of the Christian that he can reach God through Christ. He is thus quite familiar with the voice of the shepherd [76] and even more, is happy to converse with his friend who was in the bosom of the Father [77] and has concealed nothing of what he knew.[78] But let us not begin by quoting John whose words are, as it were, charged in their feeling for the Father.[79] Let us rather ask a topical question: How do we listen to God's Word? How do we read the Bible? Is it a phase in learning to love God?

Second Phase: Sacrifice

During the first phase the lover is liberated from his own small world; his heart expands. Something new has happened; someone has entered it. Yet, he soon goes away and the lover relapses more or less into his habitual state. One's ego must learn to forget itself permanently, to lose itself entirely in the other. This is accomplished by sacrifice. Love is given only to those who are capable of giving themselves. For this reason, Jesus taught an absolute detachment and was himself the model of the supreme sacrifice. This idea

[67] Lk. 14, 26-27. Note that "to hate" is the same as "to love less than."

[68] Lk. 17, 8-10.

[69] It seems to me impossible to separate the theology of love from psychology; if psychology is the knowledge of people, how can it be ignored when studying this preeminently human phenomenon called love. Anyone who thinks there is still a danger of "psychologizing" should examine whether he, for his part, is entirely free from "dogmatizing" or philo-

logizing."

[70] See pp. 62-66 which should be reread at this point.

[71] Lk. 11, 28; 8, 21; cf. Mt. 7, 24-26.

[72] Mt. 13, 18-23.

[73] Lk. 12, 56; 11, 20.

[74] Mt. 13, 16-17.

[75] Mt. 11, 27-30.

[76] Jn. 10, 3-5; 27-28.

[77] Jn. 1, 1.8.

[78] Jn. 15, 15.

[79] This will be discussed in detail on pp. 179ff. concerning Jesus' devotional life.

is so extraordinary that we must analyze it in another "component" of the Christian: generosity.

Let us mention here only the two wings needed by the sense of sacrifice, desire and hope. The desire for God which imparts a willingness to sacrifice is a mixture of enthusiasm and pain—enthusiasm because of its power of attraction, pain because one knows oneself to be so unworthy, since all the world is so far from God and so reluctant to accept the invitation to work in his kingdom. Paul on the road to Damascus, Peter in his boat and so many others know that one cannot approach Jesus without being wounded by that, as it were, contradictory desire which says, "Depart from me, for I am a sinful man." [80]

The situation could scarcely be more contradictory and yet it is so. In a certain sense, one cannot endure God and yet, he is the great attraction. Man desires that God should be everything, yet, it seems as though no one takes him into account. For this reason the true Christian is never without pain. He continuously prays an ardent prayer: "Hallowed be thy name! Thy Kingdom come! Thy will be done, on earth as it is in heaven!" [81] Such are the perfect desires of love.

On the other hand, there is also hope, confidence. Love without prospects fades. Jesus teaches a boundless confidence. We must ask and be certain that we shall receive; God is better than the best father.[82] Let us not imagine that the effect of our supplication depends upon its length or its difficulty or on finding the right formula. This would prove great confidence in ourselves, not in God. Everything depends on God, and he is so good. One moment is sufficient if we can truly, in a gesture of boundless surrender, detach ourselves from all our guarantees and depend solely on him.

We must depend on him for our daily bread, depend on him in all the difficulties and dangers that incessantly wait upon the poor and that can assume the proportions of a mountain.[83] But no mountain can resist faith, or, in this text, confidence in God.[84] This mountain is only a manner of speaking, but unfortunately the haughty attitude of a hardened judge is only too real. But the widow must have no fear; she may fear the judge perhaps, for he fears neither God nor man, but not God himself who is precisely the opposite of this *parvenu* bandit.[85] This parable thus is by no means a recommendation to remain endlessly beseeching. God does not allow himself to be incessantly assailed, but will *speedily* vindicate those who call to him day and night.[86]

Christians will show their love of God by having faith under circumstances that would normally cripple a man: in persecution [87] and during an even greater calamity: sin, for God grants forgiveness.[88] The sinner—and each of us is a sinner—shows his love not by sitting down under his troubles and thinking of himself as forever sullied. He must rise up and go home, equipped with no other valid argument than the goodness of his Father.[89]

He who perceives at the feet of Christ, with or without aromatic ointment, that God is infinitely forgiving; he who is deeply conscious of the many sins for which he has been forgiven, such a one has loved greatly.[90] Jesus' theory is that one can know the intensity of love by the depth of that awareness of sin and thus by the confidence that bridges this abyss.[91] We must have so much trust, sinners though we are, that the absence of fear displays the depths of our love.[92]

The union of desire and hope has given rise to yet another phenomenon in the heart of the Christian: homesickness for God. It is impressive how an adult, intensely active man like Paul can long to depart, to be with Jesus and with God.[93] Whence does this longing arise?

One assumption, which should not be lightly rejected, although it cannot be definitely proved by reference to the synoptics, is that the disciples, living and working with Jesus, noticed in him such a great longing for the Father that they perforce communicated it to others later, when all had been made plain. When he, who characteristically raised his eyes to heaven in order to pray,[94] had vanished from their midst, there began in the world a movement of exiles, of pilgrims.[95] "My love is crucified and no fire remains to me now

[80] Lk. 5, 8.
[81] Mt. 6, 9-10.
[82] Mt. 7, 8-11; Lk. 11, 9-13.
[83] Mt. 6, 11; Lk. 11, 3.
[84] Mt. 17, 20; cf. 1 Cor. 13, 2.
[85] Lk. 18, 1-8.
[86] Lk. 18, 8.
[87] Mt. 10, 28-31; cf. 1 Pet. 3, 14.
[88] Mt. 6, 12; 9, 2.
[89] Lk. 15, 11-24.
[90] Lk. 7, 47.
[91] At first sight, Jesus appears to say

that the woman is forgiven *because* of her great love, but in this case, the parable of the remitted debt is entirely misplaced. The great love must therefore be a sign of the forgiveness granted.
[92] 1. Jn. 4, 18.
[93] Phil. 1, 21-26.
[94] Mt. 14, 19; Jn. 17, 1.
[95] Cf. 2 Cor. 5, 1-10; 1 Pet. 2, 11; and also the chapter on Jesus as pilgrim, pp. 227-249.

which seeks to nourish itself upon matter; but I have living water
that bubbles within me and speaks to me in my inmost heart: 'Come
to the Father.' " [96] This was written in the 1st century. What follows is more feminine, but what a personality it reveals! "O my
delight, Lord of all creation and my God! How long must I watch
for your presence! Must I perhaps desire not to desire you? O my
God and my creator, how you wound without anointing, how you
hurt with no wound visible, you kill a person and leave him with
more life." [97] One could quote page upon page, and not only of
those sixteenth-century mystics who "died that they might not
die." [98] A later evolution one might think, with no immediate basis
in the life of Jesus? Before coming so smugly to this conclusion let
us give a thought to the theme of John who is often so generous in
his use of symbols and anecdotes to convey the *atmosphere* that
Jesus left behind.

According to John, Jesus did cause water to well up, fresh-flowing
water to continue forever to quench our thirst. And what is this
water but the desire for God? [99] If anyone is thirsty let him drink
now, for out of the heart of Jesus shall flow rivers of living
water.[100] Just as bread is undoubtedly the symbol of the *will of the
Father* [101] so is water the symbol of the religious thirst after the
same God.

Philip must have suspected this, for he asked: "Lord, show us the
Father and we shall be satisfied." [102] This assumes an ever frustrated
desire to know God, to see him and understand him. And Jesus
answers that he is the *way;* [103] signposts are unimportant for those
who do not look forward to the goal. Jesus knows their longing for
God, but to his mind it is not yet ardent enough, hence his complaint: "But now I am going to him who sent me, yet none of you
asks me 'Where are you going?' " [104] This is as much as to say: "The
Father has given you all to me: You must desire much more to be
with me where I am going." [105] According to John, Jesus has taught
and given us an intense desire for God; this is an essential aspect of
our love of God.

Third Phase: Union in Joy

He who has learned to give must go to the uttermost limit, must
give his passion, his pleasures, the deepest joy of his being. Our joy
is the deepest ground of our being. We are what we desire. He who
has given his joy, has given all. This is no longer a sacrifice, for the

gift of joy comes from where pain can no longer enter. The highest love is spontaneous, joyful. Those who have one joy are perfectly one. These are, to my mind, indisputable psychological facts, applicable as much to human love (which so seldom attains this level) as to the love existing in God (where the union of the three Persons is a mutual ecstasy of happiness). This is also true of the love of man for God. One has only to think of the Old Testament "rejoicing in God" and the most remarkable comparison that Paul makes between *love* and *joy*.[106] They are even interchangeable. Let us now see how Jesus taught this union with God in the joy of mutual happiness. In the first place as always, but here more than ever, Jesus taught through his *life*. Later we shall discuss in more detail his life of prayer that was above all a eucharist, a prayer of thanksgiving. This thankfulness consists in being joyful because the other is good, being happy and content on his account. The apostles saw Jesus' infinite happiness revealed in his praying eyes, the holy, almost singing peace from which his words arose, the long periods of prayer, the extraordinary prayer of thanksgiving of the Last Supper. This is suitable material for later, but is already the essential here.

Let us pick out a few extremely significant statements on this subject. Already in the Sermon on the Mount, the apostles are called happy and blessed because they place all their reliance on God's goodness, because they are contented with God. This is especially striking in the last beatitude, where the *persecuted* must rejoice and be glad, "for their reward is great in heaven." [107] Here we find, even more acutely than in the preceding beatitudes, the use of the Jewish reward-terminology. The word, "reward," however, had lost so much of its original meaning that it had come to signify something like "value," "satisfaction," "effect." [108] In our case the accent lies on the *origin* of that reward; "the great reward in heaven" is roughly equivalent to the "great value for God" and even more accurately perhaps, "the great joy of God." We find this expressed literally in the parable of the talents, where the servant who is

96 Ignatius of Antioch, *To the Romans*, 7, 2.
97 Teresa of Avila, *Cries of the Soul to God*, VI, 1.
98 Teresa of Jesus and John of the Cross: "Muero porque no muero."
99 Jn. 4, 13-14.
100 Jn. 7, 37-39.
101 Jn. 4, 34.
102 Jn. 14, 8.
103 Jn. 14, 6.
104 Jn. 16, 5.
105 Cf. Jn. 17, 24.
106 Cf. Rom. 14, 17 (Instead of faith, hope and love, he has: hope, joy, faith); 2 Cor. 1, 24; 8, 2; Gal. 5, 22.
107 Mt. 5, 12.
108 Mt. 5, 46; 1 Cor. 9, 18; Jn. 4, 36.

rewarded "enters into the *joy* of his master." [109] This not only means that God grants us happiness, but that *he is* joy, and that we enter into this joy, become one with him in this joy.[110] The reward of which Jesus speaks is "the affirmative of God's love, over which man can have only joy and happiness." [111]

The parable of the prodigal son which is "the Gospel within the Gospel" and thus always significant, shows what should have been the attitude of the elder son, who thought that he possessed perfect love. He should have realized that all the goats in the shed, all that the Father has and is, also belongs to him: "All that is mine is yours." Most especially he should have joined in the rejoicing and feasting on account of all the good the Father does, especially for every conversion.[112] To be a Christian is to have the same joy as the Father.

This thesis is propounded in particular by John, the theologian of love, who knows that God is love and represents the whole of Christian life as an abiding in love.[113] He gives the typically Christian aspect of this love. All the words that Jesus spoke were intended to convey his joy to us, that our joy too might be perfect.[114] Christian love is the sharing in the joy-in-God of him who is one with God and who does always what is pleasing to God.[115] This is the same as the vision of a man like Paul, mature in love, for whom the essence of life consists in thanking God the Father through Jesus in word and deed.[116] He repeats incessantly that we should be thankful, be joyful.[117] To understand this properly, we would have had to be present at the eucharistic celebrations, those schools of love, organized by the first Christians.[118] There it was not only the memory of Christ's passion that was kept alive; [119] could any apostle ever forget the ineffable smile on Jesus' face when he spoke of his Father?

It was not the evangelists' intention to paint portraits of the Christian and his love of God. Their figures are rather contrast persons, uncomprehending or dull, like Nicodemus, or hovering on the threshold of love like the Samaritan woman, the man born blind and Lazarus' sister, Martha.

Anyone, however, who is familiar with Luke must be reminded of one positive example of the true love of God, of the true Christian in whom the three phases of love spoken of above are so splendidly realized. She is called blessed because she believed with all her being and carefully kept and pondered in her heart all that God had revealed: Mary, the attentive.[120] Her willingness to make any sacrifice, her faith unto death, all the more terrible since it was the martyr's death of her own son, made her the obedient handmaid of the Lord [121] who also gave proof of a boundless confidence,[122] even going so far as to expect miraculous solutions. Finally, she was someone who *entirely* forgot her own insignificance in order to rejoice with endless joy in God her Savior whose mercy drew forth in her soul a spring for a *Magnificat* that would endure from generation to generation.[123]

SECOND FOCAL POINT: LOVE OF MANKIND

Let us begin by reiterating our agreement with the synthesis John left us. Brotherly love was Jesus' special characteristic, a *new* [124] commandment, *his* commandment.[125] It was so central to his teaching that after a few years the Christian community already considered it an old commandment.[126] And here too the theologian to whom we are giving so much credit, stresses that Jesus' doctrinal force must be sought rather in his life than in his words: ". . . even another." [127]

Later we shall examine how Jesus put this love into practice; [128] let us now listen to a few of his words. They concern both quality and quantity; regarding this first aspect let us once again apply the psychological data of the preceding section. The three phases may

109 Mt. 25, 21.

110 "This detail (concerning the *joy*) may have been inserted by Matthew, but it opens such deep perspectives with regard to the eternal life that we may safely attribute it to Jesus himself." (Lagrange, *Comm.*).

111 Cf. H. Preisker, E. Würthwein, "Misthos," in *TWNT*, 4, 699-736; quotation 703.

112 Lk. 15, 31-32.

113 Cf. Especially 1 Jn. 4, 7 to 5, 4.

114 Jn. 15, 11; 16, 24; 17, 13; cf. Jn. 1, 4.

115 Jn. 4, 34; 8, 29; 16, 15.

116 Col. 3, 17; Eph. 5, 20.

117 Col. 3, 15; Phil. 4, 6; 3, 1; 4, 4.

118 Cf. Acts 2, 46; Lk. 24, 30-35.

119 Cf. Lk. 22, 19; 1 Cor. 11, 24-25.

120 Lk. 1, 45; 2, 19, 51.

121 Lk. 1, 38; Jn. 19, 25-27. Luke's influence can be detected in John's text; see Vol. 2, pp. 116-120; and especially M. E. Boismard, "Saint Luc et la rédaction du quatrième évangile" in *Rev. Bibl.* 69 (1962), pp. 185-211.

122 Jn. 2, 4-5; see preceding footnote.

123 Lk. 1, 45-55.

124 Jn. 13, 34.

125 Jn. 15, 12.

126 1 Jn. 2, 7; 2 Jn. 5.

127 Jn. 13, 34; 15, 12.

128 Cf. pp. 127ff.

be summed up in one rule: "Do unto others as you would have them do unto you." Jesus calls this "golden rule" the quintessence of the whole of revelation.[129] To be able to put it into practice one must first give the other one's full attention, put oneself in his place, view and consider him from his point of view. Then one must *do* what he wants, in other words sacrifice oneself, which amounts to a real desire for his good and is only possible when we have a hopeful prospect with regard to him. Finally, one can put oneself in another's place to such an extent that *his* good becomes one's own happiness. This is union, the highest degree of love.

Now for some examples for each phase. The classic case of the clerics who evidently "saw nothing" on the road from Jerusalem to Jericho illustrates the way in which attention for others should detach us from our own egotistical preoccupations. A common Samaritan did see and pity entered his heart through his eyes.[130] Here, we could quote a dozen anecdotes, especially from St. Luke's gospel, where Jesus constantly suggests or requires that we must *look*. We must look at the beggar at the door [131] and at the swarming city with its beauty and tragic recalcitrance.[132] We must notice the crowds of people on the hill slopes, talking and scurrying about, but aimless as sheep without a shepherd; [133] we must have an eye for a little man like Zaccheus in the tree [134] and for a woman who in a very special manner was brought to the attention of the illustrious host: "Do you see this woman?" [135]

We may as well close our list there; everyone can supplement it as he wishes and we can end together with the last judgment, where the judge will have convinced us that we did not see well at all. Perhaps we will not immediately understand and say: "Lord, when did we see thee hungry . . . and when did we see thee a stranger? . . . and when did we see thee sick or in prison?" [136] There will be a painful examination of what we did see. Naturally, we will remember having seen people who were poor and sick, but all too seldom did we put ourselves in their places, so that, in fact, we saw only rags and a sorrowful expression or statistics in the paper. If we had really looked we would have discovered a brother, not our brother alone, but a brother of the Lord Jesus himself. Then our love would have been quite different.

Certainly, Jesus did not verbally emphasize that we must be especially concerned with the *spiritual* needs of our brothers and that we must admire beauty of soul. He preferred to teach such delicate things through his actions and his way of being.[137] For the moment it is sufficient to point out that he did not ask that we should walk through life with our eyes shut or retire into the desert because the world is evil.

Paul and the saints imitated him and saw the wretchedness, the sin, the destruction. Their gaze was naturally not superficial. They were not eager after sensation, full of a secret pleasure in evil, or indifferently analyzing wretchedness—for it is possible to contemplate misery yet close one's heart [138]—their seeing was merely the prelude to the involvement of their hearts.

We spoke of sacrifice as the second phase. Now it is one of the basic principles of Jesus' spirituality, revealed in all the gospels, that there is no greater proof of love than the giving of one's own life.[139] This is how the disciples saw Jesus: as the suffering servant of Yahweh who came not to be served but to give his life for others; [140] as the good shepherd who willingly lays down his life.[141] In this he is a constant lesson for us: "By this we know love, that he laid down his life for us, and we ought to lay down our lives for the brethren." [142]

Such a heroic ideal is attractive. Who would not wish to enter upon eternity in the same way as Maximilian Kolbe or Damien de Veuster? But were we to wait for such a great opportunity we might be sadly disappointed. Jesus passes on to a more tranquil routine, with many tiny pricks. Let us begin by helping the helpers, thus with no expectation of eventual profit. Let us, for example, go to the assistance of those who will never be able to repay; [143] let us lend where the money is lost.[144]

Let us, in brief, give so that our left hand does not know what the right hand gives.[145] True sacrifice is completely disinterested, otherwise one is simply headstrong or a good accountant. A special case is surely the willingness to sacrifice our own liberty for the wellbeing of others; lest the little ones be scandalized.[146] Paul, the

---

129 Mt. 7, 12.

130 Lk. 10, 31-33.

131 Lk. 16, 20-21.

132 Cf. Lk. 19, 41.

133 Mk. 6, 34.

134 Lk. 19, 5.

135 Lk. 7, 44; one must not, of course, exaggerate this detail; it may very well be Luke's literary style.

136 Mt. 25, 37-39.

137 Cf. pp. 113ff.

138 1 Jn. 3, 17.

139 Mk. 10, 45; Jn. 15, 13.

140 Cf. p. 272.

141 Jn. 10. 11. 15.

142 1 Jn. 3, 16.

143 Lk. 14, 12-14.

144 Lk. 6, 34-25.

145 Mt. 6, 3.

146 Mt. 18, 8.

champion of Christian liberty, heroically applied this rule by making himelf a slave for all, despite his freedom, in order to win all.[147]

Indeed, it was in order to *win* all, for every sacrifice is fruitful. Contrariwise, sacrifice is ultimately impossible where no hope exists. Love is patient, love hopes for all things and can therefore bear all things.[148] Such patience obtains all things.[149] Jesus too explains "and you will have gained your brother." [150] Patience is viewed in a concrete manner though, this is by no means so easy, since it means being willing to forgive again and again, unto seventy times seven,[151] and moreover, to take the first step oneself.[152]

On the religious plane this hope makes us pray the Lord of the harvest that he may send laborers,[153] and for forgiveness for the sinner.[154] For to the Christian, sin is a wound; the Christian cannot possibly rejoice in injustice, perfidy or evil.[155] Jesus himself was saddened by the hardness of heart of the pharisees [156] and by the lack of generosity on the part of the rich young man on whom he had gazed affectionately a short time before.[157] The desires for spiritual love and the actual experience of it lead to the painful conclusion that it is very difficult to enter the kingdom of God. And yet, love never despairs, for to God everything is possible.[158]

The reason for love's perpetual optimism my be found in the third phase of its development: love continues to bear all pain and setbacks because a deeper *happiness* dwells within her. True love is always happy. This is why sacrifice is not the highest degree of love; that is, if one regards sacrifice more or less as an achievement. A person can give away all he has and still not love, says Paul.[159] He can even allow his body to be burned and still not love.[160] What then is lacking in such a disinterested person?

Paul answers with a poetic list of qualities which together form the canticle of love. In modern terms it could be summed up in a word: the gift of *self*. Love is never content with any gift; it desires the person. And to give oneself means to say to the other that you are happy on his account, that you find your happiness no longer in yourself but in him. Jesus expressed it thus in a parable: to love the prodigal son as a brother is to be glad to go into the house and dance at the feast.[161] His hyperboles carry the same message: Go two miles when only one is asked for; offer the undamaged cheek after receiving the blow on the other.[162] This amounts not to a greater sacrifice but to an entirely different spirit. It is no longer the law of strict retribution that must reign but the law of pleasing others.

To do a favor was the simple motto of a great, if youthful, saint. One must ask oneself time and again as did the Carmelites of Lisieux: "How can I do the other a favor?" until it has become a reflex to find one's own happiness in others and to share it with them.

If we now pause to consider the *quantitative* aspect of brotherly love, we see that Jesus applies all this, which is merely an elucidation of the golden rule, to all possible human relationships; in other words, to all sorts of societies.

Beginning with marriage, which Jesus considers as a matter of love, he will reform marriage, restore its unity and indissolubility. But it is not his intention merely to be strict. On the contrary, his disciples must learn to love each other with the love that God had foreseen from the beginning: "For this reason a man shall leave his father and mother and be joined to his wife, and these two shall become one.[163] One flesh means one person, in other words, one being; a spiritual and physical entity. Such a union naturally involved a revision of the attitude towards women, a revision indeed initiated by Jesus.[164]

The law of love must extend to cover the whole of family life. With regard to parents this means the abolition of the hateful korban practice.[165] Whatever our age we must honor and love our parents as people, as Jesus himself did.[166] The same holds good for children, who are also people. Assuming that the apostles were not particularly ill-natured it is striking that Jesus should have given them a stern lesson on the love of children.[167] Young people, who are seldom treated with true understanding—it is not always easy to find sympathy for "difficult" teenagers—possess the right to determine their own future and to follow their own vocations.[168]

We have already dealt with the application of this law of love on a social and international level; it followed directly from the preaching of a kingdom of God of justice and peace and with universal

147 1 Cor. 8, 13; 9, 19.
148 1 Cor. 13, 4. 7.
149 Cf. "La esperanza todo lo alzanca" (famous saying of Teresa).
150 Mt. 18, 15.
151 Mt. 18, 22.
152 Mt. 5, 23-24; 18, 15-17.
153 Mt. 9, 38; Lk. 10, 2.
154 1 Jn. 5, 16.
155 1 Cor. 13, 6.
156 Mk. 3, 5.
157 Mk. 10, 21-22.

158 Mk. 10, 24-27.
159 1 Cor. 13, 3.
160 1 Cor. 13, 3.
161 Lk. 15, 32.
162 Mt. 5, 39-42.
163 Mt. 19, 3-9.
164 Cf. pp. 119ff.
165 Mk. 7, 8-13.
166 Lk. 2, 51-52; Jn. 19, 25-27.
167 Mk. 10, 13-16.
168 Mt. 10, 35-36; Mk. 3, 21, 31-35: cf. 1, 16-20.

dimensions.[169] We also touched upon the important place given to enemies in Jesus' teaching on our neighbor. At all times people have doubted whether such a rule could conceivably be put into practice. "It is not an impossible thing but a perfect thing," says Jerome. Here we see then that "love is the greatest folly imaginable" (G. Fessard). And yet, it is essential in order that peace shall reign in a country of imperfect people.[170] What indeed can we oppose to Jesus' dialectic when he says that brotherly love does not consist of loving those who love you.[171] But if we must also love those who are imperfect what reason have we for refusing love to those who happen to exercise their imperfection with respect to *our own* persons? This may be irrefutable logic, but it is hard to accept, as Jesus naturally knows. This is why he says that those who pray for their enemies and bless them are "sons of God," and on the way to attaining perfection.[172] He himself set the example by granting forgiveness to his enemies and executioners.[173] The first Christian martyrs imitated him in this[174] and the entire apostolic Church considered this commandment as an important rule for being a Christian.[175]

The radiation of brotherly love is thus boundless, infinite. And yet, an even more important infinity must be mentioned here, for the object of our love is not confined to the finite. In our neighbor, we meet God. To employ one of the happy formulas of theology: Brotherly love and love of God together form one theological virtue. The Gospel speaks of Jesus' presence in the needy and where two or three are gathered together in his name.[176] The liturgy sings: *Ubi caritas et amor, Deus ibi est . . . Gaudium quod est immensum atque probum.*[177] This brings us immediately to a new component of Christian man.

JOY

In analyzing Jesus' message concerning the two focal points of our lives, we have already discussed the qualities that determine the atmosphere of Christian life: joy, generosity and humility. These are but three facets of love, but they are so important that they deserve to be considered separately.

There is scarcely any mention of the word, "joy," or its synonyms in Bible concordances and dictionaries. Indeed, such terms occur only rarely in the gospels and in the entire Bible. One of the reasons for this is their abstract character. Instead, Jesus gave his peace which has an almost tangible quality for the Jews.[178] Very probably he also presented his mission literally as a "joyful proclaiming" [179] (Is. 4 off.), but it is much less certain whether he ever used the expression, "joyful message." [180] In any case it was joyful news; the name of the gospels was not conjured out of thin air.

Yet, this was no cheap or tawdry happiness, still less an advertising stunt or a beautiful veneer. From the very beginning a certain severity characterized the movement; *conversion* was the first and most necessary requirement.[181] It is a message for people familiar with real life, with all its miseries and limitations, for people willing to give the whole of themselves. For those prepared to sell everything it is a pearl that is bought with joy.[182] The true Christian is joyful while fasting and denying himself.[183] The paradox goes even further. To our certain knowledge (we are told so by Jesus himself and by the apostles) Christian joy may go hand in hand with persecution.[184]

This last fact provides us with the basis and explanation for this apparent contradiction; for we are again referred back to the Sermon on the Mount and especially to the beginning: the beatitudes. The "rejoice and be glad" seems like a later addition, but it is completely in keeping with the preceding beatitudes and faithfully reflects what Jesus intended.[185] All beatitudes are exhortations to joy. This emerges more clearly in Luke, who in this case always seems closer to the original form, particularly in the contrast with the fourfold "Woe!" [186] So must it have sounded across the slopes

169 Cf. pp. 41-51.
170 Cf. pp. 47-51.
171 Mt. 5, 46-47.
172 Mt. 5, 44-45. 48.
173 Lk. 23, 34.
174 Acts 7, 60.
175 1 Cor. 4, 12; Rom. 12, 14; 1 Pet. 3, 9; 1 Jn. 4, 10-11; Jas. 3, 17.
176 Mt. 25, 35-45; 18, 20.
177 Cf. "Where charity and love are, there is God . . . an infinite and pure joy" (liturgical hymn).
178 Mt. 10, 3; Lk. 24, 36; Jn. 20, 19. 26.
179 Mt. 10, 26. 28. 31; 14, 27; 17, 6; Lk. 5, 10; 12, 32.
180 Cf. J. Van Dodewaard, "Jesus

s'est-il servi Lui-même du mot 'Evangile'?" in *Biblica* 35, (1954), pp. 160-173.
181 Mt. 4, 17.
182 Mt. 13, 44.
183 Mt. 6, 17.
184 Mt. 3, 11-12; Lk. 6, 22-23; Acts 5, 41; Col. 1, 24; Jas. 1, 6; 1 Pet. 1, 6; 3, 14; 4, 13.
185 On the beatitudes, cf. J. Dupont, *Les béatitudes. Le probleme litteraire. Les deux versions du sermon sur la montagne et des béatitudes*, (Louvain, 1958²).
186 Lk. 6, 20-23.

and across the lake: "Rejoice, you who are poor! Rejoice, you who weep! I say that you are happy, you that are hungry. Happy too when men mock you and reject you and hate you."

And why is this? Because God is there. Not a distant God, whose existence is shown in the same way as one can prove the presence of a painting in a museum from catalogues. This is an active God who "rewards," who, in other words, from his infinite, compassionate love will shower mankind with happiness through the coming of his kingdom. For all beatitudes are literally "contained" in this one motif: "For God gives you the kingdom of God." [187] The Christian's joy is a joy on God's account and for what God does.

Because it is so deep, it comes only rarely to the surface. It is the entire Gospel that breathes joy as ozone. Jesus cannot say that men must rejoice for this particular reason or that, for he himself is, after all, the nucleus of the kingdom of God and the living joyful message. This is why the personal face of Christian joy is revealed only after the resurrection: "I will see you again and your hearts will rejoice and no one will take your joy from you." [188] When, in his epistle, Paul repeats: "Rejoice in the Lord," [189] he is speaking of a joyful message not only *as* the Lord, but also on the Lord's account, in union with the (risen) Lord.

Paul *exhorts* his hearers to be joyful. For although joy is by definition spontaneous (Who has not experienced the sadness of *forced* joy?) it is possible and necessary to grow in it. Joy in persecution does not grow as if by miracle in the leather of the scourge or on the point of the sword. It is the crowning of a life of joyful submission in the hands of the Father, with no fearful care about tomorrow.[190]

Because we Christians have made too little progress in this school and also perhaps because his diagnosis was only partly correct, Nietzsche waxed indignant over the fact that Christian joy was so timid. He is right in demanding a more robust joy, for joy is a sign of sanctity. "A saint who is sorry would be a sorry saint," says Francis de Sales. Thomas Merton is more positive: "In the supernatural order joy is only one aspect of love." This is why I can never believe in those medieval *Vitae* in which Jesus is said never to have laughed.[191] I prefer to think that from his more than human joy flowed what a beautiful book has called "The joyful existence of the Christian." [192]

GENEROSITY

Jesus made no secret of the fact that his preaching led to a narrow and difficult way.[193] The kingdom of God demands *everything* of a person.[194] Love of God and of our neighbor are hollow words if they are not linked with sacrifice; we have already underlined this in what we called the second phase of love.[195]

It is sufficient here to recall a norm and a concrete application that must both originate from a young person and one who is not afraid to unleash a revolution. For what else can one say of this norm: that we can only be his followers if we are willing to carry our cross after him?[196] This is a terrible statement, for at this period, the Jews were all too familiar with the spectacle of people dragging their crosses. It was enough to make them faint with terror, for anyone seen going along the street with the tree on his shoulder was on the way to execution. In a few moments he would be fastened to the cross and left hanging there for days to languish and to die. What Jesus demands thus is that we should be ready to die for him; otherwise, we are not worthy of him. The prophets had never demanded this, even when most extravagant. The joyful message is no laughing matter.

A concrete application of the radical involvement, which is naturally only possible when it proceeds from the joy of love, may be inclined to offend our ears: "There are eunuchs who have made themselves eunuchs for the sake of the kingdom of heaven. He who is able to receive this, let him receive it."[197] The eunuchs were decidedly not classed as likeable figures; they were mocked and pitied as people who possessed nothing of life. And yet, Jesus employs this Arabic term in order to invite us to a life in which the kingdom of God has conquered and concentrated all thoughts, convictions and affections to such an extent that nothing more is desired, not even, by way of symbol, that finest gift of all for which a man leaves father and mother. . .

Jesus did not speak in vain. His vocabulary, which I have not

[187] Mt. 5, 3. 10.
[188] Jn. 16, 22; cf. 15, 11; 17, 13.
[189] Phil. 3, 1; 4, 4.
[190] Mt. 6, 25-34.
[191] See Vol. I.
[192] By P. Schruers, (ed.) (Antwerp,

Patmos, 1962).
[193] Mt. 17, 13.
[194] Cf. pp. 66ff.
[195] Cf. pp. 87ff.
[196] Mt. 10, 38.
[197] Mt. 19, 12.

been able to find in the classical literature—the heroes there are also
great but not in love of God or of their neighbor—I now hear from
the mouths of students who refuse to submit their favorite paper to
ecclesiastical censorship and make full use (some are inclined to
term it "abuse") of their freedom as students, yet still are heirs of
Christ:

"Years ago a sensational occurrence was reported in the south of
our country. A large number of people had set out in a boat. A
thick mist covered everything. Suddenly, there was a dull thud and
the boat overturned, throwing everyone into the water. Most of the
people, children and country-women, were unable to swim. Those
who could, swam fruitlessly toward the center of the lake, for this is
where the boat had overturned. There was one man who knew the
place well; he knew that the nearest shore at that point was only
about twenty yards away. He swam toward it with a child in his
arms. Not content with this he returned to the lake. He went back
again and again until he was exhausted. He had saved six lives.
People begged him not to go back in the water, but the cries of the
drowning moved him too much, and he cast himself into the water
again. He did not return. After many hours his body was brought
ashore still clasping the seventh he had tried to save. This is the
measure of our answer to humanity-in-need. To give *everything* in
order to lead them to the truth, even death, if necessary. This is our
personal and unassailable mission and we must measure up to it
consistently at every moment of our lives in order to make our
world, our fatherland Chile, a foretaste of heaven." [198] Camillus de
Lellis seemed completely mad when, centuries before the Red Cross
existed, he ventured onto the battlefields with a great cross painted
on his habit and with no other intention than that of assisting the
dying and wounded. Damien de Veuster loved the lepers to the
point where he could say: "*We, lepers . . .*" There are the Little
Sisters of Jesus who live voluntarily in the prisons, sharing the life
of the prisoners, with no reward but their friendship. This, I think,
is enough, for these are better exegetes.

HUMILITY

All the components discussed are intimately connected. Humility,
for example, is truth, and thus proceeds from sincerity. Still more, it

is the fruit of love. If you love God, how can you help being aware of your weaknesses, your spiritual torpor? In this way you may become one of the poor in spirit, and this is the first beatitude.[199] You will feel yourself a brother of the publican who scarcely dares address himself to God.[200] If you love your fellowmen, you will feel the urge to serve them, to prefer them to yourself, and inevitably you will think of what Christ did when (in modern terminology) he threw his jacket on a chair, rolled up his sleeves and began to wash the feet of his disciples: "I had given you an example." [201]

We are not speaking of that cool humility, which is the result of inferiority, timidity, or skepticism. We refer rather to the mild warmth that glows from the great fire of inner love called meekness. It reminds us of Jesus' marvelous phrase, one of the few in which he speaks of his own personality: "Learn from me; for I am gentle and lowly in heart." [202]

To the apostles it was precisely this attitude we must imitate in Christ. Peter thus speaks of Christ who, when he was reviled, did not revile in return, and when he suffered, did not threaten: ". . . leaving you an example, that you should follow in his steps." [203] Paul, too, states decidedly: "Have this mind among yourselves which you have in Christ Jesus. He humbled himself and became obedient unto death, even death on the cross." [204] Therefore: "Do nothing from selfishness or conceit, but in humility count others better than yourself." [205]

And Jesus' criterion was proved right: the world is willing to learn from those who are truly meek and humble. The whole world learned from Paul, a giant even in humility, who did not think himself worthy to be called an apostle.[206] It learned from Francis Xavier, a rising star among the professors of the Sorbonne, who went to Goa and taught the slum children songs with the words of the *Ave Maria*.

Even closer to home, was not the world willing to learn from the "little Theresa" who confessed that she could have fallen lower than the Magdalen and who yet, by her whole life attempted to refute the words she had once heard that a pure soul had never yet loved as

---

198 Alvaro Barros, Vice-president of the Student Federation of the Catholic University of Chile, Santiago, in *Machitun*, 19.8. 1962.
199 Mt. 5, 3.
200 Lk. 18, 3.
201 Jn. 13, 15.
202 Mt. 11, 29.
203 1 Pet. 2, 21-24.
204 Phil. 2, 5. 8.
205 Phil. 2, 3.
206 1 Cor. 15, 9.

greatly as a soul that had been converted. This is not correct, she said, for is not purity of soul a result of the *protective* (and thus even greater) love of God? [207] Just because she was so humble, this young religious, so intelligent and sensitive, was able to exercise an untold influence, despite certain bourgeois limitations, as do all who understand that "Jesus made so certain to take the lowest place that no one can take it away from Him." [208]

THE BOND WITH JESUS

Yet all that we have mentioned, no matter how closely connected, would lack the intimate factor of unity were it not for the personal bond with Jesus. The whole of history proves it. Paul expresses it magnificently in the Epistle to the Philippians: "For to me, to live, is Christ." [209] For John, Christ is the whole of truthfulness,[210] all love is in and with Christ,[211] the generous gift of life,[212] humility —all are directly inspired by Christ [213] and no joy can be truly perfect without the testimony of the Word of life which he has heard and seen.[214]

According to Peter, the entire life of the Christian is animated by a belief in Christ as he reveals himself: "Without having seen him, you love him; though you do not now see him, you believe in him and rejoice with unutterable and exalted joy. As the outcome of your faith you shall receive the salvation of your souls." [215] James, too, views everything, from social problems to personal illness, against the background of the Lord's coming, which is close at hand and which gives us "patience" and courage.[216] How can we explain this "*consensus*"?

One might of course cite friendship. These people had known Jesus and had remained faithful to him. History, indeed, tells us of great and splendid friendships, but this was something more: it was the permanent relationship to a crucified rabbi of these apostles and of millions of others after them. There is no similar phenomenon in the history of the world. The explanation cannot be in the friends themselves; it must be found in the one friend. Can the gospels enlighten us as to how it all came about?

It was in any case done less with words than with deeds. From the very first meeting it may have been clear to the twelve that they had embarked on something that would last forever. John recounts how two disciples fell completely under his spell and even sets down the exact hour.[217] Jesus knew what they needed and Mark indicates the basis of their training as follows: "And he appointed twelve to be with him."[218] This beginning will confirm and intensify the further course of that training. For whereas the crowd considered Jesus a prophet, a man who spoke with authority and demanded belief in God,[219] without considering that from henceforth a religious life also implied living with Jesus, the twelve grew ever closer to him.

Certain miracles, such as those of the loaves and fishes, would normally have inspired everyone not to direct political decisions such as that Jesus should be crowned king but to an extraordinary confidence in him; this man is greater than the prophets, greater than Moses, almost equal to God, who sent the manna.[220] But the crowd cannot see further than the end of its nose, and even the disciples to whom Jesus reveals himself in a number of extraordinary events—the stilling of the storm, the walking on the waters [221] —even they do not understand. With rather cruel insistence Mark's dialogue makes the disciples furnish the details themselves; they must say how many baskets they have recovered each time: the first time—"twelve", and the second time—"Seven." "And do you not yet understand?"[222]

It was the disciples expecially who heard the infrequent yet astonishing statements in which Jesus, quite differently from the prophets, demands attention *for himself*. He invites men to follow him on condition that they shall be faithful unto death.[223] Persecutions indeed are inevitable, not only for God's sake, as in the time of the Maccabees, but *for his own sake*.[224] He dares to refer to his own personality as a recommendation for his function of teacher, not because this personality is so "strong," but "because I am gentle

207 Cf. *Geschiedenis van een ziel*, IV, 19. Eng. trans: *The Story of A Soul* (Westminster, The Newman Press).

208 Saying by Abbé Huvelin which made a deep impression on Charles de Foucauld.

209 Phil. 1, 21.

210 Jn. 18, 37.

211 1 Jn. *passim*.

212 Jn. 15, 13.

213 Jn. 13, 15.

214 1 Jn. 1, 1-4.

215 1 Pet. 1, 8-9.

216 Jas. 5, 7-9. 15.

217 Jn. 1, 38-39.

218 Mk. 3, 14.

219 Mk. 1, 15; cf. 11, 22, and the chapter, "Jesus Bearer of a Message," pp. 250-273.

220 Jn. 6, 15; Mt. 14, 22 (He *compelled* them).

221 Mk. 4, 35-41; 6, 45-53.

222 Mk. 8, 17-21.

223 Mt. 4, 19, etc; 10, 38.

224 Mt. 5, 11.

and lowly in heart."[225] Here Jesus is almost diametrically opposed to the prophets whose sole desires are to be voices, of God, zealous for the true yoke of the law, whereas Jesus speaks of *his own* yoke that is sweet, and his burden light.[226]

This almost intolerably original approach can be justified only by the fact that no one can know God except through him: "All things have been delivered to me by my Father; and no one knows the Son except the Father, and no one knows the Father except the Son and any one to whom the Son chooses to reveal him."[227] For this reason he dares to utter an invitation that would not have been tolerated from any prophet: "Come to me, all who . . ."[228]

Such an utterance was undoubtedly a highlight. Luke makes the occasion the return of the seventy-two disciples from their first trial journey.[229] Normally Jesus was not so explicit, but life with him was always an adventure during which he trained the naïve and the skeptics. The apostles undoubtedly contained both, with Thomas and Philip perhaps as extreme examples.[230] Doubtless, too, he was able to speak more clearly when he ate with them for the last time. One of those present expresses it thus: "I am the vine, you are the branches . . . Apart from me you can do nothing."[231] ". . . he who loves me . . . I will love him and manifest myself to him . . . and my Father will love him and we will come to him and make our home with him."[232] "I will not leave you desolate; I will come to you. Yet a little while and the world will see me no more, but you will see me because I live and you will live also."[233]

Here we should rather write out the parting words in their entirety and not simply refer them to the imaginary world of the fourth evangelist. John ponders long, reasons deeply, and edits very freely, but his historical background is solid. In any case on this evening the hour had come for the eucharist, the solemn celebration of the heavenly Father in the most intimate union possible with Jesus who was ready to depart: "This is my body . . ."[234] No matter what interpretation one gives to these words, it will henceforth be impossible to separate religious experience in its most intimate form from the Person of Jesus. The sober synoptics who describe this most extraordinary meal for us, already give evidence of a Christ-mystique. John will put it more explicitly: "He who eats my flesh and drinks my blood abides in me and I in him. As the living Father sent me, and I live because of the Father, so he who eats me will live because of me."[235]

With these few details and the culminating point of the evolution we shall have to be content. Not even the most inventive exegete will ever be able to describe to us how the whole of Jesus' life led to that final result. Certain details in his parables, a mysterious note in his way of speaking, something indefinable in his face, a seemingly careless gesture, a glance, or the simple attitude of his body—a thousand signs might insinuate what the disciples were later to experience and to understand.

John has expressed that idea, perhaps in an oversimplified way, in a series of self-definitions of Jesus in which it is shown that to be a Christian is the same as to belong to Christ. "I am the bread of life . . . I am the light of the world . . . I am the door of the sheep . . . I am the resurrection and the life . . . I am the way, the truth and the life . . . I am the true vine." [236] That God is a shepherd was one of the themes of the prophets; [237] now Jesus, too, is the good shepherd.[238]

Jesus does not replace the Father, but his coming signifies a new phase in the history of sanctity: "Hitherto you have asked nothing in my name; ask, and you will receive, that your joy may be full." [239] Henceforth, men will approach the Father with boundless confidence *in his name*, that is, in his spirit, with his mentality, united with him. ". . . believe in God, believe also in me." [240] In these short words is contained the greatest religious revolution in history. It would be fascinating, but take far too long, to examine the course of this revolution, which is still in progress. Since the passing of the young teacher from Galilee, a Christ-experience has taken place on earth. Active and, for the rest, completely normal people confess that they wish to die "in order to be with Christ." [241] An aged bishop like Ignatius of Antioch desires to be ground by the teeth of the lions, because the voice of his "crucified love" calls to him: "Come to the Father," and he begs his Roman friends not to intervene in his favor.[242] Others are prepared, for Jesus' sake, to

225 Mt. 11, 29.
226 Mt. 11, 30.
227 Mt. 11, 27-28.
228 Mt. 11, 28.
229 Lk. 10, 21: "at that hour."
230 See Vol. I.
231 Jn. 15, 1-8.
232 Jn. 14, 21-24.
233 Jn. 14, 18-19.
234 Lk. 22, 19; see also pp. 194ff.
235 Jn. 6, 55-57.

236 Jn. 6, 35; 8, 12; 10, 7; 11, 25; 14, 6; 15, 1.
237 Is. 40, 11; Ez. 34, 11-23; 27, 24; cf. Mt. 18, 12-14; Lk 15, 3-7.
238 Jn. 10-11.
239 Jn. 16, 24; cf. 14, 13-14; 15, 16; 16, 26.
240 Jn. 14, 1.
241 Phil. 1, 23.
242 Ignatius of Antioch, *To the Romans*.

live in pain, with physical and apostolic crosses, until the end of the world.[243]

We must humbly confess that we, Christians, fall lamentably short in many respects, yet, we must not forget the row of marvelous figures who have filed past the eyes of the world. These were people who clung with heart and soul to Jesus' Word and life. He was the unifying factor of their existence. We cannot dismiss this as pure autosuggestion, for it seems to me impossible rather to attribute such achievements to people of our calibre, with or without autosuggestion. It is, after all, safer and more reasonable to believe in a statement of Jesus that shocks the universe: "Heaven and earth will pass away, but my words will not pass away." [244] It is indeed easier to make a universe than to reform human hearts. On this note of confidence ends our introduction to Jesus' message.

[243] Including Teresa of Avila, Charles   [244] Mt. 24, 35.
de Foucauld.

Part Two

The Personality of Jesus

The application of psychology to biblical science and especially to the interpretation of the gospels seems to be anathema to a great many exegetes, Catholic as well as Protestant. As a reaction against the entire body of *Lives* of Jesus which, since the last century especially, made use of the psychological *réveil* to elaborate romantic episodes, full of subjective interpretations, into a sort of new gospel, this chorus of protest deserves the applause of all who are concerned with Jesus and with the truth. A better insight into the *Formgeschichte* [1] invites us to be extremely cautious; it should today be a general conviction that it is highly dangerous to draw hasty and narrow conclusions from the Gospel texts.

This reaction, however, undoubtedly went too far. We must protest against it too, and, since the sense of the whole of this second part depends on it, we must first examine whether it is possible or indeed desirable to approach the figure of Jesus from a psychological standpoint.

Everything depends on what one understands by "psychology." It is naturally impossible to compile a daily record of Jesus' reactions and attitudes, explaining his words by his prevailing state of mind, as is done in psychiatric institutions. One will have to be very cautious in dealing with what dogmatic theologians call "the psychology of Christ," that is, the union that exists between his human nature and the divine Person of the Word, and the awareness of this union.[2] Yet, a third type of psychological knowledge exists, which amounts to a study of the *personality*, that is, the complex of human qualities as expressed in actions and attitudes—the way of speaking, dealing with others, mildness or severity, devotional life, in short, what is known today as being-in-the-world. In our opinion such a psychological study of Christ is both possible and desirable.

[1] See Vol. 2. [2] Cf. pp. 203ff.

It is possible because the gospels provide us with sufficient data. Indeed, without in any way denying that it was the aim of the apostles and the evangelists to preach salvation—which may then be viewed somewhat as a theological principle of a rather abstract nature [3]—and freely admitting that Jesus' words and deeds were frequently transmitted by the gospels outside their vital context,[4] we are yet positive that they wished to convey to us something about a *person*. A person is not a principle nor yet a complex of truths even be they truths of salvation. To speak of a person is to venture into the field of insight, into human nature, and to set in motion the whole machinery of psychological interest.

We admit that psychology, considered as the systematic study of human acts, with special emphasis on the inner life, did not exist at the time these documents were written. Yet even then there was considerable interest in man's basic attitudes as revealed in his actions. Jesus can be said to have interested the apostles in this way. Witness the existence of a tendency toward even a mystique of *imitation*.

It is remarkable how strongly the imitation of Christ was emphasized from the very beginning. In Paul's very first epistle he says: "You know what kind of men we proved to be among you for your sake . . . so that you became an example to all the believers in Macedonia and in Achaia." [5] The Corinthians must become imitators of Paul, just as he is an imitator of Christ.[6]

Many Protestants, justifiably resentful because in the Middle Ages the imitation of Christ seemed to be exclusively confined to "voluntary poverty" and celibacy, in other words, to the monastic life, tend to violate the texts. Certainly the term, "to follow," (*mimeomai*) in many cases expresses the duty to docility in the sense of obedience, and naturally enough the imitation of God or of Christ will differ from "pure mimicry as when, for example, a dilettante attempts to imitate the art forms of a great artist." [7] Yet, it is necessary to do considerable philological violence to the long series of texts [8] on imitation in the New Testament before one can state that "an imitation of Christ finds no support in the words of St. Paul." [9] In certain cases, this theory was even put into practice, which caused Kierkegaard to remark sarcastically, "The whole art of Christianity really consists in abolishing imitation." [10]

Happily, the swing of opinion has made rapid progress. Lately, it is above all the baptism texts and the theme of the "image" (*eikoon*) which draws the attention of exegetes to the idea of a transformation in Christ's image, with all the moral-religious consequences implied.[11]

In any case Christians must have, either in themselves or among themselves, the sentiments of Jesus himself.[12] Christ's passion, his humility and obedience, are basic themes in the first Christian exhortations.[13] This shows that people were interested in the Person of Jesus, in his personality. The gospels may contain a great amount of theology, but one cannot imitate a theology.

This does not mean, however, that it is *easy* to collect, sift and arrange psychological data concerning Jesus. It is, on the contrary, difficult, especially if one prefers truth to beautiful theories, silence to original discoveries and a humble question mark to the lucky chance to attribute impressive traits to the figure of Jesus. But this already concerns the *way* in which the investigation is carried out. What follows will undoubtedly be far from perfect, but should be taken as an honest attempt.

Since the difficulties are so considerable it might be more desirable

---

[3] On this point we advise a certain caution. Theology is all too often made so abstract that it seems to become a game of ideas. Theology is formal, but according to true philosophy, the *forma* must remain organically linked with the *materia* from which it is abstracted.

[4] In general, psychologists and men of letters (and even too many dogmatic theologians) take too little account of the very special character of our documentation on Jesus. The gospels are exactly the opposite of a number of psychological files. In the interesting work of Alejandro Roldan, S.J., *Introduccion a la ascetica diferencial* (Madrid, 1960), one finds a long analysis of the character of Jesus (pp. 290-442) in which the texts should be treated with more caution. The same must be said of other "psychologies of the gospels," which are usually quite indigestible for the exegete.

[5] 1 Thess. 1, 5-7.

[6] 1 Cor. 4, 16; 11, 1.

[7] G. Bouwman, *De Bijbel over volgen en navolgen* (Roermond-Maaseik, 1961), p. 56. This is a remarkable little book.

[8] 1 Thess. 1, 6; 1 Cor. 4, 16; 11, 1 (cf. 10, 33); Rom. 15, 3; Eph. 5, 1-2.

[9] W. Michaelis, "Mimeomai," in *T.W.N.T.*, 4 (1942), pp. 661-678; quotation p. 676.

[10] Quoted by G. Bouwman, *op. cit.*, p. 58.

[11] According to E. Larsson, "Christus als Vorbild. Eine Untersuchung zu den paulinischen Tauf- und Eikontexten," (*Thesis Uppsala—Acta. Semi. Neotest. Upsal.*, 23, Lund, 1962).

[12] Phil. 2, 6. Both meanings are possible: "Have this mind among yourselves"—"toward each other," or in yourselves, in your hearts. In any case the reference is to a psychological fact—the attitude of humility, on the part of the Philippians and of Christ (v. 8).

[13] Cf. 1 Pet. 2, 21; Jn. 13, 15; 1 Jn. 2, 6; Col. 3, 13.

to abandon any idea of a psychological study were not the matter so extremely important. It seems impossible, yet there are tomes on the market, claiming to be complete, in which the theology of the New Testament or Christology are explained without, for example, one word being said about Jesus' goodness. Quite frequently his miracles are considered exclusively as "signs," "proofs" of his divinity; his passion is the principal of our reconciliation and even in the appreciation of the resurrection, which is fortunately increasing, his Person is as good as ignored.

This trend might well be the modern docetism. If the Word truly became man, then it is a priori of the utmost importance that we should come to know something of his human personality. For it is *in* this human figure, and not somewhere behind or linked with it, that the infinite fullness of God himself was revealed to us.

The following work plan, I think, gives us a fairly complete and balanced image of Jesus' personality:

1. His true humanity.
2. His goodness.
3. His leadership.
4. The figure that inspired him.
5. His devotional life.

I
Jesus' True
Humanity

In trying to define what the Christian should be according to Jesus' message, we have not dwelt upon the limitations and defects actually found among Christians. We seldom encounter perfect harmony between the various components of the Christian human image. The fire of religious zeal that devoured and inflamed so many people throughout almost their entire lifetime seems powerless to burn away all the traces left in the human psyche by a sinful past and an ancestry of sinners. We are personally and communally tainted, and a truly supernatural life scarcely ever succeeds in illuminating our daily round. This is why so many upright Christians seem so barely "human." We protest against this spontaneously, not only out of human solidarity, but for God's sake. For "although less perfect than grace, nature too is a daughter of God. And, if it is true that God became man in order to make man a God, then it is no less true that he did so also in order to teach man to be human" (H.J. Valla).

How can we define that perfect human being who seems only to be found in Jesus? What is "true humanity"? The phrase is not in the dictionaries and it is difficult to find an equivalent. "Humanism" is not quite the same thing, apart altogether from the overtones which this word, derived from the Latin, *homo*, has acquired without aspiring to be complete. I would dare to propose that the following three factors are of decisive importance in building up a picture of someone who is "truly human."

1. *The harmonious union* of apparently contradictory qualities, such as gravity and joy, justice and goodness, perseverence and adaptability, humility and dignity, etc.

2. Pronounced *masculinity* (or femininity) and at the same time,

a noble attitude toward the other sex. In order to be truly human, one must also be truly a man or a woman.

3. *Involvement with life*, whereby the person in question does not seem to us distant and unreal, but by his unison with nature, with people, with ordinary life, attracts us and inspires confidence.

A FACT: JESUS HAD CHARM

Before analyzing the three factors listed above, we shall first establish the fact that Jesus must have been an attractive person. This can be deduced from the gospels which, without in any way setting out to describe Jesus' outward appearance or his human aspect, nonetheless, provide us as if by chance with a number of valuable indications.

His youth was described by Luke as a growth "in favor with God and man." [1] We might say, "People were pleased to see him" and this continued to be so. When he later appeared in public, people were beside themselves with wonder "at the gracious words that proceeded out of his mouth," [2] and he was generally esteemed.[3] A woman loudly sang his praises in terms which might offend the puritan ear, but which are clearly intended as congratulatory toward the person of Jesus and his mother.[4]

John relates a concrete fact: A number of representatives of the public order, sent by the pharisees to take Jesus prisoner, returned empty-handed and with their hearts full of a person who spoke as they had never heard anyone speak before.[5] Luke sketches for us the scene in which the small, caustic tax collector falls from his tree in surprise and allows himself to be completely captivated by Jesus, heedless of the economic consequences.[6]

Are these merely the personal impressions of a romantic Luke or of a John so passionately involved in Jesus' cause? All the synoptics describe how women and children approach him confidently, under the stern gaze and threatening words of the disciples (probably not the most thick-skinned—on the contrary, they appeal for reasonableness and order).[7] When rough fishermen and a phlegmatic tax collector become enthusiastic at the very first contact and leave everything to follow someone,[8] there must be a reason for it.

We see the same enchantment at work in the story of Andrew and his companion, of Philip, with a soft heart, of Nathaniel, who found himself checkmated.[9] Admittedly, only John gives this last detail, and only Luke speaks of the desire entertained by the unscrupulous Herod for a contact with Jesus.[10] *All* the evangelists, however, mention a certain hesitancy in Pilate's attitude to Jesus.[11] This man, whom history does not credit with too many scruples, was evidently quite thrown off balance by an extraordinary person like Jesus. Is this Christian apologetics? Undoubtedly. Has it any foundation?

Let us view the matter from another angle. It is a generally valid law that people who are able to win faithful friends in the midst of great difficulties, even the danger of death, must possess superior qualities. When, in addition, they make an impact from the very first contact, we are dealing with absolutely exceptional cases, for this assumes a far-reaching, extremely rare harmony between the greatness of their mission and the impression made by their concrete appearance. Both characteristics are present in Jesus' case—what loyalty, from the very beginning, and so often ending in a martyr's death! If the immediacy of his conquests is not revealed in the foregoing anecdotes, then surely it can be seen irrefutably in the disproportion between his success and the almost unbelievable brevity of his life and the few years of his public work.

Karl Jaspers, a non-Christian, does not hesitate to include Jesus in his short list of the four greatest human beings: Socrates, Buddha, Confucius and Jesus. And someone who is only concerned with "the future of unbelief" admits that the founder of Christianity was "a genius of loving-understanding" and that on account of its world-embracing message of love, Christianity has become a fact which may be considered as the zenith in the history of humanity.[12] I do not believe that unattractive personalities exercise such a deep and such a sustained influence. One must assume rather that Jesus possessed the "true humanity" of which we will now examine the aspects or qualities given above.

[1] Lk. 2, 52.
[2] Lk. 4, 22.
[3] Lk. 4, 15.
[4] Lk. 11, 27.
[5] Jn. 7, 32, 46.
[6] Lk. 19, 1-10.
[7] Mk. 10, 13-15; Mt. 19, 13-15; Lk. 18, 15-17.
[8] Mk. 1, 16-20; 2, 13-17 par.

[9] Jn. 1, 35-51.
[10] Lk. 23, 8.
[11] Mk. 15, 1-15; Mt. 27, 19-26; Lk. 23, 4. 6-12; Jn. 18, 38-40; 19, 4-16.
[12] G. Szczesny, *Die Zukunft des Unglaubens, Zeitgemässe Betrachtungen eines Nicht-christen* (Munich, 1958), pp. 51-54.

Harmony of Apparently Contradictory Qualities

In order to be truly human, one must have lived a full life. One must have taken risks and achieved a degree of harmony between the what is daringly personal (the "original") and what is peacefully general to the whole of humanity. The true man lives and moves upon the bridge between two worlds and is therefore attractive from all aspects.

This is why religious-minded persons, let us call them "saints," are often less attractive personalities. This is not because they possess fewer qualities, but because they must also acquire harmony on a new terrain. The person who heroically denies himself and sees the true face of sin is more inclined to disapprove of "the world" and become too serious in his relationships. The man fired by apostolic zeal can easily give the impression that in his feverish activity he has mislaid true peace and joy. The person who is strict with himself will readily become strict with others or, contrariwise, tend to make excuses for others and thus again fall short in appreciation of others.

It thus follows that the "saint," who naturally may have no moral defect, is confronted with the almost impossible task of spreading the weight of his inner fire over the entire fragile surface of his human appearance without breaking it. We make the distinction here between "saints" and other "great men" who are indeed expected to be magnanimous and may not strive after self-interest, but whose greatness is not destroyed by vanity and sensuality, like Napoleon and Bolivar, who were so fond of fame and women.[13] It thus happens that many saints, despite their excellent qualities, often have something lacking or exaggerated in their makeup.

Among the few in whom "greatness" and "sanctity" achieve harmony, one can think of Francis of Assisi and Gandhi. Others see in Theresa of Lisieux a masterwork of harmony between grace and nature. It would be arrogant to try to detect faults in these great ones of our race, yet, this harmony undeniably reached a higher level in Jesus, whose personality was illumined by an incomparably more intense light and "a light without shadow" (Heinrich). In him, virtue needed no onesidedness or exaggeration in order to exist.

To turn now to some of these balanced contradictions:

1. Jesus was a man of deep inner life and prayer, on the one hand, and of great drive and powerful initiative on the other. He traveled

from village to village and displayed a ceaseless activity. The forty miracles alone, mentioned in the gospels—leaving aside the general mention of "many miracles"—indicate an intense activity during the few years his "public life." Small details which give an even more vivid picture of that dynamism, and which were surely not invented by John and Mark, may be found in Jesus' "weariness from his journey" [14] and the fact that he sometimes did not find time to eat. [15]

Still less can anyone doubt the depth of his communion with God, not solely because he retired into solitude and spent whole nights in prayer even when people were looking for him, [16] and this up to the very end, in the days of the most violent polemics in the capital, when he went to pray "as usual" in the Garden of Olives, [17] but perhaps even more because all his words were undoubtedly born of a deep inner life. What Jesus says is full of life and reality, goes straight to the human heart, is simple and deep so that it can defy the centuries. How different from the rapid, nervous phrases inspired at the spur of the moment by children of activism and then gone with the wind. Had we been privileged to witness the birth of this teaching we would have seen it welling up from the infinite depths where the peace of God reigned.

2. Another of Jesus' attractive qualities is the combination of stern detachment with regard to his own person and openhanded goodness toward others, without a trace of superficiality. I cannot believe that it is purely poetical imagery on Luke's part when he says that the Son of Man on his travels had less comfort than the fox and the birds. [18] He could skip a meal and indeed did so in such a way that his friends were in despair [19]—a detail which surely no Christian could have invented—and it is also established that he began his ministry with a lengthy retreat, with a fast in the strict sense of the word, in which he stood firm against temptations. [20]

But his sobriety did not make him mean or stingy. On the contrary, the soundest evangelical traditions mention the abundance of bread with which he fed thousands in the desert. [21] John is the only one who tells us of the six hundred and twenty or so gallons of the

[13] Cf. the excellent article of A. Lasser, "El gran hombre y el santo," in *La Nueva Democracia* (January, 1962), pp. 26-33.

[14] Jn. 4, 6.

[15] Mk. 3, 20; 6, 31. This perhaps became a cliché in Mark, but only because it was based on an exact recollection.

[16] Mk. 1, 37.

[17] Lk. 22, 39; Jn. 18, 2.

[18] Lk. 9, 58.

[19] Mk. 3, 20-21.

[20] Mk. 1, 12-13.

[21] Mk. 6, 32-44; Mt. 14, 13-21; Lk. 9, 10-17; Jn. 6, 10.

finest wine,[22] but although this wedding feast has a symbolic meaning, one may not on that account deny it any historical basis. It is in
any case a fact that Jesus was repeatedly seen at banquets, so that
some even begin to grumble: "Behold, a glutton and a drunkard, a
friend of tax collectors and sinners." [23] Such disrespectful outbursts
were certainly not invented by the Christians and are completely in
accord with what the gospels tell us of "Jesus at table."

May we then believe these same gospels when they show us how
far this jovial master was from cheap cameraderie or bourgeois con-
formism. God is present at the table conversations and his kingdom
shines through. A woman who is a notorious sinner (how many men
are in the same state) goes home completely changed. On the other
hand, the rabbi will never allow himself to be persuaded by false
courtesy to disguise the truth, even though it means placing his host
in a difficult position.[24]

3. In Jesus greatness and humility went hand in hand. He
preached the most exalted doctrine in the simplest way. No philosopher or religious reformer was so profound, yet used such a simple
vocabulary as he did. This same humility can be seen in his contacts,
which were not confined to an élite. He was rather a friend to the
needy and the sick, exerting himself for an infirm old man—he had
been ill for the past thirty-eight years, says John [25]—and concerning
himself with the mentally ill and the possessed whom most must
have found repulsive.[26] He converses with women, the despised
of antiquity,[27] and speaks lovingly to the children, who were of no
account.[28]

Yet, he will not bow down to the high priest, nor to Pilate, nor to
Herod, and still less to the soldier who thought it his duty to strike
him.[29]

This greatness and humility seem bound up with the secret of his
person. He himself says that he is "gentle and lowly in heart," [30] yet,
a force goes out from him that confounds his opponents. According
to all the evangelists, this force earns them a series of defeats in
public clashes [31] and causes them to fail in a number of attempts on
his life, made, according to Luke, at Nazareth and according to
John, repeatedly in Jerusalem.[32]

4. Besides being exceedingly wise and level-headed, Jesus also
gives evidence of freshness and youth. He is loyal to the old ways,
of which nothing may be lost (although this naturally concerns
only the essential, the spirit).[33] He is prudent, does not seek futile

difficulties, as, for example, when the political climate becomes dangerous as a result of the Johannine movement [34] and he wishes to avoid a clash with the pharisees.[35] Other facets of this level-headed wisdom are the importance he attaches to parental love, the root of all tradition,[36] and, above all, the undeniable fact that he knows the human soul through and through.[37]

On the other hand, Jesus never gives the impression of being an old man. On the contrary, his remarkable daring and far-reaching demands serve as an inspiration.[38] His doctrine is new. He has not come to patch up the old garment, and he will use gleaming new bottles for his new wine.[39] His wisdom does not consist in moderation, not even in the normal. He invites his followers to abandon all their possessions [40] in order to begin a life in which the kingdom of God takes the place of family happiness.[41] Every disciple must consider martyrdom as a real possibility.[42] Above all, his enthusiasm is infectious, yields to no opposition and, even in the last desperate moments, is not soured by discouragement or bitterness. He will die full of fight. The wisdom of Seneca was unable to conquer the youth of his day, yet, that of Jesus remains today a source of inspiration for adventures that appear completely insane. In saying that the Gospel does not age, we are honoring Jesus' youthfulness and maturity.

A True Man and Courteous toward Women

G. Bichlmair devoted an entire book to "The Man, Jesus," and many other books have examined every aspect of Jesus' attitude toward women.[43] They all, however, reflect the same attitude, for only a true man can be courteous toward women, and a woman can

[22] Jn. 2, 6-10.

[23] Mt. 11, 19.

[24] Mt. 9, 9-13; 26, 6-13; Lk. 7, 36-50; 14, 1-24; 19, 1-27; Jn. 12, 1-11.

[25] Jn. 5, 5.

[26] Mk. 1, 25-26; 5, 1-8; 7, 31-37; 9, 14-29.

[27] Jn. 4, 9.27; Lk. 10, 38-42.

[28] Mk. 9, 36; 10, 13-15.

[29] Jn. 18, 22-23.

[30] Mt. 11, 29.

[31] Mt. 22, 34. 46; Mk. 12, 34; Lk. 20, 40; cf. further on Jesus as polemist, pp. 148ff.

[32] Lk. 4, 29-30; Jn. 5, 18, cf. Mt. 12, 14.

[33] Mt. 5, 17-19.

[34] Mt. 14, 13.

[35] Mt. 12, 14-15.

[36] Mk. 5, 8-13; Lk. 2, 51-52; Jn. 19, 25-27.

[37] Jn. 2, 24-25; cf. Vol. 2 (typical of John).

[38] Cf. pp. 145ff.

[39] Lk. 5, 36-39.

[40] Mt. 19, 21-23, etc.

[41] Mt. 19, 11-12.

[42] Mt. 16, 24.

[43] Cf. J. Leipoldt, *Jesus und die*

only be truly womanly by showing herself tender as a sister and solicitous as a mother (especially toward man).

It may seem a limitation and indeed it is one of the bounds inherent in the adventure of "emptying himself" begun by God's Son, but Jesus did not merely become human; he became a man. As he was bound by his incarnation to a particular point in space and a definite period in time, a choice had also to be made on his entry into humanity. He had to become either man or woman. It is doubtless more satisfactory to both sexes that the Word became man, and may even correspond more to the desire of *woman* (even after she has gained those rights so long denied her).[44] In any case, the fact remains; Jesus' entire attitude, activity and being were characterized by a firm, restrained manliness.

For years, he was engaged in an essentially masculine trade: the carpenter was the practical man of the village, something like the electrician or the mechanic of today.[45] He was made of stern stuff: loneliness did not deter him, not even in the dark of night or the desert with its wild beasts.[46] He compares himself to a good shepherd: [47] this is an image of courage, conjuring up the idea of risking one's life. There were no shepherdesses in the mountains of Juda. In the hour of approaching mortal danger, when everyone instinctively seeks support and companionship, he intervenes bravely for his friends: ". . . if you seek me, let these men go." [48]

There is no trace of softness or sentimentality in Jesus' speech or behavior, not even in Luke, who is temperamentally inclined in this direction.[49] "Those who are gorgeously apparelled and live in luxury are in kings' courts," says Jesus ironically.[50] His way of speech is neither grandiloquent nor servile; he is objective, in a masculine way. He has no need to employ emotional arguments or indulge in personal outpourings; he does not ask for pity or beg for sympathy, although he is undeniably a person with a heart. The objectivity and directness of his character shine through the pages of the Gospel, although it is possible that the very nature of our documents which, after all, offer us a stereotyped rendering of his words, has increased this impression of an almost unyielding objectivity.[51]

This objectivity, which renders Jesus independent of the opinions of others, which makes him prefer (and utter) the stern truth to any favourable impression he might create, leads, among other things, to violent exchanges with the pharisees,[52] but is also recognized by his opponents—not without sly intent—as a positive point:

"Teacher! We know that you are true and care for no man; for you do not regard the position of men . . ." [53] On reading this text, he seems to appear before us, the *man*, Jesus, with his frank, impartial, entirely upright gaze.

No less striking, however, is his spotlessly pure, wonderfully kind, and always courteous attitude to women. Considering the country and the period, it is positively amazing what a prominent place women occupy in the Gospel. A large percentage of the miracles involve women. Less sensational, but much more striking, is the fact that a whole series of parables show how familiar Jesus was with woman's work and how he appreciated it: mother and daughter grind at the mill from the early hours of the morning; [54] it is a woman who works the yeast into three measures of flour to bake the bread; [55] it is she, too, who patches the garments [56] and sweeps out the dark little room to find a lost object or coin.[57] These are all such domestic allusions, unexpected in a revolutionary message.

These details were certainly not invented by the first Christian community, for there the women played a rather retiring role. A man like Paul, who has many women helpers in his apostolate, insists that women should be silent at the meetings; they can consult their husbands at leisure when they get home.[58] It must have been Jesus himself who brought about this change. Just as people must have wondered that he did not marry—an eighteen-year-old carpenter was not a bad match in a village like Nazareth—they must also have been amazed at the emancipation he brought about.

For Jesus, woman is no longer a second-class being. The entire evangelical tradition confirms the presence of women in Jesus' public life.[59] Luke even mentions a number of names.[60]

Frauen (Leipzig, 1919); P. Ketter, *Christus und die Frauen* (Stuttgart 1944), 1949[2]. An interesting chapter, but one which should be read critically, is "Mann und Weib," in E. Stauffer's *Die Botschaft Jesu damals und heute* (Bern, 1959), pp. 68-85.

[44] Some theologians, like R. Laurentin, find in this an explanation of the exceptional place that Jesus' mother, Mary, occupies in God's plan of redemption.

[45] Mk. 6, 3; cf. the chapter on Jesus as pilgrim in this book, pp. 227ff. (with bibliography).

[46] Mk. 1, 13.
[47] Jn. 10, 11-15.
[48] Jn. 18, 8.
[49] Vol. 2.
[50] Lk. 7, 24-25.
[51] Cf. Vol. 2.
[52] Mt. 23.
[53] Mk. 12, 14.
[54] Mt. 24, 41.
[55] Mt. 13, 33.
[56] Mt. 9, 16.
[57] Lk. 15, 8; cf. Mt. 12, 44.
[58] 1 Cor. 14, 34-35.
[59] Mk. 15, 40-41; Mt. 20, 20; 27, 55; Lk. 24, 22.
[60] Lk. 8, 2-3.

The scenes with Martha and Mary [61] are absolutely amazing,[62] as is that with the (probably young) woman taken in adultery. This story, too, probably comes to us from Luke, though it is in St. John's gospel.[63] Jesus firmly and courageously embarks upon a struggle in the young girl's defense—"the guilty man had once again gone scot free"—and allows her to begin a new life with her husband. It must have been the first time in her life that this young woman encountered such a chivalrous man, and that after such a night and such a morning! [64] Even the disciples expressed their amazement at Jesus' conversation with the Samaritan woman, among themselves, for they dared say nothing to him.[65]

When Mary anoints his feet with costly ointment, in order that he shall at least have some sort of burial, for she feared he might be stoned and cast into the communal grave with the other criminals, Jesus himself defends her against the disciples.[66]

The meeting with the women on the way to the place of execution is not uninteresting, but it pales in comparison with the story of Mary Magdalen.[67] We do not know the details, but to judge from the facts we do possess, it must have been more breathtaking than the films it has inspired.[68]

Thus, we see that Jesus' attitude, though entirely devoid of anything that smacks of familiarity, or which might give rise to suspicions in a field where suspicions are all too easily aroused,[69] gives evidence of a far-reaching and reformed sympathy, of understanding and compassion, even of tenderness, as in the case of the twelve-year-old girl whom he snatches from death just at marriageable age, in the bloom of her youth, and to whom he orders food to be brought.[70] Throughout the gospels, he displays friendship, as in the case of the sisters of Lazarus,[71] and sincere love toward women.

This love must be viewed in its deepest aspect. Jesus is the redeemer of man and woman, and he could redeem only in the measure that he was familiar with the inner life of both, (with their sin and their hunger for God, for goodness and happiness) and loved them as they were.

The gospels, naturally, transport us into a world predominantly male. Yet Jesus' attention and affection are fairly equally divided between men and women. This alone should be sufficient to enable us to conclude that he was a real man, truly and completely human.

His Closeness to Life

To be truly human presumes noble sentiments, a strong will, far-reaching plans, a harmony of virtues. Yet, something is missing if we cannot clearly see that the person in question is completely involved in life, close to us, fused with all that is human and closely linked with nature. There must be no gulf between the true man and what we simply, but so evocatively, call "life."

For a man—and now we are in fact talking of a man, and of qualities that are rather rare in that sex—to be truly pleasing and to gain all hearts, he must be close to life. His lively, intuitive grasp of a situation, his directness of contact, the realism that keeps both his feet firmly on the ground, his spontaneous love of beauty in any form that inspires him to strike that note which touches the heart—these are the elements that give the "finishing touch" to true humanity.

Now, it can scarcely be doubted that Jesus was a person to whom everyone immediately felt drawn. The explanation lies in the first place in his *closeness to nature*. In this respect, the gospels differ entirely from Paul's epistles. To this very day, Jesus' parables conjure up countless little scenes for us: We *see* the sower who goes out and moves with a rhythmical motion of his arm along the road, between the rocky places, among the thistles and thorns.[72] While the farmer sleeps and rises, night and day, the seed sprouts and grows, first the blade, then the ear, then the full grain in the ear.[73] Before our eyes, we see the mowers moving over the ripe corn-fields.[74]

It would probably never have entered Paul's head to associate God's providence with birds that neither sow nor reap, or with the

[61] Lk. 10, 38-42.

[62] Lk. 7, 36-50.

[63] Jn. 8, 1-11; cf. Vol. 2.

[64] E. Stauffer, *op. cit.*, p. 81.

[65] Jn. 4, 27.

[66] Mk. 14, 3-11; Jn. 12, 1-8.

[67] Lk. 23, 27-31.

[68] Lk. 8, 2; 24, 10 par; Jn. 19, 25; 20, 1. 11-18.

[69] As far as I know, the Jewish tradition has not made any accusations of this nature against Jesus, although it has against Mary. Cf.

my article, "Maria altijd Maagd," in *Coll. Brug. Gand.*, 9 (1962), pp. 475-494.

[70] Mk. 5, 41-43; Lk. 8, 42. 54-55: "He took her by the hand."

[71] Jn. 11, 5: "Now Jesus loved Martha"; the friendly relationship is evident from the entire chapter and also from Lk. 10, 38-41.

[72] Mt. 13, 3-8.

[73] Mk. 4, 26-29.

[74] Jn. 4, 35-38; cf. Mt. 9, 37-38.

violet anemones that are more beautiful than the royal purple of
Solomon. This is probably the only page of nature poetry in the
whole of the New Testament; it is worth mentioning, particularly since it occurs in Matthew who had little or no poetical
inclinations.[75]

We cannot mention everything, for almost the whole of country
life is passed in review.[76] This abundance of images from nature is
most exceptional, not to say unique, in such short books of such
elevated content.

Even more important is the fact that Jesus is close to the real life
of the people. We have already mentioned how he realized that the
scarcely mature daughter of Jairus would need to *eat* [77] after her
sleep of death. He halts abruptly when he sees the little Zaccheus in
the tree—people surely laughed at the little man, all the more so
because he was rich—invites himself to supper, and is quick with his
repartee.[78]

He was greatly concerned with the sick, and this alone should
have sufficed to acquaint him with the sober realities of human life,
with its pains and fears, its hopes and plans. There are few utopians
among practicing doctors.

Death moves him,[79] especially the death of a friend; he is deeply
touched and weeps.[80] He himself will also feel fear and distress at
the thought of this pale, dangerous companion of every human
life,[81] yet this will not prevent him from feeling for others and
their problems, even in the most terrible moments of his own life.[82]
He finds the opportunity to cast a significant glance at the unhappy
Peter, who must surely have thought that he had fallen from grace,
and in addition, felt extremely humiliated.[83] On the point of death,
he has time to reassure a repentant thief [84] and to make some last
arrangement for his mother.[85] The fact that Mary and the beloved
disciple are here fulfilling a symbolic role should not prevent us
from seeing in this gesture another proof of Jesus' very deep and
very noble humanity. How many sons on their deathbeds have not
uttered the cry which linked them again with the sources of their
lives: mother!

We also find this awareness of life reflected in his *words*. Short
phrases like: "Let the day's own trouble be sufficient for the
day," [86] and "Where your treasure is, there will your heart be
also," [87] reveal a depth of worldly wisdom. "No man can serve two
masters." [88] must have held particular appeal for the slaves who

were dependent on two masters at once—quite a common situation.[89] One might list a whole series of such sayings, yet, they have less significance than the parables.

Certainly, the evangelists may have played some part in their presentation, especially the sensitive, artistic Luke. Yet the whole cannot deceive; Luke did not invent the parables, he inherited them from tradition. Possibly he may have embellished them here and there, but it is even more likely that, having first been simplified by tradition, then revised or even rewritten, they may have lost much of their original charm, a charm they possessed when spoken by someone who had gazed upon the life of man and who succeeded in conveying, in evocative human situations, something of the fire of his divine message.

Let us recall for a moment those scenes taken so directly from life. Can we not imagine ourselves standing close beside the Samaritan as he tends to the *half-dead* victim of the robbery, pouring oil and wine on his wounds, hoisting him onto his mount, making his arrangements with the innkeeper, and returning? [90] Who can forget that poor Lazarus' skin was covered with sores and that the dogs licked them? [91] And then, imagine a father's joy when his son suddenly returns home. He gets out the best robe, the ring, kills the fatted calf. Jesus even remembers the music.[92]

Admittedly, this is all in Luke, but Matthew's dryer style, which gives us another version of the parables, also shows the same eye for colorful detail: the man from the court seizing the poor wretch who is unable to pay by the throat, and the indignation of his colleagues; [93] the laborers bent under the leaden heat of the midday sun, who had "borne the burden of the day and the scorching heat;" the two sons, completely different in character, one fawning, the

[75] Mt. 6, 26-30; Lk. 12, 24-28. On the phlegmatic character of Matthew see Vol. 2.

[76] See Vol. I.

[77] Mk. 5, 43.

[78] Lk. 19, 1-10.

[79] Lk. 7, 13.

[80] Cf. Jn. 11, 5. 11. 33. 35. 38. These details are useless for the *theologian* John; here, it becomes clear that Jesus is life, not because he was brilliant, but because he loved the entire man with heart and soul.

[81] Mk. 14, 33-41; Lk. 22, 40-46.

[82] Heb. 4, 7.

[83] Lk. 22, 61.

[84] Lk. 22, 43.

[85] Jn. 19, 26-27.

[86] Mt. 6, 34.

[87] Mt. 6, 21.

[88] Mt. 6, 24.

[89] Cf. Strack-Billerbeck I, p. 433.

[90] Lk. 10, 23-27.

[91] Lk. 16, 21.

[92] Lk. 15, 11-32.

[93] Mt. 18, 28. 31.

[94] Mt. 20, 13.

other with a rough tongue and a heart of gold.[95] The risk one takes in playing one's highest trump: when the tenants see the son coming they may grow frightened, but they may also take the opportunity to settle the score once and for all.[96]

Matthew is just as realistic as Luke in telling the parable of the reluctant bridal guests. He mentions their excuses, that one went to his farm and the other to his business.[97] Luke goes into more picturesque detail: They want to go and inspect the field, examine the five yoke of oxen. There is a newly married man among them.[98]

We find something similar when we compare the parable of the talents with that of the pound.[99] Here we have two snapshots of ordinary life, with the same definition of a hard man—someone who reaps where he has not sown. Even more closely related are those of the waiting servants.[100] This is sufficient proof that Luke did not invent Jesus' gift of observation; on the contrary, he keeps close to his source, and this source is closely related to that of Matthew. Why then should it not be the same? The person who told of the ten bridesmaids, which only occurs in Matthew,[101] may very well be the source of the parable of the servants that we find only in Luke.[102]

These parables are so topical and true to life! The technique of deceit is described: "What is your debt?" "A hundred measures of oil." "Take your bill, sit down quickly and write fifty." This is the trick of a steward whose reasoning is repeated and applied time and again: "I am not strong enough to dig, and I am ashamed to beg."[103]

Until the contrary is proved I shall continue to maintain that a clever theorist, having no contact with real life, could not possibly have told these stories. No, Jesus stood upon this earth, with his two feet as much as with his whole divinity. When we say, joyfully and admiringly, that he was a complete human being, we are only translating into prosaic terms what John had already said in jubilant verse:

And the Word became flesh,
And dwelt amongst us . . . and
. . . we have beheld his glory . . ." [104]

[95] Mt. 21, 28-30.
[96] Mt. 21, 37-38.
[97] Mt. 22, 5.
[98] Lk. 14, 18-20. The allusion to the newly married man renders Luke anathema to E. Stauffer, *op. cit.,* pp. 79-80.

[99] Mt. 25, 14-30; Lk. 19, 12-27.
[100] Mt. 24, 42-51; Lk. 12, 35-48.
[101] Mt. 25, 1-13.
[102] Lk. 17, 7-10.
[103] Lk. 16, 1-9.
[104] Jn. 1, 14.

II
Jesus'
Goodness

"And he went about all Galilee, teaching in their synagogues and preaching the Gospel of the kingdom, and healing every disease and every infirmity among the people. So his fame spread throughout all Syria, and they brought him all the sick, those afflicted with various diseases and pains, demoniacs, epileptics and paralytics, and he healed them. And great crowds followed him from Galilee and the Decapolis, and Jerusalem and Judea, and from beyond the Jordan." [1] This paragraph taken from Matthew is, in my opinion, a theological thesis of the highest order.[2]

Before outlining Jesus' program (in the Sermon on the Mount) the most sober of the evangelists introduces Jesus as a man of surpassing goodness. Anyone who wishes to learn to know Jesus must make the effort to gain some idea of the extent of his loving activity and of its quality.

What is the measure of a person's goodness? Is this not a question more of intuition? Of course, yet, the mistakes that can be made in the name of intuition counsel us to establish a few objective norms. This may be done in various ways, yet most people will agree that the following elements are of the utmost importance:

1. The attitude adopted toward various sorts of people, notably toward the poor (the mentally impoverished as well as the materially poor), friends, the ordinary man, strangers or the unknown.

2. The quality of this love: forgetting oneself in order to think of others, a willingness to make sacrifices for others. Associated with this is the degree of hope one succeeds in inspiring. Finally, the intensity of the mental contact characterized especially by the pres-

[1] Mt. 4, 23-25; cf. Lk. 6, 17-19; also Mk. 1, 39; 3, 7-8.
[2] One will hardly find any Catholic dogmatic handbook that includes such a thesis. This study is left to spiritual writers and apologists, yet the dogmatists continue to claim to reveal Christ!

ence of a joy that must be at once intensely personal and entirely imbued with God.[3] Let us now see if Jesus fulfills these extensive and qualitative conditions of goodness.

ATTITUDE TOWARD THE (MATERIALLY AND SPIRITUALLY) POOR

Jesus did not pass through life without witnessing much misery. Those unacquainted with the harsh conditions of the world may find some of the Gospel passages unlikely or at least exaggerated. In the developing countries, however, no one will have any difficulty in believing in the presence of large crowds of sick, hungry, blind, or crippled people around someone who is reputed to be a miracle worker. Even in the developed countries, there is no lack of moral and spiritual problems arising from indifference, complacency, or skepticism.

In the general framework of Jesus' activity as described by the evangelists, it is stressed that Jesus performed many cures. More than half of the miracles recounted are cures, twenty-three in all, of which five involved driving out the devil. It may thus be definitely established that Jesus was in daily and close contact with sickness.

The gospels repeatedly state that a cure took place on a sabbath.[4] This circumstance is important, for it explains the opposition of the men of strict observance and at the same time proves the absolute credibility of the miracles, for the Jewish sources also mention Jesus' violation of the sabbath.[5] On the other hand it is unlikely that Jesus confined his care for the sick to the synagogal assemblies on the sabbath. We must thus assume *a priori* that the sabbath cures were merely an incidental and, as it were, accidental aspect of a much wider activity.

In actual fact, what concrete details we do possess transport us to all kinds of terrains. It is fairly common for a cure to be performed as a result of a meeting on the road.[6] Other cases, like that of Peter's mother-in-law [7] and the paralytic are localized in a house, perhaps the same house.[8] Sometimes considerable excitement prevailed among the suffering population of a place when Jesus passed the night there or made a longer stay.[9]

We must not view the reports of the miracles as eyewitness accounts such as we read every day in the papers. These stories were polished by tradition and edited. Yet we have no reason to doubt two characteristics that stand out in Jesus' behavior; his great sobriety—he wishes no one to know,[10] or leaves quickly,[11]—and his loving contact with the sick person.

Regarding this latter, the solicitous question to the blind man; "Do you see anything?" may perhaps be attributed to Mark's lively pen.[12] More difficult to type as a cliché is the dialogue with the old man who explained that he had nobody to put him in the pool.[13] In any case, Matthew sees in the manner in which Jesus performs his cures the fulfillment of a prophecy in which God's servant is presented as someone who neither wrangles nor cries aloud, who does not break a bruised reed nor quench a smouldering wick,[14] in other words as someone who loves the weak.

Even more terrible than sickness is *death*. The gospels preserve for us three stories, three moving cases, in which Jesus' golden heart is revealed soberly and affectionately. The raising up of the boy of Naim, the only son of a widow and thus indispensable, occurs only in Luke.[15] Some Old Testament influence, notably that of Elijah's gesture when he restores a child to life and "gives it back to its mother" [16] can be detected in the description. Such reminiscences occur most frequently in Luke and are in any case insufficient argument for rejecting the fact altogether.

Another case is that of the twelve-year-old girl, the daughter of Jairus, which occurs in all three synoptics.[17] Here the reference seems to be most precisely to Palestine: The father is ruler of a synagogue [18] and is called Jairus; [19] Jesus speaks in Aramaic: "*Talitha cumi!*" (Little girl, arise!) [20] All this sounds genuine, and indicates Jesus' intense compassion for human suffering.

Finally, there is Lazarus' raising from the dead.[21] On account of its undeniable symbolic meaning one might be tempted to deny its

[3] Cf. the laws of love which we have already quoted, pp. 84ff.

[4] Mt. 12, 10; Mk. 3, 2; Lk. 6, 7; 13, 10-14; 14, 3; Jn. 5, 9; 7, 23; 9, 14.

[5] *Sab.* 104b; *Tos. Sab.* 11, 15; cf. Th. Klausner, *Jesus von Nazareth* (Jerusalem, 1952²), pp. 55ff.

[6] Mt. 8, 1; 9, 20. 27; 15, 21; 20, 29.

[7] Mt. 8, 14-15 par.

[8] Mt. 9, 1-8 par.

[9] Mk. 6, 56.

[10] Mk. 1, 44; 5, 37-40. 43; 7, 33-36; 8, 23. This reticence is one of Mark's themes, but he did not invent it;

cf. Mt. 8, 4; 9, 30.

[11] Jn. 5, 13.

[12] Mk. 8, 23.

[13] Jn. 5, 6-7.

[14] Mt. 12, 19-20.

[15] Lk. 7, 11-17.

[16] v. 15 = 3 Kgs. 17, 22, LXX.

[17] Mk. 5, 21-43; Mt. 9, 18-26; Lk. 8, 40.56.

[18] Mk. 5, 36.

[19] Mk. 5, 12.

[20] Mk. 5, 41.

[21] Jn. 1, 1-44.

historicity. This, however, does not correspond to the mentality of the evangelists who indeed believed in the miracle: Jesus cures at a distance [22] and without a single word, with no possible symbolic significance. And even if the entire chapter is read as a call to believe in Jesus as *the* life, one must still assume that John's rendering of the atmosphere at the house in Bethany is true to life, just as in Luke 10, 38-42, so that one thing in any case remains unaffected: Jesus' intense love for his friends.

Did Jesus love the *poor?* The gospels do not mention that he organized systematic collections for their benefit. He himself had no fortune with which to help them. There was a fund, however, and everyone knew that money was regularly given from it to the poor.[23] Future missionaries were invited to transfer everything they possessed to the poor.[24]

We have already seen that Jesus' teaching on the kingdom of God had an important social dimension, and that his disciples immediately began to give shape to it.[25] Even more important, however, is the clear attitude of deep sympathy, almost of equality, that links Jesus to the poor. He, who was born poor will, in his first beatitude, joyfully congratulate the poor on their place in the kingdom.[26] He is not afraid of uncompromising parables like that of Lazarus and the rich fool who was more interested in his grain sheds than in his neighbors.[27] This is so true and so pointed that the poor when they heard it must have said: "This is our friend." And their friend would become poor as the lowest among them, shuttled from pillar to post, without a lawyer or an influential friend, and set out for death naked, between a handful of rough soldiers.

Later, we shall, discuss Jesus' attitude toward the most pernicious form of poverty: *sin.* This constituted the whole meaning of his life.[28] We wish only to emphasize here that it was an *outwardly visible* attitude that made a great impression upon the disciples and also provoked scandal. For not only did he regret, at the sight of the countless masses, ignorant and spiritually deprived, that they had no shepherds, in other words, selfless leaders,[29] he also positively promoted contacts with those who were publicly considered as "scum" and who regarded themselves as hopeless cases.[30] His behavior was judged too free and condemned as scandalous by indignant "betters." [31] Jesus answers that a doctor's place is with the sick [32] and also gives a declaration of principle: "I have come not to call the just, but the sinners." [33]

Admittedly Jesus seems not to have devoted himself to the "progressive" cities, with their paganized mentality under a varnish of hellenistic culture. He may perhaps have systematically avoided cities like Tiberias, with its lake, its hot water springs, its forum and stadium and its marvellous climate, and also Sebaste, Caesarea and the other coastal towns.

This cannot have been from any sentiment of condemnation or indifference, but the ambassador of God could not simply deny or revoke the eighteen centuries of preparation which we call the Old Testament without jeopardizing another principle, that of mediation. In order to save and to gather together all sinners the grain had to die, but not without having trained some of the sons of Abraham to carry out his task in the rest of Israel. And the fact that these, too, were sinful men, who failed him or were even disloyal, shows once again the boundless goodness of him whose entire life was summed up by either Peter or Luke in this brief but pregnant phrase: "He went about doing good." [34]

FULL OF ATTENTION FOR HIS FRIENDS

It is perhaps, more difficult to be "good" in one's own home, surrounded by friends and acquaintances, than to devote one's life to helping the needy. In applying this criterion to Jesus we have reached the limit of the possibilities offered by the sources. Only one evangelist has given us a picture of Jesus as an unforgettable friend, but he was writing sixty years later and was, moreover, inclined to write symbolically.

The question is whether we can freely and simply believe in all the traits of this friendship. The exegete must be on his guard here against too biographical an approach to the character of the Savior. On the other hand, the fact that in practically no case can a theological motive be detected in John's account of Jesus' friendship, lends credence to his story. Nor is John writing a thesis. On the contrary,

[22] Mk. 7, 24-30 par; Lk. 7, 1-10; Jn. 4, 46-54 (may be Luke's, too).
[23] Mt. 26, 9; Jn. 12, 5; 13, 29.
[24] Mt. 19, 21; Lk. 12, 33.
[25] Cf. pp. 36ff.
[26] Mt. 5, 3, and even stronger Lk. 6, 20.
[27] Lk. 16, 19-31; 12, 15-21.
[28] Cf. pp. 274ff.
[29] Mk. 6, 34.
[30] Lk. 7, 36-50; 10, 1-10; Jn. 8, 3-10.
[31] Lk. 5, 29-31; 7, 39; 15, 1-2.
[32] Mt. 9, 12 par.
[33] Mt. 19, 13.
[34] Acts 10, 38.

he is mainly concerned with small, almost useless details which, taken together, have a strong evocative force, admitting us, as it were, into the atmosphere which must have prevailed in the group of the twelve who were privileged to work with Jesus.

The image that we obtain of Jesus is then roughly as follows: he is a person who displays an extraordinary benevolence, even tenderness, toward his friends, in this case particularly, the twelve. He radiated a kind of charm, from the very first meeting: "Jesus turned . . . [they asked]: . . . where are you staying . . . they stayed with him that day . . . it was about the tenth hour." [35] The uncomplicated Philip can only answer everyone with "Come and see!" [36] It was good to live with the master, pleasant even, not without humor and a spice of teasing as with Nathaniel, who is dumbfounded [37] and Philip, who is chafed and chided [38] in a friendly way for his understandable, yet rather stupid, remark, "Lord, show us your father and we shall be satisfied." Jesus' answer, with the name and the interrogation at the end of the Greek sentence, might be rendered as, "Come, come, Philip!" [39]

The apostles loved him. When he is determined to go to the unsafe city of Jerusalem, the clairvoyant skeptic Thomas decides: "Let us also go that we may die with him." [40] He will later be proved right, at least so far as Jesus is concerned, but in the meantime, Jesus will leave them ineradicable memories of friendship. He will leave them his parting words, on one memorable occasion addressing them tenderly as "little children," [41] his heroic anxiety that they should go free, even if it means that he must go to meet his fate alone in the night, surrounded by none too scrupulous guards; [42] his disarming gesture and mild words to Thomas, who is by now completely confused; [43] especially his great delicacy toward Peter which Luke also mentions, [44] when he gives him the opportunity of effacing his triple denial by a threefold declaration of love. [45] It will be granted to Peter to be the perfect friend and follower of Jesus by dying in the same manner. [46]

His "beloved disciple," and Lazarus and his sisters, would demand a special approach. Although once again it is important to avoid sentimental outpourings, the result will indicate a considerable degree of intimacy. During the last supper, John lay "close to the breast of Jesus." [47] The modern exegete points out that this expression, derived from the manner of reclining at table, [48] means that John lay on Jesus' right-hand side. This is correct, but the expression also implies that this right hand side was a privileged place, the place of friendship, as with Lazarus "in Abraham's bosom" [49] and in John even for the Word, which was in the bosom of the Father.[50] When, moreover, a few lines further on, it is said that John "leaned back upon the bosom of Jesus" in order to ask him quietly who the traitor was,[51] there is no earthly chance of considering this merely a material detail. One would have to be very ill-acquainted with John to think that he would write here, without any particular motive: this one sat at the right and that one at the left. The entire case of the beloved disciple is rather an illustration of the general fact that the disciples are in Jesus' hands; he keeps them carefully and allows none of them to be lost,[52] calling them in all sincerity "no longer servants but friends," for they know all his secrets and are close to him.[53]

We must resign ourselves never to know the daily details of that friendship. The little attentions, the friendly greetings, the jokes and other inventive notions, the long conversations, the evenings spent together, the thousand little happenings during their communal journeys—all this is matter for speculation, not for history.

To my mind, however, the fact of Jesus' friendship can never be doubted. It is confirmed by the extraordinary devotion, literally unto death, which the disciples later displayed. The main support for this argument is Paul, who knew Jesus only after death, yet whose attitude toward the risen Christ must be termed a diffident yet deeply felt friendship: he tells him his complaints, his objections, his feelings, as he never does to God the Father.[54] One has only to read the Epistle to the Philippians to see what friendship is. It is likely that Paul would never have dared display such affection had he not heard, understood or felt that the apostles were on an intimate footing with the Lord.

In any case, and this holds good for Peter and John as well as for Paul, their undeniable friendship would be inconceivable without

35 Jn. 1, 38-39.
36 Jn. 1, 46; 12, 22.
37 Jn. 1, 47-50.
38 Jn. 6, 5-7.
39 Jn. 14, 8-9.
40 Jn. 11, 16.
41 Jn. 13, 33.
42 Jn. 18, 8.
43 Jn. 20, 24-29.
44 Lk. 22, 61.

45 Jn. 13, 23; 19, 26; 20, 2; 21, 7.20.
46 Jn. 21, 18-19.
47 Jn. 13, 23.
48 See Vol. 1.
49 Lk. 16, 22.
50 Jn. 1, 18.
51 Jn. 13, 25.
52 Jn. 17, 12.
53 Jn. 15, 14-15.
54 2 Cor. 12, 8; Phil. 4, 13.

assuming at least some degree of friendship in Jesus himself. Friendship is impossible if it is not to some extent mutual. For my part, I
assume that Jesus was not surpassed either in this matter of love.

TOWARD THE ORDINARY MAN

Influential persons who have had some success are scarcely ever
able to address the "ordinary man" without hauteur, so that each
party feels completely at ease.

It seems to me as clear as day that Jesus must have been very close
to the man in the street. The best proof perhaps, is his manner of
speech. "The style is the man," says Buffon, and we have only to
think of the parables and the countless allusions to ordinary everyday life—we have already given a few examples [55]—to realize that
all those who lived in the little country houses, in the narrow streets
of the towns or in the swarming city of Jerusalem, must immediately have felt close to him. For, apart altogether from the content
of his speech, a person's sympathies are revealed in his choice of
words, his manner of speaking, his tone of voice. The Jesus of the
gospels was never accused of grandiloquence, or of a style comprehensible only to the learned or élite.

For thirty years he had lived with very simple people in a little
village of perhaps a hundred souls: Nazareth. Most Jews did not
even know it existed, for it is not mentioned once in their great
geographical handbook, the Bible. In neighboring Cana, which was
no London or Paris, jokes were made about this hamlet.[56] Later, the
majority of his disciples, whom he chose himself, would be very
simple people: a number of fishermen, an official from the hated and
none-too-honest tax office. In his behavior, even in the days of his
success, we never notice any inclination toward the high life. On
the contrary, it is the average man, the less well-educated, who
believes and trusts in him most ardently, and Jesus is delighted. He
thanks God because it has pleased him to reveal his mystery "to
babes." [57]

Jesus knows that he is intimately bound with these ordinary
mortals. He will not forget anyone who helps the "babes"—and
these are not children, but the ordinary, simple people—even if it is
only to give them a glass of water.[58] In a more general fashion he
says that anything done for one of them, the hungry, the poorly
clothed, is done for himself.[59] He calls them "my brothers" [60] and

wherever they are gathered together in small groups, as true Christians, he, the risen Christ, will be in the midst of them.[61] They are so inexpressibly dear to him, that anyone who causes one of them to sin, will meet with a dreadful fate.[62]

There is even a formal declaration which is extremely thought provoking. Jesus addresses a special invitation to all those "who labor and are heavy laden." [63] This certainly refers to the ordinary man, not so much because he always has his problems and difficulties but because his lack of culture and training makes it impossible for him to learn complicated things, to disentangle the endless number of commandments and prohibitions, to know exactly what is lawful on the sabbath and what is not. Jesus' yoke will not be like that of the scribes, hard and unbearable.[64] On the contrary, it will be light, and easy for *all* men to bear. This carpenter does not lose himself in subtleties. Jesus may have left the village of his youth, but there was never any gulf between him and the people among whom he grew up.

Toward Strangers and Foreigners

There are two sorts of people toward whom we feel little attraction in the natural way: those whom we do not know, and those whom we know only as strangers, outsiders. Toward the first category, the spontaneous reaction, especially of the rich and introverted, is a feeling of unease, disturbance, even mistrust. Regarding the second category, there are few indeed who succeed in ridding themselves of all prejudice of race, people, town and class.

It is amazing how rapidly and deeply Jesus succeeds in making contact with strangers. We have already alluded to a number of sick people, and persons he met on the road. Not only did he show sympathy, he immediately entered into their world, often, too, raising them up to his. In any case a very natural yet intimate contact was brought about.

The most picturesque example is Zaccheus, head of the central office of taxation in Jericho.[65] Almost as clear is the sketch of the

55 Cf. pp. 123ff.
56 Jn. 1, 45-46.
57 Mt. 11, 25.
58 Mt. 10, 42; 18, 5.
59 Mt. 25, 40.45.
60 Mt. 25, 40; 28, 10.
61 Mt. 18, 20.
62 Mt. 18, 6.10-14.
63 Mt. 11, 28-30.
64 Mt. 23, 4.
65 Lk. 19, 1-10.

woman who had been bent over for eighteen years and could not straighten her head to look at people. But Jesus saw her, called her, laid his hands upon her and . . . she praised God.[66] A third case, again found only in Luke, mentions a charming woman who had misused her powers of attraction and who now intrudes upon a men-only supper, and the words Jesus finds to break the oppressive silence of the company and to compel the none-too-pure gaze of many of the guests in another direction.[67]

Luke also tells of the meeting with the mourning women [68] on the road to Calvary, and the sublime last glance of unique understanding exchanged with the thief on the other cross.[69] All such meetings indicate a great benevolence, a generous heart which enables Jesus from the very first moment to embrace the other's entire being. But is this not too modern an interpretation? Is this not more of Luke's romanticism, beautiful perhaps, but unreliable? Such an assumption may not be rejected out of hand, but first we must judge the other writers by the same standards. The three synoptics speak of a woman who had suffered for twelve years from an embarrassing and humiliating complaint. As unobtrusively as possible, she touched the hem of his garment and Jesus entered not only into the cure of her body, but into her entire spiritual life.[70] Luke here is in no way more romantic than Mark, who mentions Jesus' searching glance.[71] John, too, has testified to the ease with which Jesus could establish contact with strangers. Besides the former disciples of John the Baptist, upon whom Jesus makes a decisive impression at the first meeting,[72] and the almost comic confusion of Nathaniel,[73] we have the classic example: Nicodemus, the nocturnal visitor, who even afterwards remains a stranger, although to a lesser extent.[74]

It would be to distort the nature of our material were we to consider all these details as small segments of a documentary film which unfortunately is no longer complete. None of the evangelists directly intended to answer the following questions: What was Jesus' manner toward strangers? How did he open the door or what was his greeting? But if the incidental details all point in the same direction, there is a good chance that they give a reliable picture of the truth.

Regarding the true strangers, the foreigners, the first impression is that Jesus appears to be in default. He forbids his disciples to go "the way of the heathen," speaks coldly to an anxious mother from a neighboring country, and evidently refuses to speak to the Greeks who were passing on to Jerusalem and asked for him.[75] The man from the Decapolis, recently freed of a high degree of possession, who desired to become a disciple and to accompany Jesus met with a formal refusal.[76]

Yet this nationalistic attitude was only apparent; in reality Jesus' gaze was universal, although his own task had to be accomplished within the boundaries of the divine plan.[77] Jesus indeed desires the brotherhood of *all* and in the incidents quoted, he rejoices in the faith of the pagans, saying that it surpasses that of the Jews.[78] To the man he had rid of his devils he suggests—contrary to the normal recommendation to silence, or rather in agreement with this rule, since we are here concerned with another country—that he should go and spread the news in his own fatherland.[79]

To obtain a concrete view of the facts, we must consider the actual situation. Discrimination existed between Jews and Samaritans. Jesus seems to ignore the theoretical difference, but his practical attitude is clear enough. He tells a parable, which immortalizes a Samaritan as a model of neighborly love.[80] He does not neglect to stress the difference between the grateful attitude of a Samaritan leper, one of a group of ten, and the practical materialism of the rest. "Was there no one found to return and give praise to God except this foreigner?" [81] Finally, he soundly rebukes two still very short-tempered brothers, two of his best disciples, incidentally, for their feelings of revenge and cruelty toward the Samaritans.[82] Again, it must be admitted that all three incidents are taken from Luke, yet, I cannot imagine that Luke would have had the temerity to make Jesus initiate a policy of reconciliation with the Samaritans, if this were not based on tradition.

This does not mean that Jesus was not in heart and soul a Jew. But true patriotism is something quite different from prejudice and hostility toward others. Does not the greatness of a people lie much rather in the humble service it gives to others on the road to perfect

[66] Lk. 13, 11-14.
[67] Lk. 7, 36-50.
[68] Lk. 23, 27-31.
[69] Lk. 23, 39-43.
[70] Mt. 9, 20; Mk. 5, 25-34.; Lk. 8, 43-48.
[71] Mk. 5, 32.
[72] Jn. 1, 37-39.
[73] Jn. 1, 45-51.
[74] Jn. 3, 1-10; cf. 7, 50-52; 19, 39.

[75] Mk. 10, 5-6; Mt. 15, 23-26; Jn. 12, 20.
[76] Mk. 5, 1-20.
[77] Cf. pp. 52ff.
[78] Mt. 8, 5-13.
[79] Mk. 5, 19.
[80] Lk. 10, 30-37.
[81] Lk. 17, 18.
[82] Lk. 9, 51-56.

equality? For this cause Jesus was prepared to give his life, like a grain of wheat which brings forth much fruit. This was his answer to the famous Greeks.[83]

Once risen, he will command his disciples to go and teach all foreign nations,[84] but he himself cannot wait so long. From now on, he identifies himself in a particular way with strangers.[85] In the displaced persons, the people without home or country, the passing stranger, the student or mineworker, yellow or black, we meet, not curiosities, but him.

HIS ATTENTION FOR OTHERS

We have assumed that there are three degrees of love: attention, which makes possible an exchange of ideas and feelings; the strength to make sacrifice, born of hope and imbuing others with courage; the joy that unites the lover with the beloved in one transport of delight.[86] If this thesis is correct and meaningful, we must also apply it to Jesus' goodness—another word for love of one's fellows —which brings us to the qualitative aspect of our investigation.

The first qualitative element thus is the depth of attention. We measure a person's goodness by the intensity with which he is able to see and to meet others. Jesus' facility for making contact, often with chance passersby, shows us the depth of his self-forgetfulness and openness to others.

It would be superfluous to repeat the details here.[87] We must only stress how Jesus' gaze penetrated to the very deepest level, to the inner life with its desire for good, its indifference, consciousness of sin and thirst for God. Without for a moment losing sight of material needs, and sincerely concerned with family and health problems, Jesus still lived in too fierce a light not to see the fundamental drama of those whom he loved as brothers.

The paralytic, carried before Jesus by four valiant friends, hears him speak of a deeper wretchedness: his sins. Jesus holds no examination of conscience, but forgives.[88] John assures us that Jesus did *not* explain illness as a direct result of personal sins, or of parental wrongdoing.[89] Nonetheless, at his second meeting with the man he had cured at the public baths at Bethsaida, he exhorts him to sin no more in future.[90] In his contact with Zaccheus, with the self-assured yet completely helpless visitor who creates a furor at the supper in Simon's fine house, and with the pitiful young woman, recently caught in her misery and already all but condemned by the triumphant defenders of other people's chastity, Jesus could have contented himself with a few scraps of advice or musings on order in society. But he was never purely a moralist (just as he was never a pious supernaturalist). On the contrary, he steered the conversation toward a deeper point, the essential link with God which is damaged and in a certain sense destroyed by sin, and which only forgiveness itself can heal.[91]

Thus, the first thing that strikes us is the deep seriousness with which Jesus regards people, people with their sin which is viewed not so much as a "transgression" but as an attitude, a void. Yet his profound insight into the human soul was also positive. He saw what others had never seen, at least not so clearly.

Current rabbinic theology, for example, considered poverty as a punishment. There were not many who sought true love of God among the poor and simple, the humiliated. Never before him, in any case, had anyone said so roundly what even his disciples sometimes hesitated to repeat: "Blessed are you poor, for *yours* is the kingdom of God." [92] This is naturally not the cry of the demagogue, whose sympathy has detected unsuspected virtues in the lowest classes of society and proclaims this fact to them. For the poor too, the kingdom is a gift that only God can grant. But God is already in the act of granting it, and it is truly these ragged, worried people, who are really poor in the ordinary sense of the word, who already belong to the kingdom, are already rich in their simplicity, and become the model for all others who wish to enter.

Jesus must have seemed joyful rather than compassionate when he addressed them thus. It does not say so in the text, but this is so self-evident that we really do not need Luke's confirmation with refer-

---

83 Jn. 12, 20-24.
84 Mt. 28, 19; Mk. 16, 15.
85 Mt. 25, 35-43.
86 Cf. pp. 86ff. In explanation, it may be added here that these three degrees are only perfect if the beloved object is perfect; love of God is thus the absolute form of all love, and the three stages can then be called faith (the acceptance of God who makes himself known), hope (with its power of sacrifice), and love (to place all one's joy in

God). In the strict sense of the words, neither faith nor hope can be attributed to Jesus, although he possessed in the highest degree the positive content of these two virtues.
87 Cf. pp. 135ff.
88 Mk. 2, 5.
89 Jn. 9, 2-3.
90 Jn. 5, 14.
91 Lk. 19, 8-7; 7, 47-48; Jn. 8, 7.11.
92 Lk. 6, 20.

ence to the mission which some of these little ones have completed (relatively) successfully. Jesus rejoices, exults in the insight into God's secret that these little ones appear to possess and what is noteworthy, goes deeper than their work and gifts: "Do not rejoice in this, that the spirits are subject to you; but rejoice that your names are written in heaven." [93] In other words, more important than the most sensational apostolate is the fact that God loves you personally. If only we viewed people in this light!

EXEMPLARY AND INSPIRING COURAGE IN SACRIFICE

Loving begins with a sensitive and attentive gaze. Willingness to sacrifice goes a step further. We have already alluded to Jesus' great devotion to his task, entirely in the service of others.[94] In a separate chapter we shall have to examine the development of an idea that becomes increasingly prominent in Jesus' human psychology: that he must give his life for the salvation of *all*.[95] He will view this death with growing clarity and completely accept it, thus attaining the utmost limit of sacrifice, the gift of his life. No one can give a stronger proof of love.[96]

The very manner of this death, clearly interpreted some days beforehand as a sacrifice,[97] displayed that characteristic heroism which can only be summoned by true love. Throughout his inhuman torments he remained so still and so humble, without imprecations or bitterness, that one can only understand his fortitude as the strength of someone who at that very moment was aware that he was giving *everything for others*. "Because he did not notice that it was they who were putting him to death, but rather that he was in the act of dying for them" (Augustine).

The person who loves and makes sacrifices for the loved one always releases new powers. Sacrifice born of love is always fruitful. Thus Jesus' goodness was a fresh source of courage to face life. His detachment was not that of a young hero, who gathers together all his strength in an ultimate attempt to surpass himself and gain the crown. Jesus' sacrifice contained no element of self-glorification, nor of sickly masochism. It was born of love, because he was bound with others, in order to open new ways for others, in order to touch unknown strings deep in the hearts of others, so that they might emit the clear call to a new life of love.

Repeatedly, he tells his disciples that they must not be afraid,[98] that they must not remain men "of such little faith," [99] and indeed his proximity always filled them with courage and enthusiasm. It was not permanent, however. They had not yet received his Spirit. Peter thinks he knows by experience that together with Jesus, he can brave all things, even death.[100] In any event, the former fishermen had become totally different people in a short time. Jesus had broadened their perspectives: "I shall make you fishers of men." [101] And they will indeed be capable of great things, just like the discouraged little people who thought themselves completely marked and bound by sin and evil customs. These leave Jesus with an infinite perspective and in their memory the fullness of his wish: "Go in peace." [102]

Certainly he was not always successful. One person with many possessions and a noble disposition could not bring himself to abandon his wealth and follow him. This incident shows us the source of Jesus' confidence in spite of all. For when the young farmer had sadly departed, "Jesus looked around and said to his disciples: 'How hard it will be for those who have riches to enter the kingdom of God.'" And when the disciples, at first "amazed" and later, when they have heard of the camel and the needle, "astonished," asked for an explanation, "Jesus looked at them and said, 'With men it is impossible, but not with God; for all things are possible with God.'" [103] Ultimately thus, Jesus never loses confidence, for he sees God's work in everything. God cannot fail.

God does not fail even in the face of death. The clearest call to confidence is given precisely to those who will suffer persecution, and those who can scarcely read or write will be required to answer to the highest and most learned institutions in the land. They will be more worried about finding the right words to defend their Lord than about the consequences for themselves. And again, everything is possible with God and he will teach them what to say.[104]

It is an historical fact that Christianity washed into world history

---

[93] Lk. 10, 17-24.
[94] Cf. pp. 93ff.
[95] Cf. pp. 274ff.
[96] Jn. 15, 12.
[97] Mt. 26, 28.
[98] Mt. 10, 26.28.31; 14, 27; 17, 7; 28, 10; Mk. 5, 36; Lk. 5, 10.
[99] Mt. 6, 30; 8, 26; 14, 31; 16, 8; Lk. 12, 28.
[100] Mk. 14, 31; this emerges most strongly in Luke, where Peter declares his willingness to suffer imprisonment and death with Jesus (Lk. 22, 33).
[101] Mt. 4, 19.
[102] Mk. 5, 34; Lk. 7, 50; cf. Jn. 8, 11.
[103] Mk. 10, 17-27.
[104] Mt. 10, 19-20.

as an immense wave of courage, hope and new energy. This sum of strength, patience and the spirit of sacrifice cannot be explained without the risen Lord and his grace. Still less can it be entirely detached from the human personality of Jesus himself who in his earthly life began by raising others up to a new life. When we see around us people with whom we cannot speak without being, as it were, uplifted, or being so strengthened that we receive a fresh charge of courage and optimism, then we may say that these people have something of Christ. And it will often appear, especially when they themselves are in difficulties, that they *deliberately* strive for this resemblance.

JOY ON MAN'S ACCOUNT

Can one truly hold that Jesus was joyful on man's account or that he placed his joy in people? The question is of capital importance, for the greatest gift that anyone can give (or receive) is his own joy. Sorrowful love, no matter how willing to sacrifice, can never be called perfect. Acts of love "against the grain" are an inner contradiction. One begins by seeing and ends by identifying the other person with what one desires. Was Jesus literally glad to see people?

The first hesitation before answering in the affirmative, may be of a theological nature. Is it possible that someone who is God takes pleasure in creatures? A second cause for doubt could be the lack of texts. Have we any facts that prove irrefutably that Jesus found his joy in people?

One would indeed be justified in supposing that people were nothing but a source of suffering to Jesus, nothing but opposition, incomprehension and sin. On at least one occasion, Mark expressly states that Jesus was "grieved at their hardness of heart." [105] Another time he even mentions a cry of impatience: "How long am I to bear with you?" [106] On the other hand Jesus regarded his mission as the bringing of a *joyful* message. In order to carry out such a task the messenger himself must be joyful. How can one say: "Go in peace! Peace be with you!" without oneself sharing this peace with others? How can one begin a sermon with "Blessed are you! Rejoice, you poor!" without oneself rejoicing for these poor?

The entire Gospel breathes an atmosphere of joy, Jesus' joy for the people to whom it had pleased the Father to grant the kingdom and to reveal his mysteries. The cry of joy arises, not as an exceptional attack of enthusiasm in a usually more introverted nature, but as a singing bird in a landscape where everything tells of spring. Jesus does not grumble or grow bitter because men thwart his plans or because his disciples do not immediately understand. Even when he is obliged to withdraw, he does not lose his peace, but devotes himself quietly to training his followers and they are happy together.[107]

To some this basis may appear narrow, but one must take into account the thesis of St. John. This theologian among the evangelists has condensed the entire revelation of Jesus' love in the Last Supper. There Jesus will give his commandment of love and put it into practice himself: "'He loved them to the end,'" [108] and, just as it was the evening of the sacrifice: "For their sake I consecrate myself," [109] so also was it the evening on which Jesus' joy was revealed. He speaks of what fills his heart and asks that they abide in his love as he abides in the love of the Father, "that my joy may be in you, and that your joy may be full." [110] Today, they are still sorrowful, but he will see them again, and no one will be able to deprive them of their joy.[111] This is the last thing he wishes to do in this life, he explains in his prayer to the Father: "But now I am coming to thee, and these things I speak in the world, that they may have my joy fulfilled in themselves." [112] The aim of his life was to share but one joy with them, that of the Father. No one is so glad to see us as he.

Since John confirms it, theology can no longer deny it. It must be possible for a God to find his happiness in people. John points the way to the solution by saying that Jesus loves with the love (and the happiness) of the Father himself. God is the origin and also the end of his love. And yet people are not merely glasses through which Jesus' love can pass, simple "opportunities" of loving the Father. God's love indeed rests in the people themselves. He is the real cause of their existence; in their personalities, they are the object of his creative will and pleasure.

[105] Mk. 3, 5.
[106] Mk. 9, 19.
[107] Mt. 15, 21; 16, 13: with the contexts!
[108] Jn. 13, 1.
[109] Jn. 17, 18.
[110] Jn. 15, 11; cf 14, 17.27; 6, 32-33.
[111] Jn. 16, 22.
[112] Jn. 17, 13.

Jesus loves us. But he does not falter in his love, not even in the smallest detail that is not purely from God. His love knows no self-seeking, no self-interest (for self-love is a contradiction in terms) and thus no single shadow exists in his joy. In this way, Jesus reveals his love for the Father in his love for us, in a manner which is completely human and at the same time completely divine. Not only may we say that we ourselves are pleasing in Jesus' sight; we must say that an ocean of happiness rests upon us, as we are and as we ought to be. For nothing renews us quicker, or speeds us with more magnetic force toward love, than the consciousness that Jesus brought, more by his life than by his parable, the joy of the Father in the prodigal son.[113]

According to tradition, John is the apostle who best understood Jesus. If this is true, there dwelt in our world so full of darkness a boundless goodness which was not only perpetually concerned for man and prepared to sacrifice everything for his sake, but was also able to communicate to us the essence of his own being—his joy. Not in order to enrich us from without, but to make us one with himself and the Father in a common joy.

There are many who find the way of religion stern and monotonous. Everywhere one hears or senses the complaint: If only somebody understood me . . . If only I could meet a truly good person. But have we already tried to expose ourselves to the warmth of that light?[114]

---

[113] Cf. Lk. 15, 22; cf. the joy in the two preceding parables—that of the shepherd, that of the woman (and the angels): vv. 6.9-10.

[114] Cf. Jn. 1, 4-5.14.

III
Jesus
the Leader

In general, the word, "leader," is not found in the Dutch bible translations. The Concordance of Trommius gives only one text (Is. 9.15) compared with nine cases in the New Testament with "guide," "pioneer." [1] The word does not occur either in the *Bible Dictionary*. The question thus arises: Is not this title too modern, and inapplicable to Jesus if one wishes to remain faithful to objective data?

It goes without saying that in the trade unions, politics and youth movements of today, the term has acquired a meaning and all sorts of nuances that do not correspond to any term as employed in antiquity because the sociological situation is completely different. However, we should not, for this reason, reject it out-of-hand, for if we simply adopt the old term, "shepherd," which is closest in meaning to the quality we intend to discuss in this chapter, we shall still be confronted with a variety of short circuits and false derivations.

The word, "shepherd," especially in a religious context, lacks the overtones of struggle, courage and initiative it once possessed, and conjures up an image of sweetness, unknown in Jesus' time. Without then attaching too much importance to the rendering of "shepherd" by "leader," or "captain," we shall search for a series of realities that characterize an important aspect of Jesus' personality, namely, his attitude toward others as one holding authority and responsible for them. In other words, we shall attempt a short study of Jesus as leader.

Before examining the realities, let us first establish the fact itself: the first Christians regarded him as a great leader. Matthew views

[1] Mt. 2, 6; 15, 14; 23, 16.24; Acts 1, 16; Rom. 2, 10; 12, 2; Rev. 7, 17.

Jesus as the realization of the prophecy which promised Bethlehem a "ruler," who "will govern my people Israel." [2]

During the passion, when the disciples are dispersed, another prophecy is fulfilled: "I will strike the shepherd and the sheep of the flock will be scattered." [3] Here the little group of disciples is clearly thought of as a flock. Luke indeed, says it in so many words. They are the "little flock" [4] and Jesus is their "shepherd," which *we* must translate as chief, captain, leader.

The Johannine tradition is even more explicit: Jesus calls himself the "good shepherd" and analyzes the import of this term,[5] and after the resurrection, he hands over to Peter the task of "feeding his sheep," which clearly indicates leadership.[6]

Admittedly it is above all the glorified Lord who is in this way a "shepherd," for he was born of woman and pursued by the dragon, and must "rule all the nations with a rod of iron." [7] At the impressive battle of Armageddon, too, he appears as a horseman riding a white horse, with eyes like a flame of fire and diadems on his head. The armies of heaven, arrayed in fine linen, white and pure, follow him on white horses. On his robe is written, "King of kings and Lord of lords." He judges righteously and wages war against the armies that have gathered against him and his host. All this means "to rule the nations with a rod of iron." [8] In Matthew, too, Jesus appears as a shepherd at the last judgment when he will separate the sheep from the goats.[9]

Yet, according to the earliest traditions, the crucial point (and it could scarcely be more crucial) of Jesus' pastorship is the cross. The Epistle to the Hebrews calls him "the great shepherd of the sheep" with an allusion to the blood of the eternal covenant.[10] Peter is thinking of the passion and earthly life of Jesus when he glorifies him as the "shepherd and guardian of your souls," [11] or as we would say "your leader." In John, too, the good shepherd is the earthly Jesus who is prepared to give his life for his sheep [12] in direct contrast to the hirelings, who symbolize other leaders.[13]

All this authorizes us to examine Christ's role as leader. If many of the qualities we assume in a "leader" are already inherent in the term, "shepherd," as expressly applied to Jesus, we may well be able to discover other aspects which correspond to leadership in the modern sense of the term.[14]

First, however, we must agree on the qualities essential for leadership. Thus far, the following list seemed to withstand the test of criticism, so that we may consider it as representative and fairly complete:

1. A leader must possess a great ideal.
2. He must be the living embodiment of that ideal.
3. He must be able to bring it alive for others.
4. He must be worthy of their blind loyalty,
5. He must mold them to collaborate in and carry on his task.

JESUS POSSESSED A GREAT IDEAL

We have no need to repeat here what we have already said about Jesus' ideal, the kingdom of God.[15] Each must decide for himself whether such an ideal is "great" enough.

HE WAS THE LIVING EMBODIMENT OF IT

It is a basic principle of Christian leadership, that no one is above this law. Life and teaching must complement each other. Jesus, whose own life was summed up in these words, "He did and taught," [16] criticized the scribes, who with their complicated sophistry turned God's law into an insupportable yoke *which they themselves were unwilling to bear;* "practice and observe whatever they tell you, but not what they do." [17] Therefore, they are not true leaders, but blind guides.[18]

[2] Mt. 2, 6 = Mic. 5, 1; cf. 2 Sam. 5, 2 where "to be shepherd of Israel" parallels "to be leader of Israel."

[3] Mt. 26, 31; Mk. 14, 27 = Zech. 13, 7.

[4] Lk. 12, 32.

[5] Jn. 10, 11.

[6] Jn. 21, 15-17.

[7] Rev. 12, 5.

[8] Rev. 19, 11-17. cf. 16, 16 for the "place."

[9] Mt. 25, 32.

[10] Heb. 13, 20.

[11] 1 Pet. 2, 25; "your souls" = "yourself"; cf. also 1, 9; 4, 19.

[12] Jn. 10, 15; cf. 15, 13.

[13] Jn. 15, 12-13.

[14] Here, one can appreciate the dangers and the novelty of the method used deliberately in this book.

Whereas "classical" biblical theology analyzes the use of a *biblical* notion (e.g., shepherd) in its origin and ramifications, here, we also take into account, where this seems helpful, our present-day categories (e.g., leader). This may be justified by a simple proposition: What if I find it interesting to know whether Jesus was a leader or not? The danger consists in introducing modern notions into old texts, but this danger can be avoided if every text is understood in its context.

[15] Cf. pp. 36ff.

[16] Acts 1, 1.

[17] Mt. 23, 3-4.

[18] Mt. 15, 4; 23, 16.

In order to be able to show the way, one must have followed it oneself. And when Jesus calls himself "the Way," [19] this also means that he is the living embodiment of the Christian's journey through life, although naturally, the phrase here has a much wider connotation.

The apostles, too, will have to be leaders according to this same principle. They will owe their influence to their *works*.[20] They will never become great lords and dominate their followers, but will be living examples for the flock. This at least was the ideal of the first Christian leader after Jesus.[21] Here too we shall not repeat how Jesus himself put his principle into practice. The two focal points of the life prevailing in his kingdom, i.e., love of God and love of one's neighbor, could only be properly evaluated with reference to his example.[22] We have just dealt with the second aspect, his goodness toward man,[23] and we shall examine the other aspect, his religious life, in a subsequent chapter.[24]

JESUS BROUGHT HIS IDEAL ALIVE FOR OTHERS

"And at once his fame spread everywhere, throughout all the surrounding region of Galilee." [25] To what did Jesus owe this great and rapid success? It would be as wrong to seek to explain it by a multitude of miraculous inner illuminations granted to his hearers, as by the self-interest of those who sought only the healing of their body. The main factor was certainly the content of his preaching: could any message be more full of promise than the approach, indeed the immanence, of the kingdom of God? Yet even the best cause can be undermined by mediocre advocates.

Anyone who wishes to be a leader must be able to put his message across; he must possess some talent as a speaker. This Jesus certainly had. Although it is not always easy to decide, from a critical point of view, what exactly was the contribution of the evangelists in the preparation of the present Gospel text, we can state without hesitation that in the cases indicated below it was not the evangelists or tradition but Jesus himself who contributed most to the oratorical value of our texts.[26]

One of the first requirements of the leader as a speaker is that he should be able to move his audience; and while the gospels do not show that Jesus was brilliant, they do tell us that he was captivating, clear, sound and attractive. Various people found him interesting to listen to. Even now, in a completely different milieu, and after so great a lapse of time, we are amazed at the appropriate sayings, the agreeable presentation, and the forceful images which the evangelists selected and preserved. Among the most striking of these we mention:

1. Parables which sparkle with life. Let us modernize their titles: [27] "The Robbery," [28] "The Miser," [29] "The Miser and the Beggar," [30] "In the Court of the Temple," [31] "The Friend," [32] "A Father and his two Sons" (in two versions),[33] "Invitation to the Wedding,"[34] "The Wedding Procession," [35] "The Cunning Administrator," [36] "Two Colleagues," [37] "The King's Journey," [38] "Sowing," [39] "The Enemy's Tactics," [40] "The Marvelous Vital Force," [41] "Invitation to the Jobless." [42] Countless poets and writers have come under the influence of Jesus' literary genius, and to this very day, with a little trouble and imagination, the gospels can provide magnificent material for both sermons and meditations.

2. Pithy Sayings are numerous: "Let the day's own trouble be sufficient for the day"; [43] "All who take the sword will perish by the sword"; [44] "No one can serve two masters"; [45] "Let the dead bury their dead"; [46] "Render to Caesar the things that are Caesar's and to God the things that are God's"; [47] "I will make you fishers of

---

[19] Jn. 15, 6.

[20] Mt. 5, 14-16.

[21] 1 Pet. 5, 5.

[22] Cf. pp. 36ff.

[23] Cf. pp. 127ff.

[24] Cf. pp. 179ff.

[25] Mk. 1, 28. Our translation opts for the normal meaning of *epikures* (surroundings) and finds support in the parallel text of Mt. 4, 24; it is also possible to translate "over the entire region," i.e., Galilee (cf. *The Jerusalem Bible*, etc.).

[26] In many cases, we possess texts that closely approach Jesus' own words. Each text would have to be examined separately for traces of influence by tradition or the evangelist. This is beyond the scope of this book and, in any case, opinions are often divided. Cf. Vol. 2.

[27] The titles given here are not arbitrary; they reflect, after the modern literary fashion, the content of the parable. The "classical" titles are sometimes less neutral and not

always entirely accurate. For example, "the prodigal son" should rather be "the merciful father," otherwise, the important second half dealing with the elder son is omitted.

[28] Lk. 10, 30-37.

[29] Lk. 12, 13-21.

[30] Lk. 16, 19-31.

[31] Lk. 18, 9-14.

[32] Lk. 11, 5-11.

[33] Lk. 15, 11-32; Mt. 21, 28-32.

[34] Lk. 14, 15-24.

[35] Mt. 25, 1-13.

[36] Lk. 16, 1-13.

[37] Mt. 18, 23-25.

[38] Lk. 19, 12-27; cf. Mt. 25, 14-30.

[39] Mt. 13, 1-9.

[40] Mt. 13, 24-30.

[41] Mk. 4, 26-29.

[42] Mt. 20, 1-16.

[43] Mt. 6, 34.

[44] Mt. 26, 52.

[45] Mt. 6, 24.

[46] Mt. 8, 22.

[47] Mt. 22, 21.

men"; [48] "You received without pay, give without pay"; [49] "Where your treasure is, there will your heart be also." [50]

3. There are many *lovely comparisons:* the lamp in the dark house,[51] the eye as lamp of the body,[52] the city on the hill,[53] birds which (naturally) do not sow,[54] the loveliness of the flowers of the field which need no beauty treatment or sewing lessons,[55] sheep in the midst of a flock of wolves,[56] the tree and its fruits,[57] the treasure in the field and the pearl offered for sale,[58] the sheep that is lost out of a flock of a hundred,[59] the birds in God's hands,[60] drinking the chalice and being baptized with a (blood red) baptism,[61] the temple of the body,[62] casting fire upon earth,[63] the signs of the times,[64] the children on the market place, etc.[65]

4. A considerable number of *hyperboles and paradoxes* lend spice to Jesus' speech: Cutting off a hand and plucking out an eye if they cause one to commit sin,[66] the millstone round the neck,[67] adding a cubit to one's span of life,[68] offering the left cheek after a blow on the right,[69] your left hand may not know what your right hand does,[70] I have not come to call the righteous, but sinners,[71] he who finds his life shall lose it and he who loses it shall find it,[72] God has numbered the hairs of your head,[73] the camel which tries to get through the eye of a needle, etc.[74]

5. There is no lack either of the *rhythm* and *parallelism* of which the Jews and Semites in general are so fond:

Ask, and it will be given you.

Seek, and you will find,

Knock, and it will be opened to you.[75]

It is worth the trouble to examine several cases in more detail. The following, for example, consists of two parallel verses, the first negative, the second positive; the first deals with the earth, the second with heaven; in each verse lines 2 and 3 are parallel, with 2 subjects and one predicate in line 2 and one subject and two predicates in line 3:

Do not lay up for yourselves treasures on earth,

Where moth and rust consume

And where thieves break in and steal,

But lay up for yourselves treasures in heaven,

Where neither moth nor rust consumes

And where thieves do not break in and steal.[76]

Passing now from the form, in the strictly literary sense of the word, we now turn to another important quality expected in a religious leader—realism. For though theorists are necessary, they cannot (at least in that capacity) become leaders.

It is striking that Jesus never makes long speeches about God and general principles. Everything he says is directly bound up with life, and his choice of words and manner of speaking grip his audience and lead it inevitably to practical decisions. A leader must be in contact with reality, and this grip on reality must be demonstrable in certain basic ideas frequently repeated in vivid and fairly short addresses. The words of a leader, especially a religious leader, must well up from a deep fount of long meditations, but to his hearers they appear as arrows which strike as if by magic into their inmost hearts, leaving a wound which in its turn impels them to reflection and meditation.

It is an excellent thing, though rare, if the leader can carry out this meditation together with a staff of intimate collaborators,[77] but when he appears in public he must possess powers of conviction more forceful than diffuse reasonings. He must produce a program that can immediately be put into practice.

It would not be difficult to show by concrete examples that Jesus' words possessed this quality. This was expressly acknowledged from the middle of the 2nd century: "His talks are short and succinct, for he was by no means a sophist, but his word was a force of God." [78] The same author offers an explanation for the remarkable fact that

[48] Mt. 4, 19.
[49] Mt. 10, 8.
[50] Mt. 6, 21.
[51] Mt. 5, 15.
[52] Mt. 6, 22.
[53] Mt. 5, 14.
[54] Mt. 6, 26.
[55] Mt. 6, 28.
[56] Mt. 10, 16.
[57] Mt. 12, 33.
[58] Mt. 13, 44-46.
[59] Mt. 18, 12-14.
[60] Lk. 12, 6-7.
[61] Mk. 10, 38.
[62] Jn. 2, 19; cf. Mt. 26, 61.
[63] Mk. 12, 49.
[64] Lk. 12, 54-56.
[65] Mt. 11, 16-17.

[66] Mt. 5, 29-30.
[67] Mt. 18, 6.
[68] Mt. 6, 27.
[69] Mt. 5, 39.
[70] Mt. 6, 3.
[71] Mt. 9, 13.
[72] Lk. 17, 33.
[73] Lk. 12, 7.
[74] Mt. 19, 24.
[75] Lk. 11, 9.
[76] Mt. 6, 19-21. One can similarly analyze the close of the Sermon on the Mount, with slight variations between Mt. 7, 24-27 and Lk. 6, 47-49.
[77] This, too, we find in Jesus; he reviews the apostles' lives with them.
[78] Justin, *Apologia*, 14, 5.

among Jesus' followers a radical conversion often seized the illiterate, the blind, the crippled.[79] Unlike the success of Socrates, for
whose teaching no one was ever willing to risk his life, one finds this
willingness to die for Christ not only among philosophers and cultivated people, but also among workers and the completely uneducated.[80] The reason is that Jesus was not a vessel of human ingenuity,
but a *force*, the force of the ineffable Father.[81] This is the completely human yet strictly supernatural explanation of the enthusiasm Jesus succeeded in arousing.

The last quality that contributed to this enthusiasm is that he was
a *clever polemist*. A leader cannot allow himself the luxury of being
beaten three or four times in open debate. The gospels testify that
Jesus was a formidable, dauntless debater when attacked. The most
vivid examples of his powers of argument are his replies to the
accusation of complicity with Beelzebub,[82] the question about the
origin of his authority,[83] and two particularly thorny problems:
the delicate subjects of national pride concerning the payment of the
imperial taxes [84] and the resurrection of the body. Here, his opponents started out with all the laughers on their side, with the
ridiculous situation of a woman with seven unsuccessful marriages.[85] In fact, Jesus always emerged so successfully from these
contests that in the end no one dared attack him.[86]

If, therefore, Jesus saw his success gradually diminishing, it was
not because his followers ever saw him humiliated in public debate.[87] Rather he was humiliated in the same way as Gandhi, because his ideal was too high, his method too peace-loving and his
enemies self-assured to the point of fanaticism. It is perhaps for this
reason that God wished these discussions to be preserved although,
in themselves, their content is not always so important for us. The
sabbath quarrels are merely incidental—now at least we know that
Jesus was nor is no milquetoast.

The result of our examination agrees entirely with the details
given by the evangelists. Jesus really knew how to inspire people.
From the very first moment, the people were dumbfounded by his
teaching.[88] In his own district, people could not understand where
he got it from, coming as he did from an ordinary family.[89] Until
the very end, the people supported him, so that the scribes hesitated
to take him prisoner.[90] In the fourth gospel, it is the officers who put
John's thesis into words: "No man ever spoke like this man." [91]

HE WAS WORTHY OF THE LOYALTY OF HIS FOLLOWERS

There are many glittering talents that appear and vanish, like comets. They are unaccountable and thus, unfitted to be leaders. One must be able to count on a leader; his followers must be able to trust him blindly, without having to reflect. To inspire such loyalty, a leader requires selfless dedication, steadfastness of purpose, and the courage to make decisions.

We have already shown that Jesus *dedicated* his whole person, his life, and his talents to his task.[92] In the synagogues—where he reached practically everybody from the surrounding districts—in the open air, when he addressed great crowds, and when he travelled from town to town, until he and his disciples grew weary, constantly preaching and healing the sick, Jesus succeeded in awakening a great response. In eastern countries, the pace of life is usually more relaxed, but this was certainly not so with Jesus. Everyone knew that he was working with might and main, as in a great undertaking. Everyone knew that he would continue to do so. He would do everything to win the people. "Jerusalem, Jerusalem! How often would I have gathered your children together as a hen gathers her brood under her wings, but you would not!"[93] This is the language of a leader, of someone who has devoted himself passionately to his task, so much so that he will die in public, like someone paying the toll of his life's effort.

A second basis for loyalty is *steadfastness*. Jesus always remained himself. He changed no jot of his message even when circumstances began to look unfavorable. Undoubtedly, he adapted himself to circumstances, refrained from provoking useless conflicts and was unwilling to cast pearls before swine.[94] But he refused to be deterred by fear or favor. It was generally admitted that he played up to nobody.[95] This gave the disciples an extraordinary advantage, only

[79] Justin, *op. cit.*, 60, 11.
[80] Appendix of the *Apologia*, 10, 8.
[81] Justin, *Apologia*, 60, 11; Appendix, 10, 8.
[82] Mt. 12, 24-29.
[83] Lk. 20, 1-8 par.
[84] Mt. 22, 15-22.
[85] Mk. 12, 27.
[86] Mk. 12, 34.
[87] Mark gives the longest list of disputes: from 2, 1 to 3, 6; also 3, 22-30; 7, 1-23; from 11, 27 to 12, 37.
[88] Mt. 7, 28; Mk. 1, 22; Lk. 4, 32.
[89] Mk. 6, 2-5.
[90] Mk. 11, 18.
[91] Jn. 7, 46.
[92] Cf. pp. 33ff.
[93] Mt. 23, 37.
[94] Mt. 7, 6.
[95] Mt. 22, 16.

too rare with great leaders, in that they were not obliged to change their programs or tactics. No one needed to fear being disowned from one day to the next for what the leader himself had yesterday taught and asked.

Finally, we can establish that Jesus was not afraid to assume *responsibility*. Jesus seeks no shelter in various arguments on authority and devious considerations, which would be Greek to the ordinary man. He is not in favor of the umbrella system (whereby the water pours off sideways onto lower and lower roofs) with no one responsible for the entire procedure but everyone pushing responsibility onto the higher or lower grades.[95] He speaks with authority, plain and clear, like the prophets, and the people can appreciate this.[97] When the occasion arises, he can issue a very valuable invitation: "Come and follow me," and at once, people leave their work, their families, even their recently dead fathers.[98]

On the other hand, a good leader is no casuist. He may not lose himself in details and cavilling. Even when he urges concrete decisions, he must leave the practical details to his followers. Their degree of independence reflects greatly on the quality of their leader. This is why Jesus will not intervene to settle questions of inheritance.[99] He keeps to his own terrain, and this is so painfully clear that his words of necessity give rise to doubts and hesitations, as in the case of the likeable young farmer who was after all too rich,[100] or even to family quarrels because some are for him and the others against.[101]

Clear standpoints will always provoke opposition. During the trial period through which humanity is passing, even the best and most peace-loving leader will never succeed in realizing all forms of peace. Even Jesus says that he has come to bring the sword.[102] Everything depends on how this sword is used. If this sword is the truth of God, even the meekest and most humble of heart cannot insure that it will never give pain.

HE TRAINED COLLABORATORS TO CARRY OUT HIS TASK

A leader's task must surpass his person in space and outlive him in time. Thus, anyone who thinks that to be a leader means taking everything upon oneself is sadly mistaken. Jesus took care to train people to collaborate in and continue his work, otherwise the Church could never have existed.

Less attention has been paid to this point than one might think, for modern biblical scholars have devoted themselves particularly to the problem of the relationship between the "twelve" and the "apostles."[103] This tends to obscure the actual history of these twelve. In my opinion, we can safely distinguish six phases in the training of these collaborators:

1. Jesus immediately began to *invite* some men in a particular manner to follow him. Where, in general, the crowd had to rely entirely on its own initiative, there are thus occasions on which Jesus himself intervenes. The accounts of these callings which have come down to us are quite astounding.[104] It is quite possible that some of those "called" did not, in fact, become apostles, while on the other hand, not all the apostles were specially called by Jesus to follow him.[105] It is still difficult to decide to what extent Jesus' initiative in this matter differed from the custom of the rabbis and the prophets.

2. At a certain moment Jesus proceeds to train a clearly defined group; the twelve, whose names are carefully noted down by all the synoptics.[106] Mark especially stresses this fact. We see Jesus going up into the hills and calling those whom he desired in order to create a personal bond with himself before he could send them out.[107] The entire description is parallel to the Sermon on the Mount, which is absent in Mark, and obviously holds the same interest for him.[108] It is clear that this collegial structure of Jesus'

---

96 It is difficult to forget the terrible application of this system in the recent past, whereby millions of innocent people, especially Jews, were put to death with no other excuse than, "An order is an order."

97 Mt. 7, 29.

98 Mt. 8, 22; 9, 9; 19, 21; Jn. 1, 43.

99 Lk. 12, 13-14.

100 Mk. 10, 21-22.

101 Mt. 10, 32.34-38.

102 Mt. 10, 34.

103 V. Taylor, "The Twelve and the Apostles," in his *Commentary on St. Mark* (1952), pp. 619-627; H. Von Campenhausen, "Das urchristliche Apostelbegriff", in *Studia Theologica*, 1 (1947), pp. 96-130; R. Harris, *The Twelve Apostles* (Cambridge, 1927); O. Hopman,

De Apostelen (Haarlem, 1948); K. H. Schelkle, *Jüngerschaft und Apostelamt. Eine biblische Auslegung des priesterlichen Dienstes* (Freiburg im Br., 1957); G. Klein, *Die zwölf Apostel, Ursprung und Gehalt einer Idee* (Göttingen, 1961); articles by A. Verheul in *Sacris Erudiri*, 1 (1948), pp. 380-396; 2 (1949), pp. 5-43; and *Studia Catholica*, 22 (1947) pp. 65-76; 23, (1948), pp. 147-157; 26 (1951), pp. 171-184.

104 Mt. 4, 18-22; 9, 9-13, Jn. 1, 35-51.

105 Cf. the unknown or failed vocations of Lk. 9, 57-60 (less clear in Mt. 8, 19-22); Mk. 10, 20 par.

106 Mk. 3, 16-19; Mt. 10, 1-4; Lk. 6, 12-16.

107 Mk. 3, 13-14.

108 Cf. Mt. 4, 23-25: the same "gen-

closest associates was so strongly emphasized by Mark because the results were later to be important.

3. The twelve were now sent out, equipped with special instructions, on journeys that were at once preparatory tours and trial trips for later on. It is difficult to distinguish between the two. Historically, their main task will have been to prepare the coming of Jesus, but they will have shared this mission with others. Luke speaks of "seventy-two others," who were sent on ahead of him, "two by two, into every town and place where he himself was about to come." [109] This does not exclude the possibility that Jesus had already given thought to their future task, and given them special pointers, although it must be admitted from the critical point of view that several of the tips that point toward the future cannot be attributed to Jesus himself. They are derived from tradition, or from Matthew himself, in the spirit of Jesus, but bearing evidence of experience acquired later. This comes rather from the idea of trial trips.

However this may be, the apostles will have learned a great deal on these expeditions and will have come to realize afterward exactly what Jesus had done. He had, in fact, founded a school of action, and it is worthwhile to consider some of its aims.

The nucleus, indeed, the whole content of their message must be: "the kingdom of God." [110] Their task was lavishly and freely to distribute the gifts of grace: "You received without pay, give without pay." [111] They must not worry about finances, but rely on God and the goodness of the people, who will see to it that they do not want.[112] They must lose no time: "Salute no one on the road." [113] They must not be capricious in changing lodgings. They must first decide where they want to stay, then bring peace to that house and remain there until they depart.[114] Finally, they must be prepared for great sacrifices and make ready for persecutions.[115] Concerning this last point, there is clear evidence of later elements, since there is mention of testimony before kings and Gentiles,[116] whereas at the beginning of the discourse, and undoubtedly, thus, in historical reality, they are forbidden to leave Palestine.[117] Nonetheless it would be wrong to assume that the Palestine trips were all smooth going: a number of violent incidents bear witness to the contrary.[118]

4. The twelve were initiated by Jesus in an extraordinary manner into the "mysteries of the kingdom of heaven" from the moment that the crowds began to prove less receptive.[119] Private teaching

among themselves became more frequent.[120] At the same time Jesus, who up till then had performed miracles only for the "people," began to reveal himself in an extraordinary manner to the disciples. Standing up in their boat, he calms the storm; [121] and on another occasion, he walks to them across the water in order to tell them; "Take heart, it is I. Have no fear." [122]

These two phenomena are complementary, for the revelation of the "mysteries" will be intended to prepare them for the fact that the kingdom must pass through a phase of extreme smallness and humiliation; it is only a mustard seed, an invisible leaven, a grain that pierces the ground unnoticed.[123] This will shock the disciples, especially when they hear that the leader of the kingdom will die an inglorious death after having been publicly chastized. Indeed, their special instruction is chiefly concerned with the predictions of the passion.[124]

The miracles quoted, and especially the transfiguration, counterbalance these sombre perspectives.[125] They give a foretaste of the glory of the resurrection, and of the efficacy of the Lord who has gained power through the cross.[126] John sums up all these elements (apocalyptic parable of the grain, humiliation of Jesus, glorification) in the affirmation: "The hour has come for the Son of Man to be glorified. Truly, truly, I say to you, unless a grain of wheat falls into the earth and dies, it remains alone; but if it dies it bears much fruit." [127]

5. Did Jesus grant special authority to his helpers? It is not difficult to imagine a theory whereby the first Christians, suddenly bereft of their leader and completely unprepared for this new situation, would have been quite ready to accept the authority of a small group that had usurped a "mission"—hence the name, "apostles."

Such a theory not only assumes that Jesus was utterly mistaken about the future and that the apostles were unforgivably arrogant; it

---

eral survey" as in Mk. 4, 3, 7-8, and also at the foot of a mountain (Mt. 5, 1).
[109] Lk. 10, 1.
[110] Mt. 10, 7.
[111] Mt. 10, 8.
[112] Mt. 10, 9-10.
[113] Lk. 10, 4.
[114] Mt. 10, 11-15.
[115] Mt. 10, 16-34.
[116] Mt. 10, 18-19.
[117] Mt. 10, 5-6.
[118] Lk. 9, 49-54.
[119] Mt. 13, 10-18.
[120] Mk. 7, 17; 9, 27-32; 10, 10-16.
[121] Mk. 4, 35-41.
[122] Mk. 6, 45-53.
[123] Mt. 13, 31-33; Mk. 4, 26-29.
[124] Mk. 8, 31; 9, 31; 10, 32-33.
[125] Mk. 9, 2-13 par.
[126] Cf. Rom. 1-4; Lk. 24, 26, 46.
[127] Jn. 12, 23-24.

is in complete contradiction to Jesus' method of procedure insofar as this can be deduced from historical texts. All believing Christians (Protestants, Orthodox, Anglicans, Catholics) oppose any such thesis, which is untenable from the psychological and sociological points of view, and accept that Jesus himself granted an unparalleled authority to the apostles.

It is less easy to decide, however, exactly *when* this occurred. A number of exegetes hold the opinion that the essentials were only communicated after the resurrection. From a dogmatic viewpoint, this is roughly the same, for everyone accepts that the resurrection and the intervention of the Holy Spirit form an essential turning point. It is the risen Lord who appears to the twelve, and "not to all the people" [128] and gives them great powers and authority.[129] John speaks of the risen Lord's special dealings with Peter, who receives a particular mission with regard to his sheep.[130]

From this, the theory has evolved that the famous "rock" text is another tradition of the same fact, but now inserted in the public life.[131] Leaving aside the debatable nature of this thesis, it must be observed that the facts of the resurrection were already prepared during the earthly life of Jesus. The twelve, for example, could not arrive anywhere in a village to prepare for their master's arrival, without a commission in the style of the following: "He who hears you, hears me, and he who rejects you, rejects me." [132] Peter especially already had a privileged position during the public life, and a certain amount of authority over the Twelve. This is shown many times.[133]

This authority is practically limitless. In a certain sense, it will be greater than that of Christ himself, since it will be exercised in the age of the *glorified* Christ, who possesses divine power [134] and who sends his Spirit to enable them to understand what formerly passed their comprehension [135] and to perform greater miracles than Jesus himself.[136] For this reason, it is an advantage that Jesus should go.[137] One thing, however, remains constant: whatever the apostolic power may be, Jesus alone is our mediator,[138] our high priest,[139] our light, the way, the truth and the life.[140]

Peter's task was to strengthen his brethren,[141] and these brothers themselves may also have been apostles. He must feed Christ's flock, and this time the reference is certainly to the whole of the Christian community.[142] He is the rock of the Church, to which Jesus promises immortality.[143] He receives the keys of the kingdom of God, and special power to "bind and loose" truly and effectively, so that this binding and loosing will also be valid for God ("in heaven").[144] This typically rabbinic expression is fairly clear: "to bind" is to exclude, to excommunicate, while "to loose" is to raise the anathema. Such disciplinary powers naturally assume the necessary authority to interpret the doctrine, for otherwise, no norm and thus, no judgment is possible.

On the other hand, this certainly does not signify that Peter is free to invent what theories he likes. On the contrary, Peter himself must be converted, and only then will he be able to strengthen his brethren;[145] he must be obedient thus to the person and teaching of Jesus; a conversion presupposes a norm independent of the person converted.

Further definition of the apostles' authority is a point of dispute among Christians. All accept that the apostles had received something they could not communicate; revelation finished with them. The Catholic and Orthodox Churches and a number of Protestants believe that the apostles transmitted a real authority to the college of their successors, and in particular, to the successor of Peter, since Jesus when imparting this apostolic authority envisaged that his Church would last throughout the centuries.

Catholics believe, moreover, that in certain cases, this authentic interpretation of Jesus' revelation attained the degree of infallibility. This is also accepted by the Orthodox, but with certain reservations concerning the ultimate responsibility of Peter's successor in this respect.[146]

[128] Acts 10, 41.
[129] Mt. 28, 18-20; the wording is influenced by the later situation, Mk. 16, 15-16 (the "second ending" of Mk.); Lk. 24, 49; Jn. 20, 23-24.
[130] Jn. 21, 15-17.
[131] Similarly, the power to forgive sins (Mt. 18, 15-18) would anticipate Jn. 20, 22-23.
[132] Lk. 10, 16.
[133] Mt. 15, 15; 17, 1.24; 18, 21; 26, 37; Mk. 5, 37; 10, 28; 11, 21; 16, 7; Lk. 5, 3; 8, 45; 22, 8; 24, 34; Jn. 6, 68.
[134] Rom. 1, 4; Mt. 28, 18.
[135] Jn. 16, 13.
[136] Jn. 14, 12.
[137] Jn. 16, 17.

[138] 1 Tim, 2, 5; Heb. 8, 6; 9, 15; 12, 24.
[139] Heb. 3, 1; 4, 14-55; 8, 1; 9, 11.
[140] Themes of John.
[141] Lk. 22, 32.
[142] Jn. 21, 15-17.
[143] Mt. 16, 18.
[144] Mt. 16, 19.
[145] Lk. 22, 32.
[146] Cf. O. Cullmann, *Saint-Pierre, Disciple-Apôtre, Martyr* (Paris, 1952); "Petra and Petros," in *TWNT*, 6 (1959), pp. 94-112; "L'Apôtre Pierre, instrument du diable et instrument de Dieu; la place de Mt. 15, 16-19 dans la tradition primitive," in *New Testament Essays, Studies in memory of T. W. Manson* (Manchester,

It was, indeed, necessary to mention this fundamental point of our tragic division. Rather than bring apologetic considerations to bear, we merely reiterate that this disunity cannot possibly have been according to Jesus' will. All of us must thus zealously seek to learn exactly what Jesus intended when he imparted particular authority to the apostles. Whatever we assume, we must end by deciding that Jesus acted as a truly detached and far-sighted leader by binding people to him who would be no blind automatons, but living persons, invested with an incomparable prestige and authority. For is it not moving to think back on these simplest of people who went by the names of Peter, John, James, and Paul, and who became the foundation of the entire structure of the Church? [147]

6. Finally, Jesus gave his "testament." This, too, was in keeping with leadership. The leader who is passing away and wishes to insure the continuance of the communal task, will make use of the pathetic character of the last moments of a human life to imprint more firmly in the hearts of his collaborators his main ideas and the measures to be taken. Such a last disposition is called a "testament." It was even an honored literary genre among the Jews, and it is as such that we find it in John's parting words. Here, we are taking the word in a more objective sense without attempting to decide if we are dealing in every case with measures taken at the very last hour. We find, indeed, at least four "testamentary dispositions" that are dated by at least one of the evangelists on the evening before Jesus' death. This does not mean that certain of these points may not be the expression of a measure taken earlier or later. The four points are as follows:

(a) There is a "new commandment," which must be the sign of recognition among his followers, and which must counterbalance the persecutions.[148] Jesus urges this "unity among the Christians." [149]

(b) To those who had helped him and were to continue his task, Jesus left an unforgettable lesson, which stressed for them that leading consists in serving. Both John and Luke give an entirely different version of this testament of humility. To the washing of the feet in John [150] corresponds the strong statement in Luke: "Let the greatest among you become as the youngest, and the leader as one who serves . . . I am among you as one who serves." [151] We shall not go into the question of how far Luke here reflects historical reality, although the other evangelists have very similar statements in a different context.[152] This in no way detracts from the importance of this provision of the will.

(c) The testamentary dispositions we have just dealt with may be only "words," but a third, ultimate provision—the historical reality and localization of which cannot this time be doubted—concerns an institution: the eucharist. This is a commemoration of his Person,[153] and embraces a real proclamation of his passion.[154] By consuming that "blessed" bread (i.e., bread as eucharist) and that equally "blessed" chalice of wine, man shares in the redeeming passion and supreme "blessing" (i.e., eucharist) of Jesus himself, for that which is eaten and drunk is his body and his blood, that is, himself, in his capacity of sacrificial offering for the forgiveness of sins.[155] Here, we are concerned with a testament in the strict sense of the word, for Paul says that Jesus desires that his eucharist should continue to be celebrated "until he comes." [156]

(d) Finally, there is a testamentary gift, the "other helper," the Spirit of truth, who will be granted to all the faithful, but in particular to the apostles. All our sources indicate that the effective granting of Jesus' Spirit took place *after the resurrection*.[157] Both Luke and John, however, speak of a previous promise, which according to John's scheme must be situated during the Last Supper,[158] and was made according to Luke between the resurrection and the ascension.[159] Once again, therefore, we must leave an open space, but we

---

1959). H. Strathmann, "Die stellung des Petrus in der Urkirche. Zur Frühgeschichte des Wortes an Petrus Mt. 16, 17-19" in *Zeitschr. system. Theol.*, 20 (1943), pp. 223-282; J. Ludwig, "Die Primaworte Mt. 16, 18-19, in der neuesten Forschung", in *Studia Theologica*, 2 (1950), pp. 110-165; C. Journet, *Primauté de Pierre dans la perspective protestante et dans la perspective catholique* (Paris, 1953); F. Obrist, *Echtheitsfragen und Deutung der Primastelle Mt. 16, 18f. in der deutschen protestantischen Theologie der letzten dreissig Jahre* (Münster, 1961). The best contribution since Cullmann is that of F. Refoulé, "Primauté de Pierre dans les évangiles," in *Rev. scienc. rel.*, 38 (1964), pp.

1-41.

[147] Cf. Eph. 2, 20; Mt. 19, 28.

[148] Jn. 13, 34; 15, 9-17. This commandment differs from that of general brotherly love and we may take it as an historical fact that it was given in the form of a testament.

[149] Jn. 17, 20-23.

[150] Jn. 13, 1-17.

[151] Lk. 22, 24-27.

[152] Mt. 20, 25-27; Mk. 10, 42-44; cf. Mt. 18, 1-5; Mk. 9, 33-40; Lk. 9, 46-48.

[153] Lk. 22, 19.

[154] 1 Cor. 11, 26.

[155] Mt. 26, 28.

[156] 1 Cor. 11, 26.

[157] Jn. 7, 39; 20, 22; Acts 2, 1-13, 17.38; Eph. 4, 7-16 (cf. 3-4).

[158] Jn. 14, 16-17; 15, 26; 16, 7-15.

[159] Lk. 24, 49; Acts 1, 5. 8.

have, nonetheless, established that up to the very last, Jesus was concerned that the spiritual equipment of his "helpers" should be complete.

To sum up, we return again to the Johannine idea of the "good shepherd." It is not difficult to show how many traits of that image correspond to what we have found in Jesus, proceeding on the basis of the qualities required by a good leader (from the modern viewpoint). The good shepherd is dedicated: he does not leave his flock in the lurch.[160] His only concern is *their* welfare,[161] and for this he is prepared to risk his life.[162] The good shepherd, moreover, knows how to speak to his flock and to encourage them so that they desire to hear no other voice but his; they have a blind confidence in him.[163] Finally, the shepherd is concerned for the welfare of *all;* he strives for the union of sheep and shepherd.[164] Such a union is based in the first place on the shepherd's sacrifice of his own life,[165] but also comprises the service of his helpers, through whose words people will believe in him so that all may be one as he is one with the Father.[166] In the same spirit, Peter also links the image of the good shepherd with the existence of subordinate shepherds.[167] It is precisely they who set such great store on preserving Jesus' theme of the "good shepherd," painting it on the walls of the catacombs and incorporating it in the liturgy. Today, there are hundreds of thousands who feel especially attracted to the liturgy of the good shepherd. These are the priests, whom Jesus had in mind when he founded his Church.

160 Jn. 10, 12.
161 Jn. 10, 16.
162 Jn. 10, 11. 17-18.
163 Jn. 10, 3-5. 14-15.
164 Jn. 10, 16.

165 Cf. parallelism between Jn. 10, 16 and 11, 52; 1 Pet. 2, 24-25.
166 Jn. 17, 20-21.
167 1 Pet. 5, 1-4.

IV
The Figure
Who Inspired Him

Jesus, like every other person, possessed a deep secret. As in every human heart, there echoed in his own an ever-recurring theme which dominated his entire life. This was something more personal than his life's work, the preaching of the kingdom of God, and more important than character and influence, although these were in Jesus' case no less than his peerless goodness and his splendid leadership. We carry our secret in that deep zone which we call the "inner life." We touch the deepest ground of this when we enter upon the domain of prayer, for there is, in truth, nothing deeper than religious promptings. Nothing can be more basic than our relationship with God. We shall return to this aspect in the last chapter on Jesus' personality. In this section, we are dealing with something that is intimately bound up with it: the idea we have of our own lives, our exact view of our life's work, or, thinking once again in musical terms, the theme that inspires one's whole life.

Those who can be considered truly "great" have always had a fairly clear idea of their task, or "vocation," for within the great cause, upon which they had embarked, they always had their own definite task. Often, it was a figure or a small number of figures who inspired them in this, in whom they saw the projected image of their own "egos." Such a figure may be an historical personage, or may be entirely fictitious: personal contacts, reading, meetings, dreams and all sorts of combinations play a role. It goes without saying that any such figure does not detract from personal freedom; it is merely a means, a way of realizing this freedom.

Did such a figure exist in Jesus' life? Naturally, the evangelists never put the question in this way. As believing Jews, they would not have dreamed of painting or sculpting a physical portrait of Jesus—it was against the ten commandments—and the spirit of the times was unfavorable to a spiritual portrait. It would be some time before this literary genre came into favor. Nonetheless, they provide us with enough data to attempt something in this line ourselves.

THE BASIC THEME

There can be no doubt that Jesus learned the Scriptures as a growing boy—there is evidence enough of this in his public life. It is also probable that he meditated on the Scriptures and made use of them in his prayer and thoughts on life. Among the texts that interested him, we should like to concentrate on those that constituted the theme of the last years of his life. We have in mind a number of poems, the origin and meaning of which have not yet been definitely established; the Ebed Yahweh songs that form the principal portion of the second part of the Book of Isaiah.[1]

It is probable that Jesus knew and repeated these songs as a child, although it does not appear that the Jews of Jesus' time attached great importance to them. They may well, however, have been honored in certain circles, among the "poor of Yahweh" as material for meditation and an inspiration for prayer. They may be said to have influenced Mary and Joseph, who undoubtedly influenced Jesus' religious training.

It is certain that the milieu into which Jesus was born was marked by this spirit of the poor of Yahweh. They were simple people, fervent in prayer, placing their trust in God, materially poor and spiritually nourished by the Scriptures. Although the gospel accounts of Jesus' childhood are by no means eyewitness reports with literal dialogue,[2] we cannot doubt the essential traits of the characters. Joseph is a holy man, compassionate, simple in his obedience and sorrow;[3] Zachary and Elizabeth are pious people, prayerful people who have known their share of trouble;[4] Simeon and Anna are filled with the Holy Spirit[5] and are worthy successors to the poorest of all, the shepherds.[6] The manner in which Mary is described typifies her as someone completely steeped in the literature of the Old Testament. She is modest and meditative, prepared for everything, and sings to God her joy, her insignificance and her gratitude.[7]

Therefore, while it may be rash to greet the *Magnificat* as a prayer composed word-for-word by Mary, it would be equally reprehensible to assert that we know nothing more of the spiritual climate of "Nazareth." It would seem, on the contrary, an obvious conclusion that the hymns of the Suffering Servant were heard and memorized by Jesus in the house of his parents.

Let us suppose that Jesus was fascinated by the question of who the Suffering Servant was, what exactly God expected of him, what he looked like. These questions will, in any case, help us to understand the songs better. He must thus have imagined someone to whom God himself had given a command, someone who understood his task, and was able to put it into words himself, someone whose history could be outlined by the prophet in roughly this way:

The Servant Seen by God Himself

Behold my servant, whom I uphold,
my chosen, in whom my soul delights;
I have put my Spirit upon him,
he will bring forth justice to the nations.
He will not cry or lift up his voice,
or make it heard in the street;
a bruised reed he will not break
and a dimly burning wick he will not quench;
He will not fail or be discouraged
till he has established justice in the earth;
and the coastlands wait for his law.

(Is. 42, 1-4)

The Servant Himself Sees His Vocation Thus

Listen to me, O coastlands,
and hearken, you peoples from afar.
The Lord called me from the womb,

[1] Cf. J. S. Van der Ploeg, *Les chants du serviteur de Jahvé dans la seconde partie d'Isaïe* (Paris, 1936); C. R. North. *The suffering servant in Deutero-Isaiah* (Oxford, 1948); H. W. Wolff, *Jesaja 53 in Urchristentum* (Berlin, 1950[2]); R. J. Tournay, "Les chants du serviteur dans la seconde partie d'Isaïe," in *Rev. Bibl.*, 59 (1952), pp. 384, 481-512; H. Cazelles, "Les poèmes du serviteur. Leur place, leur structure," in *Recherches sc. rel.*, (1955),

pp. 5-55; V. Van de Leeuw, *De Ebed Jahweh—profetieen* (Assen, 1955); J. Coppens, "Le serviteur de Jahvè," in *Sacra Pagina*, 1 (1958), pp. 434-454; O. Cullmann, *Christologie du nouveau Testament* (Neuchatel, 1958).

[2] Cf. pp. 210ff.
[3] Mt. 1, 19-25; 2, 13-14.
[4] Lk. 1, 6-25.
[5] Lk. 2, 22-38.
[6] Lk. 2, 8-20.
[7] Lk. 1, 38; 46-56; 2, 19. 51.

from the body of my mother he named my name.
He made my mouth like a sharp sword,
in the shadow of his hand he hid me;
he made me a polished arrow,
in his "quiver" he hid me away.
And he said to me, "You are my servant,
Israel, in whom I will be glorified."
But I said, "I have labored in vain,
I have spent my strength for nothing and vanity;
yet surely my right is with the Lord,
and my recompense with my God."
For I am honored in the eyes of the *Lord*
and my God has become my strength.
And now the Lord says,
who formed me from the womb to be his servant,
to bring Jacob back to him,
and that Israel might be gathered to him . . .
"It is too light a thing that you should be my servant
to raise up the tribes of Jacob
and to restore the preserved of Israel;
I will give you as a light to the nations,
that my salvation may reach to the end of the earth."

(Is. 49, 1-6).

His History

For he grew up before him like a young plant,
and like a root out of dry ground;
he had no form or comeliness that we should look at him,
and no beauty that we should desire him.
he was despised and rejected by men;
a man of sorrows and acquainted with grief;
and as one from whom men hide their faces
he was despised, and we esteemed him not.
Surely he has borne our griefs and carried our sorrows;
yet we esteemed him stricken,
smitten by God, and afflicted.
But he was wounded for our transgressions,
he was bruised for our iniquities;
upon him was the chastisement that made us whole,
and with his stripes we are healed.

All we like sheep have gone astray;
we have turned everyone to his own way;
and the Lord has laid on him the iniquity of us all.
He was oppressed, and he was afflicted,
yet he opened not his mouth;
like a lamb that is led to the slaughter,
and like a sheep that before its shearers is dumb,
so he opened not his mouth.
By oppression and judgment he was taken away;
and as for his generation, who considered
that he was cut off out of the land of the living,
stricken for the transgression of my people.
And they made his grave with the wicked
and with a rich man in his death,
although he had done no violence,
and there was no deceit in his mouth.
Yet it was the will of the Lord to bruise him;
he has put him to grief;
When he makes himself an offering for sin,
he shall see his offspring, he shall prolong his days;
the will of the Lord shall prosper in his hand.

(Is. 53, 2-10)

Yahweh's Concluding Promise

He shall see the fruit of the travail of his soul
    and be satisfied;
by his knowledge shall the righteous one, my servant,
make many to be accounted righteous;
and he shall bear their iniquities.
Therefore I will divide him a portion with the great,
And he shall divide the spoil with the strong;
because he poured out his soul to death,
and was numbered with the transgressors;
yet he bore the sin of many,
and made intercession for the transgressors.

(Is. 53, 11-12)

We shall not venture to guess the place these songs had in Jesus'
mind during his youth; whether he sang them aloud, or murmured
them quietly to himself, or whether he knew them by heart (which

would be by no means remarkable for a Semite). We can only imagine how attractive he found the ideal and the characteristics of the figure portrayed—a tower of strength to the poor, a meek prophet, intimately close to God in carrying out his will, yet carrying his human solidarity so far that he gave his life for man's sins.

We cannot describe the history of our hymns in Jesus' psychology, all the more so since we are here repeatedly confronted with the mystery of the human and the divine in him. Yet, in any case, his divine nature did not prevent him from finding this generous gift of self attractive, and from making it his own in acquired knowledge. What was crystal clear to him from the very first moment concerning his own nature and mission, would grow increasingly more concrete and be expressed in human concepts and figures.[8] In this, the Ebed Yahweh songs will have played an important role, something of which we can deduce from the great turning point of his life, and from a number of scattered references.

FIRST CRITICAL MOMENT: IN THE JORDAN VALLEY

It was a decisive turning point in Jesus' life when, attracted by the preaching of John the Baptist on the approaching kingdom of God, he left the land of his youth to travel to the burning valley of the Jordan. Like thousands of others, he allowed himself to be baptized in the swiftly flowing water. Then something occurred that we cannot quite define, but which must have been a most extraordinary experience for him. While the divine light continued to burn as fiercely as ever in the depths of his being, the scene of which he was the object, as he stood in the water, cast whole rays of new light into his ever-quick and receptive intelligence.[9] Closely and carefully we shall attempt to follow him in this "acquired knowledge" as the theologians call it, in contrast to the "blessed contemplation of God" which never left him and which is, by definition, total.

The baptism—experience recounted by the three synoptics [10] must have been communicated in some way or another by Jesus himself, otherwise the apostles would never have known of it, for it is quite clearly a theophany addressed to him, and not to John the Baptist, as is sometimes said. Mark leaves not the slightest doubt on this subject for, although "he saw the heavens opened" is undefined, who *he* is is clearly indicated by the use of second person: "Thou art my beloved son." Only Luke tells us that Jesus was praying; the other evangelists assume that this was so.

But what actually happened, and what do the evangelists wish to tell us about Jesus? It cannot be said that all exegetes are in agreement regarding the answers to these two distinct questions.[11] It is, however, clear to everyone that there is a marked similarity to the visions with which so many prophetic missions began: those of Samuel, Isaiah, Jeremiah, Ezekiel and later Paul.[12] It is indeed the expression of a new experience, and surely remains forever imprinted in the memory as with Paul who, many years after his Damascus experience, still felt himself "struck" by this initial theophany.[13] For Jesus, too, it is a psychological starting signal for his public work. Yet it is much more than that.

It is more than a prophetic calling; it is a real investiture. But of what? There are two theories that seem most likely to be correct. Jesus can be identified with the son of man (Daniel 7, 13-14) and the apocalyptic, visionary framework, as in the Book of Daniel, supports this idea. One may, on the other hand, make the identification with the Suffering Servant of Yahweh and this is certainly how Matthew saw it.[14] In any case, Jesus now knows, in a manner clearly expressed in human terms, that he will have to carry out his messianic mission as God's messenger, having full powers, who will inaugurate God's kingdom on earth (Dan.), or else as the boundlessly good prophet who even takes the sins of others upon himself and does penance for them (Is.).

It may be that the two possibilities should not be strictly separated. In my opinion, however, it seems likely that not only Matthew but Jesus, too, thought, at least obliquely, of the figure of the Suffering Servant. For according to Matthew the heavenly voice says the following:

[8] See further on Jesus' divine and human knowledge, pp. 203ff.

[9] Cf. Lk. 2, 47; receptive = "religious, pliant"; Lk 2, 52.

[10] Mt. 3, 16-17; Mk. 1, 10-11; Lk. 3, 21-22.

[11] Cf. the penetrating article (with bibliography) by M. Sabbe, "Het verhaal van Jesus' doopsel," in Coll. *Brug. Gand.*, 8, (1962), pp. 456-474; 9 (1963), pp. 211-230, 333-365.

[12] Cf. 1 Sam. 3, 1-21; Is. 6, 1-8; Jer. 1, 4-10; Ezek. 1-2; Acts 9, 1-19; 22, 5-16; 26, 12-20; Gal. 1, 12-24.

[13] Cf. Phil. 3, 12; 1 Tim. 1, 12-17.

[14] See also; the difficulty with regard to the son of man interpretation is especially that there is no direct reference to the son of man (or to Daniel) in the actual text, nor is there any mention of a transfer of the kingdom.

"This is my beloved son,
  in whom I am well-pleased" (Mt. 3, 17),
which is a clear allusion to the Ebed songs. "In whom I am well-
pleased" is a literal quotation from Isaiah 42, 1.[15] The term, "son,"
was practically equivalent to "servant." [16] The apposition, "beloved," occurs in the text which Matthew possessed of Isaiah 42, 1-4,
for he quotes him thus in another context.[17] The divine Spirit,
which descends symbolically in the form of a dove, again recalls the
Spirit of Yahweh which will descend upon the Suffering Servant
according to the same text of Isaiah.

If this is so, then the Person of Jesus is suddenly confronted with
very clear perspectives. For although it is a hazardous task to make
many assumptions concerning Jesus' psychological experience and
development, such an experience must surely have left its own imprint upon the perfect humanity of our Lord. His imagination, the
random thoughts that passed through his head were no longer the
same. The *image* of his mission became more clear-cut, for it is not
the same to know a thing according to eternal principles, and to
recognize a particular figure with very individual traits like that of
the Suffering Servant, as the identity card given you by God.

The effect is immediately obvious with the temptation in the
desert.[18] If Jesus is a messiah according to the policy of the Suffering Servant, then all the devil's suggestions must conflict with this
image. For he will have to be a poor fellow, incapable of playing
sensational tricks and still less of subjecting all the glory of the
kingdoms of the world. The spirit of the Servant of Yahweh is
humility, toil, dishonor; not to rule over others, but to save them.

Jesus will speak several times of his mission in the same vein with
reference to another text of Isaiah closely related to the Ebed songs,
in which it is said that the Spirit of Yahweh sent him to bring the
joyful message to the poor.[19]

When Jesus begins his Sermon on the Mount with a beatitude for
the poor, when he seeks contact, in a truly surprising manner for a
messiah, with the sick and with sinners, is this not in order to "bear
our iniquities"? When he champions righteousness, is this not
"bringing justice to the nations"? Do not his remarkable, conscious
humility and meekness reflect the attitude of someone who "will not
break a bruised reed, or quench a dimly burning wick"? We would
need to consider the whole of Jesus' life anew, with special refer-

ence to the Ebed-Yahweh songs. This is what the first Christians did; the clearest proof of this is Matthew, who twice quotes our hymns in connection with Jesus' work of healing.[20]

SECOND CRITICAL MOMENT: UPON A HIGH MOUNTAIN

Many months, indeed probably two years later, when the great concourse of the multitudes was a thing of the past, a new theophany took place.[21] This time, it was upon a high mountain, which late tradition identifies with Mt. Thabor. There are now witnesses to the event, the three principal disciples.[22] The pertinent words are the same as at the baptism: Jesus is the beloved son, in whom God is well-pleased. Leaving aside what this may have meant for the disciples—and this time it *was* intended for them, although they were asleep for part of the time,—it now seems indisputable that Jesus' mission is still further orientated toward the figure of the Suffering Servant. The fact that this story takes place immediately following the first prediction of the passion is significant enough to allow us to rely on the details peculiar to Luke. According to him, it was the middle of the night, a night of prayer for Jesus.[23] All that is human in him is suddenly transfigured, and the two greatest prophets of the Old Testament come to speak with him about his mission, telling him of "the passion which awaits him in Jerusalem." [24]

[15] At least according to Matthew who also diverges from the text of Is. 42, 1-4 and 12, 18-21; he follows not the LXX but Theodotion and Symmachus.

[16] Cf. the "servant" of the centurion of Capernaum: in Mt. 8, 6. 8 and Lk. 7, 2-3 he is called *pais* which can be translated as either "child" or "servant"; in Lk. 7, 2-3 he is *doulos,* which means only "servant"; in Jn. 4, 46.53 he is *huios* which is only "son." A similar case may thus easily be assumed in the translation of Is. 42, 1. The Hebrew had *ebed* (servant); the LXX translated *ebed* everywhere by *pais* (child or servant). When one remembers that in writing their gospels, the evangelists definitely believed in Jesus' divine sonship, the

rendering of *pais* by *huios* (son) is easily explained.

[17] Cf. Mt. 12, 18-21.

[18] Mt. 4, 1-11.

[19] Is. 61, 1-3; quoted in the synagogue at Nazareth (Lk. 4, 16-21) and to the messengers sent by John the Baptist (Mt. 11, 2-6; Lk. 7, 18-23).

[20] Mt. 8, 17 (quotes Is. 53, 4); Mt. 12, 18-21 (quotes Is. 42, 1-4).

[21] Mt. 17, 1-8; Mk. 9, 2-8; Lk. 9, 28-36.

[22] This fact alone creates a great difficulty for those who interpret the transfiguration as an anticipation of the resurrection story. There are also many other indications which would seem to rule out such an interpretation.

[23] Lk. 9, 28-29.

[24] Lk. 9, 31.

We have here a closer definition of the fate of the Suffering Servant. The redeeming suffering is given the name of a locality—Jerusalem—and undoubtedly the disciples could also identify already the instruments of this persecution. They were enormously impressed, but this was nothing new for Jesus. And yet, he cannot have been quite the same when he descended from the mountain. From now on, he was to live under the shadow of the cloud which enveloped him entirely, with that clear and deliberate awareness of his coming passion which would henceforth never leave him.

A Dark Cloud of Terrifying Allusions

A period of great distress had now dawned for the disciples. A short time before, Jesus had told them that his life would end tragically. Their spontaneous reaction, most vehemently expressed by their spokesman and leader, Peter, was a violent protest: they did not agree with this at all! Jesus contented himself with an equally sharp answer, accusing them of thinking in too human a fashion and of not being willing to cooperate in *God*'s plans.[25]

After the transfiguration, the allusions will become more frequent, although only three formal predictions of the passion are mentioned; they will accompany the disciples like a threatening cloud as they make their way to Jerusalem. This sadly unenthusiastic procession is described by Mark as follows: "And they were on the road, going up to Jerusalem, and Jesus was walking ahead of them; and they were amazed, and those who followed were afraid. And taking the twelve again, he began to tell them what was to happen to him." [26]

These allusions do not only testify to Jesus' human insight, for it was to be foreseen that the pharisees would whip up their opposition to the uttermost, nor are they merely a proof of his divine knowledge of the future. It is also impossible to consider these "predictions" as an invention of the first Christians, who sought to protect themselves against the Jews' allegations concerning Jesus' slavish death by saying that he himself had predicted it.

No, these texts truly form part of the historical life of Jesus. The fact alone that not always a victory is foretold,[27] and that some texts like "the bridegroom is taken away" [28] are left fairly general and obscure, should be proof enough that they were not written later. Some of the "predictions," moreover, give a somewhat false impression, since they appear to say that his death would be by stoning,[29] or that he would be left unburied.[30] This is not to mention the stern rebuke addressed to Peter.[31] This is surely no "community theology," but harsh reality.

What all these predictions have in common is a deliberate or implicit reference to the Scriptures. Jesus says that he *must* suffer. This "must" is clear to every Jew, even where it is not expressly stated that it is so written in the Scriptures, as we find on one occasion.[32] The question is, however, *which* Scripture texts express this will of God, which includes *having to suffer*. So few Old Testament texts can be considered as predicting a violent death for the messiah. Still less do they suggest that this Savior would be an outcast.

It was only in the Ebed Yahweh songs that we found a clear description of the passion, of a suffering for others, yet even they did not state that it was the messiah who would embody this servant figure. It is, in any case, to these songs that Jesus refers, sometimes quite clearly. In almost every allusion to the passion there is a word or phrase that recalls our songs: the bridegroom shall be *taken away*,[33] the son of man will be *delivered* into the hands of his enemies,[34] and especially, he did not come to be served, but to serve, and to give his life *as a ransom for many*.[35]

It can thus scarcely be doubted that during this rather fearful period Jesus was constantly preoccupied with that mysterious figure. He must become the Suffering Servant; he was prepared; he also made this known to his disciples. The atmosphere in which he lived was that spirit which the Christians would later define as the "spirit of sacrifice."

[25] Mk. 8, 31-33.

[26] Mk. 10, 32. When Luke (9, 51) also mentions the journey to Jerusalem, he says that Jesus "set his face," an expression taken from our hymns (Is. 50, 7). Jesus not only knew what awaited him, but he went of his own accord to meet his opponents, as was expected of the Ebed Jahweh.

[27] Without allusion to the resurrection: Mk. 9, 12; 14, 8; Lk. 9, 44; 12, 50; 13, 33.

[28] Mk. 2, 20; Mt. 9, 15.

[29] Mt. 23, 37-39; Lk. 13, 34.

[30] Mk. 14, 8.

[31] Mk. 8, 32-33.

[32] Mk. 9, 11.

[33] Mk. 2, 20=Is. 53, 9.

[34] Mk. 9, 31=Is. 53, 6, 12 (in the Greek and the Hebrew text).

[35] Mk. 10, 45; Mt. 20, 28=Is. 53, 8. 10.12.

At the same time, we see in this Jesus' basic optimism. For the songs of the Suffering Servant hold out the prospect of complete victory, which will be nothing less than universal salvation. His own death is balanced by the life of the "many," a formula which we must translate by "all." [36] This same positive conviction is moreover inherent in the title, "Son of Man," which Jesus so often applies to himself, especially when he is predicting his passion, for the Son of Man in Daniel is a figure of victory, God's chosen instrument in establishing his kingdom.[37]

It has been said that, viewed from the Old Testament, Jesus' originality consisted in combining the figure of the Son of Man with that of the Suffering Servant. It must not be forgotten, however, that both "identifications" and their "combination" require a supernatural insight on his part.[38] The most original factor, that which is most profoundly characteristic of Jesus, is undoubtedly the figure of the servant, for the glorious aspect of the Son of Man was expected by all the messiah-circles, but it was in deep contact with the Ebed songs, which formed the theme of his life, that Jesus experienced the expectation of so many humiliations (with redeeming solidarity, he would take the evil of others upon his own shoulders and so enter into his glory).

All this, however, does not signify that Jesus mechanically executed the gestures of a literary model. This was no copy which detracted from his spontaneity, but just as country life determined the metaphor and the climate of his preaching, the Suffering Servant of Yahweh was the inspiring figure which so vividly evoked his own destiny and thus was constantly in his mind. Jesus' loyalty and spontaneity will be even more clearly expressed in the climax of his life, the passion.

THE LAST CRITICAL MOMENT: THE PASSION

Jesus had ardently longed to celebrate this last Passover.[39] It will have been Thursday evening, and everyone did his best to carry out the prescribed ceremony as well as possible.[40] The lamb, which had been slaughtered in the course of the afternoon in the temple square, and brought home wrapped in its own skin, now lay roasted on the table: a substantial quantity. The climax of that evening, however, would not be the eating of that Paschal lamb. Jesus took bread, then wine and proceeded to an absolutely personal act not prescribed in the ritual. Also, it was not predicted in what a sublime manner this linked the spontaneous depths of his heart with two of the most exalted figures of the Old Testament: the paschal lamb of the Exodus and the Suffering Servant of Yahweh.

The evangelists mention an extraordinary prayer of thanksgiving, a eucharist, which undoubtedly corresponds to the moment in the long, prescribed prayer when the father of the household gave thanks for the deliverance from Egypt. They do not give us the literal content of this prayer, but the essentials, expressed in somewhat differing terms, are all directly linked with his death: "This is my body, which is *given* for you . . . This is my blood which shall be *poured* out for you." [41] Luke's formula is a clear reference to the Suffering Servant who is "given over" and who says that he dies *for others*. The texts of Mark and Matthew are even clearer: the blood is poured out "for many," [42] "for the forgiveness of sins." [43] The essence of the Suffering Servant, the sacrifice of his own life in place of others, is rendered forever in these brief words.

This was, indeed, a breathtaking moment in festive Jerusalem. Jesus was thus consciously celebrating a new pasch, that of the new covenant [44] and he was completely bound up in this event. He

---

[36] "All" as a personal pronoun does not exist in Hebrew in the plural; instead the Hebrew uses "many"; cf. the prophecy of Caiaphas: "One dies for *all the people*" (Jn. 11, 49-52).

[37] Cf. Dan. 7, 13-14.

[38] On the son of man in the gospels, cf. E. Sjöberg, *Der verborgene Menschensohn in den Evangelien* (Lund, 1955); P. Vielhauwer, "Gottesreich und Menschensohn," in *Festschrift G. Dehn* (Neukirchen, 1957), pp. 51-59; O. Cullmann, *Christologie du nouveau Testament* (Neuchâtel, 1958), pp. 118-166; H. E. Tödt, *Der Menschensohn in der synoptischen Überlieferung* (Gütersloh, 1959); J. Coppens, "Le Fils de l'homme daniélique et les relectures de Dan. 7, 13 dans les apocryphes et les ecrits du Nouveau Testament," in *Ephem*

Theol. Lov., 37 (1961), pp. 5-51.

[39] Lk. 22, 15.

[40] There is still dispute about whether this was the passover rite or not. Jaubert's new hypothesis concerning the day has not made the problem any easier. Cf. G. A. Jaubert, *La date de la Cène. Calendrier biblique et liturgique chrétienne* (Paris, 1957); "Jésus et le calendrier de Qumran," in *New Test. Stud.* (1960-1961), pp. 1-30; the thesis is entirely disproved by the criticism of writers like P. Benoit, in *Rev. Bibl.*, 65 (1958), pp. 590-594; and J. Leal, "Feria Quinta: dies ultimae coenae," in *Verbum Domini*, 1 (1963), pp. 229-237.

[41] Lk. 22, 19-20.

[42] Mk. 14, 24.

[43] Mt. 26, 28.

[44] Mt. 26, 28 par; 1 Cor. 11, 25.

would initiate this covenant by giving his life, like the Suffering
Servant. Tomorrow blood will be seen to flow; from today he gives
himself, in a new religious act, using the bread and the wine, which
may represent his inner thankful submission, but which are above all
necessary in order to allow his followers to participate in his sacrifice and in his prayer of thanksgiving. He himself will be the Suffering Servant in them, with them, in the deepest possible communion
with them. Throughout the centuries the Christians will continue
this eucharistic celebration in commemoration of him. And in his
own brief life, which will last but one more day, the Suffering
Servant is working more urgently than ever to become reality.

The Ebed songs, which up till now reflected the deep *meaning* of
his life, suddenly imprint their smarting pain in his flesh and in his
senses. It is a delicate task to determine exactly what Jesus felt and
thought and what later Christian tradition saw realized in him. It is
possible, even certain, that in describing Jesus' passion, Christian
tradition has borrowed too freely from Isaiah 53, the Ebed song
most closely related to what was known to have happened during
Jesus' last night and day. And yet, one may be sure that Jesus went
to meet his death with the mind of the Suffering Servant.

"Now I am reckoned with the transgressors," he remarked before
leaving the house for the last time,[45] and this is a literal quotation
from our hymns.[46] Very soon it becomes brutal reality, when he is
arrested in the dead of night, like a dangerous bandit, so that the
Scriptures should be fulfilled.[47] A few hours later, he hangs dying
on the cross, between "two others," after a last attempt to exchange
him for a notorious criminal, Barabbas, had failed.[48]

Another oppressive detail is Jesus' silence before the Sanhedrin,
before Pilate, before Herod, on the way to Calvary.[49] It is impossible not to recall the Suffering Servant, who went "like a lamb . . . to
the slaughter . . . so he opened not his mouth." [50]

We possess no further direct testimony concerning Jesus' most
intimate feelings during these hours of anguish. What thoughts,
desires, intentions, prayers, can have filled his human heart! Undoubtedly he was possessed by a peerless love for all men; the
Suffering Servant is the great embodiment of solidarity, who loves
others to the extent of bearing their sins. He must also have felt an
unequalled, intimate love for the Father that was completely personal, free and true. It is quite impossible to reduce Jesus' inner
experience to an imitation of any precursive figure, fictitious or not.

More than ever, he was himself. And yet, we may also assume that more than ever, he found a source of inspiration in the six-centuries-old Ebed songs, which he had learned and hummed as a child, and which provided at least one human outlet for the divine fullness of love that had to burst forth from him. This is how Luke saw him, for one of his last acts was to pray for his enemies. "Forgive them." [51] Thus were fulfilled the last lines of the closing hymn of the Ebed: ". . . yet he bore the sins of many and made intercession for the transgressors" (Is. 53, 12).

"HE REVEALED TO THEM THE SCRIPTURES"

To Cleophas and his companion, who made no secret of the fact that they were disillusioned by the tragic end of their master, Jesus, before making himself known to them, revealed the key of his life. "O foolish men, and slow of heart to believe all that the prophets have spoken. Was it not necessary that the Christ should suffer these things and enter into his glory?" [52] Luke adds that Jesus interpreted the Scriptures to them.[53] He is, indeed, the great exegete of the Old Testament, as Justin will repeatedly proclaim a century later. This attests to the fact that the predictions and prefigurations of the Old Testament were fulfilled in him, and the fact that the disciples had not understood this while Jesus was still with them, at the moment they were being realized. Whether it was the risen Christ himself or the Spirit whom he promised and who played the leading role in this subsequently granted insight is purely incidental.[54] In any case, the Christians now knew something of the basic theme of Jesus' life.

It is not only the evangelists who describe Jesus' state of mind with reference to the Ebed Yahweh figure. For Peter, the matter is crystal clear; speaking of the way in which a Christian must meet suffering, he recalls the example of Jesus and quotes a long extract from the most typical Ebed song.[55] So far as Paul is concerned, it is known that he seldom refers to Jesus' earthly life. It is thus all the more significant that, in one of his most brilliant passages, which

45 Lk. 22, 37.
46 Is. 53, 12.
47 Mk. 14, 48-49 par.
48 Mk. 15, 6-15, 27-28.
49 Mk. 14, 61; 15, 5; Mt. 26, 63: 27, 12-14: Lk. 23. 9: Jn. 19, 9.

50 Is. 53, 7.
51 Lk. 23, 24.
52 Lk. 24, 25-26.
53 Lk. 24, 27.32.44-47.
54 Jn. 14, 26; 16, 13.
55 1 Pet. 2, 22-25 (=53, 4-9).

rightly forms the heart of the Easter liturgy, he exhorts the Philippians: "Have this mind among yourselves which you have in Christ
Jesus." What was this mind? That he humbled himself, took on the
form of a servant (or slave) and was obedient unto death, even
death on a cross." [56]

Another text of the Pauline tradition describes the purpose of
Jesus' coming into the world as a fulfilling of God's will, with the
human nature prepared for him by God: "A body hast thou prepared for me . . . I have come to do thy will." [57] This obedience
unto death also became the source of inspiration for Paul himself,
who wished in his life to complete what is lacking in the Lord's
passion.[58] Paul sees himself truly proceeding in the footsteps of the
Suffering Servant in order to become "a light for the Gentiles." [59]

[56] Phil. 2, 5-8.
[57] Heb. 10, 5-7.
[58] Col. 1, 24; cf. 1 Cor. 11, 1.
[59] Acts 13, 47 (=Is. 49, 6); 18, 9-10 (=
Is. 41, 9-10); 26, 16-18 (=Is. 42,
7.16); Gal. 1, 15 (=Is. 49, 1); 2
Cor. 6, 2 (=Is. 49, 8); Phil. 2, 16
(=Is. 49, 4). Cf. L. Cerfaux, "Saint
Paul et le Serviteur de Dieu", in
Recueil Lucien Cerfaux, 2 (1954),
pp. 439-454.

V
Jesus
in Prayer

To know a person's devotional life is to enter upon the most secret ground of his being. We can never contemplate that secret in the full light of day. With the best will in the world we cannot reveal it ourselves, for there are so many obscure, impenetrable aspects to prayer, besides those aspects which are too ambiguous to be expressed in black and white.

Who can describe precisely what occurs during long hours of "aridity," and brief moments of "mystical communion"? How can we define that vague awareness of God's presence, our despairing cries for help, a sudden glow of happiness that fills our entire being? We have scarcely words to express the content of our prayer. What does it mean to us when we say, "Father," or hold a conversation with the Lord Jesus, or turn with childlike trust to the Virgin Mary, assumed in the glory of her Son?

The case of Jesus is much more complicated. His constant union with the Father, in the clarity of the infinite warmth of the divinity, is a profound mystery. Nor is it entirely possible to distinguish Jesus' "divine life" from his human experience. In him, the divine and human are inextricably linked. We can only approach the psychology of Christ and in particular, his devotional life (which is, by definition, the most intimate expression of his contact with God) with a feeling of great helplessness.

And yet, there are certain advantages. Others before us have already selected the principal points: the evangelists offer us a first-rate evaluation. It seems to me that we can gain more insight into Jesus' devotional life than is generally thought.[1] The evangelists

[1] Cf. E. von der Goltz, *Das Gebet in der ältesten Christenheit* (Leipzig, 1901); F. Heiler, *Das Gebet* (Munich, 1923⁵); J. M. Nielen, *Gebet und Gottesdienst im Neuen Testament* (Freiburg, 1937); A.

provide us with all the elements necessary to make our knowledge of Jesus, especially in prayer, an ever-growing discovery.

We shall attempt first to give a general and almost material survey of Jesus' devotional life to determine when and how he prayed. Then, we will deal with the *content* or qualitative aspect of his prayer. This, finally, should give us a better understanding of his last communal evening of prayer: the *eucharistic meal* which, exceptional though it was, can nonetheless be considered as the climax of a progressive habit of prayer.

Prayer Customs

In Jesus' time, the devotional life of a good Jew was enacted on four levels: the temple square (for the majority three times a year; for those who lived in or near Jerusalem, almost daily); in the village synagogue every Sabbath, and for the devout a couple more times a week, the daily prayer in the family circle; and, finally, the personal, individual prayers.

The gospels give us to understand that Jesus took a normal part in the official services in the temple. Jesus was brought up by religious people who journeyed every year to Jerusalem.[2] This seems to imply that neither Joseph nor Mary nor later Jesus himself, went to Jerusalem more than once a year, a custom which was in fact not counted a sin for the Galileans. Jesus made at least five pilgrimages during his public life: John describes Jesus' presence in Jerusalem during two Passovers,[3] for the celebration of Pentecost,[4] the feast of Tabernacles,[5] and for the dedication of the temple.[6]

Did Jesus feel *obliged* to go? John describes a great miracle in Galilee around the feast of the Passover.[7] By this he almost certainly wishes to show that the miracle of the loaves and fishes, as a pre-figuration of the eucharist, refers to a more exalted and definitive Passover, but this is not sufficient to prove that Jesus deliberately evaded the law of pilgrimage. The uncertainty about whether he would or would not attend the Feast of Tabernacles [8] seems to indicate that he possessed a greater freedom, although, too, it appears that he was normally expected to attend.[9]

It is even more important for us to know exactly how Jesus participated in these feasts. Two short but eloquent texts suggest his great fervor. Even from childhood he desired "to be about his Father's business," [10] and later he forcibly drove the merchants from the sacred enclosure, an act that reminded his disciples of the psalm verse: "Zeal for thy house will consume me." [11] An answer like that given to the Samaritan woman, set down by John at a period when there was absolutely no cultural contact any longer between Christians and Jews, also throws light upon Jesus' zeal for the ceremonies in Jerusalem, for "we worship what we know." [12] From this, I think we may conclude with certainty that Jesus sang along with the hymns and followed the priestly acts, while his heart was already filled to overflowing with that true adoration, "in spirit and truth" which he came to introduce.

One must arrive at roughly the same conclusions concerning the Sabbath gatherings in the synagogues. Until his thirtieth year, Jesus will have listened, together with the simple people of Nazareth, to readings and explanations from the pulpit and joined in the communal prayers. Most likely, he himself never asked to speak, nor was he invited to do so, so that later people wondered how he came to know so much.[13] All this changed, however, during his public life. The synagogue became one of his chosen places for teaching. We learn that he did not hesitate to cure the sick in a crowded synagogue,[14] although this was forbidden according to the usual interpretation of the Sabbath law, but we hear not a word of criticism of the synagogal ceremony itself.[15]

In Jesus' time, it was difficult to separate family and personal prayer. The prayers said at table had, in any case, a true family character.[16] Although we may assume that Jesus usually said the ordinary prescribed prayers over the various dishes, he nevertheless, on certain occasions, imparted a special cachet to them. The evangelists, for example, mention his prayer of thanksgiving (or blessing, not of the food, but of God who gave it) at the miracle of the loaves and fishes. The disciples of Emmaus, too, "recognized" him at

---

Hamman, "La prière", in *Le Nouveau Testament*, Vol. I (Tournai, 1958).

[2] Lk. 2, 41.

[3] Jn. 2, 13.23; 13, 1; 5, 1 is doubtful.

[4] Jn. 5, 1, at least according to the most accepted explanation of "a feast."

[5] Jn. 7, 2.

[6] Jn. 10, 22.

[7] Jn. 6, 4.

[8] Jn. 7, 1-10.

[9] Jn. 7, 11.

[10] Lk. 2, 49.

[11] Jn. 2, 17.

[12] Jn. 4, 22.

[13] Mk. 6, 1-6.

[14] Mt. 12, 2, etc.

[15] Cf. Mt. 6, 5; 23, 6.

[16] On these customs and the entire historical context of this section cf. Vol. I.

this particular moment, less undoubtedly from any special manner of breaking the bread than from the way in which he prayed.[17]

There seems no reason to assume either that Jesus neglected or abandoned the *Eighteen Prayers*, which had to be said three times a day, and were by no means mere ejaculations. In their definitive form drawn up shortly after Jesus' time, these prayers took up eighty lines of typescript. Admittedly the "Our Father," like this prayer, is composed in the first person plural, but this is insufficient reason for considering it a replacement. It is much more likely that Jesus faithfully but unobtrusively said this long prayer wherever he happened to be at the prescribed times.[18]

The same is undoubtedly true of the prayer, "Hear O Israel," or the "Shema," for Jesus quoted from this glorious profession of faith in answer to the question regarding the principal commandment: "You shall love the Lord your God with all your heart . . ." [19] Here, this prayer is in no way treated as a formula, but as something vividly present in the mind and perfectly expressing the only divine commandment.

Frequent Personal Prayer

According to a rabbinic saying, a good Jew prayed more than a hundred blessings a day, and, indeed, a deeply religious person is always finding opportunities to meet God in his life, to thank him and to implore him. It is remarkable how often the evangelists mention that Jesus prayed.[20] Even in a milieu in which prayer was an essential element of daily life, Jesus was conspicuous for his intense piety. He usually prayed alone, either in the early morning, as we are informed by Mark in a brief but unforgettable scene,[21] or when the day's task was done.[22] Luke even speaks of whole nights of prayer.[23] It was these long periods of prayer which especially attracted the attention of the disciples.

They may well have heard something of the content of that prayer, for like all his contemporaries, Jesus seldom prayed in complete silence. Part of his prayer was certainly "oral" and said out loud. In any case, they were firmly convinced that their master possessed a personal, distinctive manner of praying. One detail, which Luke either derives from tradition or which perhaps expresses his own theological vision, tells how Jesus taught the Christians' own prayer, the "Our Father," after having spent some time praying alone.[24] We may undoubtedly conclude from this that it reflects his own devotional life. It thus echoes Jesus' own ardent longing, first and foremost in his prayer, for the coming of the kingdom, and his deep solidarity with all mankind.

Without wishing, at the moment, to analyze the content of these prayers, we stress the fact that the atmosphere of Jesus' prayer recalls in a peculiar way what the moderns call "retiring." Jesus goes to pray when the people have departed;[25] he withdraws to a world where one can meet God, as it were, more intimately. This last statement may not be completely acceptable, for one cannot say that the eucharist and certain prayers, performed during moments of great emotion, either of sorrow or rejoicing, show us a Jesus less deeply absorbed in God.

Jesus, in any case, was not the person to restrict his prayer to the prescribed formulas, no matter how long they took. In his daily life, he did not forget God. Here, we are referring not so much to the general, vague and scarcely definable presence of God, which characterizes a contemplative disposition, as to the deliberate prayer which is the condition and consequence of such a disposition.

Jesus could begin to pray at any moment. One feels it in his words, which are imbued with piety. Moreover, the evangelists have cited certain instances that illustrate Jesus' perpetual contact with God and the ease with which he prayed. These instances were either important or merely caught the disciples' attention.

Characteristic, yet not so very important, was, for example, the "blessing" of the children. This certainly does not mean that Jesus made the sign of the cross over them, but rather that he gave them what the Jews considered a "blessing," in other words, a prayer of praise to God on the occasion of a meeting or event. Here, undoubtedly, Jesus lovingly rested his hands upon the little heads,[26]

---

[17] Cf. Mt. 14, 19; Lk. 24, 25; the "breaking of bread" is a formula which refers equally or even more to the prayer pronounced by the head of the family at the breaking, than to the breaking itself.

[18] Cf. Mt. 6, 6.

[19] Mt. 22, 37.

[20] Here is a complete list of the synoptics, in which the explicit prayers to be discussed later are omitted: Mt. 14, 19.23; 15, 36; 19, 13; 26, 27, 36-44; Mk. 1, 35; 6, 41.46; 8, 6; 14, 32-39; Lk. 3, 21; 5, 16; 6, 12; 9, 16.18.28-29; 11, 1; 22, 17.19.41-44; 24, 30.

[21] Mk. 1, 35-36.

[22] Lk. 5, 16.

[23] Lk. 6, 12.

[24] Lk. 11, 1-4.

[25] Mt. 14, 23.

[26] Mt. 19, 13.

which naturally pleased the mothers. In Jesus' answer to the protesting disciples we can perhaps assume something of the words he addressed to the Father: "To such belongs the kingdom of heaven." His warm voice, which the mothers heard, must have thanked the invisible Father for the kingdom, for the gift to the little ones. And so this blessing, mentioned in passing on a busy day, differs little from the "cry of rejoicing," a cry of deep thankfulness and exalted contemplation, with reference to the other "little ones," this time surely adult disciples, to whom the Father had revealed the things of the kingdom.[27]

Jesus' baptism, on the other hand, his temptation, the transfiguration and the passion were all important events and each was characterized by a special prayer. Prayer was also associated with decisions of vital importance for his own task and for others: Jesus prayed before appointing the twelve,[28] when the missionaries returned from their journeys (at least according to Luke)[29] before the miracle of the loaves and fishes—an event of exceptional symbolic import[30]—before Peter's recognition of him as the messiah and Jesus' far-reaching reaction,[31] and at the resurrection of Lazarus.[32]

All this shows us someone for whom God is always there, someone who constantly moves in an atmosphere where the human factor is not the only or the most important. Jesus lives in a presence.

A CONTEMPLATIVE ATTITUDE OF MIND

If we wish to learn to know the *content* of Jesus' devotional life, it is essential to distinguish certain aspects of it. In the following pages, we shall confine ourselves to four: the contemplative attitude of mind, supplication, the prayer of submission, and finally the pure prayer of praise. It should not be difficult to show how all essential elements are contained in these four types.[33]

A contemplative attitude of mind consists in the constant contemplation, admiration and awareness of God. Contemplation is never blind, but has always an object. It is scarcely ever entirely "general," for in this case its object can be nothing but "God." Our earthly knowledge of God is too meagre, too negative, to occupy us entirely for any length of time without including what God does. There can thus be no doubt concerning the object of Jesus' contemplation: God, who grants us the kingdom. We have already pointed out earlier how Jesus sees the Father at work in every-thing.[34] A short outline will thus be sufficient here.

Jesus sees God at work from the very birth of the kingdom; a true birth from the infinite compassion of God's loving gaze, re-flected in Jesus' own pity: two shepherds in search of the lost sheep.[35] He sees him, too, in the modest creatures which are none-theless eloquent witnesses of a God who has infinitely more care for people. For what are flowers, birds, ripe harvests and blue-green vineyards but means of showing us the Father and the kingdom? For Jesus, sunshine and rain are God's gifts to all men.[36]

Jesus must be truly accustomed to see all things in God when he can meet the sinner in a paralytic [37] and detect repentance and a secret love of God in a notorious woman,[38] just as he rebukes the foolishness of the farmer who boasts of his record harvest but is so poor "with God," [39] like the almost almighty judge who "fears not God" [40] and the young adventurer who has forfeited his own honor and the family's good name by sinning "against heaven" and before the face of his (earthly) father.[41]

Nothing moves Jesus so much as the people, especially the simple people, who are in God's hands. His harmonious love for mankind, closeness to nature and deep feeling for God are all eloquently expressed in the question: "Are not two sparrows sold for a penny? And not one of them will fall to the ground without your Father's will. But even the hairs of your head are all numbered. Fear not, therefore; you are of more value than many sparrows." [42] In the parallel text, Luke speaks of five sparrows sold for two pennies.[43] Some will say merely that sparrows are evidently cheaper in fives,

---

[27] Mt. 11, 25-27; Lk. 10, 17-24.

[28] Lk. 6, 12. In Matthew the episode comes immediately after Jesus' ex-hortation to pray to the Lord of the harvest, that he should send laborers (Mt. 9, 37-38; Mk. 3, 13 says that Jesus went before them up a mountain [prayed there?] and called them from there).

[29] Lk. 10, 17-24; the parallel context of Mt. is different.

[30] Mt. 6, 46.

[31] Lk. 9, 18.

[32] Jn. 11, 41.

[33] Cf. what has already been said about the degrees of love; the con-templative attitude of mind is the

same as attention for God; suppli-cation and submission are expres-sions of hope, while the prayer of praise is a pure experience of love, i.e., of joy in God. Cf. pp. 84ff.

[34] Cf. pp. 163ff.

[35] Mt. 9, 36-38; 18, 12-14; Jn. 10, 11.28-30.

[36] Mt. 5, 45.

[37] Mt. 9, 2; Jn. 5, 14.

[38] Lk. 7, 47.

[39] Lk. 12, 20.

[40] Lk. 15, 18.21.

[41] Lk. 15, 18.

[42] Mt. 10, 29-30.

[43] Lk. 12, 16-7.

while others will decide that there is some confusion about the
state of the sparrow market. What is certain is the extent to which
Jesus had become one with God. The expression, "Not one hair of
your head will fall to the ground," was not unknown to the Jews,[44]
but this in no way detracts from the piety of a Jewess' son.

The strongest expression of Jesus' contemplative attention for
God is found in St. John's gospel. It is a theological expression,
reflecting not so much the letter of his words as the meaning of his
entire life. This Johannine vision could be summed up in one sentence: All of Jesus' senses are anchored in the Father.

Jesus *sees* his Father; no one has ever seen God but he.[45] Nothing
of what he says is his own invention, but only what he has seen by
the Father.[46] He can do nothing of his own accord, except what he
has seen, for the Father loves the Son and shows him everything that
he does.[47]

Jesus continually *listens* to his Father. He speaks as the Father has
told him,[48] and his judgment is always infallible since he judges
according to what he has heard.[49] It is not necessary for God's
voice to be physically heard, although this does occur,[50] for everything that Jesus says has already been pronounced and listened to on
another plane; his teaching is not his own but the Father's.[51] What
preacher gives so little of himself while giving his all, because he is
like a microphone entirely directed toward another which vibrates
with the speaker?

The other senses, too, although less delicate, help to show the
contemplative union of Jesus with the Father. Since we humans
spend almost the entire day wondering what we shall eat, the feeling
of hunger may help us understand what takes place in the heart of
him whose food it is to do the Father's will, although the disciples,
with the bread in their hands, stand looking on in perplexity.[52]
Even more than this, Jesus feels the Father; it is like the touch of his
fingers which carefully placed the disciples in *his* hands [53] so that
both watch to insure that no one snatches them from those protective hands.[54] This is why Jesus himself will not feel lonely when all
his tangible friends abandon him. He knows that the Father is with
him.[55]

In Jesus is realized the intense yet despairing dream of the religious person: never to speak of God as of someone one remembers,
for true prayer never says "yesterday" or "last year," but is a looking upward *now* and *forever*.

VEHEMENT SUPPLICATION

"I came to cast fire upon the earth and would that it were already kindled. I have a baptism to be baptized with; and how I am constrained until it is accomplished." [56] Despite the uncertainty regarding the exact meaning of the fire referred to here,[57] these exceptionally vehement words allow us to gaze into the heart of Jesus, where powerful desires mingle and find an outlet in his prayer. There is tension in Jesus' life, and we know both the cause and the moment. The cause is the coming of the kingdom, the moment is the cross. Then he will be plunged into that baptism, in which he will be immersed as in a sea of bitter suffering. This tension, too, was not purely external, physical. It existed deep within him and found expression in that form of prayer which is essentially incomplete and will have no existence in eternity: the prayer of supplication.

As we all do, Jesus prayed for himself. It is highly likely that he too asked for his daily bread as he taught his disciples to do.[58] He never asked forgiveness for his own faults; he never showed any trace of repentance or of sin, but it is a positive truth that he begged the Father to lighten his agony.[59]

Yet Jesus' supplication is above all a passion for the kingdom. Until the end of the world his disciples will pray, "thy kingdom come," and this is not intended as an abstract, idealistic wish as when a person longs for a "better world" or the "sanctification of all." Jesus' prayer is concrete, addressed to a living person whose name must be glorified and who must be spoken to directly: "Father, hallowed, (glorified) be thy name!" This Father has a saving plan, a will to redemption: "Thy will be done." [60] Jesus undoubtedly betrays something of his own devotional life when he counsels us: "Pray therefore the Lord of the harvest to send out laborers." [61]

44 Cf. 1 Sam. 14, 45; 2 Sam. 14, 11; Acts 27, 34.
45 Jn. 1, 18; 6, 46.
46 Jn. 8, 38.
47 Jn. 5, 10-20.
48 Jn. 12, 50.
49 Jn. 5, 30.
50 Jn. 12, 30.
51 Jn. 7, 16-17.
52 Jn. 4, 34.
53 Jn. 3, 35; 13, 3; 17, 2.
54 Jn. 10, 28-29.
55 Jn. 16, 32.
56 Lk. 12, 49-50.
57 Among the explanations given: violent dissensions among families, etc. (cf. 51-53), the coming of the Spirit, the cleansing of all evil, spiritual ardor (cf: "then Elias rose up, a prophet as fire, and with words like a burning oven"; Jesus Sirach 48, 1).
58 Mt. 6, 11; Lk. 11, 3.
59 See also pp. 274ff.
60 Mt. 6, 10; Lk. 11, 2.
61 Mt. 9, 38.

These laborers are people like Peter, for whom he makes special supplication to the Father.[62] The harvest, however, is the whole of mankind, even the executioners who crucified him and for whom he puts in a good word.[63] When Paul sees anyone made to fall, he burns with indignation.[64] Day and night he was mindful of all the Christian communities, ardently begging for their salvation, their love and their happiness.[65] What then, must have been Jesus' intentions? Our imagination could not possibly encompass them all; it would not be able to bear their diversity, their multiplicity and above all their intensity and would become unhinged by the glowing desires that consumed the endless spaces of his wishes and affections. People are thin in their longings and fat with desires. How have we loved our nation, and loved all peoples, and begged the Father? We may even be disconcerted by the violence of some of the synoptic texts. Was Jesus really so vehement? Let us then read the theological supplications of John so that all may be one.[66]

SUBMISSION

The prayer of supplication is almost instinctive to human nature. It can adopt magical or worshipping forms and seems to be the most common religious phenomenon of all times. For who does not desire help, even from the gods? One can even say that almost all peoples have good desires, although they are too few and too brief. Was there ever a young generation that did not dream? But the transition from the broad terrain of desires to the confined and difficult world of reality can be made only via a steep and narrow bridge. Every affirmative step on that bridge brings us higher. Every hesitation halts the machine and every "No" sets us back a pace. If Jesus truly so desired the kingdom, his prayer of supplication would have to be transformed into acts of submission, of acceptance.

The prayer of submission not only caused Jesus to see the Father, but to long for him. It was a perpetual exchange, a complete transference. For submission means that an "I" gives itself to a "you," thereby accepting the will of the beloved as a source of its own strength. But this concerns only the *beloved*, for only love is capable of such sacrifice. This obedience is even the measure of our love. Jesus' measure was infinite, not only because each of his acts proceeded from a divine fullness, but because there was no limit to his gift of self. He was obedient unto death; he even gave his own life; no limit could withstand the force of his dedication to the Father.

Did Jesus find this easy or difficult? In all probability his life of submission was normally joyful and spontaneous. He had come to do the will of the Father, this was his calling from his entry into the world; [67] it was a daily act, like eating bread.[68] We may assume that for Jesus ,too, "to eat bread" was normally a pleasant thing.

In any case, we do not know if in his youth he sometimes found it hard "to be about his Father's business." [69] It is quite possible that conflicts sometimes arose, such as that mentioned on the occasion of a pilgrimage.[70] We do not know, however, whether the years of puberty, the arduous work, the contact with people who undoubt-edly were not all perfect, the growth of his own body and mind, made it difficult for Jesus to follow the way of his Father. It does not seem so. His resistance to the heavy temptations in the desert appears to have caused him no great strain.[71]

Jesus feels himself intimately related to all those who hear the will of his Father and carry it out. They are like brothers and sisters to him; it is a bond that makes him happier than the affection for a mother.[72] This tends to suggest that Jesus was unreservedly a "joy-ful giver" [73] whose will did not experience his submission to the Father as a perpetual struggle. It must even be said that Jesus was so deeply happy in the gift of himself that from this happiness could well up the stream of grateful homage which was his prayer of praise.

It therefore seems all the more strange, although one of the best founded facts of evangelical tradition, that Jesus passed through certain extremely difficult moments toward the end of his life. If we possessed only the scene in the Garden of Olives, described for us by the synoptics,[74] there might still be the small possibility that this was merely intended as encouragement for the faltering Christians who hesitated at the thought of martyrdom, although this would

[62] Lk. 6, 12; 9, 18; 22, 31-32.
[63] Lk. 23, 34.
[64] 2 Cor. 11, 29.
[65] From the first epistle (1 Thess. 1, 2) to the last (Col. 1, 9.)
[66] Jn. 17 *passim.*
[67] Heb. 10, 5-7.
[68] Jn. 4, 34.
[69] Cf. Lk. 2, 49.
[70] Cf. Lk. 2, 48-50.
[71] Mt. 4, 1-11; Lk. 4, 1-13.
[72] Mt. 12, 46-50.
[73] Cf. 2 Cor. 9, 7.
[74] Mt. 26, 36-46. par.

weaken its historical character. But what then are we to think of the
loud cry on the cross,[75] the psalm, "My God, my God, why hast
thou forsaken me?" which betrays a terrible torment of soul? [76]
Luke knows of another cry, evidently made months earlier, when
Jesus longs for the baptism of his passion while feeling "constrained" at the prospect.[77]

John, who is not inclined to obscure Jesus' majestic divinity,[78]
nonetheless mentions another incident, scarcely a few weeks before
Jesus' death. A number of Greeks wish to speak with Jesus, who
takes the opportunity to speak of the necessity for his sacrifice, his
falling into the earth like a grain of wheat in order to bear fruit. At
that moment Jesus prayed as follows: "Now is my soul troubled.
And what shall I say: 'Father, save me from this hour?' No, for this
purpose I have come to this hour. Father, glorify thy name." [79]

Perhaps the strongest exhortation not to gloss over the seriousness
of Jesus' struggle may be found in the Epistle to the Hebrews, in
which Jesus' solidarity with us is based on the fact that "in the days
of his flesh, Jesus offered up prayers and supplications, with loud
cries and tears, to him who was able to save him from death, and he
was heard for his godly fear. Although he was God's son, he learned
obedience through what he suffered." [80] This may be an allusion to
Gethsemane.

Jesus cried, and thus reached, according to the rabbinic scale of
values, the third degree of prayer: "There are three sorts of prayer,
and each is more lofty than the one before: prayer, cries and tears.
Prayer is performed in a low voice, cries with a loud voice and tears
are stronger than all." [81] A text like Hebrews 5, 7-8, is certainly no
pious invention: "The intense faith, the courage and the pitiable
condition of Jesus will have made a great impression on the writer.
No mere theoretical consideration of the priestly qualities or the
perfection of the messiah could inspire passages like this."

How could it be otherwise if Jesus is truly man? For that he was
truly man does not alone mean that his body was hardened by
physical toil or by his work for the apostolate; it means even more
than the bloody destruction of his physical heart which so soon
ceased to beat. More than anyone Jesus had to desire love and happiness, for the flame of his life had remained completely pure and he
was more aware of the happiness which the Father has prepared
for us. He stood in the midst of this seeking, unwilling humanity,
linked to it with all the fibres of his sensitive heart in everything

except sin. "The fear of suffering and death shown by Jesus in this supplication, proves how much he shared in the most natural and deepest feelings of man." [82]

Jesus' prayer was granted; during those dark hours in which every tender joy and enthusiasm was taken from him. "He learned (in a new manner, the perfect) obedience," which the Epistle to the Hebrews ascribes to his "godly fear." [83] He therefore becomes, not idyllically but in a real manner, a living model and the principle of salvation for all who wish to obey him.[84] Luke is right in presenting Jesus' last moment as a prayer of perfect submission: "Father, into thy hands I commit my spirit." [85]

PRAYERS OF PRAISE AND THANKSGIVING

To praise God and to glorify him is to transfer all our joy, our enthusiasm, our admiration, to him. From his early childhood Jesus was familiar with the ancestral "blessings" that are in fact prayers of praise. But since Jesus' time a special category of prayers of praise has developed, or at least a particularly warm although less "poetic" note can be discerned in the praise that man can offer to God. Christian prayer will become essentially a prayer of *thanksgiving*.

The prayer of thanksgiving, viewed here not as the friendly appreciation for a favor received, but as a grateful recognition of what God in the fullness of his love discovered and accomplished for us, differs from the prayer of praise only in nuances. Its object is slightly different. Whereas the prayer of praise is principally concerned with commemorating God's greatness and beauty in nature, and is thus more poetical in expression, the prayer of thanksgiving deals with facts: creation, the redemption, the story of salvation. Subjectively, too, there are nuances: the special characteristics of the prayer of thanksgiving are joy, humility, affection, perfection—

---

[75] Mk. 15, 37.

[76] Mk. 15, 35; Mt. 27, 46; the confusion of Eloi/Elias underlines the historical authenticity.

[77] Lk. 12, 50; that this baptism is martyrdom is sufficiently evident from Mk. 10, 38.

[78] Cf., for example, the scene of Jesus' arrest in Jn. 18, 4-8, with that of the other evangelists.

[79] Jn. 12, 27.

[80] Heb. 5, 7-8.

[81] Quoted by Schoettgen; cf. C. Spicq, *L'Epître aux Hébreaux* (Paris, 1953), Vol. 2, p. 113.

[82] C. Spicq, *op. cit.*, p. 114.

[83] Heb. 5, 7-8.

[84] Cf. Heb. 5, 9.

[85] Lk. 23, 46; this, too, is from the Psalms (Ps. 31, 6).

one has first meditated long and deeply on the goodness of the giver—in short, the typical warmth that wells up from a grateful heart.

Such prayers of thanksgiving are the highest form of human prayer, since they entirely correspond to the abiding relationship between ourselves and the Father.[86] Heaven is not a place, but life in a climate of ineffable thanksgiving. This gratitude can so detach us from our own egos that we become thankful for *all* that God does, even though we are not directly concerned, even for all that he is, for himself: "We thank you for *your* great glory." It can thus be safely assumed that this form of prayer was especially characteristic of Jesus, all the more since he, according to the New Testament theology, is the firstborn of the whole of creation,[87] the only high priest,[88] who knew that it had pleased his Father that in his humanity the whole of the fullness dwelled, to bring peace, through the blood of his cross, to all creatures, on earth as in heaven.[89]

This assumption is richly confirmed by the facts. Admittedly there are very many aspects of Jesus' prayer of praise and thanksgiving of which we know nothing. We know little of the words, the style, the images, the rhythm and the development of his devotions. It is not given to us to follow the young worker during a free evening or a pilgrimage to Jerusalem. We possess but little information concerning the content of his long hours of prayer during his public life. Nonetheless, it seems to me that there can be no doubt that the silent stones and rocks were witnesses then to something quite different from (fraternal) supplication. Jesus' words are too imbued with a deep, contemplative peace, and the effect of his presence, wherever he is and whatever he does, is too much an enthusiasm for and glorification of God [90] not to conclude that the tree that bears such fruits must be filled with such sap. Only those who are filled with God's glory can make others glorify God.

We have already spoken of the pure joy in God which echoes in Jesus' words and was noticed by his disciples.[91] It is this joy even more than sacrifice which transforms recognition into gratitude and determines the measure of our love. According to this positive fact, Jesus' most perfect prayer must have been his prayer of thanksgiving, and we would have to accept this even though no concrete description of such prayers had been preserved. But in actual fact, we do possess prayers of thanksgiving, naturally in an abbreviated form: the cry of rejoicing, the prayer of thanksgiving by Lazarus' tomb and the eucharist.

In his cry of jubilation, Jesus expresses his joy that a number of simple people, who had had no opportunity to study the Scriptures like the wise and understanding, had understood God's plan.[92] Thus, it has pleased the Father! Jesus expresses his joy, his thankfulness, in words that seem to be derived from the Song of Thanksgiving of the young men in the fiery furnace who had also understood the secrets of God.[93] Luke, who situates the episode after the return of the disciples, sees in this what we might call an "apostolic" prayer of thanksgiving.

With the resurrection of Lazarus, we have a different situation, one emotionally charged by the death of a friend whose passing brings so much grief that even Jesus weeps. The evangelist gives us to understand that Jesus had offered a supplication beforehand: "I thank thee that thou hast heard me." [94] Now he prays out loud, so that all will attribute the miracle to God. At once we see that such an intimate bond exists between him and the Father that he is certain in advance of the miracle: the Father always hears him. Jesus has never asked for anything and not received it. And what sort of things does he ask for? We may draw some conclusions from the bearing of the entire Lazarus episode, which projects far beyond Bethany. Jesus desires to be "the resurrection and the life" for all mankind.[95] We may say that Jesus gives thanks because in him the Father conquers death in the absolute sense of the word.

The third prayer is of such capital importance that it received the simple name of eucharist (the prayer of thanksgiving). We shall devote the whole of the following section to it.

---

[86] It would not be difficult to show that the "classical" division of prayer into four types (supplication, reconciliation, thanksgiving, and adoration) is far from perfect. Reconciliation is a form of supplication; adoration must be present in every prayer, and there is an infinite variety of prayers of thanksgiving so that some of them form the most lofty prayers of praise.

[87] Col. 1, 15.

[88] Heb. 3, 1; 4, 7, etc.

[89] Col. 1, 19-20.

[90] Cf. especially in Lk. (2, 20; 5, 25; 13, 13; 17, 15; 18, 43; 23, 47).

[91] Cf. pp. 90-93, 98-100.

[92] Mt. 11, 25-27; Lk. 10, 21-22.

[93] Cf. L. Cerfaux, "Les sources scripturaires de Mt. 11, 25-30," in *Eph. Theol. Lov.*, 30 (1954), pp. 740-746; 31 (1955), pp. 331-342; he defends the historicity of this prayer, its independence of John and its scriptural background.

[94] Jn. 11, 41.

[95] Jn. 11, 25.

THE MOST PERFECT PRAYER IN THE HISTORY OF THE WORLD

Every Christian knows that Jesus' Last Supper had a quite extraordinary significance, and that the most characteristic part of that supper was the twofold eucharist—thanksgiving over bread and then over wine—with what came afterward.[96] This fact clearly reveals the extent to which we are "historical beings." No one can contain or fix his existence in one moment; however it may annoy us or offend our taste for logic and deduction, we are made for *facts* and these always contain a sizable number of unforeseen elements. We cannot say because human nature is thus, the history of the world will evolve in this way or because this man's nature is thus, the course of his life will be such and such. In the same way we cannot say since Jesus is both God and man, his activity, his death, his prayer . . . will assume certain forms.

The Last Supper was one of these totally unforeseen and decisive events—in my opinion the most important moment in world history, so far as prayer is concerned. On the one hand, it is merely the continuance and normal climax of Jesus' devotion. Even in the brief outline given here, it will not be difficult to detect the various elements we have come across before: contemplative attention for God, supplication, submission, thanksgiving. On the other hand, however, it was a great surprise. If it is true that at certain moments a man can concentrate the whole of his vital force, and synthesize the entire wealth of his feelings and his will in one new and mighty gesture, then this must certainly have been so for Jesus during that night.

No one will ever be able to reconstruct the exact sequence or the precise words of this celebration. The evangelists' accounts are brief and scarcely give the impression of a real prayer. Moreover, our present liturgy makes us take it for granted that the wine prayer immediately followed the bread prayer although this cannot have been so. In any case the entire event centers around two prayers of thanksgiving. What was the content of these prayers and what was the significance of the consumption that followed?

It may be helpful to point out that, just before the paschal meal officially began, one of those present had to ask the head of the table why this night was different from the others, why, for example, unleavened bread was eaten. It seems obvious to assume that already at this moment Jesus may have said something of the bread he was about to eat, seeking his explanation not in the haste with which the Jews were obliged to leave Egypt, but in his own body and life.

In any case it seems likely that he spoke of the new meaning of the bread when, during the last thanksgiving, he held up the bread in his right hand, as prescribed. After this, he gave the "eucharisticized" bread [97] to his disciples, perhaps repeating what had already become clear: "This is my body," which for a Semite means roughly the same as "This is myself." Not one of them doubted that by eating, they also shared in that gesture, in Jesus' prayer of thanksgiving. Certainly, they all understood the allusion to the liberation, but this time not from Egypt: the bread of the true redemption is Jesus himself. This is as much as we can know, and for the apostles themselves it may all have been very hazy. They will understand better an hour or so later, when Jesus again departs from the ritual prayer, this time at the blessing of the cup with wine.

This thanksgiving over the wine, which was normally supposed to last several minutes, and was regarded as the most solemn and joyful moment of the feast, toward the end of the celebration, after the meal, will surely have enlightened them. We do not know if Jesus alluded, as was customary, to the deliverance from Egypt. In any case, he pronounced words of prayer that will have conjured up for all those present the scene on that same afternoon, when thousands of animals were slaughtered on the temple square and much blood had flowed and rows of priests caught the blood in gold and silver dishes, passed it on and finally poured it over the foot of the altar. This was a ceremony of "spilled blood."

[96] Cf. H. Lietzmann, *Messe und Herrenmahl* (Bonn, 1926); W. Gossens, *Les origines de l'Eucharistie, Sacrement et Sacrifice,* (Gembloux, 1931); E. Schweizer, "Das Abendmahl, eine Vergegenwärtigung des Todes Jesu oder ein eschatologisches Freundemahl" in *Theol. Zeitschr.*, 2 (1946), pp. 81-101; F. J. Leenhardt, *Le sacrement de la sainte cène* (Neuchâtel, 1948); H. Schuurman, "Eine quellen-theologische Untersuchung des lukanischen Abendmahlsberichtes" in *Neutest Abhandl.*, 19, 5; 20, 4-5, (Münster, 1953-1957); J. Jeremias, *Die Abendmahlsworte Jesu,* (Göttingen, 1960³); M. De Tuya, "La doctrina eucharistica de los sinopticos," in *Ciëncia Tomista,* (1957), pp. 217-282; P. Benoît, "The Holy Eucharist," in *Scripture,* 8 (1956), pp. 97-108; 9, (1957), pp. 1-15; J. P. Audet, "Literary Forms and Contents of a normal Eucharistia in the first century," in *Stud. Evang.*, 73 (1959), pp. 643-662; J. Steinbeck," Das Abendmahl Jesu unter Berücksichtigung moderner Forschung," in *Nov. Test.*, 3 (1959), pp. 70-79.

[97] An expression of Justin's, Apologia, 66, 2; 67, 5.

There stood Jesus now, with the chalice filled with red wine raised in his right hand, speaking of his own spilled blood in an ardent prayer of thanksgiving to the Father. Never before had the disciples heard so impressive a prediction: something terrible was about to happen, a bloody death. And how was it possible for someone to express so much submission to God's dispositions that he offered this "shed blood" in advance, in thanksgiving. For we must assume that it was not only after the thanksgiving that Jesus said: "This is my blood." Such a phrase would have been incomprehensible without an introduction. It seems more like the conclusion, which the others must immediately associate with the paternal and priestly task: to celebrate and give thanks to God.

The apostles will perhaps have been most struck by the painfully direct allusion to the bloody execution of their master. Yet, there were other, vital associations that must immediately have sprung to mind: "This is the blood of the covenant" [98] recalled all too clearly the covenant of blood, when Moses said: "Behold the blood of the covenant which the Lord has made with you." [99] This is the fulfillment of the promise of a new and eternal covenant.[100] It will be a covenant for all: "for the many," as the Servant of Yahweh intended it. This opened horizons of which they perhaps had never dreamed. Their dreams had always been much too small. But Jesus gave thanks, with his whole heart, with his whole body and blood. He was certain of the moment, certain of what God was doing now, and this filled him with joy. And he wished that all should share as closely as possible in his feelings and his prayer at that moment. He gave them the "eucharisticized" wine, which penetrated to the depths of their being, as an intimate bond with him.

Considerable dispute has grown up among Christians, especially since the Reformation, concerning the manner in which Christ was (and is) present in these "eucharisticized" foods.[101] Were bread and wine purely symbolic? Did they contain the power of Christ? Was he personally present, albeit in a mysterious, extraordinary, "sacramental" manner? It seems to me that the synoptic texts do not contain sufficient data to settle the matter one way or another. The gospels do not describe the reaction of those present, and in any case the abundant blood that flowed beneath the cross of Calvary will have deepened the apostles' insight. Would they ever have begun to celebrate that same supper with thanksgiving had they not witnessed the appearances of the risen Christ and the extreme ease with which he moved among his followers?

We are thus thrown back on other testimonies of the apostles, for only they can enlighten us. The earliest source is Paul, who shows little inclination to overestimate Jesus' earthly actions. That precisely he demands such deep respect for the bread and wine of the eucharistic blessings should cause us to reflect. "Whoever, therefore, eats the bread or drinks the cup of the Lord in an unworthy manner, will be guilty of profaning the body and blood of the Lord." [102] There seems to me no other explanation for this than a contact with the truly present Lord, all the more since Paul goes on to say that one must "discern" the body, and attributes physical consequences to its consumption because the Corinthians show too little respect for this body: "Many of you are weak and ill, and some have died." [103] The same realism is found in 1 Corinthians 10, 14-17, and is not at all weakened by the fact that Paul continues to speak of "bread" and "wine." [104]

Another of the disciples, too, confronts us with the mystery of the "real presence," for John's bread-speech, especially the last part, can scarcely be understood otherwise: "Truly, truly, I say to you, unless you eat the flesh of the son of man and drink his blood you have no life in you . . . for my flesh is food indeed and my blood is drink indeed. He who eats my flesh and drinks my blood abides in me, and I in him." [105] John realizes how difficult it is to believe this and speaks himself of the disbelief of his audience and the hesitation of the disciples: "How can he give us his flesh to eat?" [106] And Jesus says not a word that might resolve their difficulty.

[98] Mt. 26, 28; cf. Lk. 22, 20; 1 Cor. 11, 25.

[99] Ex. 24, 8; cf. Heb. 9, 15-22 with explicit quotation from Ex. 24, 6-8.

[100] Jer. 31, 31; cf. Heb. 8, 8-13.

[101] A detailed review of the theories on transubstantiation may be found in C. Vollert, "The Eucharistic Controversy on the Transubstantiation," in *Theological Studies*, 22, (1961), pp. 391-425. Cf. also the double number of *Summa Eucharista* (July-August, 1963) (*Praesentia Realis*, Nijmegen, 1963) (articles by B. van Iersel, W. Driessen, P. de Haes, and R. Vosse-Brecher).

[102] 1 Cor. 11, 27.

[103] 1 Cor. 11, 29-30.

[104] He follows the normal mode of expression as authors will continue to do who positively accept the *praesentia realis*. Similarily, Luke, who formally teaches the virgin birth of Jesus, continues to speak unconcernedly of "his parents" (Lk. 2, 41) and "his father" (Lk. 2, 33, 48).

[105] Jn. 6, 53.55-56.

[106] Jn. 6, 52.60.66-67.

We see thus that the Pauline and Johannine churches confessed and experienced the real presence of Jesus. So did the other churches, insofar as we possess any testimony concerning their eucharistic celebrations. We must thus conclude that for us, too, it will be an important step toward knowledge of Jesus when we consume him as food and drink in order to be included in his prayer of thanksgiving. For, although there have always been community prayers, if Jesus is truly present here, and especially present in those who take him to themselves (for all the texts show that this is precisely the intention,) we have here a unique manner of prayer upon which each person must take a stand, especially if he is convinced what gratitude he owes to God and how incapable he is of rendering it.

Because this last eucharist of the Lord is so unforgettable and so important, it is all the more regrettable that we should possess so little textual evidence for it. The synoptics are laconic in the extreme, they give us scarcely one sentence, although this contains the most essential words, which seem to have been pronounced (or repeated) after the prayer of thanksgiving proper. Luke suggests that Jesus incorporated a supplication in the solemn prayer of thanks: "Simon . . . I have prayed for you . . ." [107] When did Jesus pray for Peter if not just beforehand, out loud? This may seem a daring assumption to many. Do we then know nothing else about Jesus' prayer to his Father, standing, with the bread, and especially the chalice, in his hands?

Perhaps we do possess a prayer that closely approaches the letter of that prayer. If so, we find it in John. For it is, after all, remarkable that he, the only evangelist who alludes several times to the sacraments,[108] who wrote the eucharistic bread-discourse and devotes entire pages to the parting words, should pass over the Last Supper in silence. This omission has never been satisfactorily explained. Let us therefore venture a hypothesis: the privileged text, the most faithful rendering of Jesus' first and normative bread and wine thanksgiving, is John 17!

We may begin by noting that this prayer has always been thought to have a priestly character; it is even known as "the prayer of the high priest." [109] An acute author like Bultmann asserts simply that "the actual supper of the Lord was replaced by Chapter 17." [110] Others call John 17 "a sort of preface," thus the beginning of the solemn prayer of thanksgiving of the Mass [111] or of a "liturgical consecration." Thus encouraged, let us proceed to examine the details.

In the first place, it is remarkable in the extreme that John should describe Jesus' exact attitude: [112] . . . "he lifted his eyes to heaven." [113] The synoptics mention this same gesture at the miracles of the loaves [114] and, despite its absence from the synoptic accounts of the institution, it has found a place in our Roman consecration text! We shall establish on several occasions that John 17 coincides with our earliest liturgical Mass formulas, especially with the Didaché.

"The hour has come" seems entirely to correspond with Jesus' great desire to keep this Passover with his disciples.[115] The deepest intent of his prayer and of his whole life is immediately expressed in one phrase: "that the Son may glorify thee." [116] This became the refrain of the prayer of thanksgiving in the Didaché: "Thine is the glory, forever and ever," [117] and forms the conclusion of the Roman canon: "By him and with him and in him is to thee, God the Father, all honor and glory, world without end." With this mind Jesus' prayer could only be thanksgiving, although he never utters that word. Only he knows what the Father does through him, granting eternal life to all whom he gave him,[118] and what he himself was able to do for the Father: the work has been accomplished,[119] his name has been manifested,[120] the Father's message has been proclaimed . . . [121]

The prayer of thanksgiving also contains a supplication: "I am praying for them [122] (just as in Luke: Peter, I have prayed for you) that thou shouldst keep them from the evil one," [123] as in the Didaché.[124] For that matter, several other particular expressions like "Holy Father" (again in our prefaces) [125] and "your holy name" recall the Didaché.[126] What Jesus asks for his disciples is that they should be with him, wherever he is, to behold his

107 Lk. 22, 32.

108 Cf. Jn. 2, 1-12; 3, 3-9; 10, 34.

109 Since David Chytraeus, one of the founders of Lutheranism (1600).

110 Comm. on John, 1952[13], p. 351.

111 H. van den Bussche, *Jesus' woorden bij het afscheidsmaal* (Tielt, 1955) p. 166.

112 Durandus.

113 Jn. 17, 1.

114 Mk. 6, 41 par.

115 Lk. 22, 15.

116 Jn. 17, 1.

117 *Did.* 9, 2.3.4; 10, 2.4.5.

118 Jn. 17, 2.

119 Jn. 17, 4.

120 Jn. 17, 6.

121 Jn. 17, 8.

122 Jn. 17, 9.

123 Jn. 17, 15.

124 *Did.* 10, 5.

125 Jn. 17, 11; *Did.* 10, 2.

126 Jn. 17, 6; *Did.* 10, 2.

glory.[127] This is, in Johannine terminology, the same as we read in Luke: "So I appoint for you that you may eat and drink at my table in my kingdom . . ."[128] and both cases reflect the will of the Father: "The glory which thou hast given me I have given to them,"[129] which is the same as: "As my Father appointed a kingdom for me, so do I appoint for you . . ."[130]

But does this prayer of thanksgiving contain a sacrifice, a consecration? Undoubtedly: "And for their sake I consecrate myself to you."[131] This consecration is a gift of the entire person, a setting-apart. Bultmann, who is not concerned with finding a Palestinian origin for John, considers the allusion to the words of the Last Supper *doch wohl unbestreitbar*.[132] H. van den Bussche speaks of a "prayer of consecration."[133] To consecrate oneself is indeed the same as giving one's body and blood. Where the synoptics say that this was done "for the many"[134] or "for you"[135] our present consecration links both: "for you and for many." In John we find this same typical *for:* "For them, for their sake," further clarified with "so that they also may be consecrated in truth,"[136] which corresponds to Matthew's formula: "for the forgiveness of sins."[137]

Finally, there is the communion, which is recalled by the prayer, "I in them and thou in me, that they may become perfectly one."[138] This is a Johannine equivalent of "Eat, this is my body," and entirely in agreement with "He who eats my flesh and drinks my blood abides in me and I in him. As the living Father sent me and I live because of the Father, so he who eats me will live because of me."[139] And this communion idea merges into the longing for the definitive gathering, with the Father, as found also in the Pauline tradition, celebrating the eucharist "until he comes."[140] There is also a profound awareness of this oneness through this "one loaf"[141] which is even more strongly emphasized by the Didaché.[142]

We have thus two certainties and one question:

1. The high-priestly prayer of John contains all the essential elements concerning the eucharist known to us from other sources.

2. It contains these elements in an original form insofar as they are comprised in a solemn prayer of thanksgiving, and are not found only as an explanatory statement after the actual prayer as in the synoptics, who uncontestably offer an abbreviated form.

3. The question remains: How literal is John's rendering of Jesus' prayer of thanksgiving? Undeniably, the style is that of John himself, but "it would be reckless to consider this prayer merely as a

composition of the evangelist." [143] Here we approach very closely the attitude, the sentiments and, though this is less easy to determine, the words of the first canon of the Mass.

It would be a good thing to read John 17, bearing in mind an image of Jesus at prayer with the bread and especially the chalice in his hands. It would perhaps be even better to celebrate the eucharist now, especially from the preface onward, with the mentality and attitude of John 17, although the complicated structure, the use of a dead language and the air of mystery [144] which is hard to justify render this a difficult proposition to carry out. And even if it were easy, it would take a whole lifetime of religious experience before we could gradually come to realize what this prayer must have meant to Jesus. For to my mind this act had the most far-reaching consequences of any in the religious history of mankind.

[127] Jn. 17, 24.
[128] Lk. 22, 30.
[129] Jn. 17, 22.
[130] Lk. 22, 29.
[131] Jn. 17, 19.
[132] *Op. cit.*, p. 391, n. 3.
[133] *Op. cit.*, p. 168.
[134] Mk. 14, 24; Mt. 26, 28.
[135] Lk. 22, 20.
[136] Jn. 17, 19.
[137] Mt. 26, 28.

[138] Jn. 17, 23.
[139] Jn. 6, 56-57.
[140] 1 Cor. 11, 26.
[141] 1 Cor. 10, 17.
[142] *Did.* 9, 4; 10, 5.
[143] H. van den Bussche, *op. cit.*, p. 166.
[144] In the Eastern liturgy, on the contrary, the central part of the eucharist, i.e., the prayer of thanksgiving section, is sung aloud.

Part Three

The Mystery of Jesus

There is a law that dominates all human progress and all forms of knowledge—scientific, historical, psychological or simply the mutual knowledge of lovers. This is the law of simplification through intensification. Nothing and no one can resist this law of our spirit that desires always to progress toward a deeper zone while wishing at the same time to sum up everything in an ever simpler, more lucid and stronger synthesis.

It follows that the knowledge of God, which we call theology, and which is in concrete terms a pondering (meditation) on the history of salvation, will strive after depth. When it takes Jesus as its object, it cannot be content with analyzing his message; even his personality, as revealed in his actions, cannot be the tranquil destination of theology. From the question, "What were you like?" we must press on to "Who are you?"

This leads us to considerations that concern the deepest secrets of Jesus' being. We are attempting to penetrate a zone where the darkness is so great, or rather where the limitations of our own powers become so evident, that we can see no further, that is, to the mystery of his Person. A mystery is a reality pregnant with possibilities, a light so bright that we can no longer see the dividing line between what lies within our grasp and what surpasses human understanding, even when this is illuminated by faith. For this reason, the "mystery of Jesus" is a critical factor in every Christology.

It must be admitted that many Christians nowadays experience a strong and permanent feeling of "unreality" on reading many Christological treatises. They have the impression of living in two totally distinct worlds. The world of faith tells us of the incarnation of the Son of God, the infinite value of the redemption, our divine life as the result of the active presence of the risen Christ, our eucharistic community, the mystical body of Christ, the coming parousia. Yet when we are among people, watching the farmer at work, chatting with the worker at his machine, or squatting in front of the factory gates, when we see the rapid typist, the hordes of waiting passengers at the bus stop or station at six o'clock, everything surely appears different. Where now are the exalted reflections of the morning's meditation?

Where, even among the clergy, can we discover the face that conjures up for us the presence of Christ and transports us spontaneously into his world? It is very seldom that we meet the sort of smile which we feel must bear witness to an intense inner life by its imperturbable peace and communicative strength. Even in prayer, when we wish to test what we really believe of this incarnate one who carried on his presence into the eucharist, are we not troubled by doubt, uncertainty, a feeling of emptiness, of distance, of absence? And when we leave the church, with the firm intention of carrying on the love of Christ, as instruments of him who dwells within us, how often are our loftiest intentions not washed away by the first contact, the first word, so that we soon return to ourselves, taking pleasure in the purely human or somewhat less than human in a world without any flicker of redemption?

The explanation lies, in the first place, in the unavoidable darkness of our faith. We live in a time of trial, without the "light of glory" which will raise our understanding to the full contemplation of God. This obscurity, though, is made darker by guilt. It is we ourselves who have grown to live with, or even helped to construct, the dividing wall, by "retreating" from one world into the other and resigning ourselves to an ever divided and ever provisional existence. It is hard for us to live constantly in the one, great reality. When we give a party, what becomes then of the redemption? And when we enter the ball park or the factory, do we still believe in the risen Christ? It seems to us that it is easier to live "unconcerned," although we are willing to devote a minute or perhaps longer every now and then to religious matters. This means, therefore, that we accept an exception to the general law of love which states that love is always progressing either toward union or toward annihilation.

There is a third reason, more or less linked with these two: it is possible that our Christological concepts and the basic aspirations of our considerations (and theology) may be harmful. We must be particularly careful not to fall into one of these two abysses: interest in the *purely static*, and absorption in an *impersonal* direction, as trying merely to decide what "merit" is, or studying the history of the terminology. Before embarking on our project, we should first decide what exactly are the points of interest and choose a suitable direction for a profounder study of Christology.

POINTS OF INTEREST

To which centers of the mystery of Christ must we devote our attention? On the one hand, such a center cannot lie in any particular anecdote from his life, in a miracle or a debate; love, of necessity, demands synthesis. On the other hand, Christology consists in the knowledge of a Person, someone who had and has a history. It is impossible to reduce this personal knowledge to an "essential."

In order to know a person—and it would be heretical not to view Christ though his humanity—we must consider the development of his existence. The "mystery" of a person must well be deeper than the succession of facts concerning his life and the sum total of his qualities, but it can never be condensed into a fixed concept. For what date could one choose to perform this total survey of a being: birth, childhood, the decisive hour of adulthood, death. Any lover would consider it an intolerable mockery were we to say: "I know your loved one; he is a created being, consisting of soul and body; this is the essence of him." With certain nuances, this criticism is also valid of an exaggeratedly essentialistic view of the Christ-mystery: "I know Christ: he is a divine Person joined in hypostatic union with a human nature."

Nor can this term, "hypostatic union," ever clarify for us the mystery of Christ. It is a principle, an important one at that, which throws light upon the various phases of Christ's existence just as do the other principles: that he was wise, that he had a heart. Yet, while a principle can explain a great deal, it cannot sum up the essence of a human existence.

Unfortunately, we are not tilting at windmills.[1] How many treatises deal with the "knowledge of Christ" without distinguishing between "Christ before death" and "Christ in glory," between the knowledge he acquired as an adult man and what he possessed in his mother's womb? It is still very easy to find books that explore the "being of Christ" without even mentioning his resurrection, as though it were uninteresting to know the Lord as he is.

[1] On the two trends, one essentialist the other dynamic, at the Second Vatican Council, P. Schillebeeckx wrote in *Evangèliser*, 101,

We must not view the matter so statically; pinpointing one moment is insufficient to know a person, especially when that person is
Christ. Our points of interest will be widely distributed in a manner
coinciding with the plan of the earliest converted philosopher and
with the traditional structure of the "Apostles' Creed." [2] To know
Jesus in the various phases of his existence is to follow him in his
incarnation, his growth, his mission, his passion, his glorification and
his parousia. These will form the six chapters of this section, taking
as our two poles the birth and resurrection or, in liturgical language,
Christmas and Easter.

In Which Direction Shall We Explore?

Theological reflection, like any other, follows, either deliberately
or not, a particular intention that will decide in which direction the
various themes will be developed. The dogmas of the incarnation
and redemption, for example, lend themselves to considerable *philo-
sophico-historical* deliberations on the meaning of terms like "incarnation," "person," "nature," "substance," "consubstantial," "hypostasis," "satisfaction," "sacrifice," "penance," "evolution" and their
associated controversies.

One can also explore the mystery of Christ in an *ethical* direction
and examine in what manner this is a liberation and a task for will
and heart progressing toward peace and goodness. Even in an ethical
direction, it is possible to discover how in the prism of Jesus' humanity the entire human nature is infused with the light of his
divinity, to see what nobility the new creation conjures up before
our eyes. Nor should we neglect the *cosmic* approach: What is
Jesus' place in the evolution of the cosmos and particularly in the
framework of "the phenomenon of man"? Even when we have
exhausted the possibilities of one direction, there may still be much
to do elsewhere.

Which direction must we choose? This depends partly on the
circumstances. In the East, an aesthetical exploration may be considered of vital importance. The natural philosophers—as we all are
to a certain extent—attach particular significance to the cosmic
radiation of the "Light of the World."

And yet, we are not so much concerned with a contemporary
elucidation. The malady is more deeply rooted and the remedy is
simpler. We must decide what is *objectively* the indicated direction

for the further development of Christology and to this end we possess an indisputable norm. For though all points of view are interesting they are not all equally connected with the aim. And the aim of Christology can only be to know Christ. If, then, we assume that Jesus is a living Person, who clearly became man in order that we might attain his deepest mystery through his humanity, then the basic rule of all insight into human nature holds good for him too: "Love in order to know." Only the love of Christ grants the intuition that leads to a true knowledge of Christ. That in Christ which is a cause and consequence of greater love, is interesting to us.

This seems self-evident, yet, so many works run counter to this principle—slavishly following the "classical handbooks" or puzzling over the most complicated side issues—that a profane example is not out of place. What must I study in order to learn to know my parents? It is fascinating to trace the whole family tree, but it is much more fascinating to read their love letters when they were first engaged. It may be useful to go into the problems of the market, transport, the stock exchange because my father is in business, but I shall get to know more about him from one glance into his prayer in church or travelling. Everything concerning my father is interesting, but love tells me that some matters take preference. And what are they? Is the decision purely subjective? Not at all, for nearly everyone agrees on the best way to get closer to our parents, and simple psychology also expresses it as a principle: "To learn to know a person, become interested in what interests him."

Jesus was animated by love for the Father and for humanity. A Christological theme will be interesting in the measure that it reflects and clarifies this double love. A practical guide is the confrontation with what appeared fascinating to those who noticeably excelled in this love: the saints and the mystics. This makes it all the more disquieting that such a gulf should exist between the themes and treatment of the theological treatises and the spiritual writers. Theology has begun only very recently to free itself of the shackles of a slavishly adopted table of contents, padded with intellectualistic subtleties as in a geometry textbook. These works were moreover compiled in Latin and destined almost exclusively for seminarians and (to a much lesser extent) the clergy. On the other hand, the genre, "spirituality" has grown much closer to theology. This evo-

---

(1963), pp. 343-350 ("Impressions sur Vatican II").

[2] Justin, *Apologia* 31, 7 (the plan of his entire book); 42, 3-4, etc.

lution is a hope and a light: theological exploration must be so
directed that the hunger of a religious person is at once satisfied and
intensified. But this may not serve as an excuse for obscure, inac-
curate language. And the difference between theology (directed
toward the object) and spiritual training (directed toward the subject) must also be retained. In all this, the clarity and the objectivity
must bring us as close as possible to the stupendous mystery that is
God.

THE MYSTERY OF CHRIST IN THE GOSPELS

These reflections concern Christology in general. Can they also be
applied to the gospels? Undoubtedly! In the first place their arrangement: their scheme is exactly that which we proposed. The
Credo and the gospels are based upon a common project which may
be called "apostolic" in the full sense of the term. Both John and the
synoptics begin with Jesus' birth; Luke then deals with his growth
and they continue on with the identical sequence: public life, passion, resurrection, prospects of the parousia.

Concerning the direction, I think that the close of the last gospel
may well serve as our guide. John wrote that his readers might
believe that Jesus is the Christ, the Son of God, and that believing
they might possess *life* in his name.[3] His choice was limited but
anyone who thinks he has anything different to contribute, or that
he can elaborate, must do so in the same spirit. According to John,
that faith and that life are a personal, vital contact with love: "For
God so loved the world that he gave his only Son, that whoever
believes in him should not perish, but have eternal life." [4] "And this
is eternal life, that they know thee, the only true God, and Jesus
Christ, whom thou has sent." [5]

It seems to me that this goal cannot be attained by a purely
thematic grouping of the principal ideas and trends of the gospels.
Such a form of study is necessary as a technical basis, even for the
nonspecialist, but has little appeal for the whole person as an introduction to the *message* of the gospels.[6] For this one needs a contemporary approach. We need a bridge to integrate Jesus' message into
our view of the world, or rather one which links our problems to
the plan that God accomplishes through his Person. Integration of
necessity leads to confrontations with philosophy, mysticism and

the catechical experience of the Church through the centuries, and finally, with contemporary poetry, science and climate of life. Yet it may not lead us so far that we cannot recognize the gospels on rereading them. An easy and spontaneous return, in other words, an uninterrupted contact with the sources themselves should characterize any *Introduction to the Gospels*.

In actual fact, this will mean that every now and then we shall gaze far into the future while remaining too substantial for a reader trained in philosophy. It will also be necessary to situate the evangelical data within the New Testament milieu as a whole. We may certainly not allow ourselves to be tempted into coordination and concordism, but on the other hand, it is equally erroneous to isolate what one evangelist says (for example, Mark on the resurrection) from what we know from other sources concerning the faith of the community of which he was a member. This was not entirely possible in the preceding sections, since other sources tell us nothing of Jesus' preaching and little about his personality. Now however, regarding the mystery of Jesus, there is fortunately sufficient material on hand to approach the sparse and regrettably brief indications in the gospels in religious depth, and to gain a more accurate estimate of their bearing. Anyone who accepts this plan will be sadly compromised. The reader must be prepared to abandon the innocuous intellectual terrain and to see Jesus in *his* life, in our world. The writer himself is in a thankless position, for in every paragraph he will be found at fault. He can never achieve technical correctness; it could always have been done differently and, above all, better. It is almost impossible to speak of a fixed, uniform method of introducing "a true reading of the Gospel, at once exegetical and spiritual." [7] But there are times when one must make the attempt.

[3] Jn. 20, 31.
[4] Jn. 3, 16.
[5] Jn. 17, 3.
[6] We dare to refer to our little thematic studies and "exercises for self-study" in the two preceding volumes of *Inleiding tot de lezing van het evangelie* (Antwerp); a brief motivation in Vol. 1, pp. 8-10.
[7] See L. Cerfaux in the Preface to Vol. 1.

I
The
Incarnation

An educated and balanced person acquainted with the firm laws of sociology and the long history of "myth-creating activity" among all the peoples of our planet, must view with extreme suspicion any belief in an incarnation.[1] That God "came down from heaven and dwelt among men" is, after all, an almost universal theme of legends and mythologies. And even if one purifies and demythologizes the language, removing any suggestion of an airtrip and abandoning an antiquated view of the world, it still sounds unbelievable: "a divine person 'becomes' human."[2]

It is no wonder that theologians and apologists pile up proofs in order to render this fact "credible," but this is not our intention. We must attempt to grasp the meaning of this mystery, and to this end we will follow step-by-step the belief of the early Church.

This belief grew; it is much more evident in the fourth gospel than in Mark's. Can this not be considered suspicious? Legends, after all, tend to inflate their heroes, in this case even to the status of divinity. Yet, on the other hand, direct and completely unambiguous language, referring, for example, to Jesus as a child or to his very first public sermon, would tend to be even more suspect. Let us assume that a boy of eighteen, give or take a few years, declares without any preamble that he is God, and backs up his statement with the most impossible and scientifically unverified miracles. One might speak in such a case of a unique circus, but a religious person would probably not give the performance another thought. It is in Jesus' favor that in his case the procedure was entirely different. He left an impression which was hard to define. After his departure, people began to reflect, and the divine nature of his actions and his being became increasingly clear.

The same principle of gradual growth may also be applied with reference to an objection very current in the Graeco-Roman world: "If you believe that Christ is God, how can you explain that he only became man now?" [3] Here we have the enormous difference with pagan mythologies, the fact that the incarnation dates from a time when information could be documented and verified.

Let us consider the course of the world, hypothetically at least, from the evolutionist point of view: the painfully slow rise of life from a state of lifelessness, the sluggish growth toward the mammals, the extremely late appearance of *homo sapiens*, the prehistoric

[1] The bibliography on the dogma of the incarnation is naturally very extensive, but the critical study of the gospels under this aspect might almost be called slight. Cf. F. Tillmann, "Das selbstbewusstsein des Gottessohnes auf Grund der synoptischen Evangelien," in *Bibl. Zeitfragen* IV, 11-12 (Munster, 1911); E. Norden, *Die Geburt des Kindes, Geschichte einer religiösen Idee* (Leipzig-Berlin, 1924); A. Janssens, *Het mensgeworden Woord* (Antwerp, 1929); M. Lepin, *Le Christ-Jèsus Son existence historique et sa divinité* (Paris, 1929); L. Bieler, OEIOE ANHP, *das Bild des "gottlichen Menschen in spätantike und Früchristentum* (Vienna, 1935); W. Goossens, "De divinitate Christi juxta evangelia synoptica," in *Coll. Brug. Gand.*, 28 (1945), pp. 12.24; F. M. Braun, *Jésus, Histoire et critique* (Tournai, 1947); G. Sevenster, *De christologie van het Nieuwe-Testament* (Assen 1948²); F. Ceuppens, *Theologica biblica III: De Incarnatione* (Torino, 1950²); J. Dupont, *Essais sur la christologie de saint Jean* (Bruges, 1951) J. Guitton, *Le problème de Jésus Divinité Résurrection* (Paris, 1953); P.A.M. Henry and others, *Initiation théologique, IV: L'économie rédemptrice* (Paris, 1955²); W. Grundmann, "Sohn Gottes," in *Zeitschr. f.d. neut. Wiss.*, 47 (1956), pp. 113-

133; B. Lemeer and others," Jesus Christus," in *Theol. Woordenbock*, 2 (1957), cols. 2467-2541; P. Schoonenberg, *Het geloof van ons doopsel, III: De mensgeworden zoon van God: het derde geloofsartikel* ('s Hertogenbosch, 1958); V. Taylor, *The Person of Christ* (London, 1958); W. Marsen, *Anfangsprobleme der Christologie* (Gütersloh, 1960); H. B. Kossen, *Op zoek naar de historische Jesus* (Assen, 1960); B.M.F. van Iersel, *"Der Sohn" in den synoptischen Jesuworten, Christusbezeichnung der Gemeinde oder Selbstbezeichnung Jesu* (Leiden, 1961); W. Marchel," Abba Pater! La prière du Christ et des chrétiens. Étude exégétique sur les origines et la signification de l'invocation à la divinité comme père avant et dans le Nouveau Testament" (Diss. Pont. Inst. Bibl. Rome, 1961); Garcia Cordero, *Jesucristo como problema: Los grandes interrogantes en torno al Hombre-Dios* (Salamanca, 1961); T. De Kruijf, *Der Sohn des levendigen Gottes* (Anal. Bibl. 16, Rome, 1962); G. Schreiner, "De historische Jesus en de Kerygmatische Christus" in *Bijdragen*, 24 (1963), pp. 241-279.

[2] For more on this see p. 337.

[3] Cf. Celsus' difficulties in Origen's *Contra Celsum*, II, 1-8; Justin, *Apologia*, 46, 1ff.

periods, lasting hundreds of thousands of years, almost without culture, without writing, finally arriving at the era of the community, art, learning, high roads . . . If God wished to come among the people, this era was not the worst to choose. At this time, a few centuries after Abraham, it was possible to prepare a people which would be truly conscious of its sin, be capable of believing the impossible and of looking forward to a positive and definitive intervention by God in world events. All this, of course, does not necessarily "prove" that Abraham's faith was necessary or that a people of God had to be formed before the Son of God. It may however, lead us not to reject as abnormal a gradual clarification of the religious acceptance of a supernatural fact like the incarnation.

THE IMPRESSION THAT JESUS LEFT

What impression did Jesus make upon his contemporaries? What did he say of himself? Did people think that he was, or claimed to be, "God"?

The gospels, written by people who undoubtedly believed in his divinity, give us not a single pronouncement whereby Jesus would have simply stated "I am God." We may therefore safely conclude that Jesus never did make such a statement. The same holds good for "the Son of God," a title that was, in fact, used as a laudatory reference to persons who were in no way considered as divinities.

This truthful discretion on the part of the evangelists strengthens our confidence in the impressive series of indirect indications which they do give us.[4] These we can classify under four headings.

In the first place, we find ourselves in the company of someone who repeatedly makes such audacious claims that logically he must be considered higher than the prophets (including John the Baptist), than David, the temple or the angels.[5] Jesus is more powerful than Moses and assumes the right to perfect the Law [6] even on a very concrete and important point: the Sabbath.[7] Naturally, the evangelists regard all this from their new, Christian viewpoint, but we may certainly give them enough credit to conclude that Jesus acted differently from the prophets who always justified their interventions by referring to God, who had spoken to them. The prophets delivered a message, but Jesus never claimed to be a prophet. He calls himself the son of man, thereby recalling the puzzling figure of the Book of Daniel, whose origin is shrouded in mystery.[8] Jesus does not seem much concerned with justifying his actions and his attitude. He says what he says, he is what he is.

Even more daring and better founded from the critical point of view are Jesus' *actions*. We may be sure that he was in no way fond of instituting discussions on his "titles" or "dignity" which are such essential features of later Christologies. He did, however, intervene, often quite unexpectedly, in the history of his people or of some particular person. He forgives sins.[9] With astonishing spontaneity he performs a great series of miracles and considers himself as the only one stronger than Beelzebub; he constantly drives out the devil and shares his miraculous powers with his disciples.[10] He is everything in the life of these disciples: "Come and follow me," is in itself a daring invitation, but what are we to think of someone who dares to demand voluntary poverty, who even proposes family dissention and martyrdom for his sake.[11] We are instinctively cautious when faced with world-shocking claims to be the judge who will pass judgment on all: Can a person with such comparative power and success have really said such a thing openly? Yet the diversity of the texts and the extremely original form of some of them tempt us to conclude that Jesus himself insinuated that he possessed this supernatural authority.[12]

Nonetheless, all this could still be considered as merely "functional." It is conceivable that God might give a man a higher mission than that of prophet and messiah. This is why the third indication is the decisive one. There is a mystery inherent in Jesus' *religious* attitude, which allows of no solution within a purely human per-

---

[4] For the most part we possess on this subject only the arguments of the apologetics handbooks which are not exactly renowned for their critical sense. Even the list of indications provided by B. Rigaux in *Apologétique* (Paris, 1948[2]), pp. 1058-1059, glides too smoothly over the difficulties; the most serious of the recent Catholic contributions are those of Van Iersel (see footnote 1), Feuillet (see footnote 19), and P. Benoît, "La divinité de Jésus dans les évangiles synoptiques," in *Lumière et Vie*, 9 (1953), pp. 43-74.

[5] Mt. 11, 9.22.43; 12, 6.41; 13, 41.

[6] Mt. 5, 21-38.

[7] Mt. 12, 8 and the miracles on the sabbath; on the scandal they caused, cf. Jn. 9, 16.

[8] Dan. 7, 13-14. The term is found 13 times in Matthew, 14 times in Mark, 25 times in Luke and 11 times in John, and each time used by Jesus himself.

[9] Mt. 9, 2 par.; Lk. 7, 48.

[10] Mt. 10, 1.8; 12, 28-29; Lk. 10, 17-20.

[11] Mt. 5, 11; 10, 18.25-35.38; 16, 24; 19, 21.

[12] Mt. 7, 22-23; 13, 41; 16, 27; 19, 28; 25, 31-33.

spective. He who constantly stresses the equality of all men before
God, and criticizes any form of paternalism, especially in the religious domain, since we are all "brothers," [13] nonetheless arrogates for
himself a distinctive place when he speaks of his life with God.
Why is he accustomed to speak of "my Father" instead of "our
Father" or "the heavenly Father"? [14] From whence comes the
strange expression, "your Father," as though he himself belonged to
a different category from us? [15] And there is the most extraordinary detail, yet historically very difficult to refute: he calls himself
"the Son." [16]

What were the apostles to conclude from this? Can we accept
that a person—be he the noblest, the most brilliant of men, bur-
dened with the most exceptional task—should so set himself apart
from others? And he is at the same time the humblest of rabbis, the
intimate friend. It must inevitably have seemed strange to the disciples, some evenings, when they pondered on the events of the day.
Jesus' opponents pondered, too, and came to the conclusion that
Jesus was a blasphemer.[17] "This was why the Jews sought all the
more to kill him, because he not only broke the Sabbath, but also
called God his Father, making himself equal with God." [18] This
sentence of John's is more than a theological thesis ("Jesus is God");
it also synthesizes an historical revelation.

Finally, one must mention here a series of subtle *allusions* that
succeeded in creating a particular atmosphere, a dangerous atmosphere at that, for nothing less was involved than the personification
of Yahweh. Various Old Testament authors had had the idea of
introducing "divine wisdom" in a very concrete and demonstrable
fashion, as a person distinct from God, a daughter of Yahweh,
playing before his face, communicating with the people, plying
them with gifts, instructing and inviting them. No one had misin-
terpreted this literary game, but still less had any man of God ventured to apply it to himself. Yet, this is exactly what Jesus did.[19]
Wisdom claims the love of all men, and requires of her lovers that
they should value her more than any treasure, in order to be
"worthy of her." [20] These are also the terms in which Jesus demands love for himself.[21]

"And now my sons, listen to me: happy are those who keep my
ways . . . He who finds me finds life." "Come to me, all you that
desire me, and be filled with my fruits. To think of me, is sweeter
than honey." [22] Do we not hear an echo of wisdom's invitation in

Jesus' summons: "Come to me all who labor and are heavy laden, and I will give you rest. Take my yoke upon you and learn from me . . . and you will find rest for your souls. For my yoke is easy and my burden is light." [23]

Only wisdom enjoys the privilege of communion with God; she knows his secrets. No one can know God's plans but he to whom that wisdom is granted. No one knows God except he who abides with wisdom.[24] The celebrated "word of John" of the synoptics is in a similar vein: "All things have been delivered to me by the Father . . . and no one knows the Father except the Son, and any to whom the Son chooses to reveal him." [25]

"Wisdom cries aloud in the streets; in the open square, she raises her voice." [26] Jesus compares his generation to children sitting in the marketplace who are also not prepared to listen, and he concludes: "Yet wisdom is justified by all her works . . ." or ". . . by her children." [27] Here we have the term itself. Jesus is thus, in a certain sense, wisdom. He shares her fate, and those who refuse to hear will equally share the fate of those who reject the advice of wisdom when she calls and holds out her hand. "Distress and anguish will befall them; doom will approach like a whirlwind, they will seek her, yet not find her." [28] This, indeed, seems very similar to the lament over Jerusalem.[29]

One does not seem justified in attributing all these discreet plays upon words to the first Christians; yet, if it was, indeed, Jesus himself who knew that he was wisdom, one can go even further. "Come, eat of my food and drink of the wine I have mixed" [30] may throw a light upon the miracle at Cana, the miracle of the loaves and fishes and the eucharist. Jesus says that here is someone of more significance than Solomon, whose wisdom was sought after and

13 Mt. 23, 8-11.
14 Mt. 7, 21; 10, 32; 11, 27; 12, 50 etc.
15 Mt. 5, 16, 45; Lk. 6, 36; 12, 30.32.
16 Mk. 13, 32; Mt. 24, 36; Mt. 21, 37 par. Mt. 11, 27; Lk. 10, 22.
17 Mt. 9, 3; 26, 6; Jn. 10, 33.
18 Jn. 5, 18; cf. 7-8; 11, 53-57.
19 Cf. A. Feuillet, "Jésus et la sagesse divine. Le 'logion Johannique' et l'ancien Testament," in *Revue Bib.*, 62 (1955), pp. 161-196; "Les thèmes bibliques majeurs du discours sur le pain de vie," in *Nouv. rev. theol.*, 92 (1960), pp. 802-822;

918-939; 1042-1062.
20 Prov. 8, 17; Wisd. 8, 2; Wisd. 6, 16; cf. 3, 5; Prov. 3, 14-15; 8, 10-19; Wisd. 7, 8-10.
21 Mt. 10, 37.
22 Prov. 8, 32, 35; Eccles, 24, 26-27.
23 Mt. 11, 28-29.
24 Wisd. 8, 3-4; 9, 14.17; Eccli., 7, 28.
25 Mt. 11, 27.
26 Prov. 1, 20.
27 Mt. 11, 19; Lk. 7, 35.
28 Prov. 1, 24-28.
29 Mt. 23, 37-39; Lk. 13, 34-35.
30 Prov. 9, 5.

admired by the queen of Sheba.[31] He also refers to the fulfillment of
a promise made repeatedly in the Old Testament, that in the last
days the people would be instructed directly by God.[32] Now,
says Jesus, the rabbi is no longer needed; everyone is taught by
God.[33] Only if we recognize in Jesus the divine wisdom can we
discover the sense of this apparently anarchist statement, which entirely conflicts with the figure of a person who acted "with authority." [34] We thus arrive at a conclusion that Paul also reached by
completely different methods: Christ became for us the wisdom of
God, in him are concealed all the treasures of wisdom.[35]

WITH NO HUMAN FATHER

The strictly supernatural impression that Jesus had left upon his
disciples soon gave rise to curiosity concerning his origin. The accounts of his childhood by Matthew and Luke, John's prologue and
a number of texts by St. Paul, in particular the hymn to Christ of
Philippians 2, each gives a slightly different approach to this question, and so helps to clarify the mystery of Jesus.

Matthew possesses a number of details which he employs with
definite intent. We learn, for example, that the newly born fulfills a
number of prophecies; he is born in Bethlehem, he is descended from
David through his mother's husband. The strongest thrust in this
sober account, which by its very structure shows that the author
possessed no detailed information,[36] is the closing sentence of the
genealogical table: "And Jacob was the father of Joseph, the husband of Mary, of whom Jesus was born, who is called Christ." [37]
This seems plainly to indicate that Joseph was not the father of
Jesus. Was he then born of an adulterous relationship as was claimed
in Jewish circles? Matthew rejects such a suggestion; this conception is the work of the Holy Spirit.[38] God's creative power has led
to the fulfillment of yet another prophecy: "A virgin shall conceive
and bear a son." This must be considered as a climax to the series of
miraculous births in the Old Testament, for this child is not born of
aged parents or a barren mother. It has, in fact, no human father.

Let us try to imagine what this means to a Semite who is not
acquainted with modern biology and for whom "conception" is
something quite different from the union of two cells. For him a
new human being is created because the father, the active factor in

procreation, plants one of his own vital seeds in the womb of the mother who is almost as passive as the earth, a mere matrix. The child is not so much hers as the father's, upon whose knees she will lay it after birth. Where now this masculine intervention is replaced by a direct power from God, one must unavoidably think of a divine fatherhood, so the child is really "Emmanuel," God-with-us; an abiding presence of God in our midst.

THE SON OF THE MOST HIGH

Luke enlightens us further upon the milieu in which Jesus was born, although of course one must not judge this childhood gospel in the same way as one evaluates a modern reportage with flashlight photos. Jesus was born in a poor milieu (out of doors, laid in a manger, visited by a handful of wretched shepherds) and greeted in the temple by a greybeard and a still older widow.

But who is it who was born in this way? Luke is no more explicit than Matthew. Like the latter, but more picturesquely and with particular attention to Mary, he makes it clear that he is speaking of a virgin birth. Yet, the words he employs in order to reveal this mystery are the fruits of profound reflection. Without trying to decide here from whom these words were ultimately derived (from Luke, from his sources of information, from Mary herself), we shall content ourselves with stating the result.

In the first place, it is remarkable that the titles given to "the Son of the Most High" are precisely those which were traditionally reserved for Yahweh: He will be "great" and "holy"; "he is the "Savior,' " [39] For a Jew, the only one who can "save," especially in

[31] Mt. 12, 42; Lk. 11, 31.

[32] Is. 2, 2-4; Jer. 31, 31-34; Ps. 51, 8, 119.

[33] Mt. 23, 8-10; Jn. 6, 45.

[34] Mt. 7, 29 par.

[35] 1 Cor. 1, 24-30; Col. 2, 3.

[36] J. Racette, "l'Evangile de l'enfance selon Saint Matthieu, in *Sciences Ecclésiastiques*, 9 (1957), pp. 77-82; S. Muñoz-Iglesias, "El Evangelio de la infancia en San Mateo," in *Estudios Biblicos*, 17 (1958), pp. 234-273 cf. *Sacra Pagina*, II, pp. 121-149; G. Phillips and others, *De*

Mariapassages uit het Mattheus evangelie (Verslagboek Mariale Dagen, 1961; Tongerlo, 1962); F. Hofmans, "Maria altijd Maagd," in *Coll. Brug. Gand.*, 8 (1962), pp. 475-494; (1963), pp. 53-78; A. Vögtle, "Die Genealogie Mt. 1, 2-16 und die Matthäische Kindsheitsgeschichte," in *Bibl. Zeitschr.*, 8 (1964), pp. 45-58; 239-262.

[37] Mt. 1, 16.

[38] Mt. 1, 20.

[39] Lk. 1, 32; 1, 35; 2, 24; 1, 32.47.68; 2, 11.30.

the eschatological times, is God himself. This is why John the Baptist was also greeted as a precursor of God.[40] In addition, the newly born will not only be the "Christ of the Lord"; [41] he will be "Christ the Lord" [42] so that Mary can be greeted by Elizabeth as "the mother of my Lord." [43] Of what man can it ever be said that he will reign forever and especially that he will be the light of the peoples and the glory of Israel? [44]

For Luke's bible-reading public, the whole of this "theology-by-allusions" must have been extremely fascinating and significant.[45] But the artist who composed Luke, 1-2, went even further. His meditations—his poetical game, his theological theses; who can draw the distinguishing line—lead him to an even closer parallelism that seems to dominate and lend unity to his entire composition. His train of thought is roughly as follows: Mary is the daughter of Sion, image of the People of God, and to her comes Yahweh. He covers her with his shadow just as the glory of God filled the temple, and takes up his abode permanently among us, as in the ark.[46] I give here a list with the most striking parallelisms:

"Sing aloud,
O daughter of Zion . . .
The Lord, your God,
is in your midst,
a warrior who gives you victory"
                    (Zeph. 3, 14.17).

"Hail,
O favored one
the Lord
is with you.
Do not be afraid, Mary . . .
you will conceive . . .
and bear a son
and you shall call his name
Jesus"
                    (Luke 1, 28-31).

"Then the cloud covered
the tent of meeting
and the glory of the Lord
filled the tabernacle
and Moses was not able
to enter the tent of meeting
because the cloud abode
upon it and the glory of the Lord
filled the tabernacle"
                    (Ex. 40, 34-35 LXX).

"The Holy Spirit
will come upon you
and the power of the Most High
will overshadow you.
Therefore the child to be born
will be called holy,
the Son of God"
                    (Luke 1, 35).

"And David was afraid of the
Lord that day, and he said:
'How can the ark of the Lord
come to me . . .'
And the ark of the Lord
remained three months

"In those days . . .
Elizabeth exclaimed with a
loud cry:
(Blessed are you among women
and blessed is the fruit of
          your womb)"

in the house of Obededom	Why is this granted me, that
the Gittite,	the mother of my Lord
and the Lord blessed	Should come to me? . . .
Obededom	And Mary remained with her about
and all his household"	three months.
(2 Sam. 6, 9.11 LXX).	(Luke 1, 39-42, 56).

THE WORD BECAME FLESH

Not everyone will be equally attracted or convinced by Luke's artistic contemplation. Of more direct and universal appeal, within the grasp of businessman and thinker, are Paul's sublime phrases in the hymn to Christ of Philippians 2. It has now been fairly well-established that they assume Jesus' previous existence.[47] We might also mention various other "attempts" to put this mystery into words, but will confine ourselves here to what might in a certain sense be termed the climax of the apostolic penetration: the prologue of St. John.

Many generations of Christians have attributed an almost magical significance to this prologue; reading it would heal the sick, touching with this page would drive out evil spirits and bring peace to children affected by a mysterious fright . . . Why was this passage

[40] Lk. 1, 17.76.

[41] Lk. 2, 27.

[42] Lk. 2, 11.

[43] Lk. 1, 43.

[44] Lk. 1, 33; 2, 32.

[45] We sympathize with, but are not entirely convinced by, the suggestions of Laurentin (see footnote 46).

[46] According to S. Lyonnet, *Le récit de l'annonciation et la maternité divine de la Sainte Vierge*, (stencilled Rome, Bible Institute, 1954 and published by l'Ami du clergé, 1956), pp. 33-46; J. P. Audet, "L'annonce à Marie," in *Rev. Bibl.*, 63 (1956), pp. 346-374; S. Muñoz-Iglesias, "El Evangelio de la Infancia en S. Lucas y las infancias de los héroes biblicos," in *Estudios Biblicos*, 16 (1956), pp. 329-382; R. Laurentin, *Structure et théologie de Lc. I-II* (Paris, 1957), especially pp. 120-131; G. Philips and

others, *Maria in het boodschaps-verhaal* (Verslagboek Mariale Dagen, 1959; Tongerlo, 1960); J. Hermans, *De Bijbel over Jesus' geboorte en jeugd* (Masseik, 1960); J. Gewiesz, "Die Marienfrage, Lk. 1, 34," in *Bibl. Zeitschr.*, 5, (1961); pp. 221-254; H. von Campenhausen, "Die Jungrauen-geburt in de Theologie der alten Kirche," in *Kerygma und Dogma*, 8 (1962), pp. 1-26.

[47] Among the wide range of literature we mention P. Henry, "Kénose (Phil. 2, 6-11)," in *Dict. Bibl. Suppl.* 5 (1957), pp. 7-161 and the interesting comparison of the interpretations of L. Cerfaux, O. Cullmann and V. Taylor by W. Neill in *Expository Times*, (Nov. 1962), pp. 40-42. Cf. also M. E. Boismard, "La divinité du Christ d'après Saint Paul," in *Lumière et Vie*, 9 (1953), pp. 75-100.

thought to possess such powers? Perhaps on account of the first three lines alone, for they contain such an audacious renewal in the titles given to Jesus that only a strong apostolic personality would possess the authority to sustain them: Jesus is called "the Word." Can we detect here the influence of Greek speculations on the Logos ("the Word"), a sort of intermediary divinity between the supreme God and the people? Did the Mandeans perhaps play a part? This was a gnostic sect found east of the Jordan in which the personified Savior bore the name, "Knowledge of Life" (*Manda da Hayyâ*). Or can John simply be explained as giving inner force and religious depth to purely Jewish and Christian data, notably God's affirmative reply to his promises, the "Word" of God predicted by the prophets and finally become reality? [48]

One thing is clear from the beginning: the Word existed previously. This is the first thunderbolt in a series of three: "In the beginning was the Word." This brings to mind the first sentence of the Bible and at once links Jesus with the whole of preceding creation. "And the Word was with God": not, therefore, some more or less independent intermediate deity, but someone who enjoyed the intimacy of God. The Jesus whom you have seen walking and perhaps touched with your hands, came from the bosom of the Father. And now, finally, after two gigantic steps, which at the same time are still hesitations, the third step: "And the Word was God." This is blindingly clear. This Jesus of whom I am speaking now was God. No one has put this more strongly than John.

From this fact all our gifts proceed. With Jesus came life, which was after all nothing other than fullness of being. This was the light that shines so bright and crystal clear in the blue Palestinian sky and casts its limpid fullness over every landscape and every human face; [49] life, that compresses into one word all that a man desires, in contrast to the nothingness, which is death; [50] the glory, which literally contains and radiates the whole "weight" of the divinity. God cannot or will not give this glory to anyone; it is strictly personal, noncommunicable property, but Jesus came among us with that glory which the only Son receives from the Father.[51]

John has given several very striking interpretations of this "coming" of the Word. The first, in the prologue itself, describes, as it were, the cosmic drama: the light that seeks a way through the darkness and meets with sombre resistance. Yet, in this struggle those who are receptive are born to a new life, derived purely from

God, through a mysterious birth that must be like that of the break-through of light.[52] Realizing this, the evangelist reaches a peak of jubilation in which he directly links the two extremes in a cry of grateful faith: "And the Word was made flesh!" [53] The "Word," the greatest dignity (divine self-awareness, loftiness, and power) is here linked most intimately with "the flesh," the most realistic term to express our weak humanity, our smallness and limitations. An infinite distance is bridged; not in space, for John is not thinking of someone descending through the air from afar, but in quality. The disciple must think of the enormous difference between the law, and grace.[54] Hitherto, humanity possessed no true revelation of the invisible: no one has ever seen God, but in Jesus, united with the Father, God has revealed himself.[55]

The entire gospel of St. John is filled with the most remarkable expressions. Jesus is the "one who is sent." [56] This is not intended in the general sense, as someone who is convinced that he has a task to fulfill. Jesus comes from somewhere. Before his appearance in the world, even in such a way that he is not of the world, he witnessed "heavenly things." [57] He has seen the Father and comes only to impart what he then heard and saw.[58] He comes "from on high," has "descended" and is "not of this world." [59] It follows from this that even were one to trace the course of Jesus' life, from birth, one would still be far from knowing his origin.

John puts it even more strongly: Jesus was before Abraham, and Isaiah saw his glory.[60] What glory was this? Isaiah knew no other than that of the temple vision.[61] The glory that awaits Jesus in the future is essentially the same as what he possessed before the creation of the world.[62]

One might sum up John's vision of Jesus as follows: "He is the Son of God, who has come into the world." [63] It would, however, be exaggerating, even incorrect, to assume that John has always in

48 Cf. Deut. 30, 11-14; 32, 47; Lk. 1, 2; Phil. 2, 16 (cf. 1 Jn. 1, 1); 2 Cor. 1, 19-20.

49 Jn. 1, 4; 5.7.8.9; 8, 12 etc.

50 Jn. 1, 4; 6, 35; 8, 12; 11, 25; 14.6.

51 Jn. 1, 14.

52 Jn. 1, 4-5. 11-13.

53 Jn. 1, 14.

54 Jn. 1, 17.

55 Jn. 1, 18.

56 Jn. 3, 17-34; 5, 36.38; 6, 29.57; 10, 36; 11, 42; 17 *passim*.

57 Jn. 3, 12.31-33.

58 Jn. 6, 46; 8, 38.

59 Jn. 8, 23; 17, 14; 18, 36.

60 Jn. 8, 56; 12, 41.

61 Is. 6, 1-4; note the quote from Is. 6, 9-10 in the preceding verse (Jn. 12, 40).

62 Jn. 17, 5.24; cf. 6, 62.

63 Jn. 11, 27; cf. 1, 9; 3, 19; 9, 39; 12, 46; 16, 28; 18, 37.

mind the moment of the *incarnation*. Even when he writes of the Word that "became flesh," he is perhaps not thinking specifically of what took place in Mary's womb, or indeed of Bethlehem. He even speaks repeatedly (at the resurrection of Lazarus for example) of him who *comes* into the world, using the present tense.[64] It is in the *adult* Jesus that John contemplates the Word. It must even be added that the fourth gospel shows a great straining toward the future: the cross and the glory. Both constitute Jesus' "hour." Nonetheless, we are fully justified in continuing to speak of "the gospel of the incarnation," since this magnificent book is truly dominated by the idea of the union between that life that was with the Father from all eternity and that sensitive and vulnerable existence which we know so well from experience and which we call "humanity."

If we follow John we shall not linger with the bewitching tableau so sensitively depicted by Luke: an angel bearing a message to a holy virgin. The beautiful dreams that surround every cradle with glory, fear and hope are only a beginning. Although it is true that in every child is concentrated a family's dreams and aspirations for the future, in this case, our thoughts must penetrate deeper, past even that selfless virgin who so purely symbolized the rest of Israel. In this Jesus, we must see the Word, in our dark human community, the light.

On the other hand John is not satisfied merely to contemplate the result of this union between the Word and the Flesh. We must look past what is human in Jesus to the divine, to the God. This is an exceptionally difficult task: psychologically, because it costs us a considerable effort to wrench ourselves from our own little world, and theologically, because one can easily be mistaken in defining and expressing what, in fact, was united in Jesus. This did indeed happen, although even the mistakes contributed to the gradual intensification and clarification of the Christological dogma, as we shall briefly show.

CHRISTOLOGICAL DELIBERATION AND DISCUSSION

It is impossible and unnecessary to give here even a brief description of the further development of Christology. It would be wrong, however, to separate this further development from our gospels and to consider it as resulting from the conflict of later philosophies or trends. It is the gospels themselves which gave rise to it and which require the illumination of that dogmatic growth in order to be fully understood today.[65]

The school of Antioch, for example, clearly proceeded from the "ordinary, human" Christ, as he appears in the synoptic gospels. The Alexandrian school prefers the vision of John, that of the risen Christ, the God who comes into the world and irradiates it with his own being. Neither school was able to remain completely free of error. The pupils of the admirable Diodorus will see in Jesus' humanity a source of nobility of purpose and spiritual maturity, but sometimes tend to forget the mystery of their model's being. The admirers of Athanasius and Cyril of Alexandria, on the other hand, will often be so lost in their mystical and intellectual reflections that they, unlike John, lose sight of the insignificance of the concrete reality.

But before these two trends came into violent conflict with the names which they immortalized (Nestorius and Eutyches), the importance of Johannine terms had already been established in the summer palace of the emperor Constantine in Nicea, where in the Bythinian spring of the year 325 some 250 bishops held the first ecumenical council. A man fairly advanced in years—he must have been about sixty-five and had only been ordained at fifty,—was called upon to explain why he felt it necessary to teach that Christ was a pure creation of the Father. Arius, as he was called, was repudiated and exiled (this last by the emperor). He died eleven years later, days before his solemn reinstatement, but it is doubtful whether he would have endorsed the Nicean profession of faith: "the Word is consubstantial with the Father."

The further struggle, waged with pamphlets, treatises and patriotic and cultural incidental motives, would gradually clarify the concepts "substance," "nature," and "person," among others. But before this, Nestorius, Patriarch of Constantinople, would be called

[64] Jn. 1, 9; 3, 19; 11, 27.

[65] Cf. E. Hendrix, "Kerkelijke leer en theologie over Christus. De leer der Kerk in haar historische ontwikkeling," in *Theol. Wdnbk.*, 2 (Roermond-Masseik 1957), cols. 2489-2516; P. Smulders, "De ontwikkeling van het Christologisch dogma," in *Bijdragen*, 22 (1961) pp. 357-424; H. Grass-W. G. Kümmel, "Jesus Christus." Das Christus verstandynis im Wandel der Zeiten. Eine Ringvorlesung der Theol. Fak. Marburg," (1963).

upon to give an account of himself. The overimpetuous Cyril would insure that Nestorius would be condemned even before he arrived, and before the arrival of the other Eastern bishops and even of the papal legate (Ephesus 341). He was accused of "splitting Christ into two persons" and consequently of allowing Mary only the name *Christotokos* (mother of Christ) instead of *Theotokos* (mother of God). The historians must now try to decide, especially now that a sort of autobiography of the unfortunate bishop has recently been discovered, if his doctrine was really not open to an orthodox interpretation. In any case the struggle would continue to flare up again intermittently. Sometimes fortune favored the "Antiochians," sometimes the incorrigible "Cyrillians." Toward the end of the 5th century, many points had been cleared up: there are two natures in Jesus, a human and a divine, yet they neither mingle nor are separated. Each has its own viewpoint, and they are united in the union of the person or hypostasis.[66] In the 7th century, it was further decided that this double nature also implies a double will.[67] Scholasticism, from Peter Lombard (ca. 1150) onward, was to go more deeply into the principle of hypostatic union and determine the philosophical assumptions and consequences to be derived from it, although the two chief protagonists, Thomas Aquinas († 1274) and Duns Scotus († 1308) will not agree entirely on this point. Both assume that there are two natures and one person in Jesus, but Thomas, who evidently leans toward the Alexandrian school, views it more as one act of existence whereby the Word "assumes" the human nature, whereas Scotus, leaning toward the Antiochian dualism, postulates two acts of existence and an independent human nature "assumed" by the divine nature.

We mention this development here, not so much because both trends exist up to the present-day and have far-reaching results in practice, both within and outside the Catholic Church, but as a warning. Our Christological treatises urgently need renewal. The fact that any such renewal must be based upon the Scriptures gives me courage to frame a number of desiderata and what might be taken as a prognosis with regard to the future of Christology.

In the first place, intimate contact between dogma and Scripture must be restored. Subtle distinctions regarding the created substance, the distinction between the human nature and the human person are welcome, but they are not the last word and they tend to distract us from the object of our study unless we bear the biblical image of Christ constantly in mind. Fortunately, this "return to the sources" is now in full progress and splendid results have already been achieved in the biblical Christologies of L. Cerfaux (Catholic), O. Cullmann (Protestant) and V. Taylor (Anglican). Many dogmatic treatises are now crammed with scriptural quotations. This is an encouraging sign, but it is not yet a proof of victory, for exegesis is a scrupulous mistress and today grants admission to no one who is not, as it were, equipped with a diploma of intuition and proficiency in the matter of *Formgeschichte*.

On the other hand, there is the quite conceivable danger that students will content themselves with a fairly literal repetition of the biblical categories, somewhat classified. This is no proof of respect for the Word of God; respect for someone's words demands in the first place interest and thus, if one does not understand the language, a translation is required. Each period must translate the message of Christ anew. As far as the incarnation is concerned, which is essentially the manifestation of God's Word in a concrete person, or to put it more generally, of uncreated love in a created life of love, this translation will have to be carried out, it seems to me, on the basis of a confrontation between exegesis and psychology, mysticism, sociology, history and the natural sciences. We do not exclude philosophy, for the branches of knowledge mentioned must be considered not solely in their "experimental" aspect but also in their basic nature.

John tells us, indeed, that in Jesus "the Word of life was revealed" and that in him we "have communion" with each other and with the Father.[68] How can one comprehend the deeper significance of this without knowing how a spiritual being can reveal itself to a religious mind and what exactly are those profound relationships that bind men to each other and to God? This is a great undertaking for rational and experimental psychology, for reflections in depth psychology and a study of the mystic.

Besides this vertical dimension there is also the horizontal. According to Paul, the incarnate Word is the center and pinnacle of the ages: the one thing necessary is to know the depth, the height, the breadth and the length of Christ's love.[69] The theology of the incarnation must thus be concerned with the whole of creation,

---

[66] Decree of the Council of Chalcedon (451) (Denziger 148).

[67] Third Council of Constantinople (681).

[68] I Jn. 1, 1-4.

[69] Eph. 1, 9-11; 2, 7; 3, 14-19.

especially with the history of the human race, the efforts of the
religions, the elevation of the human body by Mary's Son, the significance of the quiet birth of the Word in a corner of Palestine for
the tremendous march of humanity toward liberty, love and happiness. The dogma of the incarnation throws light upon the dynamic
course of the entire creation, but the opposite is also true: the
incarnation can only be fathomed by those who see the bright light
of God shining upon the phenomenon of man in its widest context.

It may be that this overlong digression was not too short to express a desire which is cherished in silence by many and which can
cause seminarians to revolt against what is held up to them as the
classical "De verbo incarnato." This desire is, in the final analysis,
nothing more than the secret, sometimes sluggish, sometimes painful
process of consumption of the fascinating fire of which the first
sparks were preserved for us in the childhood gospels and in the
prologue of St. John.

II
Jesus as
Pilgrim

The discovery of Jesus as a pilgrim seems to be a grace reserved for our time. This discovery was made through experience. The famous "Wanderer of Christ" from the orthodox world,[1] the extraordinary history of the holy beggar, Benedict Labre, who scarcely reached the age of his divine model, and the wide circles that choose the "mystery of Nazareth" as the object of their meditation or the source of their inspiration in their family life or in fraternities, are all well in advance of theological reflection.

There are very few theological studies on this subject,[2] despite the fact that the gospels provide us with quite a number of data, and the first theologians—Justin and Irenaeus—devoted considerable attention to it. Their religious formulas would even lead one to assume that this point would be incorporated in the Creed.[3] Before beginning our study we must prevent any misunderstanding. We are not, under the aspect, "pilgrim," dealing merely with a number of qualities peculiar to the "wanderer." Jesus' journeys do not even come into the discussion. We are really concerned with an essential aspect of his "mystery," that is, of the deep situation and meaning of his life. For the life of man is in reality a pilgrimage: metaphysi-

---

[1] This book appeared in Russian in 1884, and was translated into German (1925), by Reinhold Walter; French: *Irenikon*, 4, (1928), n. 5-7 and at Neuchâtel (1943); English: by Dom Theodore Baily O.S.B. (1930) and Rev. R. M. French, Anglican; Dutch: by Karel Verhulst, 1941, and the Trappist Benoît De Moustier 1948. The ecumenical character is striking (Verhulst is non-Catholic).

[2] Cf. G. Brillet, *Le Sauveur, I. L'enfance et le début du ministère de Jésus* (Paris, 1956); F. J. Lustkandl, "Was wissen wir über die äussere Erscheinung des historischen Christus," (Thesis, Vienna, 1957); R. Aron, *Les années obscures de Jésus* (Paris, 1960). Particularly for the literature on Jesus' psychology, see footnotes 30 to 32.

[3] See footnote 26.

cally speaking, we are dynamic beings in transit, hovering between
nothingness and everything, bound for a mysterious destination.
Our existence is unfinished, still growing. The remarkable thing is
that this condition could be truly shared by the God-man. We are
at the same level as in the preceding chapter: what the incarnation
expresses in a rather vertical manner, has also a longitudinal dimension. This is what we mean by our "pilgrimage."

THE SITUATION OF THE PILGRIM

It is entirely clear to every thinking person that there are two
laws which give to our existence the dynamic character of a journey. The first law is that of growth; all human life is development,
biological and spiritual growth, communal development and striving. People are always on the move, looking toward the future; they
cannot possibly remain static. The second law states that they have,
personally and communally, a task, a commission. This is the law
of work. Our situation is already thus described in the first pages of
the Bible: "Be fruitful and multiply, and fill the earth and subdue it;
and have dominion over the fish of the sea and over the birds of the
air and over every living thing that moves upon the earth." [4] This
command is deeply imprinted in our nature, and in every heart and
every people dwells this longing for achievement, the desire to attain greatness through the work of one's own hands.

But completely different aspects of our status as pilgrims are revealed in the People of God, so much so, indeed, that only the
descendants of Abraham realized that they were a pilgrim people.
Since the first patriarch received the command to leave his coun-
iry,[5] the believer knows that he will be a pilgrim in a land that is
not his own.[6] For centuries, the growing people of Yahweh will be
literally guests among strangers, they will know humiliation and
oppression and when at last, thanks to their great guide Moses, they
finally come to possess their own country, they will look for a new
Moses who would lead them definitively into their new fatherland.[7]

The self-awareness of this pilgrim people is strongest among the
leaders and comes into particular prominence during moments of
crisis. How moving is Abraham's complaint at Sarah's death when in
the presence of his dead wife he explains to the Hittites: "I am a
stranger and a sojourner among you." [8] Jacob, the father of the
Jewish nation, sums up his whole life as follower: "The days of the

years of my sojourning are a hundred and thirty years; full and evil have been the days of the years of my life . . ." [9] The history of the people of the covenant, according to a splendid passage in the Epistle to the Hebrews, is one long progression of a people that walks in faith: "These all died in faith, not having received what was promised, but having seen it and greeted it from afar, and having acknowledged that they were strangers and exiles on the earth. For people who speak thus make it clear that they are seeking a homeland. If they had been thinking of that land from which they had gone out, they would have had opportunity to return. But as it is, they desire a better country, that is, a heavenly one. Therefore, God is not ashamed to be called their God, for he has prepared for them a city." [10]

Did they reach the "city"? No. For more than a thousand years, they had even no idea of an afterlife worth mentioning. But they sought peace and rest after their travels and their labors. In this too they failed to a large extent because they were not willing to follow the "paths" of the Lord. God therefore swore "in his anger" that they would not enter his rest.[11] It was Jesus, the high priest, who "penetrated to the heavens," who finally brought the redeeming solution to this painful problem of an entire people.[12] Such, at least, is the view of one of Paul's disciples, a Jew hard to identify but who undoubtedly possessed an ardent pilgrim soul. He wrote the Epistle to the Hebrews. This man had discovered Jesus and from then onward considered all his companions in the faith as pilgrims on the way to the glorious rest, in the coming city of God in which Jesus has already taken up his abode, for all Christians know that he, the firstborn of many brothers, triumphantly crossed the abyss of death and now prepares a place for us with the Father.[13]

According to this vision Jesus is our *archègos*. This is an untranslatable word combining the qualities of leader, chief, commander, guide and pioneer. An authorized dictionary defines it as: "He who, at the head of a row, sets to work and thus gives the decisive impetus." [14] In this sense Jesus' murder was an attack on the

4 Gen. 1, 28.
5 Gen. 12, 1.
6 Gen. 15, 13.
7 Deut. 18, 15-19; cf. the commentary Acts 3, 22.
8 Gen. 23, 4.
9 Gen. 47, 9.

10 Heb. 11, 13-16.
11 Ps. 95, 11.
12 Explicitly set forth in Heb. 3, 7—4, 16.
13 Rom. 8, 29; Col. 1, 18; Jn. 14, 2.
14 W. Bauer, *T.W.N.T.* (Berlin, 1958 5), col. 223.

"author of life," [15] our "Leader and Savior," [16] the "pioneer and perfecter of our faith," [17] the pioneer through whom God would bring many sons to glory.[18]

From this, we see that Jesus must be situated in, and at the head of, a pilgrim people. His journey ends with the "ascension," which we shall discuss in more detail later. The question now is: Was Jesus himself a pilgrim too, and in what sense? To obtain our answer we shall have to examine the characteristics of the people of the covenant which impart to them a mystical quality in violent contrast with all purely human myths dealing with the future. The believer walks in obedience: Abraham was the first heroic obedient servant; Israel desires with heart and soul to be dependent on God's law. The pilgrim of the covenant never acts on his own initiative.

This introduces a third factor: temptation. The chosen people were repeatedly tested, particularly during the march through the desert toward the promised land. The pilgrim is tempted by the noisy recreation facilities offered by towns and villages on his way. The tempter dwells in his own heart in moments of hesitation or discouragement or attacks him from outside, covertly or openly, suddenly or by stealth. No one escapes this law that has prevailed since Abraham, who was "tested" by God,[19] up to the last disciple of Jesus: "In the world you have tribulation." [20]

Thus we come to the last characteristic of the biblical pilgrim: loneliness. This is the heaviest trial for social man and it is inevitable. The pilgrim is a solitary even though he usually prefers to travel in a (small) group. The celebrations and the banquet will only be held when the last one has arrived; then there will be no more loneliness. But meanwhile, man must continue on through the night of loneliness, where no one really pays much attention to what is going on in the heart of the solitary traveller: he can never quite succeed in communicating his desires and longings, his deepest secrets. The doors at night are shut against him and the road, deserted. Every sensitive person must at some time or another feel a certain sympathy with Job, the classic model of the biblical pilgrim:

He has put my brethren far from me,
and my acquaintances are wholly estranged from me;
my kinsfolk and my close friends have failed me,
the guests in my house have forgotten me,
my maid servants count me as a stranger

I have become alien in their eyes.
I call to my servant, but he gives me no answer;
I must beseech him with my mouth.
I am repulsive to my wife,
loathsome to the sons of my own mother.

(Job 19, 13-17)

We can thus sum up the condition of the pilgrim in a double law, written in the very nature of our humanity, and a triple requirement of obedience, proper to those who are called by the God of the covenant:

1. the of growth,
2. the law of work,
3. obedience to God's guiding Word,
4. through the inevitable temptations
5. even in the lonely night.

Assuming that this sketch of our situation as pilgrims corresponds to reality, the confrontation of Jesus' life with these data will be a real touchstone for his humanity.

THE LAW OF GROWTH

The gospels, especially that of Luke, tell us how Jesus commenced his human existence. His mother conceived him through a particular intervention on the part of God, but afterward cared for her child like any other mother. "She was with child," says Luke, "when they set out for Bethlehem." [21] This was, indeed, a fitting birth for a pilgrim, out of doors and laid in a manger "because there was no room for them in the inn." And such a small pilgrim at that: "She wrapped him in swaddling clothes." [22]

It may appear banal to mention three times, as Luke does, that Jesus grew up and developed from a child to an adult.[23] But this was not so self-evident when speaking of a messiah. Traditions existed according to which the messiah would suddenly appear without anyone knowing where he came from. John alludes to these

---

[15] Acts 3, 15.
[16] Acts 5, 31.
[17] Heb. 12, 2.
[18] Heb. 2, 10; all the texts mentioned have the word *archègos*.

[19] Gen. 22, 1.
[20] Jn. 16, 33.
[21] Lk. 2, 5.
[22] Lk. 2, 7.
[23] Cf. Lk. 1, 80; 2, 40.52.

when he tells us that Jesus' enemies objected that they knew where he was from.[24] The fact that Jesus grew up is an important theme for the first Catholic theologian who lived a good half century after John. "Jesus grew up according to the development common to all men; used the ordinary necessities of living; ate various kinds of food and remained unknown for about thirty years." [25] This point is even included in a sort of credo, derived, according to Justin's custom, from the predictions of the Old Testament:

> We set down how it was predicted that Jesus,
> our Christ, must come,
> be born of a virgin,
> attain adulthood,
> cure all sickness and weakness and raise the dead,
> be despised, humiliated and crucified,
> die, rise again and ascend into heaven.[26]

This long journey through life reminds Justin of the phrase in Psalm 19, 5: "like a giant, joyfully runs its course." Indeed, he concludes, keeping to his custom of explaining the pagan mythologies as unsuccessful imitations of the Christian mysteries: "As a shadow image of Jesus they invented Hercules, a mighty man who travelled the whole earth as a pilgrim." [27]

A more eloquent proof of the importance of Jesus' "growth" for the theologians of the 2nd century is the testimony of Irenaeus. In his psychological view, human existence comprises five ages: man is in turn a baby, an infant, a child, a youth (between thirty and forty) and a man (between forty and fifty). Obviously, on the assumption that Jesus passed through all these ages, he asserts that Jesus, having been baptized at thirty, continued to live in Nazareth until he was forty, and died around the age of fifty.[28]

But Jesus' growth was not merely physical. Luke emphasizes that Jesus grew *in wisdom*.[29] This one word carries us deep into the heart of the mystery. How can someone, who is a divine Person from the very first moment of his existence, whose knowledge is thus not only perfect, but infinite, increase in wisdom? It is not necessary to take up a position here in the spirited debate which is being fought out on grounds of meditation and theological reflection, especially since the psychological interest of our period has begun to examine the question of Jesus' ego.[30] Leaving aside the theories of P. Parente and Bartholomé Xiberta on the one extreme and Paul Galtier, S.J. on the other,[31] we shall seek in the most direct way possible for a global picture presented to us by the Scriptures themselves. In this endeavor we feel that we have the backing of a number of excellent authors.[32]

The gospels give the irresistible impression that Jesus was in real contact with persons and things. He penetrated gradually into a new situation, made inquiries and learned, and was thus constantly acquiring new knowledge. This knowledge, usually called "acquired knowledge" by the theologians—Thomas Aquinas speaks of experimental knowledge—presumes a series of efforts, an attitude of alert eagerness to learn. His splendid parables, which bring the whole of human experience to life before our eyes, his pithy and

[24] Cf. Jn. 7, 25-28.

[25] *Dialogue with Trypho*, 88, 2.

[26] *Apologia*, 31, 7; cf. *Dialogue with Trypho*, 102, 2.

[27] *Apologia* 54, 10.

[82] *Against Heresies* II, 22, 4.

[29] Lk. 2, 40-52. Cf. G. Stahlin, "Prokopè," in *T.W.N.T.*, 6, cols. 712-713; there is literary contact with the Old Testament books of wisdom; cf. also Eph. 4, 13; the same term as in Lk. 2, 40.

[30] Good panoramas in B. Xiberta, *El yo de Jesucristo. Un conflicto entre dos christologias* (Barcelona, 1954), pp. 7-82; B. D. Dupuy, "Bulletin de théologie dogmatique," in *Rev. Sc. phil, théol.* 47 (1963), pp. 99-116.

[31] P. Parente, *L'Io de Christo* (Brescia, 1950); B. Xiberta, *op. cit.*; H. Diepen, O.S.B., "La psychologie humaine du Christ selon Saint Thomas," in *Rev. Thom.*, 50 (1950), pp. 515-562; (cf. pp. 82-118; 290-329 and 49 (1949) pp. 428-492; *La théologie de l'Emmanuel. Les lignes maîtresses d'une Christologie* (Bruges, 1960) denies the existence of any human ego in Jesus. On the contrary, P. Galtier, (*L'Unité du Christ. Etre, Personne, Conscience*. [Paris, 1939]) defends the view that humanly speaking Jesus is only conscious of his human ego.

[32] We mention especially K. Rahner, "Probleme der Christologie von heute," in *Schriften zur Theologie*, 1 (Einsiedeln, 1956), pp. 169-222, Fr. trans.: Bruges, 1959, pp. 115-181, Eng. trans: *Theological Investigations*; R. Guardini, *De menselijke werkelijkheid van de Heer. Bydragen tot de psychologie van Jesus* (Bussum, 1958); J. Galot, "La psychologie du Christ," in *Nouv. rev. théol.*, 90 (1958), pp. 337-358; Ch. V. Héris, "A Propos d'un article récent sur la psychologie du Christ" (i.e., Galot art. cit.), in *Rev. Sc. Phil. theol.*, 43 (1959) pp. 462-471; J. Mouroux, "La conscience du Christ et le temps," in *Rech. sc. rel.*, 47 (1959), pp. 321-344; F. Malmberg, "Uber den Gottmenschen," *Questiones disputatae*, 9 (Freiburg i. B., 1960); E. Gutwenger, *Bewusstsein und Wissen Christi* (Innsbruck, 1960); J. J. Latour, "La vision béatifique du Christ," (Thesis, Paris, 1960); E. Schillebeeckx, "Het bewustzijnsleven van Christus," in *Tijdschrift v. Theol.*, 1 (1961) pp. 227-251; L. Jammarme, *L'unità psichologica in Cristo*, (*Miscellanea Francescane*, Rome, 1962); Y. M. J. Congar, "Ce que Jésus a appris," in *Vie spir.*, 109 1963), pp. 694-706.

sometimes cutting sayings, testify to a great sensitivity regarding all that is human and are at once the most moving products and the most striking proofs of this sort of inner life of Jesus. He too normally expressed only what he had observed, what he had assimilated in his ever-active mind.

The gospels, in addition, bear witness to a higher sort of knowledge: Jesus read people's hearts, prophesied the future, knew secrets which even the most brilliant human intellect could not learn of its own accord. If we do not wish flatly to deny the facts we must assume a sort of insight termed "infused knowledge" by the theologians. It does not seem excessive to assume that this gift, peculiar to prophets, mystics and others who gain knowledge in a supernatural manner, was also granted to Jesus "in a richer and fuller measure than to any other human being" and that it involved not only isolated moments of inspiration but rather a habitual possession "which he could call upon when he thought fit." [33] This also explains something clearly suggested in the gospels and confirmed by the whole of tradition: Jesus never formally erred. His entire message, even viewed in the light of God and tested by the changing times, is completely trustworthy.

Yet even this "infused knowledge" was necessarily limited and conformed to the law of growth. Nothing in the gospels suggests that from his earliest childhood Jesus' head was constantly filled with the most diverse pieces of knowledge on every available subject. Such actual knowledge of past and future, of the natural and supernatural would unavoidably exclude any possibility of "acquiring" knowledge. St. Thomas, who is more inclined to underestimate the law of growth, assumes that "Jesus could experience something new every day," [34] and more modern authors find it self-evident that "during his youth he did not possess the sobermindedness of an older person, and as an adult was neither naïve nor childish" (M. Schmaus). This accords with the general atmosphere of the gospels, yet, they compel us to go one or two steps further. The limitation of Jesus' concrete infused knowledge is evident from the fact that he could suffer and feel fear and disgust. The suffering in the Garden of Olives cannot be reconciled with a perfectly pure insight and the radiant fullness of light peculiar to God and the blessed which excludes all suffering. Our joy and our grief correspond to the level and intensity of our knowledge so that the bitter grief of the son of man must be the result of a certain darkness in his range of ideas.

He, too, withstood, in his own manner, what John of the Cross has described so magnificently as "the night of the spirit."

Moreover—but this is less certain—we must assume that Jesus had no access to certain secrets which, though connected with his task, were evidently not directly essential to it. He who knew who he was and what he had to do, who saw infinitely more clearly than the prophets and astonished friend and foe with his bold statements and predictions, could not prevent one of the disciples whom he himself chose from betraying him and his work. He also expressly states that he does not know the moment of the parousia.

Jesus certainly knew beforehand that Judas would betray him, and predicted as much during the Last Supper; [35] this fact even gave confidence to the entire first generation of Christians, although they were not so much concerned with the actual case of Judas as with the growing violence of the persecutions and the defection of a great number.[36] But when John says that Jesus knew it "from the beginning" [37] this may quite easily mean from a long time ago, from the first weeks.[38] Otherwise, one is compelled to assume that Jesus deliberately chose a collaborator who would thwart him in the task imposed on him by his Father. There are indeed other "limitations" regarding Jesus' leadership of the apostles. He who selected them freely, and for a special purpose, was not in a position to allocate them the first posts. He cannot answer the sons of Zebedee on this point. Each position belongs to him "for whom it has been prepared." [39] This passive construction is quite transparent: only the Father knows and decides this.

Regarding Jesus' ignorance concerning the day of the parousia, many attempts have been made to read a different meaning into the words: "But of that day or that hour no one knows, not even the angels in heaven, nor the Son, but only the Father." [40] The unmistakable climax on the one hand, and on the other, the fact that the Father *does* know, rule out any possibility that "know" here means "know in order to communicate," as is often asserted. We must take it that this text, in which Jesus' divine sonship is emphasized as perhaps never before, means that Jesus has nothing to say about the

[33] *Summa Theol.* III q.11, a.8 ad 5.
[34] *Summa Theol.* III q.15, a.8. (Could Christ be surprised?).
[35] Especially in Jn. (6, 64.70; 13, 11.18-19, 21-30); cf. Mk. 14, 18.41.
[36] Jn. 16, 1-4, 32-33; cf. 14, 27-31.
[37] Jn. 6, 64.
[38] Cf. Jn. 15, 27; 16, 4; 1 Jn. 2, 7.24; 3, 11; 2 Jn. 5.
[39] Mk. 10, 40.
[40] Mk. 13, 32.

hour of the parousia, or that he himself had not received the revelation concerning it. This seems to me the most acceptable explanation which immediately brings us face to face, humbly and admiringly, with the mystery of God-made-man who out of love, stripped himself of all glory and adopted not only a human exterior, but true humanity with all its inevitable limitations.[41]

The gospels indeed postulate another, infinitely higher, form of knowledge in Jesus. We saw how he lived perpetually in great intimacy with his Father,[42] sometimes clearly aware of this bond and sometimes only vaguely. It is impossible to imagine an exact moment at which this awareness arose. There is no indication in any of the gospels that at a certain moment Jesus said to himself: "Well, now I really know that I am the Son of God. I didn't know it before. I thought then that I was simply a man like the others." This divine self-awareness, which Jesus thus must *always* have possessed, is called in classical Catholic theology the "beatific vision," since it corresponds in essence to the eternal privilege of the blessed: a direct, loving, contemplation of God, face-to-face, without the intervention of concepts and images. However, on historical grounds, and since Jesus' "earthly" awareness differs remarkably on several points from his later glorification and from the beatific vision of the blessed, one may be inclined to doubt whether it is, in fact, the best phrase with which to render Jesus' profound, divine self-awareness.[43]

It may well be splitting hairs, to try to decide whether it is this blessed vision of God (in which the divinity is the *object* of Jesus' knowledge) which makes Jesus aware that he is God (Galtier's argument), or does his human self-awareness *directly* attain his divine *self* (in Parente's view)?[44] In any case, this divine self-awareness seems to us an indispensable factor in the incarnation. Unless we assume that Jesus' human mind was fully aware of his intimacy with the Father and of his own divinity, then he can scarcely be called a divine Person. At the most, one might speak of a human body controlled by a divine being, in other words an apparent Person. But on the other hand, this beatific vision, with its indescribable heights of ecstasy and spontaneous glow of love, was not sufficient to illumine all the recesses of Jesus' mind. Some degree of limitation remained. Jesus was still a pilgrim.

This antinomy of fullness and limitation, a result of the union between the divine and the human in Jesus, is a mystery. It is usually formulated in these words which are directly linked with the aspect we are studying in this chapter: "Jesus was at the same time pilgrim and blessed." In the depths of his being, there dwelt an infinite peace, the light of God, yet, until his death, he was, in the real sense of the word, "journeying."

THE LAW OF WORK

The pilgrim differs from the tourist in that he has a task to perform. God, the great engineer of the universe, desires that the human pilgrimage should be characterized by the necessity to work. This world is a gigantic building yard, and even if one never leaves one's piece of ground or one's kitchen, one can help to construct a "better world." It is astonishing to see how Jesus shares in this law.

No one doubts that Jesus was a "carpenter." [45] Some suggest that he was really a smith, but we may take it as certain that he was the practical handyman who was responsible for all the complicated repairs and construction jobs in the village (something akin to the electrician or mechanic in the country villages at the beginning of the century). [46]

This fact, which inspires the progressive worker of today with courage and pride, was viewed with less enthusiasm in the Jewish world. At this period, manual work was, throughout the world, the unconsidered and humiliating task of slaves and women, and men wished to avoid it as much as possible. Even a great Christian like Origen in his polemic against Celsus denies that Jesus was a *tektoon* (worker). [47] The sophist Libanus sarcastically inquires of Julian (a Christian): "What is the son of the carpenter doing? Perhaps he is making a coffin (for Julian)?" [48]

The gospels briefly but clearly reveal to us Jesus' unknown existence at Nazareth. But even during his public life, he remained a

[41] Cf. B. Van Iersel, "De mens Jesus, in 't. H. Land," 14 (1961) pp. 97-101.

[42] See especially the article by P. Schillebeeckx, in *T.V.T.* cf. footnote 32.

[43] See Vol. 3, Chap. 1, n.4 to 35.

[44] Cf. Philippe de la Trinté, "A propos de la conscience du Christ. Un faux problèm théologique," in *Eph. Carm.*, 2 (1960), pp. 1-52.
Mk. 6, 3 (Mt. 13, 55: "the son of the carpenter").

[46] Cf. H. Hopfl, "Nonne hic est fabri filius?" in *Biblica*, 4 (1923), pp. 41-55; V. McCowan, "O tektoon," in *Stud. in Earl. Christian*, (1928), pp. 173-189; E. Lombard, "Charpentier ou Macon" in *Rev. Sc. theol. phil.*, 81 (1948), p. 4.

[47] Contra Celsum, VI, 34-36; cf. Höpfl, *op. cit.*, 45, pp. 42-43.

[48] Quoted by Theodoretus, *Eccl. Hist.*, III, 18, pp. 82, 1116.

worker. His apostles (and also the priests and laity of today) must know that they are laborers at the peak of the harvest,[49] sowers and reapers with a backbreaking job [50] for which there are few volunteers.[51] The apostles remain fishermen,[52] and in those days that calling bore no resemblance to a hobby.

Jesus' self-portrait, as presented by John, depicts him as the true shepherd.[53] Not as the kind shepherd and still less as the nice, sentimental shepherd. The Palestinian shepherd's job is heavy, despised and dangerous. He sets out into the mountainous solitude; everything depends on his sense of responsibility. He cannot be checked up on and, in fact, everyone knew that the majority of these people were completely unreliable.[54] But the true shepherd is constantly occupied in searching for the best places to graze, concerned for all his animals which he knows by name and habit, and for which he is prepared to risk his life.

The apostolate is a labor for which the wages are low, or rather for which the effort required is immense: "Do you not know," says Paul, "that you were bought with a price?" [55]

The priests may rightly say that they, too, are laborers. For us, too, May 1 is a great feast, for God's providence "which laid on the human race the law of labor" (Collect from the Mass of St. Joseph the worker) makes no exceptions. Not even for Jesus "who was considered as a carpenter and who, while he lived among men, wrought products of that craft—ploughs and yokes—whereby he taught us the symbol of justice and showed us what a life of labor is." [56] This text from the middle of the 2nd century is still valid today.

THE OBEDIENCE OF THE NEW ADAM

To work is to serve, yet, for the "nonbelievers" the ultimate aim of work may lie in his own development, the happiness of his family, etc. For sons of the covenant, however, life's task is signed by the guiding finger of God, by the forceful and enticing, admonishing and commanding, "words" of God. The pilgrim has been told his destination, the eternal city, and he must obey. His "obedience," too, must be something quite different from a family virtue. It is nothing less than the conscious receptivity of the creature to the saving plan of uncreated love. The fact that we thus, of our own free will, may comply with the carrying out of God's plan, is our greatest claim to nobility.[57] The fact that humanity resists this love is our tragedy. Adam's life, therefore, was a lost journey, but Jesus' obedience restored the harmony and made him the new Adam, the leader of the true pilgrims.[58] In this way, we were again united under one head [59] in a new creation.[60]

The life of Jesus was a continual and incomparable story of obedience.[61] The incarnation was nothing but the initiative which brought him to this condition. In this way he realized and revealed, silently, the aim and essence of the covenant. For the best that a person can do is not, as many thought, to bring a series of irreproachable sacrifices to the temple. "Therefore, he (Jesus) said, *when he came into the world:* 'Sacrifices and offerings thou has not desired, but a body hast thou prepared for me . . .' Then I said: 'Lo, I have come to do thy will.'" [62] This is the definition of obedience: to do the other's will. We find this same view expressed in Philippians 2, where the essence of Jesus' act of salvation is said to be that he emptied himself, took on the form of a servant and, being born in the likeness of man, humbled himself by becoming obedient unto death.[63]

In this attitude of obedience, one can, as it were, distinguish three degrees. At the highest level, we have the goal. In this respect, obedience is nothing less than agreement with, and complete devotion to, God's plan of salvation, which consists in "the desire to save all men and to bring them to a knowledge of the truth." [64] To work for this aim is no small thing. Jesus called the ideal the kingdom of God. It was his whole life. He was by no means a scrupulous little man carrying out orders from above at a given signal. Perfect obedience is free, creative, inventive, effective. Nowhere in the Old Testament—for

49 Mt. 9, 37; 20, 1-16.

50 Jn. 4, 35-38; Mt. 20, 12.

51 Mt. 9, 37; Lk. 10, 2.

52 Lk. 5, 10, and all symbols derived from boat and net.

53 Jn. 10, 11-18.26-29.

54 See Vol. 1, chapter "Village life."

55 1 Cor. 6, 20.

56 Justin, *Dialogue with Trypho*, 88, 8.

57 The scholastics speak of the *potentia oboedientialis*, literally: the power to obey.

58 Rom. 5, especially v. 19.

59 Eph. 1, 10: the theme of the "re-

capitulation" of all things in Christ is magnificently dealt with by Irenaeus (end of 2nd century).

60 2 Cor. 5, 17; cf. Gal. 6, 15; Col. 1, 15; Jas. 1, 18; Rev. 3, 14.

61 Cf. J. Guillet, "L'obéissance de Jésus-Christ," in *Christus*, 2 (1955), pp. 298-313: S. Gross, "Der Gehorsam Christi," in *Geist und Leben*, 29, (1956) pp. 2.11.

62 Heb. 10, 5-7.

63 Phil. 2, 6-8.

64 1 Tim. 2, 3-4.

where would the orders come from—do we read how the messiah had to set about choosing and training disciples, what parables he should think up, what his plan of action, his sacraments, his circle of friends, his feelings should be like. On these matters, the Person Jesus made his own independent decisions, brilliantly conceived and touching in their simplicity. It was precisely in such matters, which were of vital importance (and which in our situation find a pale reflection in the choice of partner, profession, undertaking or adventure) that Jesus showed himself to be most obedient. Here, he revealed the measure of his love.[65] The adult person can never wager his liberty and spontaneity for another's plans unless love is involved. If Jesus could say that his food,[66] i.e., his constant desire and his strength, was to do his Father's will, this implies that he had the joy of loving him.[67]

How uplifted must Jesus have been and how encouraged he is now when even his sinful disciples ardently desire to become, as far as possible, obedient instruments of the beloved who awaits the pilgrim.

And yet, it was not always easy for him. On a less exalted, but just as real plane which in a particular manner typifies the situation of the pilgrim, obedience is a difficult and sometimes thankless task. The great decree had to be carried through on a limited terrain, bounded in space and time, by someone with well-defined qualities, in a milieu, for the most part, independent of him. For Jesus, too, obedience meant accepting these limitations. He already began to do so as a child—Luke tells us that he was subject to Mary and Joseph.[68] Later, he became "a sign that is spoken against," [69] but he would never allow himself to grow embittered by unjustified allegations nor at the least partial failure of his mission.

He showed how absolute his obedience was on this level by integrating this persecution in his mission. His being revolted against the injustice with which he was treated and the grief it caused him, but his will dictated the answer. It was not, "Father, save me from this hour," but "For this purpose I have come to this hour." [70] This text may perhaps reveal something of that mysterious progress in obedience mentioned in the Epistle to the Hebrews: "Although he was a Son, he learned obedience through what he suffered." [71] The author is certainly not referring here to becoming morally perfect. Suffering is not capable of invariably making us more obedient, but it may give to anyone who accepts it in the right spirit a greater maturity, meekness and tenderness—all of which characteristics Jesus, in fact, possessed. When Paul searches for a concrete example of a meek person, the figure of Jesus comes, as it were, automatically to his mind (Jesus, obedient unto death).[72] Jesus himself was conscious that everyone could learn of him because he was gentle and lowly in heart.[73] This "learning" certainly does not involve absorbing, interesting facts of a religious nature,[74] but a basic attitude in which Jesus preceded us, namely, obedience to the Father. He even assures us that whoever is obedient to his Father's will is like a member of his family, and may consider himself his brother.[75]

There is yet a third level of obedience: the free bond of submission to a human person as a means toward the end, which is obedience. For fallen and wounded people, this is most useful and necessary. The Gospel itself advises us to practice brotherly instruction, and confession, taking stock of one's life, the vow of obedience and spiritual guidance are all in the same line. Jesus, moreover, instituted a hierarchy, people whom we must obey if we wish to be obedient to God. He himself, however, did not practice this form of obedience. It would have been impossible for him. He did not need this means, and it would have been false on his part to pretend that he did. He could not confess to any sin and no spiritual stock-taking or advice could be of any positive help to him.[76] Concerning his relationship to God, John's words regarding his knowledge of humanity are even more valid: He needed no one to bear witness.[77]

The unique character of Jesus' sanctity thus created a sort of barrier which his desire to be as we are could not penetrate. This at least is true of his adult life, for regarding his childhood Luke again insinuates his growth in favor with God and man was not unconnected with his submission to Mary and Joseph.[78] We are not justified in imputing any moral defect to the growing boy, but on the other hand, we may yet assume that his religious education had a positive content. As a son, he received the benefit of his parents'

---

[65] "Obedience is the measure of love" (Charles de Foucauld).

[66] Jn. 4, 34.

[67] Jn. 14, 31; cf. 8, 29.

[68] Lk. 2, 51.

[69] Lk. 2, 34.

[70] Jn. 12, 27.

[71] Heb. 5, 8.

[72] Phil. 2, 1-5: the inspiration for the christological hymn.

[73] Mt. 11, 29.

[74] To obey is, for example, not the same as saying "Lord, Lord" (Mt. 7, 21).

[75] Mt. 12, 50; Mk. 3, 35; Lk. 8, 21: with minor variants.

[76] Jn. 8, 46; cf. the contrast Jn. 16, 8.

[77] Jn. 2, 25.

[78] Lk. 2, 51-52.

mature insight and experience. In this respect, his relationship with them was that of pupil and master. His confrontation at the age of twelve with the teachers in temple—and the general astonishment underlines the extraordinariness of the situation—is a proof rather than a denial of this.[79]

HIS TRIALS

In biblical language, trial is the same as temptation. Both have to do with obedience in difficult circumstances. The temptation aspect, however, tells us that the difficulties proceed from a deeper source than our own evil nature or impotence. Our Lord, who had no faults, could be terribly tempted. Why was this? Because there is a tempter. The bible says that he was involved in the very first human sin, and that the struggle will only cease at the parousia.[80]

It is a hopeless undertaking to try to take the devil out of the bible. Jesus did not regard the devil as a fairy-tale figure or as the personification of evil. It is significant, however, that the devil's first appearance is only mentioned at the beginning of his public life. "Then Jesus was led up by the spirit into the wilderness to be tempted by the devil." [81] A maximum interpretation regards this temptation as the sole and decisive one, upon the result of which depended the whole further course of events.[82] It is, on the other hand, an unjustified minimalizing to see in this story nothing but a model discussion, on the rabbinic pattern, in which two opponents try to confound each other with arguments from the scriptures.[83] The true perspective will be more in keeping with Jesus' words at the Last Supper as recorded by Luke: "You are those who have continued with me in my trials." [84] This signifies that these trials were frequent, even the normal condition of Jesus' public life: Jesus "was tempted in every respect." [85]

This does not mean that the tempter does not resort to tested weapons or neglects to probe the weak spots of our system. He lurks in hunger, in the lust for power, in the desire for happiness, or the aversion to death; we see this in the temptations in the desert and in the Garden of Olives. He is even more skillful at making use of disillusionment, avarice, and jealousy, thereby poisoning human relationships so horribly that—even taking into account personal weakness and malice—they lead to such incomprehensible results as this: the righteous one was disposed of with the connivance of a traitor, a high priest, members of the councils, the mob, and a fairly important Roman official.

Just because the devil knows how to mobilize and maneuver the forces of evil, Jesus' victory has a cosmic effect: the ruler of this world is cast out; [86] his power is broken. Jesus is the cause and model of our victories over the tempter, [87] for, whether we are speaking of Jesus or ourselves: "We are not contending against flesh and blood, but against principalities, against the powers, against the world rulers of this present darkness, against the spiritual hosts of wickedness in the heavenly places." [88] Here we have the term, "darkness," which is so typical of the pilgrim who feels himself isolated in temptation as Jesus was in the desert, when even during his agony he could not find one of his closest and most beloved disciples to watch one hour with him.

Before examining this loneliness, it is necessary to point out one difference between Jesus and ourselves: "He was in every respect tempted as we are, but without sinning." [89] This does not merely imply that Jesus did not, in fact, commit a sin. Without making any formal declaration, the gospels suggest that it was impossible for Jesus to sin, for usually, temptation finds in us a certain complicity in that more or less accepted and even cherished pleasure which we call desire and of which James says: "each person is tempted when he is lured and enticed by his own desire. Then desire, when it has

[79] Lk. 2, 47-48.

[80] Gen. 3, 1 Hff; Rev. 20, 10.

[81] Mt. 4, 1. Cf. E. Fascher, *Jesus und der Satan, Eine Studie zur Auslegung der Versuchungsgeschichte* (Halle, 1949); J. Dupont, "L'arrière-fonds biblique du récit des tentations de Jésus," in *New Test. Stud.*, 2 (1956-57) pp. 287-304; G. Vann-P. K. Meagher, *Stones or Bread. A study of Christ's temptations* (London, 1957); M. Steiner, "La tentation de Jésus dans l'interpretation patristique de Saint Justin à Origène," in *Et. Bibl.* (Paris, 1962).

[82] H. Seeseman, "Piera," in *T.W.N.T.*, 6, pp. 33-37. He asserts that at this time Jesus could sin. Nevertheless, this is not a condition of a true

struggle nor of human freedom. It is, on the contrary, impossible for a divine Person to commit a sinful act; to assume the possibility of sin is to rule out a true incarnation.

[83] Cf. K. S. Kuhn, "Pierasmos-hamartia—sarx im N.T. und die damit Zusammen-hangenden Vorstelllungen," in *Zeitschr. f. Theol. u. Kirche*, 49 (1952), pp. 200-222.

[84] Lk. 22, 28.

[85] Heb. 4, 15 (Kata panta); cf. O. Michl, *Der Brief an die Hebräer* (Krit. exeg. Komm. N.T., 7th imp.), p. 55.

[86] Jn. 12, 31.

[87] Heb. 2, 18; 4, 15.

[88] Eph. 6, 12.

[89] Heb. 4, 15.

conceived, gives birth to sin . . ." [90] But there was nothing low in Jesus, no surge of reprehensible desires, no trace of yielding to the tempter: "The ruler of this world has no power over me." [91] The scene in Gethsemane and the impressive passage of Hebrews 5, 7, prove that this total purity of heart could be reconciled with an experience in which extreme moral distress, occasioned partly at least by devilish intervention, compelled the lonely tempted one to exert every effort of his will, to exhaust all his powers.[92]

LIKE THE LONELY BIRD

In the famous passage which we shall discuss, St. John of the Cross compares the mystic who has attained the highest stage with a lonely bird.[93] This is also applicable to Jesus whose dark night we can to some extent gauge through the medium of mysticism.

From the social point of view, Jesus lived in extreme isolation. This does not mean to say that he lived withdrawn or was by temperament an introvert. But his phenomenological situation, the bearing and influence which his words and actions could have upon others, are truly surprising when we reflect that we are dealing with the Son of God. He spent about thirty years—more than ninety percent of his life,—in a hamlet which is not even mentioned in the Old Testament. His fatherland was an insignificant spoke in the wheel of the Roman Empire which was itself only one of the culture centers of the world, although this was only discovered more than a thousand years later. Almost two centuries passed before the Romans, who aspired to be in the know about everything, devoted a couple of lines to the figure of Jesus. And this was the man who knew that he had come for all men of all lands and all ages!

If this "light of the world" is thus extremely singular, there is something which isolates him even more: incomprehension. Jesus was like a stranger: "Out of Egypt I have called my Son." [94] He worked in the Galilee of the Gentiles, in the midst of a people that sat in darkness, in the region and shadow of death.[95] The Galileans were looked down on in the capital [96] and they in their turn spoke ironically of Nazareth, insofar as they knew of its existence: "Can anything good come out of Nazareth?" [97] He met with so much resistance that it seems at a certain moment as if his followers can be counted on the fingers of both hands. And even this confused little group has to be asked: "Will you also go away?" [98] A few months later occurs the scene which every generation of Christians will recall with a feeling of desolation, whenever they read the passion according to St. John: "He went out, bearing his own cross, to the place called the place of a skull." [99] Here a man enters upon the most terrible isolation as a prey to his fate and to cold mockery. Nature, too, played her part and although it was scarcely noon, Jesus died in the midst of darkness.[100] To end it all his body was laid to rest in a tomb intended for another.[101]

More important still, however, was Jesus' spiritual isolation. Here we distinguish, first of all, a negative aspect: total emptiness. He lived in the world, but so simply and so detached that no possession could ever bind him. The pilgrim must hasten onwards, he must deal with the world as though he had no dealings with it.[102] There is no indication in the gospels that Jesus was attached to anything, nor that he ever desired to gain or to keep anything for himself. Everything in his words and actions, his eating and drinking, is pure and limpid. We never detect in him any of the small vanities or the mighty ambition (sometimes even conducive to heroism) which we meet so often even in the most advanced.[103] He himself considered only one thing necessary.[104] He knew nothing other than the kingdom, and there his heart found its treasure.[105] Neither his teaching nor his works nor his disciples are his; everything belongs to the Father.[106]

In the evangelical image of Jesus, we have at length met somebody whose eyes are pure lamps, "whose memory (mind) has renounced all forms and memorable things which are not God." He is someone entirely orientated towards God, who lives completely

[90] Jas. 1, 13-15.

[91] Jn. 14, 30.

[92] Cf. H. Strathmann, *Der Brief an die Hebraeer* (N.T. Deutsch), 1954,[7] p. 99: On the development of the ethical personality of Jesus.

[93] *Geestelijk Gezang*, 14th & 15th verses nr. 24.

[94] Mt. 2, 15; cf. Hos. 11, 1.

[95] Mt. 4, 15-16.

[96] Mt. 26, 73.

[97] Jn. 1, 46.

[98] Jn. 6, 67.

[99] Jn. 19, 16.

[100] Mt. 27, 45.

[101] Mt. 27, 60; Jn. 19, 41-42.

[102] 1 Cor. 7, 29-31.

[103] Everyone could give a thousand examples. We need only recall the statement of a pure heart like little Theresa concerning the temptation to assert her right of ownership in the matter of good ideas and beautiful thoughts.

[104] Lk. 10, 41.

[105] Mt. 5, 33-34; 13, 44-45 etc.

[106] Jn. 7.16; 14, 10; 17, 9 etc.

"empty" before his face," in order to receive from him the fullness of his mind." He practiced spontaneously what the mystical doctor counsels: "Therefore, the more the soul strips the mind of forms or memories which are not God, the more it will direct the mind towards God, making it all the more empty in order to hope for the fullness of his mind. What one must do in order to live in complete and pure hope of God is to direct the soul immediately towards God in a feeling of love whenever ideas, forms, and various images crowd in, without dwelling on them, and neither thinking of these things nor paying to them more attention than is necessary to recall them in order to know and to do one's duty, if this is involved." [107]

This total nakedness corresponds to the characteristic virtue of the pilgrim: hope. Theologians, however, state that Jesus could not possibly possess the virtue of hope (or that of faith), for he already enjoyed the chief object of Christian hope, the beatific vision. Yet, on the other hand, there were pilgrim qualities which prevented this blessedness from constantly overflowing into his inner life, his senses, and his experience of happiness, so that the inner freedom he displayed is, in fact, related to what with us is the theological virtue of hope.

The wretchedness, the injustice, the sluggishness and cowardice of the leaders, the baseness and filth of sin concealed beneath a colorful façade or insolently displayed in public, wounded him deeply, made him more alone and deserted than anyone ever felt before. He knew only too well what a perfect world should and would one day be like to let himself be won over by tinsel and gilt. In this sense, the *Imitation* is right in saying that Jesus' life was one long cross and martyrdom. The gospels have recorded literally the original sound of that loneliness: "My God, my God, why hast thou forsaken me?" [108] This is not hopelessness, nor an intrusion into his divine sonship, for he continues to say, "*my* God." It is, however, the profoundest expression of spiritual poverty and loneliness that we know.

There is, however, also a spiritual loneliness which has a positive basis: the exaltation, the intensity of love and joy so great that it becomes incommunicable. Jesus loved his Father, knew him, contemplated him, was loved by him, but no one showed any understanding of this union or asked him about the Father.[109] He, with the meekest and humblest of hearts, stood absolutely alone, and about him swarmed and writhed a humanity which was "of the earth." Perhaps the mystic, whose life can be compared with a lonely bird on a house roof, can give us an idea of Jesus' loneliness:

"St. John of the Cross states that a lonely songbird has five characteristics.[110] We assert that all five are eminently applicable to Christ during his mortal life.

"The first characteristic is that the lonely bird usually perches as high as possible: Never was there a higher nor a more uninterrupted contemplation than that of Jesus during his entire lifetime. He was ever absorbed in God, far removed from the ordinary, always in prayer.

"The second characteristic is that it always points its beak towards the direction of the wind. Similarly, Jesus was every moment dependent on what the Father said, on his commands, on the joy he gave him.

"The third characteristic is that the songbird sits alone and tolerates no other bird near it, but flies away as soon as another wishes to alight beside it. Can we imagine a greater anxiety than that of Jesus not to be deprived by any company of the treasure of his loneliness in God?

"The fourth characteristic is that it sings very sweetly. Jesus' song was extremely sweet, for it enchanted the Father who had eyes and ears only for him.

"The fifth characteristic is that it has no definite color. Jesus too displayed no tint of particular attachment or subservience to a higher or lower degree. He gave away his love, as the Father had commanded, and loved all with unchanging generosity. These are, according to our mystic, the five qualities of the lonely songbird. The Son of God possessed them as no other during his stay here on earth. When he expired in the hands of the Father, he must have received him as someone picking up a wounded bird." [111]

This loneliness makes the mystic infinitely poor and infinitely rich. Rich, in the exceptional hour when God reveals himself and halts and absorbs the whole of his inner life. Then the privileged one knows that everything belongs to him: God, the heavens, the earth,

---

[107] *Ascent of Mt. Carmel,* Third book, 15, 1.
[108] Mk. 15, 34 (= Ps. 22, 1).
[109] Mt. 11, 27; Jn. 14, 31; 17, 25; the complaint: 16, 5.

[110] See footnote 93.
[111] M. M. Cabodevilla, "Christo vivo. Vida de Christo y vida cristiana" (BAC), Madrid, 1963, pp. 270-271.

the angels, everything.[112] Yet, he is poor because he knows so well that nothing but God is worth a fig, and God himself withdraws, leaving his loved one in a state of aridity. The mystical life is nothing but a see-saw between these two lonelinesses and Jesus, who in the deepest core of his being was exalted above this up and down movement, still shared our pilgrim condition to such an extent that his mind, too, was subject to that feeling of unutterable loneliness, since man cannot express how poor everything is without God and how great is our wealth in him. From time to time, the disciples suspected something of all this, particularly when Jesus was at prayer,[113] yet, even then he was forced to conclude: "Have I been with you so long, and yet you do not know me." [114] Thus spoke a lonely pilgrim on the evening before he reached home.

CONSEQUENCES OF THE CHURCH

The fact that all the foregoing statements could be interpreted in the individualistic sense justifies their being applied to the Church, from whence it appears that Jesus' being a pilgrim gloriously illuminates and confirms the nature of the Christian community.

Jesus is the captain of the Church. Not only is he her actual head and leader, he has also shown her the way. Since he was a pilgrim, we form together a pilgrim Church. During this provisional, incomplete existence, we must be re-created after the perfect image of the Father, which He, as the new Adam, as it were, carried before us to our goal. We shall examine in the following chapter how each of us must experience this personally, but it is also important to view the ecclesiastical aspect founded on our common status as pilgrims.

The Church is indeed subject to the law of growth: she begins as a mustard seed, as a leaven; she must grow as a body.[115] The law of work also applies to her, too; she is a vineyard, a harvest, a fishing enterprise.[116] Her nature and vocation is obedience, listening to God's word, entirely dependent on him in a manner most forcefully expressed by the comparison with the marriage relationship: "For the husband is the head of the wife, as Christ is head of the Church, his body, and is himself its Savior. As the Church is subject to Christ, so let wives also be subject in everything to their husbands." [117] This attitude of obedience is so striking and categorical that all "powers" in the Church must be considered as humble services rendered [118] and must be constantly exercised in dependence on the Spirit who is the true builder of the community[119] and the inner and lifegiving Law of the new covenant.[120]

The Church's temptations are described in the Apocalypse. The letters to the seven Churches mention particularly loss of the first love, disloyalty, false wealth, and lukewarmness.[121] This struggle confronts her with the dragon, and she must flee into the wilderness.[122] The wilderness signifies loneliness. Indeed, the followers of Jesus form a small flock,[123] and the kingdom of God grows "by night and by day" while the people sleep or wake, but in any case, so that no one seems to notice it.[124] The Church's union with Jesus already exists, but it is so intimate that it is not noticeable from outside and will only become public at the parousia.[125] Therefore, the bride and the Spirit continue to repeat in a voice full of homesickness, the word of the pilgrims: "Come!"[126] There was once a young man who lived on an island. Every evening he set out with a band of comrades round and round the island. Sometimes, he leaped into the boat alone, like a lonely swan, and sailed far away from the island, dreaming under the stars; and sadly he returned. One day he realized that he was lacking in love and courage. Then, he sailed in the opposite direction, towards the mainland. He first steps were difficult, as a swan waddling making an effort with each step. But he persevered, searching for the city, a pilgrim among the people. And we, a holy nation of "aliens and exiles," living among the heathen,[127] must know that "we are away from the Lord while we are at home in the body."[128] "Therefore let us go forth to him outside the camp (that is, abandon the security, the sufficiency and the mutual flattery), bearing abuse for him. For we have here no lasting city, but we seek the city which is to come."[129] The mystery of the great pilgrim is burningly topical.

[112] Cf. the "Prayer of a Soul Inflamed with Love" by John of the Cross: "To me belong the heavens, to me belongs the earth," etc. Cf. Rom. 8, 32.
[113] Cf. Jn. 17, 2.
[114] Jn. 14, 9.
[115] Mt. 13, 31-32; Eph. 4, 16.
[116] Mt. 20 1-16; 21, 28-46; 9, 37; Jn. 21, 5-11.
[117] Eph. 5, 23-24.
[118] Lk. 22, 26.
[119] Eph. 2, 18.21; Rom. 8, 14; 1 Cor. 12, 3-13.
[120] Acts 1, 5.28; 20, 28; Rom. 8, 2.
[121] Rev. 2, 3.
[122] Rev. 12.
[123] Lk. 12, 32.
[124] Mk. 4, 27.
[125] Rev. 21, 2; Col. 3, 3; 1 Jn. 3, 2.
[126] Rev. 22, 17.
[127] 1 Pet. 2, 9-12.
[128] 2 Cor. 5, 6.
[129] Heb. 13, 13-14.

III
Jesus, Bearer
of a Message

Every person is a messenger and has something to tell us from God. Since he is free, his voice is unique, irreplaceable; a spark that glitters with its own light in the glowing symphony of flames which reflect and celebrate the uncreated love.

Every person believes or would like to believe that he has his own particular mission, and the scriptures bear him out. This is not so much because every period has seen the emergence of people charged with a particular task: prophets, kings, priests, sages, or, more generally, poets, explorers, demagogues, mystics. There is a more general and more fundamental mission, since man, as such, is God's proxy on earth. Man and woman are created after God's image and likeness, and it is their vocation to represent him, to govern the earth in his name. By our very being we are the bearers of a message.

This applies to Jesus with the full weight of the law of incarnation. His incomparable mission was not given him *despite* his humanity; on the contrary, it shows how intensely human he actually was. One is precisely human insofar as one brings a message, while the only person who cannot possibly be given a mission or be a messenger is God himself. Jesus, on the contrary, is "the one who is sent." [1]

Jesus' "special assignment" which naturally occupied his adult years and his public life, can be given the names of "prophetic mission" and "messianic task," a function exercised by no other person and not even by an angel. And yet, his mission was simpler, more universal and more revolutionary than any other; as the new Adam, he came to restore the image of the Father. These are the three main aspects which we have to examine.

In Jesus' time there was no proliferation of prophets. Prophets are always exceptional cases, not at all like the "good comrade" who pats you on the shoulder and leaves you in peace. The prophet provokes a reaction, thrusting himself forward, willingly or not, on the stage of history. It would thus be fascinating to review the whole of Jesus' activities and the response of the various institutions from a prophetic standpoint. Only *this* perspective reveals the style of many of his pronouncements—joyful message, threat, prophetic parables—his reading of men's hearts, and the miracles which recalled Elisha, to their full advantage. Interest in this point is rapidly increasing among exegetes.[2]

What interests us at the moment, however, is not the content and style of his message, not even its historical evolution or the psychological problems connected with it. We are not interested in whether Jesus began with a joyful message and ended with threatening speeches. Furthermore, we are not interested in the meaning of the vision in the Jordan valley, or whether he received a new task by means of the transfiguration. Finally, we are not interested in what type Jesus represents in the series of prophets, since he was at the same time an apocalyptic visionary (which connects him with the learned intellectuals, whereas the prophetic genre is essentially popular), and even had something of the rabbi about him and was practiced in sapiential instruction.[3] The only facet we wish to explore is the significance and manner of this prophetship in the global mission and the mystery of Jesus' Person. We establish that our sources adopt different standpoints and indicate a maturing process.

The synoptics, who reflect essentially the broad stream of tradition, deal with the extraordinary authority and special power emanating from Jesus' words.[4] In this, he differs from the rabbis

---

[1] A particular theme of John.

[2] P. E. Davies, "Jesus and the role of the prophet," in *Journ. Bibl. litt.*, 64, (1945), pp. 241-259; J. Daniélou, "Le Christ prophète," in *Vie spir.*, 78 (1948), pp. 154-170; H. Riesenfeld, "Jesus als Prophet," in *Spiritus et Veritas* (Mel. Kundzviwis), 1953, pp. 135-148; G. Gils, *Jesus prophète d'après les évangiles synoptiques* (Louvain, 1957); G.

Friedrich, "Profètes," in *T.W.N.T.*, 6 (1959), pp. 782 (bibliography) and pp. 842-849 (Jesus as prophet).

[3] How complex this is emerges perhaps most clearly from the existence of three sorts of parables: sapiential, prophetic, and apocalyptic, cf. Vol. 1, chapter on "The Cultural Situation."

[4] Mk. 1, 22.27; Mt. 7, 29; Lk. 4, 32.

and takes his place among the prophets, for the message of these
latter derives its power not from any dialectic force but from the
simple fact that it comes from God. It is powerful because "Yahweh
lets none of his (prophet's) words fall to the ground." [5]

It is therefore quite possible that the people will put Jesus to
death, for this seems to be the fate of the prophets,[6] but no one
will be able to change the fact that his words "will not pass away." [7]

The words of the prophet are like a sharp sword [8] with which
Yahweh can destroy people and nations, yet his "judgments" are
greeted as the morning light.[9] Matthew and Luke say something of
this kind when they sum up Jesus' mission as "a sign that is spoken
against, set for the fall or rising of many in Israel," [10] or speak of
him as someone who begins preaching in Galilee of the Gentiles and
thus brings a great light to the people who lived in darkness.[11]

We know little of the psychology of Jesus as a prophet. How did
he know what message he had to bring? The gospels, even that of
St. John, give us to understand that Jesus never spoke "of himself."
His message came from the Father. Yet, they also indicate, at least in
one of the synoptic texts and constantly in John's theological docu-
ment, that Jesus' case was unique. Not one of the prophets, not even
Moses, had ever seen God, whereas Jesus enjoyed the perfect vision
of the Father,[12] knew him, and communicated only what he had
seen,[13] so that only he was capable of revealing to the little ones
that which was hidden from the wise and understanding.[14]

Do the gospels enlighten us about the response which such
prophetic words must surely have evoked? In a certain sense, they
tell us very little. On a few occasions, they mention that his preaching was greeted with enthusiasm by the crowd, but nowhere do
they tell us that the people returned home greatly moved. They are
very sparse with their descriptions of sudden or gradual conver-
sions. Still, a few examples, like that of Zacheus or the notorious
lady who burst in on the supper party, and especially the tone of the
gospels, give some indication of the incomparable virtue and creative force which emanated from his words. These four little books,
quite devoid of any literary ostentation, are dominated by an atmosphere of boundless confidence and triumphant certainty that is
positively astonishing. The tradition which thus preserved and
transmitted Jesus' words, already knew that they were capable of
changing history and transforming human hearts.

This realization developed particularly after the resurrection, under the influence of the Spirit who "brought Jesus' words to remembrance" and revealed their full significance.[15] The converts will witness in joyful surprise how these words, despite their brevity, are capable of curing all sorts of people of all sorts of defects. "We who formerly took our pleasure in ravishments, magical practices, jealous love of our own wealth, hate and violence, have completely changed our way of life since we came to believe in the Word." The only explanation for this, Justin goes on, is that Jesus "was not a sophist, but that his word was a power of God." [16]

This expression "the Word," perhaps reflects the deepest and most perfect insight into Jesus' prophetic function. In order to understand it properly, however, we must first mention another ripening process, for any reflection on Jesus' prophetic activities must of necessity lead to a review of the concept of covenant. The prophet, by definition the man of God's word, was always in the service of the covenant, especially since Jeremiah. It was his task to purify the people and constantly to summon them to fidelity to the past and future commands of the God of the covenant. A desire for, and certainty of, a new and permanent phase in this history gradually developed. People spoke of a "new covenant." [17]

Jesus is the prophet of this new covenant. In him God has given his definitive yes and ratified and fulfilled all former promises.[18] He is therefore the prophet of the last stage, or simply *the* prophet (of the messianic times), of whose coming the people had more than once shown a premonition.[19] In him, we are no longer dealing with a prefigurative sign, a messenger; it is God himself who visited his people.[20] When Jesus goes to die in Jerusalem, as befits a prophet, it will become clear that he was the servant of a new and much more exalted covenant [21] which admittedly would be sealed more by his blood than by his oracles.[22]

[5] 1 Sam. 3, 19.
[6] Lk. 13, 33.
[7] Mk. 13, 31.
[8] Is. 49, 2.
[9] Hos. 6, 5.
[10] Lk. 2, 34.
[11] Mt. 3, 15-16.
[12] Jn. 1, 18; 6, 46; 1 Jn. 4, 12; cf. Ex. 33, 18-33.
[13] Jn. 7, 28-29; 8, 38.55; 15, 15 etc.

[14] Mt. 11, 25-27; Lk. 10, 21-22.
[15] Jn. 14, 26; 16, 13-15.
[16] *Apologia*, 14.
[17] Jer. 31, 31 (34); Ezek. 16; 36, 25-29; Hos. 2, 16-25.
[18] 2 Cor. 1, 19-20.
[19] Mt. 21, 11; Lk. 7, 16; Jn. 6, 14; 7, 40.
[20] Cf. Lk. 7, 16 with 1, 68.78.
[21] Heb. 8, 6-18.
[22] Heb. 9, 12.15; 12, 24.

The unique character of Jesus' prophetic task led the first Christians—with the exception of the Ebonites and various groups of Jewish Christians—almost systematically to avoid the title, "prophet." A sublimation was necessary and unavoidable. One form of it led to Jesus' being known not so much as someone "Mighty in word and deed" [23] but as "the Word" itself. Whatever influences may have contributed to this concept being applied to Jesus,[24] the identification with the *Logos* is in any case a most felicitous invention, which most evocatively renders Jesus' function as climax and completer of prophetism.

JESUS THE MESSIAH

All the trends and publications of the New Testament testify that Jesus is the messiah. This is so plain as to render all the more remarkable the number of modern authors—including the most reputable and competent—who forcefully deny that Jesus fulfilled any messianic task during his earthly life. Still less, they maintain, did he possess any such insight into his life's work in his awareness as a *mortal* man. Since the first year of our twentieth century, Wrede's thesis has dominated a good deal of the New Testament exegesis: the *Easter-certainty* comprises two things: (1) the belief that Jesus lives; (2) the belief that Jesus is the messiah.[25]

This thesis is correct in what it states positively. The first Christians were, as it were, aroused from sleep by the events of Easter, and regarded the resurrection in some way as Jesus the messiah ascending to his throne. Peter, in his Pentecost address, clearly states: "Let all the house of Israel therefore know assuredly that God has made him both Lord and Christ (messiah), this Jesus whom you crucified." [26] But it is impossible, even little short of absurd, to assume that this assertion could be a conclusion drawn by the disciples after the resurrection, on the basis of the scriptures, but *without antecedents* in the actual life of Jesus. Is it really conceivable that all the disciples accepted Jesus' messianic dignity with such conviction that it now, as it were, forms part of his name "Jesus Christ" (literally Jesus messiah) if Jesus himself were entirely unaware of it and never made the slightest claim to it? [27]

It falls outside the scope of this section to *prove* that Jesus was aware of being the messiah and voiced this awareness. Any such proof would have to fulfill all the critical requirements and take into account the data of Form Criticism. One might perhaps derive a possible argumentation from the brief data which follow and which aim to show *how* Jesus revealed himself as the messiah. After this we shall devote a little more time to the problem—too rarely raised by the dogmatists and biblicists—of the meaning of this messiahship.

How Did Jesus Reveal Himself as the Messiah?

Our present day world is not accustomed to seeing great leaders act in a humble, quiet, almost mysterious manner. Weeks beforehand, newspapers and radios inform us of the approaching arrival of political and religious leaders, complete with their (romanticized) biographies. Candidates for office make nationwide tours and everyone is familiar with their programs. Jesus, however, only said on very few occasions, and then only towards the end of his life, that he was truly the messiah.

Why all this secrecy? Some maintain that he simply never thought of proclaiming himself the messiah; such an idea never entered his head. Such an "explanation," which seems little in accord with our concept of biblical inspiration, meets with a number of critical objections.

Various details lead us to decide that Jesus was unwilling or unable, at the beginning of his public life, to declare that he was the messiah. Caution counselled against it, for the Romans were not inclined, out of the goodness of their hearts, to let themselves be deprived of the interesting bulwark that Israel represented for them, for the sake of these messianic goings-on. Obedience prevented it, for it was the will of the Father, expressed in the scriptures, that the

23 Lk. 24, 19.

24 Cf. pp. 219ff.

25 W. Wrede, *Das Messias-geheimnis in den Evangelien* (Göttingen, 1901), p. 166. The bibliography on this point has assumed the proportions of a deluge. We mention two important collective works: *Der historische Jesus und der kerygmatische Christus* (Berlin, Evanglische Verlagsanstalt, 1960); *Der historische Jesus und der Christus unseres galubens. Eine katholische* *Auseinandersetzung met den Folgen der Entmythologisierungstheorie* (Vienna, 1962). (Cf. especially the article by F. Mussner, pp. 103-128). Cf. further "La venue du Messie," *Recherches bibliques*, 6 (Louvain, 1962); the number "Le Christ Roi" of *Lumière et Vie*, 57, Vol. 11 (1962).

26 Acts 2, 36.

27 This is even more striking in Spanish: Jesucristo.

messianic age should not be exactly what most contemporaries dreamed of; immediately to proclaim himself as the messiah would be equivalent to canonizing the widespread, excessively nationalistic and limited idea of the kingdom of God. Finally, filial devotion required that it should not be Jesus himself who took the initiative, for the role of messiah was so great and so divine that "no one might claim that honor for himself," as was said of the high priesthood, a less important office. "So also Christ did not exalt himself . . . but was appointed by him who said to him: 'Thou art My Son, today I have begotten thee.' " [28] Only the Father could enthrone Jesus, so that dramatic declarations had to be avoided as much as possible.

And yet, Jesus had to make himself known by word and deed, as a leader who knew what he wanted, yet, whose activity only gradually attained full development and revealed its purpose. Provided we bear the necessary distinction in mind, we may be able to learn something from a modern leader who spoke on the evolution of his mission in an important address. This is the speech given by Fidel Castro on Dec. 1, 1961 for the pupils of the "School for Revolutionary Instruction":

> I believe in Marxism. I believe absolutely in Marxism. Did I believe on the first of January? I believed on the first of January. Did I believe on the 26th of July? I believed on the 26th of July. Did I understand it as I understand it today? Comparing what I understood then with what I understand now, I see a great difference. Was I prejudiced? Yes, I was prejudiced. On the 26th of July? Yes. Could I call myself a true revolutionary on the 26th of July? No. Then I could not call myself a true revolutionary. Can I call myself a true revolutionary today? That would mean that I am satisfied and naturally I am not satisfied. Have I any doubts about Marxism or do I think that certain interpretations are wrong and need to be revised. No, I have not the slightest doubts . . ." [29]

Turning to the case of Jesus, we find that he was very quickly received with great enthusiasm by the people. The main reason for this was not exactly his spirituality. Jesus performed miracles and this was a clear portent of the incomparable happiness the messianic kingdom was to bring. He performed exorcisms, like David, the only Old Testament figure said to have driven out an evil spirit as an anointed one (messiah) and favored of the Spirit.[30] It is thus that the first to greet Jesus in a messianic manner will be the sick and the possessed. They know that he is the "son of David," the "Son of God." [31]

But Jesus himself offers no such explanations. On the contrary, he imposes silence on all those who feel themselves bound to proclaim him the messiah. Yet, he continues to act and to preach. If the finger of God is at work and displays greater power than the devils, then this is a sign that the kingdom of God has come.[32] And if the messianic kingdom has arrived, who then, logically speaking, is the messiah? If the Pharisees persist in demanding a sensational sign, that is their business.[33] And if the people draw too political a conclusion from a truly messianic miracle which recalled the miracles of the Exodus and the manna, he will radically oppose it, oblige his disciples to leave the overenthusiastic crowd and withdraw to the hills, far from any royal claims.[34]

The situation was, in fact, constantly ambiguous. Jesus called himself the "son of man," a title which while not messianic did not exclude the possibility of that dignity, since a text from the Book of Daniel described him as a figure to whom God handed over the *kingdom*.[35] We meet the same situation when two overenterprising disciples come up against an evasive answer and are firmly put in their places in connection with their eventual positions in the kingdom.[36] And yet, neither the sons of Zebedee nor the other disciples could be compared with the ordinary rabbi-students. No, something was happening. A movement impossible to halt had begun in the history of salvation and they themselves would be seated upon thrones when the twelve tribes of Israel solemnly came together.[37]

On a few rare occasions the veil of secrecy was lifted. An impressive landscape near Caesarea Philippi, capital of a zone which had remained outside Jesus' normal sphere of activity, would be witness

---

[28] Heb. 5, 4-5.

[29] Pro memoria: July 26, 1953: unsuccessful invasion of Cuba; Fidel Castro captured, Jan. 1, 1959: entry into Havana and triumph of the revolution. The text of the speech may be found in *El Imperio de la Ley en Cuba*, published by the International Commission of Jurists (Geneva, 1962), pp. 77-81; the quotation is on p. 79.

[30] 1 Sam. 16, 13-23.

[31] Mt. 9, 27; cf. 12, 23; 15, 22; 20, 30; 21, 9-15. Mt. 8, 29; Mk. 3, 11; Lk. 4, 41.

[32] Mt. 12, 28.

[33] Lk. 17, 20-21.

[34] Mk. 6, 45-46; Jn. 6, 15.

[35] Dan. 7, 14. 18. 22.

[36] Mk. 10, 35-45.

[37] Mt. 19, 28.

to Peter's profession of faith. There the spokesman and leader of the disciples affirms that Jesus is the messiah, and is congratulated by the master in person since only divine revelation can have revealed this to him.[38] Nothing gives rise to the assumption that this peculiar place must have been selected by "popular theology" for such a role. We are dealing with history.

Less deliberate—at least at the time it occurred—was a more or less parallel reaction by the people a few months later. Now we are in the capital and Jesus rides through the streets mounted upon an ass. He has nothing of the fighter, the general or the guerilla leader —they would at least have chosen a horse—yet, nonetheless, he is greeted by messianic cries of welcome: "Hosanna to the son of David." This could mean that the king of peace came to the daughter of Sion in order to inaugurate the kingdom, but in fact "his disciples did not understand this at first. When Jesus was glorified, then they remembered that this had been written of him and had been done to him." [39]

The most solemn affirmation comes during Jesus' trial when the high priest formally puts the question: "Are you the Christ, the Son of the Blessed?" [40] The question is plain, but many scholars deny that this trial had a messianic character. Could it be blasphemy, they wonder, to pose as the messiah? And what has the accusation concerning a rebuilding of the temple to do with all this? [41] This matter has been adequately dealt with.[42] Naturally enough, the fact that a person is the messiah or claims to be the messiah is not blasphemy. What the jury did regard as blasphemous was the fact that this claim was made by a poor Galilean, with no powerful backing, who had to rely on future greatness ("You *will* see the son of man sitting at the right hand of power") and who thus rendered the blessed God ridiculous and despicable by his affirmative answer. As regards the allusion to the temple, this can be clarified by the first great messianic prediction made by the prophet, Nathan, who promised not only the kingdom but the rebuilding of the temple to David's descendant.[43] Jesus fulfilled this prophecy: the new temple will be none other than his glorified body.

The reaction of the Sanhedrin proved that Jesus' cautious attitude had been the only correct one. He had now exposed himself and must pay the price, which was death. Yet once again the darkness of ambiguity would envelope Jerusalem when someone either as a joke, or to discourage other adventurers, composed the inscription:

"Jesus of Nazareth, King of the Jews." [44] His impotence, so horrible in contrast with the assumed or hoped for messianic glory, caused the onlookers to cry mockingly: "Aha, You who would destroy the temple and build it in three days, save yourself and come down from the cross . . . Let the Christ, the King of Israel, come down now from the cross, that we may see and believe." [45] But Jesus clung heroically to the cross, for he was indeed the messiah, but in his own manner.

NATURE AND SIGNIFICANCE OF JESUS' MESSIAHSHIP

As the messiah, Jesus was the bearer of the most passionately longed for message in the world. Centuries of promises, prospects, prophecies, dreams and prayers were concentrated in him. A rabbinic saying maintains that God began to reign visibly on earth from the time of Abraham; all blessings since that time were a prefiguration of, and a preparation for, him. It is with this grandiose vision that Matthew begins his gospel: "The book of the genealogy of Jesus Christ, the son of David, the son of Abraham." [46] His name will be Jesus, for he will save his people from their sins. [47] The most magnificent accomplishments of the kings of Israel, in particular of the admirable and popular hero David pale in comparison with his mission: "He will be great and will be called the Son of the Most High; and the Lord God will give to him the throne of his father David and he will reign over the house of Jacob forever." [48]

We have already indicated some of the chief characteristics of the kingdom of God which Jesus preached and brought. [49] But to what extent did he realize this kingdom and what is its precise significance? If Jesus is a messiah, i.e., if he is anointed, he must take his place among the kings of Israel, and in those days the kings were the great accomplishers, the reformers, the strong men of the community. Israel knew that what was a myth for many other countries would

---

[38] Mt. 16, 16-17.

[39] Mt. 21, 9; Jn. 12, 16.

[40] Mk. 14, 61.

[41] Mk. 64, 57-58.

[42] Cf. O. Betz, "Die Frage, nach dem messianischen Bewusstsein Jesus," in *Nov. Test.*, 6 (1963), pp. 20-48, especially pp. 34-37.

[43] 2 Sam. 7, 13.

[44] Jn. 19, 19.

[45] Mk. 15, 29-32.

[46] Mt. 1, 1; cf. the reference to Abraham in the Magnificat (Lk. 1, 35).

[47] Mt. 1, 21.

[48] Lk. 1, 32-33.

[49] Cf. pp. 36ff.

become reality for her: she would see the appearance of an ideal
king, of *the* king, *the* anointed. As chosen representative of a mighty,
enterprising God who intervened in history, he would re-create the
earth. He would usher in nothing less than a return to the conditions
of paradise not so much in order to excuse the disillusionment of
Jesus' contemporaries as to insure that we ourselves do not underestimate what is at stake here; we should constantly refer back to
the numerous prophetic pages which nourished and sustained the
Jewish people's unquenchable thirst for happiness, for peace, for
human solidarity, and religious depth. When the messiah comes,
sang Isaiah, the wolf will dwell with the lamb and the leopard lie
down with the kid. Calf and lion will graze together and be so tame
that a little child will lead them. The suckling child will play un-
harmed over the hole of the asp and put his hand on the adder's den.
Then "they shall not hurt or destroy in all my holy mountain; for
the earth shall be full of the knowledge of the Lord as the waters
cover the sea." [50]

An introduction to the gospels, is perhaps not quite the place to
ask what we ourselves are doing to accomplish our mission of "messianic community" or even to begin to fulfill the expectation of the
peoples. Enormous promises will have to be made good, and not
only in the hereafter. But to return to our immediate subject; what
did Jesus himself do? Did people see in his frail unassuming figure
the messenger who had come to convey the infinite riches of God to
a hungry humanity? Was he a king? Can we maintain now, looking
back and without deluding ourselves with soothing incidentals that
he did not fail to realize the age-old dreams which the real prophets
of Yahweh had also cherished and encouraged? If we wish to prove
that we for our part are really not disillusioned, we must be able to
cite a number of accomplishments or at least a collection of signs
which allow us to affirm that Jesus is the messiah. If the Feast of
Christ the King—a tautology which doubly affirms the messianic
reality—is not to be a hollow mockery, we must be able to describe
that king.

In the course of this investigation we must remember to bear in
mind that the real king of the kingdom is not Jesus, but the Father,
who literally does everything. It is also essential that the kingdom
should pass through a phase of smallness and humiliation before the
transfer of power.[51] But on the other hand, Jesus himself asserts
that the kingdom has already come. This being so, we can find no

other yardstick to measure his messianic quality than the real influence which he exercised in order to make of men a community of brothers in which peace and justice prevail, based upon and orientated towards the love of God the Father. In the light of history then, it seems we must inevitably conclude that Jesus' influence in this respect really defies all comparison.

The gospels show us his methods:

1. The preaching of the "truth." The parables give us to understand that the kingdom begins with the sowing of the Word, and Jesus is the sower.[52] Before Pilate, he maintains that he is king because he has come to bear witness to the truth.[53] And if we examine the facts, and perhaps our own lives, must we now wonder if there is any greater power in the world than Jesus' Word?

2. His literally miraculous goodness was indeed a great solace to the masses, and continues to move the Gospel reader even up to the present-day. The delicacy of his attitude and its healing effects are sufficient cause for believing in him.[54] John calls them "signs," or "works" and mentions the question: "When the Christ appears, will he do more signs than this man has done?"[55] The evangelists contented themselves with a limited selection, but these signs were nonetheless written "that you may believe that Jesus is the Christ, the Son of God."[56] Until the parousia the people will desire and obtain signs from Jesus: liberation, healing, an alleviation of their needs.

3. He suffered out of solidarity. For a world that requires deeds rather than words, the gesture of the servant of Yahweh was decisive. We shall have to deal with this in more detail, but it forms an intrinsic part of his messiahship. The voluntary acceptance of a harsh existence and especially of excruciating suffering from a spirit of solidarity with all his fellowmen has proved the most powerful spiritual lever in the history of the world, assuming that one considers other things than battles, change in the economy, and new trends in art. "I, when I am lifted up from the earth, will draw all men to myself."[57] At that moment, the ruler of this world was cast out.[58]

4. His Church. This is Jesus' last means of carrying out his mes-

[50] Is. 11, 6-9.
[51] 1 Cor. 15, 24; cf. pp. 336ff.
[52] Mk. 4, 14.
[53] Jn. 18, 37.
[54] Jn. 3, 2; 10, 38; 14, 11.
[55] Jn. 7, 31.
[56] Jn. 20, 31.
[57] Jn. 12, 32.
[58] Jn. 12, 31.

sianic task. It was devised by him and already commenced to exist
during his earthly life. The messianic kingdom was indeed granted
by the Father to this small flock.[59] Jesus also solemnly confirms that
Peter, who is the rock of his Church, possesses the keys of that kingdom.[60] The Christians, therefore, will have to incorporate the three
aforementioned means into their daily lives, with the support of
their serving leaders: the proclaiming of the Word, a brotherly love
which is inventive, and with God's help is capable of miracles, and a
completing in their own existence what is lacking in Christ's afflictions for the sake of the Church.[61]

We know only too well that all this has been but imperfectly
realized and attracts scant attention from press and radio, mass meetings, and everything that influences public opinion. The kingdom of
God is still that mustard seed and that mixture of good and evil. We
form a pluralistic world, and never so much as now when "good"
and "bad" live together indiscriminately, and Christianity and
paganism dwell together in the hearts of those who are inside the
Church and those who seem to be outside it.

And yet, the situation is not so undecided. The press does not
report everything that goes on and the radio does not use every
wavelength. At the last judgment the records will mention not
only the "Christian civilization" (which was not after all the worst
in the world) but also those details that escape the eye of the his-
torian: the sensitive acts of charity of people who, being illiterate,
are not even on the electors' register, certain gestures of forgiveness,
marital fidelity, apostolic heroism, concealed from a natural sense of
simplicity or hermetically sealed off from the outside world by
refinement of persecution. The number of cheers for Christ the
King will cause a sensation. It may therefore be said that despite the
urgent need for conversion of which we ourselves are conscious,
the Christian people is nevertheless truly what Christ intended: his
Church,[62] that is, the "collection" of those who make God's dominion visible and tangible on earth, just as and slightly better than was
done by the "assembly" of the Jewish people in the temple which
was erected on Sion.

In this connection, it must be observed that Jesus, messiah, is an
absolutist king, since the kingdom of God covers the whole of
human activity and the whole of history. But this in no way justifies
the theory of the two swords or any form of clericalism whatever.[63] May one then say that the messiah has nothing to do with

social reforms or political systems? Absolutely not! The celebrations of Christ the king were perhaps a little romantic and pathetic, laid too much emphasis on "our schools" or waved too insistently their Catholic colored flags, but in their hymns and even more so in the intuition of the faithful, they expressed a pure truth. Institutions are not indifferent authorities; nothing is equal to the kingdom, Jesus possesses *all* power.[64] He *must* adopt positions which affect the kingdom of peace and justice, the deepest happiness of the family of God. He is not outside or above the kingdom.

But Jesus exercises his direct sovereign authority through the means indicated above. He does no arrogate to himself the place of civil authority. In this sense, his kingdom is not of this world.[65] In this dramatic statement, face-to-face with death, he addresses an encouraging yet solemn word to those in authority: their mission is not a game, or a profit-making affair or a means of passing the time; they are not above the truth and one day, they will be called to account for the manner in which they freed freedom within the limits of their function.[66]

If, therefore, to conclude we take as our definition of "king" someone who is capable of radically reforming human society—a quality particularly essential in a messianic ruler—then it may indeed be applied to Jesus. He was unique in fulfilling the role of God's delegate, and that without palace or army or even a white collar.

JESUS AS IMAGE OF THE FATHER

Jesus was God's messenger through what he said as a prophet and even more by what he did, as messiah. Two lines which crisscross the whole of the Old Testament converge in him. But now we are faced with an idea which is more novel and unexpected: Jesus is a messenger by what he is: the image of the Father. Everyone is aware of the significance of this. Having spoken on countless occa-

---

59 Lk. 12, 32.

60 Mt. 16, 19.

61 Col. 1, 24.

62 Mt. 16, 18; cf. Col. 1, 18.24; Eph. 1, 22; 5, 23-32.

63 Cf. Lk. 22, 38; the medieval jurists saw in the two swords the symbol of the two powers, (civil and ecclesiastical), which must both be given by (through) the Pope, just as Jesus was permitted to receive two swords.

64 Mt. 28, 18.

65 Cf. Jn. 18, 36.

66 Jn. 18, 37.

sions through his prophets, God spoke at length through his Son: "he reflects the glory of God and bears the very stamp of his nature." [67]

The apostles, but especially the Fathers, expressed this fact in forceful synthetic terms. Jesus is not so much the messenger as the message. Not only were his words unique, he is the unique Word of the Father. He gave us not so much a kingdom as himself. We could continue like this indefinitely and perhaps end by merely playing with words if we do not make the effort to penetrate to the heart of these traditional antinomies.

If then, we examine the true significance of the fact that Jesus came to proclaim himself and to grant us himself as the best message of all, we immediately arrive at the category, "image of the Father." This is, according to the New Testament, the profoundest essence of the Lord, and this was already visible, although not completely, during his mortal life. In what way? In two ways especially, which are, in my opinion, complementary and irreducible. One line is drawn through the new Adam and in a second direction we are confronted with the glory of the Father. The contemplation of the new Adam, naturally a more human view, quickly lends itself to concrete application in our own lives, so that we, too, might be new people. The second line, more strongly focused on God, results from a vision of faith and leads to contemplative absorption. The champion of this latter is St. John, while Paul tended more to develop the first. We find both trends, however, reflected in the synoptics, who offer us an earlier tradition despite the redaction.

1. *The New Man*

Man, the only animal which regards itself speculatively with a profound metaphysical gaze, is not satisfied with himself. There are, of course, some cries of admiration: "Man is a noble animal" (Sir Thomas Browne). "What a piece of work is man!" (Shakespeare) and a series of definitions, from "a reasonable animal" to the more modern "a naturally religious animal" (Charles Lamb) which all extol the greatness of our species. Yet, the cool, penetrating English gaze cannot possibly compare with the passionate hunger of Hölderlin or Unamuno, nor cause us to forget the accents with which countless numbers since Plato, Augustine, and Theresa have sought an outlet upwards. Is a German invitation to rise above man (which does not necessarily mean the creation of an *Ubermensch*) so exaggerated? In any case, we see again in our time the story of Diogenes repeated, who went out with his lamp in the bright midday sun looking for "a man."

The Bible, too, is conscious of that longing for a perfect man.[68] The first pages of the book are devoted to the figure of Adam, literally, "the man." The old story reveals to us the double basis of our inborn dissatisfaction and homesickness. On the one hand God, has bestowed on us an infinite, divine nobility by creating us "in his image and likeness," [69] but on the other, we seek in vain within ourselves and all about us, for we have sinned. In fact, we are nothing but a handful of poor, weak, miserable, naked creatures, who are often clumsy and unfortunate in handling the best things we have: love, creative work, union with God. Israel was always conscious of this drama; certain anonymous great ones of our race had felt it in the very fibre of their beings and set it down under divine inspiration so that it remained recorded in the beginning of Genesis. A prophetic voice had promised redemption: God would create "a new heart" in a future generation,[70] but meanwhile Job bewailed his limitations and his nakedness in beautiful, heart-rending songs.

In reality, we already formulated our thesis when we dealt with Jesus' personality, in particular with his pure humanity: Jesus is the perfect man. We can, however, express ourselves more accurately now. The question is this: was this nobility and this pure humanity a particular case, an admirable yet temporary realization, or do we possess in Jesus a definitive model, approved and sent to us as a message? Was Jesus a messenger from God through his harmonious character, his goodness, his qualities of leadership, his dedication, his life of prayer? Has God taught us through him what a human being should be like?

[67] Heb. 1, 13.

[68] Cf. P. Galtier, *Les deux Adam* (Paris, 1947); C. R. Smith, *The Biblical Doctrine of Man* (New York, 1951); L. Cerfaux, *Le Christ dans la théologie de Saint Paul* (Paris, 1951), pp. 176-187; 324-328; F. W. Eltester, "Eikon im N.T.", in *Beihefte Z.N.W.*, (Berlin, 1958); J. de Fraine, *Adam et son lignage* (Bruges, 1959); J. Jervell, *Imago Dei, Gen. 1,26f. im Spätjudentum, in der Gnosis und in den paulinischen Briefen* (Göttingen, 1960);

H. Crouzel, "Image de Dieu," in *Catholicisme*, 21 (1960) pp. 1238-1240 (with bibliography, especially for the Fathers); E. Brandenburger, *Adam und Christus* (Neukirchen, 1962); E. Larsson, "Christus als Vorbild. Eine Untersuchung zu den paulinischen Tauf und Eikontexten," (Thesis, Lund, 1962); T. Aerts, "Le verbe 'suivre' dans la tradition synoptique," (Thesis, Rome, 1962).

[69] Gen. 1, 26; cf. 1 Cor. 11, 7.

[70] Jer. 31, 33; cf. 2 Cor. 3, 3.

If we leave aside any prejudice for or against and take care not to use an *a priori* approach, we find that the Word of God does not provide a completely unambiguous answer. What is clear, however, is that Jesus is the image of the Father.[71] Paul, moreover, expressly develops the theme of the first and second Adam.[72] Yet, here, he is referring in the first place to a *heavenly* image, that is, to the *risen* Christ.[73] This should preserve us from cherishing arrogant dreams, from striving after a Utopian perfection which is out of keeping with our limited existence, or from inhaling an overworldly spirit. No, we must lift up our eyes and, like the young Pharisean disciple of Gamaliel, contemplate the glory of the glorified Jesus, as in a mirror, in order to be changed into his likeness from one degree of glory to another.[74]

This last text already contains the admission that it is not only in his risen form that Jesus is the image of the Father. If we can already imitate him now, he himself must have been worthy of imitation when he was a pilgrim. Indeed, the theme of the image leads spontaneously to practical exhortations to imitate and practice as underlined by Kierkegaard with his trenchant words and his biting irony, Bonhoeffer by his life, and now by learned theses of Protestant inspiration.[75] Paul, indeed, speaks too generally to think only of the hereafter. God predestined us to be conformed, now and forever, to the image of his Son.[76] The virtues with which the "new man," re-created after Jesus, must clothe himself are very concrete and valid for all time,[77] which inevitably recalls to mind the *earthly* figure of the Lord. How could a heavenly Christ inspire us if we know nothing of his mortal life? Could he strengthen us with his grace without touching our hearts with the memory of his own behavior during the time he dwelt among us, tangible and vulnerable? No, we must not separate supernatural metaphysics from interpersonal psychology.

Did Jesus' contemporaries regard him as the perfect or the true man? Generally speaking, they evidently did not. Even his disciples do not appear particularly sensitive to this theme. Afterwards, it is true, they began to reflect, and their retrospective insight came down to us via several more or less isolated traditions. Matthew preserved a statement of immense profundity: Jesus says to *all* that they can *learn* of him.[78] This undoubtedly embraces the humility of the teacher and the suitability of his doctrine, but testifies still more to the convincing attractiveness of his personality, for which Jesus, doing and teaching were one and the same thing.[79] Luke, too, has transmitted to us certain traditions of this kind. He links Jesus with Adam in his genealogy,[80] and his account of Jesus' childhood strongly emphasizes that Jesus grew "in grace and wisdom" with God and man.[81] The Bible employs these two terms to express the human ideal of perfection,[82] and the most striking case is certainly that of the first *martyr*, Stephen, in the version of this same Luke.[83] Finally, it is by no means certain that the title, "son of man," applied to Jesus by all the evangelists and thus based on a broad tradition, is always intended to evoke the heavenly figure in the Book of Daniel. Normally, this term is simply a more poetical form of "man." We are thus fairly safe in assuming that in this frequent use of "the son of man" vibrated something of that pride and deeply respectful awareness that we should feel on reading a modern book on Jesus in which the principal character is constantly referred to as "the man."

Under the heading, "Jesus' Personality," we have attempted to sketch a certain global picture of what, according to the indications provided by the gospels, this ideal man must have been like. And yet we cannot refrain from pointing out that all the New Testament authors refer to the following traits as outstandingly characteristic of Jesus and especially worthy of imitation: humility, meekness, obedience, in a word, the attitude of the servant of Yahweh, which is the opposite of the first human sin and has therefore power to heal the bite of the old serpent. It is through these qualities that the "perfect man" became our redeemer. We reserve the content of this particular "ecce homo" for the following chapter.[84]

2. *The Glory of God*

The fact that Jesus by his very being brought us the message of

---

[71] 2 Cor. 4, 4; Col. 1, 15; Heb. 1, 3.
[72] Rom. 5, 12, 21; 1 Cor. 15, 45-49.
[73] 1 Cor. 15, 49.
[74] 2 Cor. 3, 18.
[75] Cf. the thesis of Edvin Larsson (see n. 68) who points out that the idea of imitation must not be sought so much under the keywords *akoloetheo* (to follow) and *mime-omai* (to imitate) but rather in the texts which describe Jesus as *eikon* (image): Col. 1, 15; 3, 10; Eph. 4, 24; Phil. 2, 5-11; 2 Cor. 4, 4; Rom. 8, 28-30; 1 Cor. 15, 44-48; and in the

baptism, spirituality (Rom. 6, 1-11); Gal. 2, 19-20; Col. 2, 11–3, 4; Eph. 2, 4-7.
[76] Rom. 8, 29.
[77] Co. 3, 9-14; Eph. 4, 22-24.
[78] Mt. 11, 29.
[79] Acts 1, 1.
[80] Lk. 3, 38.
[81] Lk. 2, 52.
[82] Jas. 1, 5; Rom. 16, 19; Col. 1, 9. Eph. 1, 8; 5, 15; Acts 2, 47; 4, 33; 7, 10.
[83] Acts 8, 8-10.
[84] Especially the last paragraph.

what man ought to be like is stated more strongly, but with a completely different accent, by John in particular in those passages which reveal that in Jesus we have seen what God is like. Not a man or a people escapes the call to imitate the gods. The images of God and of man necessarily complement each other. This is why it is so important that Jesus, again according to John, was a living apocalypse, i.e., a perpetual revelation of the Father. "The perfect man" and "the glory of God" are two facets of the same reality. "No one has ever seen God; the only Son, who is in the bosom of the Father, he has made him known" concludes John's prologue,[85] a few seconds after we have rejoiced because we have beheld his glory.[86]

This assertion, that God has been seen, evokes in the normal person and especially in the religious-minded, a whole series of stubborn objections. This seems too simple to be true. God is so great! Can anyone possibly have seen that God who sows the stars in the heavens and stands beyond and above our history and succession, he who reads our deepest thoughts and holds millions of human lives in his hand, effortlessly is the God of truth and the source of all visible and invisible beauty? If we as Christians maintain what Moses held to be impossible—"No man shall see God and live" [87]—we must have serious grounds for making this assertion. Let us content ourselves with three questions: [88]

   1. When did man see God's glory (in Jesus)?
   2. Who were privileged with this vision?
   3. What is the principal quality of God that is thus "seen"?

The answer to the first question is easy. Although the fourth gospel also has Jesus speak in the present tense, as though the disciples themselves had consciously experienced the revelation of God's glory when they were travelling about with Jesus and heard him debate, the correctives employed by John himself leave no possibility of doubt; it was only afterwards that they realized it, after they had reflected deeply on all that had happened.[89] It was even *impossible* before to possess the essential spirit of Jesus because he was not yet glorified.[9]

We are thus dealing with a retrospective vision of God's glory. The disciples were not sufficiently receptive to see the full import of the most astonishing and revelatory incidents such as the miracle at Cana, whereby Jesus revealed his glory.[91] The commentary on the miracle of the loaves and fishes is in this respect eloquent enough.[92] We know a number of these sympathetic figures who were too shortsighted to realize what was happening under their very eyes and who, when all is said and done, cut a very poor figure: Nicodemus, the Samaritan woman, the man born blind, Philip: "Have I been with you so long and yet you do not know me, Philip? He who has seen me has seen the Father." [93]

We find this almost childish inadequacy in the synoptics, in the story of the transfiguration: three chosen disciples are given the opportunity of seeing something of the glory and richness of their master and they cannot keep their eyes open because of their tiredness.[94] This incomprehension is not contradicted either by the second Epistle of Peter, which asserts that they were eyewitnesses of Jesus' majesty when he received honor and glory from the Father.[95] This later insight is no denial of the preceding fact, but rather assumes it.

We are at once a step nearer to the solution of the second problem, for the foregoing implies that the vision of God's glory in Jesus is dependent on a great gift, that of faith. Without the Spirit no one would ever have seen anything. The faith of the disciples corresponds to the revelation of Jesus' glory at Cana.[96] It thus follows that the possibility of sharing in that glory is unlimited. In the story of Lazarus, Martha symbolizes everybody; the condition is universal: "Did I not tell you that *if you would believe* you would see the glory of God?" [97] This too we find in the synoptics. In the most "Johannine" text of Matthew and Luke, Jesus expresses his joy that the

[85] Jn. 1, 18.

[86] Jn. 1, 14; cf. 1 Jn. 1, 1-4.

[87] Ex. 33, 20; cf. Gen. 33, 31; Is. 6, 5.

[88] H. Kittel, *Die Herrlichkeit Gottes* (Giessen, 1934); G. Kittel, "Doxa," in *T.W.N.T.*, 2 (1935), pp. 236-258; A. M. Ramsay, *The Glory of God and the Transfiguration of Christ* (London, 1949); J. Dupont, *Essais sur la christologie de Saint Jean* (Bruges, 1951); T. Crisan, "De notione Doxa in evangelio S. Joannis in luce Veteris Testamenti," (Thesis, Rome, 1953); J. Duplacy, "L'espérance de la gloire de Dieu dans l'Ancien Testament," in *Bible et Vie chrétienne*, 8, (1954-55) pp. 40-54; "La Gloire de Dieu et du seigneur Jésus," *ibid.*, 9, pp. 7-21;

B. Bussmann, *Der Begriff des Lichtes beim Hl. Johannes* (Münster i.W., 1957); A. Feuillet, "L'Incarnation rédemptrice dans les écrits johanniques," in *Introduction à la Bible*, (Tournai, 1959), II, pp. 890-914; G. Stahlin, "Jesus Christus das Licht der Welt," in *Universitas Festschrift A. Stohr*), (Mainz, 1960), pp. 58-78.

[89] Jn. 2, 22; 12, 16; 13, 7; 14, 26; 20, 9.

[90] Jn. 7, 39; cf. 12, 16.

[91] Jn. 2, 11.

[92] Jn. 6, 26-27.

[93] Jn. 14, 9.

[94] Lk. 9, 32.

[95] 2 Pet. 1, 16-18.

[96] Jn. 2, 11.

[97] Jn. 11, 40.

knowledge of God is given to those who have the simple receptivity of the faithful: God reveals himself, not to the wise and understanding, but to the "little ones." [98] This is also in the Sermon on the Mount: the simple of heart, those who are not disbelieving or skeptical, but have a pure heart, these will see God.[99]

Faith is to such an extent the necessary and sufficient condition that even those who did not know Jesus during his earthly existence and did not eat with the risen Christ will yet see the glory of God. We are confronted here with a paradox: "Blessed are those who have not seen and yet believe!" [100]

Then comes the last question: what more do we now know about God? John answers: "We have seen his *glory*." [101] If we view this against the background of the Old Testament, this is God's most characteristic quality, something like his "holiness," entirely peculiar to him. Hence, the doxologies are too numerous (*doxa* is the Greek word for the Hebrew, *kabod*, rendered in English by *glory*) in which one "gives" to God that which belongs to him alone.[102] If this is so, we must conclude that what we are privileged to find in Jesus is nothing less than the approach to us of God's infinite majesty. What we have beheld of God is the very depth of his being come closer to us.

John has repeatedly given a more concrete form to that deepest essence of the Father, as revealed in Jesus-among-us. He suggests a gesture of endless benevolence, complete and selfless liberality, overflowing life, freely granted communion. "God so loved the world that he gave his only Son." [103] The whole adventure of living together with Jesus can be summed up in one certainty: "He loved us," [104] and this in no way divorced from the source: does not the Father himself love us? [105]

With the mentality of John, one might define Jesus' nature as follows: he who receives and communicates the glory of the Father. The glory which he gives us brings about the union with the Father.[106] The glory which he received consisted in being loved by the Father before the foundation of the world.[107] To glorify and to love are thus one and the same.[108] All the enormous weight of the divine glory—*kabod* means weight as well as glory—so passionately worshipped through ten centuries of rudimentary but intense theology upon which the Jewish people might pride itself, culminates in the definition which was only possible after Jesus had passed through the world: "God is love." [109] It is thus literally correct to say that anyone who "saw" (in other words, beheld in a spirit of faith) the fullness of grace which proceeded from Jesus acquired a new concept of God.[110]

But let us be a little more cautious in the face of such far-reaching conclusions. Perhaps these were only the elevated concepts of a high-minded theorist. This seems unlikely to begin with, for John's is a passionate temperament, lively, yet, down to earth. If he says that Jesus' earthly existence brought him to realize that God is love, then his opinion is worth pondering on. But let us also consult another tradition, that of St. Paul.

The Pauline tradition which is of necessity realistic by reason of the varied apostolate in the rough little coastline towns, provides us with a text which can rival that of John: "When the goodness and loving kindness of God our savior appeared, he saved us, not because of deeds done by us in righteousness, but by virtue of his own mercy." [111] This text admittedly comes towards the end of Paul's exchange of letters, but it is no novelty. Let us imagine ourselves striking up a conversation with one of those Christians, fairly well-to-do, generous by nature, endowed with rich spiritual gifts, but a little too free and easy: the Corinthians. We would pose them a question of interest to us, to them, and to everyone. What do you think of God? What is he like? Their answer would be a commentary on a few lines from one of Paul's epistles: "Behold the new is come and all this is from God, who through Christ reconciled us to himself . . . that is, God was in Christ reconciling the world to himself, not counting their trespasses against them." [112] In Rome, too, one might hear similar quotations, for example, that nothing and nobody will be able to separate us from the love of God in Christ Jesus, our Lord.[113]

---

98 Mt. 11, 25.

99 Mt. 5, 8; against skepticism, see Jn. 20, 27; Mt. 12, 22-30.31. 41-42; 16, 1-4; against credulity, see Mt. 23, 23.

100 Jn. 20, 29.

101 Jn. 1, 14; 2, 11; 11, 40; 12, 41; 17, 5.22-24.

102 Rom. 11, 36; 16, 27; Gal. 1, 5; Phil. 4, 20; Eph. 3, 31; 1 Tim. 1, 17; 2 Tim. 4, 18; Rev. 1, 6; 4, 11; 5, 12-13; 7, 12.

103 Jn. 3, 16.

104 Jn. 13, 34; 15, 9.12.

105 Jn. 16, 27; cf. 14, 21.

106 Jn. 17, 22.

107 Jn. 17, 24.

108 Cf. Jn. 17, 4-5 with v. 23.

109 1 Jn. 4, 8.

110 Jn. 1, 14.

111 Tit. 3, 4-5.

112 2 Cor. 5, 18-19.

113 Rom. 8, 35-39.

Paul, who cannot forget God for one moment and is in a certain sense too impatient to tarry long with Jesus alone, admits all along the line that only now do we know God. One might almost say that the famous circular for Asia Minor, which bears the name of the Ephesians, speaks of a new God, who displayed the riches of his glory,[114] of something which reduces all dimensions to zero and surpasses all mystical and rational knowledge: the love of Christ.[115] In Jesus, God showed us "the great love with which he loved us" in order that all the future might behold "the immeasurable riches of his grace in kindness toward us in Christ Jesus." [116]

Let these few texts suffice. If our hearts were humble enough, one of them would be sufficient to make us pause in ecstasy. There is only one thing we wish to add. For centuries, the glory of God has been associated with light-phenomena. God dwells in unapproachable light.[117] God is light.[118] Since Jesus is his image, the people of Capernaum saw "a great light," [119] and the shepherds were bathed in the glory of the Lord.[120] It is sacrosanct theology and not merely atmospheric imagery when John says that the light shines in the darkness and that the true light that enlightens every man came into the world.[121] And as he pens these phrases, he is most surely not thinking of a sort of floodlit crib of Bethlehem, but of a great man hurrying over the dusty roads, visiting bathing pools, and healing those blind from birth because he is the light of the world.[122]

It is essentially the adult Jesus, during his public life, who has become for us the message of a God who is love.

Anyone who has ever seen the expectant faces of parents as they lean smiling over a crib understands the urgent questions. What will become of this child? What marvellous message will its enthusiasm bring us? For how many will this new-born freedom be the beginning of a great happiness, the essential companion on the great journey?

Thus, begins the history of man, which may perhaps end in doubt or outright failure. And yet, it will have recalled the great fact which we know by faith: that God took a spark from the glowing volcano of his breast and with a mighty throw, flung that freedom into the turbulent course of human history. Man, the most evolved of creatures and God's own representative in the kingdom of matter, numbered one little spark more, a small waxing freedom in the midst of so many others. He grew up in great silence, a pilgrim like all the others, a worker like most of them. For three years, which passed like lightning, the spark flared up and glowed upon his pure and limpid features, as a lamp can burn in a mountain hut and a humble heart in a human breast. The spark was called Jesus and the moment has now come to see how after one final flickering it died out and rose again.

114 Eph. 3, 16.
115 Eph. 3, 18-19.
116 Eph. 2, 4-7.
117 1 Tim. 6, 16.
118 1 Jn. 1, 5.

119 Mt. 4, 16; cf. v. 13.
120 Lk. 2, 9.
121 Jn. 1, 4-5.9.
122 Cf. Jn. 9; connection with 8, 12.

IV
Jesus
the Redeemer

Surely, without hesitation or nuances, the Christian people confess during the stations of the cross: "We adore thee, O Christ, and we bless thee, because by thy holy cross thou hast redeemed the world." What daring, what conscious gratitude and unconscious anxiety are concealed in these words! What do we mean by the "world"? Was the redemption an automatic event? Who was truly and visibly redeemed? Why must it involve death and suffering? Must we, too, suffer in order to redeem?

Let us begin by stating that any manner of speech—theological, kerygmatic or the "ordinary" vocabulary, is unavoidably innaccurate. The mystery of Jesus can never be adequately expressed. Even to distinguish phases is to render ourselves guilty of speaking too coarsely in black and white. Hermetically divided periods do not exist: we are concerned solely with moments of climax, significant facts, and symbolic values. The mystery of the incarnation is most remarkable when we contemplate its beginnings in Mary's womb and in the crib of Bethlehem. Whoever desires to see Jesus the pilgrim will have to linger around Nazareth, since it is here that the greatest number of years and perhaps the most marvellous features of that mystery are to be found. Spontaneously, we imagine the bearer of a message as a public orator, fully conscious of his mission as messiah, whose inner being has passed beyond the powerful but uncertain headstrongness of youth. For the same reason—yet without denying that Jesus was and is the redeemer in every aspect of his life—the Christian people have always considered Jesus' suffering, and more particularly, the short span of time between the Last Supper and his death, as the basis of his redeemer's title.

In order to give our study a certain progressive line, we have divided it into four points: [1]

1. To refresh our minds concerning the reality of the passion and death.

2. A brief sketch of Jesus' passion as an historical fact, whereby a well-defined psychological attitude was evident on his part.

3. Exploration of a hypothesis: the primary effect of Jesus' death lay in the exemplary character of the new Adam. In different terminology, the entry of the new Moses as leader and priest into the land or tabernacle of the promise through the bitter waters of death.

4. A short survey of the endless horizons of "consequent effectiveness" which gradually found expression in a vocabulary which will have to be further refined. The most striking are the freeing from sin (moral dimension) and the saving of the human race from death, by death (transhistorical dimension).

SUFFERING IN HUMAN LIFE

To live is to suffer. We are all aware of this, and it is very easy to deduce from this that Jesus had to suffer if his incarnation were to be valid and complete. And yet, both theological reflection and religious meditation tend almost irresistibly to lead one to forget this self-evident fact. We are intellectuals and when once the world of ideas has been set in motion, in the brain of the theologian or in the

[1] Short bibliography: J. Rivière, *Le dogme de la Rédemption. Essai d'étude historique*, (Paris, 1905); *Etude théologique* (Paris, 1941³); K. Staab, *Die Lehre von der stellvertretenden Genugtung Christi* (Paderborn, 1908); W. Hillmann, *Aufbau und Deutung der synoptischen Leidensberichte* (Freiburg i.B., 1941); J. Pascher, *Theologie des Kreuzes* (Münster, 1948); K. H. Schelkle, *Die Passion Jesu in der Verkundigung des Neuen Testamentes* (Heidelberg, 1949); C. Novel, *Essai sur le développement de l'idée biblique de Rédemption* (Lyon, 1954); J. Jeremias, "Pais theou," in *T.W.N.T.*, 5 (1954), pp. 676-713; E. Lohse, *Märtyrer und Gottesknecht. Untersuchungen zur urchristlichen Verkündigung von Sühntöd Jesu Christi* (Göttingen, 1955); E. F. Sutcliffe, *Providence and Suffering in the Old and New Testament* (Edinburgh, 1955); E. Schweizer, *Erniedrigung und Erhöhung bei Jesus und seinen Nachfolgern* (Zurich, 1955); C. H. Dodd, *Benefits of His Passion* (Nashville, 1956); L. Moraldi, *Espiazione sacrificale e riti espiatori nell' ambiente biblico e nell' Antico Testamento* (Rome, 1956); V. Taylor, *Jesus and His Sacrifice. A study in the Passion-Sayings in the Gospels* (London, 1957²); L. Richard, *Le mystère de la Rédemption* (Tournai, 1959) X. L. Dufour, "Passion", in *Dict. Bibl. Suppl.* (1960) pp. 1419-1542; L. Sabourin, *Rédemption sacrificielle. Une enquête exégetique* (Bruges, 1961).

meditation of the inner man, they quickly lose all contact with reality. As Christians and more important still, as theologians, we should never allow ourselves to lose the intimate awareness of the whole reality of our human existence, including sin, suffering, and death. We need to have the mentality of the authors of Genesis or *The Brothers Karamazov* and *Crime and Punishment*.

How little anyone knows of life who has not intimate contact with suffering or who has not seen death gnawing away at the lives about him? How fragile life itself appears when we are wracked with pain. Suffering is universal, and yet, it is "the only thing with which we cannot sympathize" (Oscar Wilde). It fills the hospitals; we banish it to the lunatic asylums, the prisons, the red-light districts, yet, we meet it on the corner of every street and on our own doorstep. Families are afflicted and whole nations struggle in despair; old people die their lonely deaths and children pitifully cry. Each day, millions of lives provide a commentary to the Book of Job.

The two facts of suffering are called death and sin. Alexander was thirty-three years old and world famous when he cried out that he was dying despite the aid of a superfluity of doctors. Others agree with Montenaeken:

Life is vain
A little love
A little hate
And then . . . good day.

Life is brief
A little hope
A little dream
And then . . . good night.
(Léon Montenaeken)

But what really troubles us is sin; our own impotence, weakness, malice; the injustice in the world, those who commit murder so that righteousness may prevail and those who turn a blind eye to slavery in order to insure freedom. The daily victories gained by cunning, arrogance, money, disloyalty, brute force. The disillusionment because we cannot be certain that what is beautiful is also good. We know men with noble foreheads, strong arms, and capable hands; we know people of keen understanding, of artistic talents . . . and how much bitter disillusionment they have brought to others and to themselves by their caprices, their infidelity, their selfishness. We were privileged to see the beauty of a woman's face, hear the charm of her voice; we knew her graceful movements, the infectious force of her enthusiasm and her passionate love, her ability to devote herself to important matters and to bear grief, her gifts of observation, and her lightening intuition—and how much love she has forever destroyed, how many families she has broken up, what a balance of frivolity, superficiality, betrayal, she has built up.

When a man is born, he enters upon an immense stage on which good and evil are dramatically opposed and the actors are impelled by an urgent thirst: a thirst for truth, goodness, happiness, beauty, love. And no one has ever been able to satisfy this thirst without great crises and much suffering.

Even under the best circumstances, when a number of equally great and noble people meet, harmony is difficult to establish, as is graphically illustrated in O. Henry's short story, "The Gift of the Magi." Jim and Della, two nice people, are struggling against poverty. They possess two souvenirs of a happier past—Jim's gold watch and Della's magnificent long hair. They wish to buy each other a Christmas gift. Della sacrifices her long tresses and with the twenty-two dollars thus obtained, buys a platinum watch chain for Jim. He, meanwhile, sells his watch in order to enhance the natural glory of Della's hair with a pair of tortoise-shell combs. Christmas comes, but Jim is without his watch and Della no longer needs combs. The entire story symbolizes our powerlessness to live without suffering and without causing pain. This is true even of those who love most ardently and could be expected to divine the wishes of the loved one.

One might object that Jim and Della could have shown a little more insight. Possibly, yet, when love personified appeared upon the scene with unequalled sagacity, he died amid terrible torments. One might also say that the tragicomic situation in which Jim and Della found themselves on that long-awaited Christmas Eve shows even more clearly the depth of their love, and that this is enough. Certainly, but this did not prevent them both from feeling that they had made a useless sacrifice. And this is precisely the question: why can we maintain that Jesus' sacrifice was not useless?

The question itself is more topical than ever. Ours is an age of redemption, of liberation. Whole nations struggle to gain independence. For the first time humanity knows the planetary dimensions of her ills; the world's wretchedness is revealed to the eyes of the photographer and the television camera; eyewitnesses and international conferences testify to it. We have discovered powerful medicines and at the same time multiplied our capacity to harass and eliminate each other. We are beginning to discover the laws of economic progress and popular hygiene and to strive after structural reforms. Compared with such a measureless task of redemption, of what significance is that small, isolated fact that a condemned man dies of asphyxiation, at ten minutes distance from Jerusalem? Before beginning to explore this mystery, let us recall the historical facts.

THE BRUTAL FACT OF THE PASSION

The accounts of the passion occupy a very special place in the gospels and are disproportionately long. Out of sixteen chapters, Mark devotes two entirely to the passion which, historically speaking, lasted barely two days. This cannot be explained by the fact that the passion is of great importance from the theological point of view, for the gospels give us not reflections but descriptions. For the first time we are offered details, with the names of the persons, dialogue, and what might be termed a general view of events. Nowhere else in the gospels are we so conscious of dealing with reality, with an historical fact. There can be no doubt about it: Jesus suffered, and Jesus died.

It is extremely difficult to find the thread and to reconstitute it exactly. Had all this taken place in our time, the press, radio, and television would have provided us with detailed information. Following the new style, they would begin by introducing the characters. First and foremost, there are the four main characters, all equally unpleasant people who in a democratic age would find it difficult to get themselves elected and would never be reelected. In the spring of the year 30—the probable date of these events—all four found themselves in Jerusalem. The tetrarch, Herod Antipas (age fifty-one), had recently caused considerable scandal in the city by his divorce and remarriage to Herodias (age thirty-six), the wife of his half brother, whose beauty and personality had seduced him during a trip to Rome. Everyone still remembered the execution of John the Baptist, which was undoubtedly connected with this affair. More recently still, Salome (age nineteen), the daughter of Herodias, had won the heart of her uncle, Herod Philip (age fifty-two), and had departed with him as his wife to the northern provinces. Antipas was a very rich man with a yearly income of two hundred talents, or two million denarii (one denarius was roughly equal to a day's wages). Antipas was *persona gratissima* with the emperor Tiberius, and shared in the common people's hatred of the house of Herod. He did little or nothing to improve its evil reputation.

Annas (age fifty-two) had been replaced as high priest fifteen years earlier, but still enjoyed considerable influence in both Church and civic circles. Five of his sons would attain the high priesthood, and his son-in-law, Caiphas, who had already exercised this function for twelve years, confirmed the popular saying that Herod was born with a caul. His decided character, out for gain, adroit in his servile policy towards the Romans, contributed to the latent anticlericalism.

The enigmatic Pilate had arrived four years earlier from Rome and was regarded by the most moderate people as "unyielding, ruthless, obstinate" (Philo). Like the three aforementioned, he could not help but notice the festive atmosphere, but for him, this meant being prepared, cool, swayed by no religious feelings, ready only to intervene.

These then were the characters. Our reporters would next proceed to transmit the actual facts. Even those newsmen with a solid religious background would furnish their agency with fairly divergent texts. The differences between the various reports might be even greater than those we detect in the evangelists, no matter how popular the "scientific approach" nowadays. They would for example speak of the agony in the Garden of Olives, preferring either the dogmatic interpretation of John,[2] the parenthetic intent of Luke[3] or a mixture of both, as in Matthew and Mark.[4] They could most probably clear up several doubtful points; whether it was actually a troop of Roman soldiers which came to take Jesus prisoner and what motive these men had been given: the elimination of a bandit, a political rebel or a heretic. We might obtain a more comprehensive view of the sequence of events and of the respective roles of Annas, Caiphas, the Sanhedrin as a whole, Herod Antipas, and Pilate. The exact recording of the indignities and humiliations suffered by Jesus would be unbearable, even without direct trans-

[2] Jn. 12, 23-32.   [4] Mt. 26, 36-46; Mk. 14, 32-42.
[3] Lk. 22, 29-46.

mission, but each station would have its own angle and presentation. One would give the impression that certain exalted persons were entirely responsible for the whole affair; another would sketch the terrifying picture of the Syrian cohorts. Some reckless reporter would suddenly surprise his televiewers with a close-up of the scourge, clearly made of bone and leather with iron tips, while smoothly and unemotionally informing them that the dark, sticky patches are Jesus' coagulated blood.

Other pictures would resolve our doubts concerning the color of the inscription: black or red letters on the white background, and also regarding the cross: Was it a "T" or an "X" shape? They would enlighten us about the piece that Jesus carried and how he carried it: tied to his back or loose, and about the manner of the crucifixion, the size of the nails, the quality of the witnesses. An interview with the officer on duty would help to clarify the nature of Jesus' last cry. Was it "natural" or must it be considered miraculous, since the condition of the heart and of the nerves would seem to render impossible any such cry shortly before the collapse? [5] It is quite likely that we would not have to waste any more words on the shroud of Turin and we would also be able to make a clearer distinction between historical fact and theological affirmation with regard to the cosmic and religious phenomena which occurred at the sixth hour.[6] And what would be the importance of all this?

Psychology, another fashionable profession of our time, would then come to our aid. Replace the eyewitnesses and the evangelists by modern psychologists and we would have had a much better idea of Jesus' attitude, his feelings, his reactions. The text of their passion might then have run roughly like this:

"The Savior did not endure in his passion all conceivable forms of human suffering. No matter how refined the pain of crucifixion, we are familiar with the inventiveness of modern cruelty. It is therefore wrong to stress the physical suffering, where this, in fact, relates to the mental agony suffered during a drama of moral redemption. Yet, it is no less true on this account that in order to redeem us, Jesus was willing to undergo terrible tortures. Crucifixion was so devised that no part of the body escaped pain. In order to measure the depth and acuteness of Jesus' suffering, one must also take into account the extreme sensitivity of his body which was

born of the virgin Mary and exempted from the diseases which
blunt our senses. Through his will, which held his entire being
absolutely in check and raised it to an extreme of consciousness, he
was incomparably more vulnerable to all forms of suffering, whereas
with us one form excludes the other, and our wills strive to render
us insensible to grief.

"For three days, which were to be full of tragedy, the totality of
human suffering was concentrated in the heart and soul of Jesus. He
experienced the punishment inflicted by man, by foreigners and
countrymen, by strangers and dearly beloved friends, by great and
small. He knew every form of grief that the human heart may taste:
the unfaithfulness of friends, being rejected by one and betrayed by
another. No scorn was spared him; his reputation and his manly
honor were attacked. He was branded as an impostor and exhibited
naked before the eyes of his countrymen. Finally, there was an
endless sorrow in which all his courage ebbed, and, to conclude, the
apparent desertion by the Father." [7]

THE PRIMARY RESULT OF JESUS' PASSION

What we have just read gives us some idea of the depths of Jesus'
suffering. It is perhaps not so difficult to convey that his extreme
sensitivity and his loving heart rendered him more vulnerable than
anyone else. Human suffering finds its supreme expression in him,
but why do we speak in that connection of the saving of mankind?
Why is his death more effective than those of the millions who were
slaughtered on the battlefields and in the concentration camps of
this century? Surely, they, too, experienced mental agony and were
sometimes subjected to more protracted and horrible tortures?
Why has his cross become a symbol of hope in our houses and upon
our graves, while no one made a symbol of the eight hundred
crosses upon which the flower of the Pharisees died in agony a
century before Jesus [8] in the very center of Jerusalem and watched

[5] Cf. H. Modder, "Die Todesursache bei der Kreuzigung," in *Stimmen der Zeit*, 144 (1949), pp. 50-59.

[6] Cf. J. Michl, "Fragen um das Leichentuch von Turin," in *Theol. Quart.*, 136 (1956), pp. 129-173.

[7] J. Mellet, La Rédemption," in *Initiation théologique*. (I have translated from the Spanish edition (Barcelona, 1961), I, p. 150.

[8] Flavius Josephus, *Antiquitates*, 13, 14, 2; *De bello Judaico*, I, 4. 6. Cf.

by a jubilant Alexander Janneus as he sat drinking wine with his mistresses? No special power is attributed either to the six thousand slaves crucified along the Via Latina between Rome and Capua.[9] Who expected anything extraordinary of the two thousand crosses which circled Jerusalem with the terrible spectacle of so many howling and shrieking rebels, and this after Jesus' birth? [10]

Here lies the entire mystery of the passion, for it is a fact that the first Christians already attributed a most exceptional value to Jesus' suffering. They linked his passion to their own lives, and soon immortalized this connection in the phrase, "He died for us." This will soon form one of the pillars of Pauline theology and of the whole of Christian life. Let us try to trace the foundations.

A double observation can perhaps put us on the right track. First and foremost, it is a fact that the best or our race, the truly great, have always had great respect for suffering. We have only to think of the deaths of Oedipus and Socrates, of the Communist and patriot "martyrs." There is a nobility in pain which compels us to pause and think. It even, according to the pagan mythologies, characterized the lives of the gods. For this reason alone suffering is powerful. Why was Gandhi's influence worldwide?

On the other hand, we feel great sympathy for people who speak on behalf of others. The bible provides some splendid examples, beginning with Abraham and Moses; [11] the figures of Job, Tobias, and Daniel are engraved in human memory. God punishes the pitiless scoffers, but when the sufferer himself intercedes, he can obtain their pardon. The combination of these two facts leads us to the following hypothesis: in God's plan, suffering for the sake of others is exceptionally efficacious. This combination of "suffering" and "for others," brings us to a law: the law of *compassion*. Each one contributes to the salvation of mankind in the measure of his, of necessity voluntary, compassion.

If this hypothesis is valid, then Jesus' initiative in the face of the world's misery and sin is nothing but a voluntary sharing in our grief. The supreme value of *his* crucifixion lies in the exceptional measure of his compassion. We shall test this principle a little further and then follow two parallel paths which seem to characterize the mechanism of this mysterious efficacy: the way of restorative exemplariness and the path along which a guide drags all his followers during the passage through the bitter waters of our pilgrimage.

1. *Compassion, Principle of Redemption*

"The Son of God loved me and gave himself for me." [12] No other phrase perhaps expresses more clearly and more succinctly the conviction of the entire Christian tradition: Jesus was intensely compassionate towards us. The Christological hymn from the Epistle to the Philippians describes how Jesus became a slave, obedient unto death on the cross, and how God therefore exalted him and granted him divine influence.[13] Peter impresses upon his readers: "Christ suffered for you . . . He himself bore our sins in his body on the tree, that we might die to sin and live to righteousness. By his wounds you have been healed." [14] This last text is an almost literal quotation from the songs of the Suffering Servant, whose suffering saved "the many." This also brings us closer to the origin of the apostolic conviction that we have indeed been "saved."

It can have been none other than Jesus himself who revealed that in his life was now fulfilled that which the Suffering Servant had expressed as a figure or idea: that the grievous suffering of one particular person could affect the inner life of another, could purify the sinful heart and unite it with God. We have no grounds for assuming that it was some apostle's imagination, or a mutual discovery of old Scripture texts, or inflated theoretical considerations which produced such a remarkable, even unique insight. It thus seems self-evident that the identification of the son of man with the Suffering Servant, in other words, the realization that Jesus' life's work and in particular his passion could have a redeeming effect on the entire people, must have been derived essentially from the earthly Jesus.[15]

But Jesus did not say this in the manner of a teacher formulating, then proving, a thesis. It was even a long time afterwards before the apostles realized exactly what had occurred. But the new and higher light, radiating from the resurrection, brightly illumined the earlier events, words, and attitudes. What enlightened the apostles most, in my opinion, was the willingness and self-assuredness with which Jesus died.

E. Stauffer, *Jerusalem und Rom* (Bern, 1957), pp. 123-127: "Die Kreuzesstrafe im antiken Paläs-tina."

9 Cf. Stauffer, *ibid.*, p. 126.

10 Flavius Josephus, *op. cit.*, 17, 10.10;

De Bello Judaico, 2, 5.8.

11 Job. 42, 7-8.

12 Gal. 2, 20.

13 Phil. 2, 5-11.

14 1 Pet. 2, 21-24.

15 Cf. pp. 163-178.

We see indeed how, on rethinking and describing the passion, the apostles constantly stress that Jesus acted freely and in full awareness. They retain the constant memory of "the grace of our Lord Jesus Christ, that though he was rich, yet for your sake he became poor." [16] In the Pauline tradition Jesus' death is an impoverishment, an emptying of self, a voluntary humiliation.[17] In the Johannine tradition we find the same voluntary aspect but now enriched with a majestic grandeur: "For this reason the Father loves me because I lay down my life that I may take it again. No one takes it from me, but I lay it down on my own accord. I have power to lay it down and I have power to take it again, this charge I have received from my Father." [18] This basic attitude is reaffirmed in more concrete form during the Last Supper, when Jesus was aware that the hour had come,[19] in the particularly Johannine scene in the Garden of Olives,[20] and before Pilate.[21]

But the synoptics, too, whose accounts are drier and more pragmatic, provide us with touching examples of this inner firmness and submission of Jesus' will: the unshakeable decision to go to Jerusalem, nonetheless; [22] the open opposition to the Pharisees as well as to the Sadducees and the Herodians which must inevitably have made his triumphal entry the prelude to a mortal exodus; a burial accepted gratefully and in advance,[23] the revealing of the coming treachery, according to one tradition,[24] and of the traitor, according to another; [25] the complete, deliberate, yet, most painful acceptance of the Father's will during the agony; [26] the categorical refusal of human and angelic help to change the course of a drama already in full motion; [27] the voluntary loneliness which was his after he had insured the safety of his disciples—a fact particularly stressed in John.[28]

The absence of any protest when the cross is laid upon his shoulders further testifies to this spirit; on the contrary, "bearing his own cross," according to John's hieratic expression, he left the town.[29] He also refused the drugged drink [30] and successfully completed the great test, so that he could say: "It is finished," bowing his head and—again in John's words—"giving up" his spirit, as though placing something very precious into someone's hands.[31]

But for our safety his death had not alone to be self-willed; he had to be certain of his purpose. He knew that his life would serve.[32] One of the celebrated songs of Deutero-Isaiah said that the Suffering Servant would obtain great multitudes as booty [33] and, in fact, we find that Jesus, in predicting his passion, retained that perspective. In poetical-theological style this is known as dying like a grain of wheat in the earth in order to bear much fruit,[34] drawing all men to himself from the height of the cross,[35] risking his life like a courageous shepherd so that the sheep may graze in safety.[36] Luke, too, gives us another eloquent proof of this certainty: Jesus can promise someone paradise, for *today*.[37]

Common to all the evangelists and undoubtedly, too, the source of this invincible certainty on the part of Jesus and of Christianity is the language of the scriptures. Jesus is no impotent victim, the plaything of hostile forces; his death is one great Yes to a divine promise. The first Christians had the indescribable consolation of knowing from the scriptures that these were not the bitter fruits of destiny, but the fulfillment of an eternal decree. It is hence that the accounts of the passion are full of explicit and implicit references to the Old Testament.

It has even been asked whether Jesus would have found the way to the cross without the scriptures; in other words, would he have realized that voluntary suffering was necessary if man was to be redeemed. This question is most probably wrongly put. The evangelists answer only that Jesus, in fact, lived with the scriptures and saw in them the expression of his Father's will. It is perhaps the best sign of his humanity that he did not absorb God's decree in his acquired knowledge by means of an overclear intuition, but more objectively through a norm which was even set down plainly in writing. This norm, which in concrete form is above all the figure of the Suffering Servant from Deutero-Isaiah, was interpreted by Jesus' mind, assimilated by his heart, and transformed into reality by his will.

Voluntary suffering is compassion; certainty of self presupposes an awareness of victory. Jesus' willingness and sureness during the

16 2 Cor. 8, 9.
17 Cf. also Phil. 2, 7.
18 Jn. 10, 17-19.
19 Jn. 13, 1.
20 Jn. 18, 4-9.
21 Jn. 19, 10-11.
22 Mk. 10, 32; Jn. 11, 8-10.16.
23 Mt. 26, 12.
24 Mk. 14, 18-20; Lk. 22, 21-23; Jn. 13, 18.
25 Mt. 26, 21-25; Jn. 13, 21-30.
26 Mt. 26, 39-44.

27 Mt. 26, 50-54.
28 Mt. 26, 55; Jn. 18, 8-9.
29 Jn. 19, 17.
30 Mt. 27, 34.
31 Jn. 19, 30.
32 Mk. 10, 45.
33 Is. 53, 12.
34 Jn. 12, 24.
35 Jn. 12, 32.
36 Jn. 10, 11.15.28.
37 Lk. 23, 43.

passion are therefore merely expressions of what we termed "the redeeming compassion" which constituted the essence of his passion. It is thus not wrong to paint a Calvary like Roualt's, in which the dark eyes of the crucified figure penetrate deep into the heart of the spectator, with an expression of infinite thirst and indestructible sympathy (literally the same as "compassion" but in the real, noble sense). Nor is there any fault to find in the image Dostoevski left us in the purest and most "influential" figure from his works: Sonia Semionovna. This girl possesses a boundless, naked generosity and, in the passage in which she tells Raskolnikov of her horrible wretchedness, the prostitution forced upon her by her stepmother, she evokes for us the drama of the cross. When Raskolnikov brutally asks her if she loves her stepmother (Mrs. Marmeladov) she answers that she does, and defends her:

"You—you would have to know her. She's just like a child. She is almost mad with grief. And what an intelligent woman she was—so generous and kind. Ah, if only you knew everything."

Sonia said this almost despairingly. It was clear that she was deeply hurt and wanted nothing better than to defend Mrs. Marmeladov. Every feature expressed an *insatiable* (if one may use that term) *compassion*.[38]

Sonia's compassion will be the saving of Raskolnikov, an otherwise hopeless case. Jesus, who could think no evil nor utter any condemnation of his own executioners, is the highest example and the source of this same rule. Let us now attempt to penetrate deeper into that divine decree according to which a love unto death would save everyone from death.

2. Restorative Exemplariness

Even those who accept the law of redeeming compassion falter on occasions before the cross. Why did God wish that his Son should die? Was no redemption possible without suffering? Must love necessarily be accompanied by grief and pain? It has so often been repeated that "one drop of blood, even one act of love on Jesus' part would have been sufficient to save all mankind." Was Calvary then not a needless blood-spilling from hands, feet, and heart, insofar as we all now carry with us the memory of a death which resembled more a form of torture than a return to the Father's house? And, say others, if God was so good, could he not be satisfied with somewhat less suffering? And why did he not forgive unconditionally, without making any demands? Do we not sometimes see parents, spouses, and friends reconciled purely through the "granting" of forgiveness?

It is clear that God's forgiveness could be entirely free. It *is* free and necessarily so. Every page of the bible testifies that what God does is pure grace. It would be naive or blasphemous to imagine the three divine Persons debating among themselves the size of the ransom or the conditions they will demand for a reconciliation, since, after all, their prestige has been undermined or their feelings hurt.

The problem lies not in the difficulty of "stilling the divine wrath," but in the necessity for our purification. For if God has loved us enough to grant us the privilege of becoming his children, this cannot occur without our cooperation. Sin and redemption touch the very fibres of our being; they are not things which can be stolen from or returned to the safe which bears our name. It is *we* who have sinned and thus *we* who must be purified. And assuming that God were willing to remit all our sins *gratis*, the question still remains: How shall we render ourselves receptive to this forgiveness? How can this grace create us anew? If we assume in addition that God's goodness seeks the most effective manner of aiding us in this purification, the further question arises: What is the best means of raising us from the abyss of a world racked by self-seeking to the luminous heights of pure, ardent love?

It is on this well-defined point that Jesus' cross proves its particular efficaciousness in two constituent elements of our being. We are imitative creatures, hence the effects of exemplariness; we are creatures who can be urged along in groups, by a leader, hence the influence exercised by anyone willing to take the lead.

Can anyone doubt that we are essentially imitators? Everything we know we have learned by observation, adaptation, combination. We eat, speak, walk, and move because others have done so before us. Every image, every figure that appears before our eyes is already powerfully at work in us; before we realize it, we are already trying to adopt something from it. This is a law of our nature, an aspect of our social structure, a characteristic of the human race. It is the dynamo which transfers the acquired speed from one to the other, the basis of education and the explanation of the progress of peoples and of the human race as a whole.

---

[38] Cf. *Crime and Punishment*, IV, 4.

Let us apply this notion to sin, for it is nonsense to wish to deny our self-seeking. The image of the perfect man had been lost. The first Adam had turned out a failure: he was disobedient. This is to say that he desired a knowledge other than that of understanding; he wished to arouse feelings which were absent in love. This is what the old man was like, this is the picture of ourselves. What the cross gave back to us, is the complete model. It is complete and perfect not because it held itself aloof, at a safe distance from our ills and far exalted above our difficulties, but because this model became our travelling companion, sharing in the whole mechanism of our purification, even in the inevitable suffering, in the consequences of sin. It is, in fact, through the cross that Jesus became the new Adam.

This is why the apostles in chorus glorify Jesus' humility, his obedience, his meekness. They recommend for imitation in Jesus precisely those qualities which were absent in the first Adam. All can learn from him because he is humble of heart.[39] When we rebel against injustices done to us, then we must know that he suffered for our sake so that we might follow in his footsteps.[40] When we have trouble in remaining united or in refraining from bragging and boasting, then we must think of the sentiments which inspired Jesus, for he became a slave for us, obedient unto death, even death on the cross.[41] Our love for our neighbor is grudging: let us think of him who was rich and made himself poor for us.[42] Finally, when we hesitate in the face of the excessive demands of brotherly love, he once again gives us the measure: we must give our very lives, just as he gave his life.[43] These are the contexts of the model passages. Such was the mentality of Paul, John, Peter, and Matthew. This is what Jesus was like.

It is important to note, in order to understand the entire background of the passion narratives, that Jesus' model of humility was a humiliation, a cross, something costing blood and tears. For it is precisely through this that he caused new purifying springs to well up inside *us*, and these we need for we are constantly tempted to think that sin can be forgiven without "restitution." Certainly, God forgives freely and our "rehabilitation" bears no resemblance to the solemn apologies offered to an offended statesman, yet, sin left us confused, deformed, impotent, unfitted to see God's face or to be pleasant company for the fellow guests of eternity. But where would we begin with the task of purifying ourselves, left to our own resources? We need a companion in purification, someone who undergoes with us the painful process of the crucible in which raw metal is refined to the pure gold of love. We need a model which does not fade and grow blurred at the crucial moment, when it hurts. It is in such moments as these that we look up and see the cross.

Jesus knelt down, washed us, and remains with us until we are completely pure. We, forgetting our sins and failings, often judge that life falls short of our dreams, humiliates us so to speak. Jesus, forgetting who he was, thought of what we would have to endure to be happy with him in God, and he came to join us on that painful journey, to draw us along with him and to help us become what he is. This is, to my mind, the profound significance of the passion as a "model," of which the footwashing according to John is a sort of preface.[44] It will doubtless always remain a disputed but incontestable law that in order to help our neighbor effectively, we must suffer for him and with him.

3. *The Guide through the Waters*

In order to become and to live as a true son of God, the sinner must rid himself of all attachment to self; "lose himself."[45] We must take up our crosses, in other words, be prepared to die, especially in times of persecution.[46] Luke says that we must accept this torture daily.[47] Life is a hard struggle; the Christian has a difficult climb ahead of him along a narrow path in order to gain entry through a narrow door.[48] But through his suffering, Jesus has become the perfect guide for this platoon of death. He was the first to carry his cross; we need only follow him.

This is then the second way of formulating the particular effect of Jesus' crucifixion. We are not alone in the struggle and in the unavoidable suffering. The captain marches in our ranks, shares in our privations, runs the same dangers, and through a mysterious law of our human nature, this helps us immensely.

This is a biblical vision. For the Jews the great common struggle and definitive purification had been the passage through the Red Sea under Moses' leadership. Jesus is now the new Moses, not so much

[39] Mt. 11, 29.
[40] 1 Pet. 2, 18-24.
[41] Phil. 2, 1-8.
[42] 2 Cor. 8, 7-10.
[43] 1 Jn. 3, 16-18.
[44] Jn. 13, 1-15.

[45] Mt. 10, 39; 16, 25-26; Mk. 8, 35-37; Lk. 9, 24; 17, 33; Jn. 12, 25.
[46] Mt. 10, 38.
[47] Lk. 9, 23.
[48] Mt. 7, 13-14; Lk. 13, 24.

because he has given us a new law upon a mountain, but because he was the first to pass through the bitter waters of death and to open the way to the true promised land. When we became Christians through baptism, we died with Jesus and passed through that water: "I want you to know, Brethren, that our fathers were all under the cloud, and all passed through the sea, and all were baptized into Moses in the cloud and in the sea . . . Now these things happened to them as a warning, but they were written down for our instruction, upon whom the end of the ages has come." [49]

This is as much as to say that Christ was the rock [50] and that Moses was a prefiguration of Jesus. More accurately still, Jesus is the true pascal lamb who gave the pilgrims sustaining food, accompanied them, and blotted out their sins. [51] Throughout the whole of history that pascal lamb has been the living symbol of the liberating Exodus and passage through the sea; it formed the focus of the Passover celebration; the pascal lamb slaughtered in the temple was a lively reminder of the most spectacular salvation of a people and the undoubted pledge of future safeguard through all oppression. But how pale all pascal animals appear in the light of Christ, our pascal lamb that has been sacrificed. [52]

For us, who have nothing to do with the Red Sea and are not menaced by the pharaoh's chariots, this language is none the less peculiarly significant. Our sea is purification; our Egypt, the slavery of sin; our Exodus, the painful journey towards a better life; our desert, the unavoidable loneliness of this adventure; our trials, the desire to settle for a "cushy" life or spiritual aridity; our bitter waters, those which we must all pass through without exception because they are the symbols of death. [53] And our Moses showed us the way in everything, even in death.

The Epistle to the Hebrews offers us an even more striking variation on this theme. Jesus surpasses Moses, [54] for he is the high priest, he who goes before into the holy of holies, behind the curtain, [55] in the definitive tabernacle. [56] We have already followed this magnificently inspired author in previous pages, in the footsteps of Jesus, the pilgrim, [57] but it is especially in the last phase of the pilgrimage that Jesus is revealed as high priest. It is chiefly on account of his death that God designated him as high priest after the order of Melchizedek. [58] Why is this? "For it was fitting that he, for whom and by whom all things exist, in bringing many sons to glory, should make the pioneer of their salvation perfect through suffering." [59] This formidable sentence is further explained: "For he who sanctifies and those who are sanctified have all one origin. That is why he is not ashamed to call them brethren . . . since therefore the children share in flesh and blood, he himself likewise partook of the same nature, that through death he might destroy him who has the power of death, that is, the devil, and deliver all those who through fear of death were subject to lifelong bondage . . . Therefore, he had to be made like his brethren in every respect so that he might become a merciful and faithful high priest in the service of God, to make expiation for the sins of the people, for because he himself has suffered and been tempted, he is able to help those who are tempted." [60]

Yes, Christian experience proves that the crucified Christ can help, that precisely his cross is victory and strength. Hence the almost arrogant profession of confidence, the expression of our gratitude: "For we have not a high priest who is unable to sympathize with our weaknesses, but one who in every respect has been tempted as we are, yet without sinning. Let us then with confidence draw near to the throne of grace . . ." [61]

This then is our hypothesis. The primary effect of Jesus' crucifixion or, in more general terms, the principle of redemption through suffering, is linked with a basic human characteristic: solidarity. The most powerful reforming factor in the world is compassion, and the two main ways in which this finds expression are: redeeming exemplariness (the principle of imitation) and the strength emanating from a leader who is at the same time a companion in times of trial. The fact that a divine Person is acting in Jesus imparts to all this a unique, unrepeatable character. And yet the

[49] 1 Cor. 10, 1-2, 11.

[50] 1 Cor. 10, 4.

[51] Jn. 1, 29.36.

[52] 1 Cor. 5, 7.

[53] Water constantly occurs as the symbol of dire need and of death; e.g., Is. 43, 2; Ps. 18, 5; 32, 6; 40, 3; 42, 8; 66, 12 ("through fire and through water"); 69, 2-3, 15-16; 88, 18; Jon. 2, 3-7; Rev. 8, 11; 12, 15; 21; 13 ("the sea gave up the dead"); 21, 1 (destruction of the sea, symbol of the elimination of death).

One may think in this context of baptism (by immersion) as a being buried with Christ (Rom. 6, 4: Col. 2, 12).

[54] Heb. 3, 1-6.

[55] Heb. 6, 19-20.

[56] Heb. 4, 14.19.24.

[57] Cf. pp. 227-249.

[58] Heb. 5, 8-10.

[59] Heb. 2, 10.

[60] Heb. 2, 11-18.

[61] Heb. 4, 15-16.

same law holds good for us. He who wishes to redeem with Jesus must be a guide who goes before through the salt water of trial. In this sense, he "seeks" suffering. If he is rich, he will soon become poor; if he enjoys good health, he will keep vigil and fast; he will open his eyes to the misery of his fellow men; hear their complaints and organize meetings in which bitter suffering is poured from one heart into the other. For hours at a time he will expose himself to the aridity and loneliness of silent adoration and supplication for others. In any case, he will share the fate of others and in this measure communicate strength.

Let us pause a moment at the memorable passage which describes Sonia's reaction when Raskolnikov tells her that it is he who has committed the horrible murder of the old woman:

"Have you guessed?" he whispered at last.

"O God!" A terrible wail broke from her. She sank helplessly on the bed and buried her face in the pillows. But a moment later, she sat up quickly, seized his hands in her thin fingers, and stared at him motionlessly. With a last desperate look she tried to find something more, but there was nothing; it was *true*. Beside herself, she jumped up and walked to the middle of the room, but she went back quickly and sat down beside him again, her shoulder against his. Suddenly, as though cut to the heart, she started and not knowing why herself, flung herself on her knees before him.

"Oh, what have you done to yourself?" she cried in despair, and jumping up, she threw her arms round his neck and clasped him tightly.

Raskolnikov freed himself from her embrace and looked at her with a sorrowful smile.

"How strange you are, Sonia, you embrace me and kiss me after I've told you *that*—you don't know what you are doing."

"Oh, I don't think there is anyone in the world as unhappy as you are," she cried wretchedly, and burst into violent sobbing.

A feeling he had not known for a long time came over him, and his heart melted in his breast. He did not resist it; tears filled his eyes and hung on his eyelashes.

"So you won't leave me Sonia, will you?" he said, looking at her almost hopefully.

"No, no . . . never . . . never!" Sonia cried, "I'll go everywhere with you. Oh God, I'm so miserable. And why, why didn't I meet you before? Why didn't you come to be before?" [62]

Dostoevski has contemplated the cross, and Sonia has something of Jesus. He came to make the journey with us, shoulder to shoulder. Our author was a great realist, and did not hesitate to attribute miraculous power to Sonia's compassion: the surge of repentance and later—but not without having passed through the Siberian prison—the complete salvation of the universal Adam—Raskolnikov. And he is entirely justified, for the cross is almighty, or perhaps not the cross, but the love that is so filled with compassion that it ends upon it.

DIMENSIONS OF THE REDEMPTION

Although we have come to regard Jesus' redeeming compassion as the primary content of his crucifixion, this does not mean that the infinite horizons thereby revealed are to be regarded as "secondary." They are rather aspects or dimensions of the same fact. One of the first dimensions is to some extent defined by the new statute of humanity initiated by the cross. Once again the People of God dares to gaze upon the face of the Father without terror or shame. This new statute has been developed by Christian tradition into an extensive legal terminology with various nuances and interpretations. There is too another, moral dimension: the redemption throws an entirely new light on the attitude which must now be adopted towards the world, towards oneself, and towards God. Finally, there is also a transhistorical and, as it were, cosmic dimension. The redemption is the seed of a new, purer, and more beautiful world.

1. *Our New Statute in Legal Terms*

Modern man is often scandalized by what for the early Christians was a source of joy and satisfaction. In our case, the very word, "redemption," evokes a social situation, the existence of slaves whose liberty was bought by a "ransom" to be paid to their master. The modern Christian balks. Who is this stern master who demands such an excessive price? Is it God perhaps, or the devil? The very idea seems impossible.

And yet, there is a profound reality hidden beneath this legal terminology which describes our redemption as if it were a case before the courts: the joy and pride of humanity whom God's

[62] *Crime and Punishment,* V.

mercy has raised to a height where humiliation no longer reigns, but a state of near equality or at, least, intimacy. A certain feeling for justice, deeply imprinted in our being and in our sense of honor has been satisfied.

The prophets had spoken of God's wrath, provoked by the sins of mankind, which must be inevitably and universally revealed, most particularly in a punitive judgment,[63] for God is just. He remains unfalteringly faithful to the covenant and to the promises made since Abraham. This was his initiative, and it sprang only from his mercy. But if God raised man to the status of partner, he must also have rendered him capable of mutual love, of created loyalty. Yet, there came an abundance of disloyalty, of sin. The covenant was violated time and again with monotonous frequency, almost without hope of improvement. The original harmony was radically destroyed, so that the human race came to resemble a mass of rootless invalids who in their nakedness dared not raise their eyes to the spotless purity of the divine partner's face. And it was a mistake to think, like the majority of the Jews, that it was sufficient to belong to the descendants of Abraham to qualify for exceptional treatment.

Jesus' death brought about an actual revolution in this situation. The first Christians measured its consequences with the aid of a terminology corresponding to the legal relationships of the covenant. In his first epistle, Paul already writes that Jesus' death frees us from the "wrath to come." [64] It brought us reconciliation.[65] Logically, according to the logic of someone brought up on the Old Testament, the covenant was sealed by blood: [66] "For without the shedding of blood there is no forgiveness." [67] Consequently, we have been "bought" for "a high price." [68] Better still, we are "redeemed" like slaves at a market.[69] The official papers bearing the fantastic figure of our debts have been nailed to the cross, and thus violently torn to pieces.[70] Jesus' death can therefore be called "the wages of sin" [71] and one can say that he made himself sin,[72] even a curse for us.[73]

It is quite plain that such expressions are derived from a theologian whose ardent temperament in no way recoils from the paradox and the daring formula. His legal veneer is merely superficial, yet, it is in no way meaningless or isolated. John, another theologian of equal mental capacity, is also much preoccupied with the "judgment" and the radical change occasioned therein by Jesus' death.

Jesus acquits us, from this time onwards.[74] Even before John, the synoptics assure us that Jesus himself regarded his death as a "ransom for many." [75] This emerges most plainly in the institution of the eucharist with a clear allusion to the blood of the covenant.[76]

It is in particular this juridico-cultic aspect which gained success. The Epistle to the Hebrews compares Jesus' death, deliberately and in detail, with the sacrifices of the Old Testament.[77] The Fathers say that Jesus has offered a perfect sacrifice, and the councils ratify this mode of expression. By the beginning of the Scholastic Period, Anselm, in his work, *Cur Deus homo*, will pose the problem which has since become classic in the Latin Church: since man refused to pay God the honor due to him, could this infinite wrong be made good in any other way than by an act of infinite love and obedience which would be sufficiently meritorious to make satisfaction (a new term) for the dishonor?

It needs no special accent to say that this vision is one-sided. If taken without counterbalance it may even lead to a fundamental mutilation of our ideas of a divine plan or even of our very concept of God. For the only "explanation" of the redemption is the merciful love of God. There is no other "why?" Thomas Aquinas was well aware of the very special nature of Jesus' sacrifice (*quoddam sacrificium acceptissimum Deo*) [78] which proceeded from obedience [79] and in the last instance, from love.[80] It was a "true" sacrifice precisely because of, and in the measure of, that love. But lest we be tempted to use too simplistically this term, "sacrifice," which is the climax of man's soul-stirring yet sometimes perilous striving to express his relationship to God with the categories of cultic offerings and the blood of sacrificial animals, let us listen to the old master. A sacrifice in the true sense of the word is an act performed in order to render to God the honor due to him, to conciliate him:

---

63 Cf. the excellent study by S. Lyonnet, "La sotériologie paulinienne," in *Introduction à la Bible* (Tournai, 1959), Vol. 2, pp. 840-889.

64 1 Thess. 1, 10.

65 2 Cor. 5, 18-20; Col. 1, 20-22; Eph. 2, 16.

66 Rom. 3, 29; Heb. 9, 10; 13.

67 Heb. 9, 22.

68 1 Cor. 6, 20; 7, 23; Rev. 5, 9; 14, 3.

69 Gal. 3, 13; 4, 5.

70 Col. 2, 14.

71 Rom. 6, 23.

72 2 Cor. 5, 21.

73 Gal. 3, 13.

74 Jn. 12, 31; 16, 11.

75 Mk. 10, 45.

76 Mt. 26, 28.

77 Heb. 9, 10.

78 *Summa* Theol. III. q.47, a.2.

79 *Ibid.*

80 *Ibid.* q. 48, a. 3.

Hence Augustine says in Chapter X of the *City of God:*

"A true sacrifice is every work performed in order to unite us in holy union with God, related to that good aim whereby we may become truly blessed." This same saint adds that Christ: "sacrificed himself for us in his passion," and the very fact that he endured this suffering *of his own free will* was exceedingly pleasing to God, since it *proceeded from the greatest possible love.* It clearly follows, therefore, that Christ's passion was a true sacrifice. And, as Augustine says later in the same book, "The sacrifices of the saints (of the old covenant) were so many different signs of this true sacrifice . . ." [81]

In the scriptures and in the Fathers of East and West the basis for all these theories of sacrifice, merit, and satisfaction, is the grateful conviction that God did not treat man as a slave or as a vile criminal. He gave us dignity, responsibility, an active share. Jesus' death is ours, so that from henceforth, we can stand before the Father not only with the emptiness of our sins, shamefaced, with sorrowful downcast eyes, but with the fullness of hearts loving with Jesus, purified by him. It is not easy—bearing in mind God's greatness and that he is the cause of all—to explain how such dignity and collaboration between creator and created is possible, for we have absolutely no common measure. And yet God is not diminished by this; on the contrary, he becomes greater; he becomes more God, since he was mighty enough to create a community which freely, lovingly without any compulsion was capable of offering him a true sacrifice, something pleasing to him on the grounds of a certain equality: a statute essential in every loving friendship. Jesus' death is thus the touchstone of the possibility and nature of a "covenant between God and man."

2. *The Moral Effect of the Cross*

The touching confusion of a child when it realizes "all that mother has done for him" by the fact of becoming his mother; the singular powers liberated in a person's heart and creating treasures of tenderness, heroism and sacred loyalty on witnessing the suffering endured by the loved one for love's sake; the life of Paul, whose back bore countless scars, whose eyes had so often flickered in horror of the deathly scourge or filled with tears on account of so many "friends" who were enemies of Jesus' cross and who accepted all this and transformed it into a pleasant odor because he thus bore on his body the marks of the Lord Jesus [82]—these are a few examples of the moral effect achieved by the suffering of a beloved being.

The apostles, good shepherds as they were, found nothing better than the memory of Jesus' suffering to inspire their followers, who were naturally fickle and uninclined to sacrifice, to deeds of generosity and submission. We may accept that a moral force did indeed emanate from the cross. We have already mentioned the characteristic situations evoked by such references and which have given us our most beautiful texts on the cross: the requirements of brotherly love, the persecution, the trials of slavery, in particular under "stern" masters, and the mutual disputes.[83] Paul made the principle of "dying with Christ" the basis of our entire struggle against sin and egoism. "How can we who died to sin still live in it? Do you not know that all of us who have been baptized into Jesus Christ, were baptized into his death?" [84] One forceful expression says it all: "I have been crucified with Christ" [85] and anyone who desires concrete indications of what it means to crucify the flesh, with its passions and desires, can meditate on the long list of "works of the flesh" which are in inner contradiction with those who belong to Christ Jesus.[86]

Naturally, we also find this in the gospels. The general norm is "to take up one's cross and to follow Jesus." [87] But perhaps, there is nothing more striking than what we might call the first "way of the cross of the disciple of Jesus," namely, the passion according to St. Luke. For when we follow Luke we cannot continue to read as an outsider or simply contemplate Jesus and adore him (as in Matthew). We ourselves become involved and are forced to follow Simon of Cyrene. We too had other things to do, but are suddenly invited to take up our cross and "to carry it behind Jesus." [88]

The Last Supper already, which Jesus so ardently desired "before he suffered," encourages us to be humble servants, just as Jesus was among us as one who serves.[89] This is particularly true if we happen

[81] *Ibid*.
[82] Cf. 2 Cor. 11, 23-25; Phil. 3, 18; Gal. 6, 17.
[83] Cf. pp. 274ff.
[84] Rom. 6, 2-3.
[85] Gal. 2, 19.
[86] Gal. 5, 16-21.24.
[87] Mt. 16, 24; Mk. 8, 34; Lk. 9, 23; Jn. 12, 26.
[88] Lk. 23, 26.
[89] Lk. 22, 27.

to be leaders of the Christian community. We are given a definition of the true disciples: those who continued faithful to him during his trials.[90] In the Garden of Olives we are struck not so much by the cowardice of the disciples—they had only fallen asleep out of sorrow [91]—as by Jesus' attitude of prayer which we must imitate "that we may not enter into temptation." [92]

Concerning Jesus' generous goodness in the midst of his most grievous suffering, Luke has provided every generation of Christians with a number of episodes on which to meditate: the friendly treatment of the traitor,[93] the healing of the wounded soldier,[94] his glance at Peter,[95] the silence preserved in the presence of Herod,[96] his anxiety for the women who mourn him,[97] the forgiveness granted to his executioners,[98] the promise made to the thief [99] and a most edifying death, breathing his last in conscious prayer.[100]

Yet, even this is not enough: The death of Jesus makes us weep for ourselves.[101] The way of the cross is ended, and we make our way home, beating our breasts.[102] Or perhaps we did not stay until the end, but went outside like Peter, bitterly bewailing our betrayal.[103] The centurion then gives the final summation: "Truly this was a just man." [104] This means that Jesus' life is more than an edifying story. It is the generally valid model of a moral life, "Jesus is not only an example but the very type of the persecuted righteous one, who absorbs in his Person the persecutions of all times and by his triumph reveals the victory of his disciples." [105]

The stations of the cross will most likely change and, certain statues will be relegated to the loft, but the Church will continue to preach a crucified Christ, that "folly of God" which is so much stronger than the strongest human invention.[106]

3. *Jesus' Death and the Cosmos*

"So death is at work in us, but life in you," According to Paul, Jesus' passion, even in the participating form of the disciples' sufferings, exercises a vital influence upon others.[107] For Jesus' death is not merely an isolated fact to which God has attached a number of extraneous consequences. There is an inner link between the passion and the future of mankind which may be expressed in one phrase: "Jesus' dying signifies the death of death."

In the first place, it signifies the death of the religious death, which is paganism. Before Jesus' death, even in the heart of his own ministry, there was a dividing wall between the People of God and the other nations. In actual fact, these latter had never gained admittance, at least consciously. But now, at the exact moment in the afternoon when Jesus uttered a loud cry and yielded up his spirit, the curtain of the temple was torn in two from top to bottom.[108] Now we all "have confidence to enter the sanctuary, by the blood of Jesus, by the new and living way which he opened for us through the curtain that is, through his flesh." [109] There is thus another curtain, Jesus' body, and this immediately does away with the privileges of the people who alone were permitted to enter the temple precincts. "For he is our peace who has made us both one and has broken down the dividing wall of hostility by abolishing *in his flesh* the law of commandments and ordinances that he might create in himself one new man in place of the two, so making peace, and might reconcile us both to God in one body *through the cross*, thereby bringing the hostility to an end.' " [110]

This gave the officer, a pagan, the right to utter the truth: "Truly, this man was a Son of God." [111] This is Mark's way of telling us that the title which he gave to his gospel ("the Gospel of Jesus Christ, the Son of God") has reached Rome, the very center of the world.

This universalism whereby in principle the death which is paganism is abolished, applies not only to space, but to time. The dead Jesus went to proclaim salvation "to the spirits in prison who formerly did not obey, when God's patience waited in the days of Noah, during the building of the ark." [112]

It was this certainty which inspired Thomas Aquinas centuries later to develop his theory of the *gratia capitis:* Jesus possesses a grace as head of mankind, and all men without exception are dependent on him. For the same reason, the Christian people reacted

90 Lk. 22, 28.
91 Lk. 22, 45.
92 Lk. 22, 46.
93 Lk. 22, 48.
94 Lk. 22, 51.
95 Lk. 22, 61.
96 Lk. 23, 9.
97 Lk. 23, 28-31.
98 Lk. 23, 34.
99 Lk. 23, 43.
100 Lk. 23, 46.
101 Lk. 23, 28.
102 Lk. 23, 48.
103 Lk. 22, 61-62.

104 Lk. 23, 47.
105 X. L. Dufour, "Passion," in *Dict. Bibl. Suppl.,* 6 (1960), pp. 1477-1478.
106 1 Cor. 1, 17.23-25.
107 2 Cor. 4, 11-12; 2 Trim., 1, 10-11.
108 Mt. 27, 51.
109 Heb. 10, 19-20; cf. 6, 19-20.
110 Eph. 2, 14-16.
111 Mk. 15, 39.
112 1 Pet. 3, 18-19; cf. H. J. Schulz, "Die 'Höllenfahrt' als 'Anastasis'" in *Zeitschrift f. kath. Theol.,* 81 (1959), pp. 1-66.

against the Jansenists, who wished to keep the redemption within
certain limits and represented the crucified Christ with the arms
raised vertically, as though he could draw only a small group up
with him. But the heart of Jesus—for it was in this context that this
devotion originated—extends its love "from generation to generation" and grants to all veritable "rivers of grace." [113]

Second, Jesus' death also signifies the end of the kingdom of
physical death. Admittedly, death is not yet definitively eliminated
(although this too will be brought about by Jesus) [114], but a real
change has been accomplished, which is demonstrated by Matthew
and John in different ways. Matthew says that Jesus' death was
accompanied by eschatological events. "The tombs also were
opened and many bodies of the saints who had fallen asleep were
raised, and coming out of the tombs after his resurrection they went
into the holy city, and appeared to many." [115]

John for his part confirms that anyone who believes in Jesus has
already passed from death to life, and will never die, as Jesus states
in the story of the raising of Lazarus. [116] This anticipation too is
linked with Jesus' death which indeed dominates the whole of the
Lazarus story from the beginning [117] up to the resultant decision
taken by the Sanhedrin "that it is expedient for you that one man
should die for the people, and that the whole nation should not
perish." [118] One death thus saves all from death, and John assures us
that this was a true prophecy. [119]

Thus originated the glorious story of the cross with its real,
tangible, material, and spiritual influence on the history of the
cosmos. With the sign of the cross people will drive out devils, resist
persecution, heal the sick. Crosses will appear on precious metals, on
jewels, on wood; they will fill the houses, accompany travellers, bear
witness to our hope of eternity above the mortal remains of our
dead. There will be millions of crosses, yet, the loveliest of all will
appear and vanish in the air, since they are simply gestures: the
sign of the cross made before prayer or work, in moments of danger
or before a meal; in baptism, the celebration of the eucharist, confession, and in countless blessings.

Were we to follow this story of the cross, we would perhaps gain
a new insight into the reality of the cosmos. We would undoubtedly
meet with magical or superstitious practices but along with this we
would see kings kneeling to receive the cross upon their shoulders,
and we would see a great peace descend upon the houses with the

little bedtime cross made by father and mother upon the foreheads of their children. We would see the stigmata shining in the body and above all, in the soul of Francis and of others. We should then quickly forget our old notion of "miracle," for it is quite incapable of doing justice to this category. In all probability, we would fall back upon an age-old song: blessed be that night, blessed be that death, blessed be the sin of Adam which gave us such a Redeemer. And perhaps we would begin to feel a little love for that crucified love.

113 Mass text of the Feast of the Sacred Heart.
114 1 Cor. 15, 26.54-56.
115 Mt. 27, 52-53.
116 Jn. 11, 25-26; cf. 5, 24; 1 Jn. 3, 14.
117 Jn. 11, 8.
118 Jn. 11, 45-54.
119 Jn. 11, 51-52.

V
The Risen
Christ

". . . about one Jesus who was dead,
but whom Paul asserted to be alive"
(Governor Festus to King Agrippa, according to Acts. 25, 19).

"Every week, filled with study and classes, I find it a relaxation on Monday evenings to meet a group of third-year students from the Lyceum for a discussion on some religious subject. The sparkling exchange of ideas and the joy on every fact testify to the spirit of comradeship which prevails in this course. Their persistent, searching questions reveal their enthusiasm for life. For them, this course is a means of fulfilling some aspiration; they work during the day, and it is a real effort for them to come to the Lyceum in the evenings to complete their personal training.

"And so the year went by, as a brave struggle in a communal cause, with each ready to help the other. Then came the shocking news. Osvaldo, the blond, lanky young man, a very likeable lad who had perhaps worked hardest of all, had died of a heart attack which had struck him down just as he arrived home.

"Osvaldo's death was so unexpected that we could scarcely believe it. A few days before, he was there in our midst, talking like any of us. And now suddenly, he had ceased to exist.

"I myself had always spoken to them of Christ as of the hero of a better world and of Christianity as something through which man can perfect all the positive possibilities of his development: in love, in the social field, in technology . . . But confronted with this fact, now, as I stood before the pupils and saw how grieved and almost despairing they were at the death of their companion, I had to admit that I had never gone more than halfway. I had not given testimony of my own faith or at least of the central point of my faith. No testimony of mine had proclaimed the *risen* Christ, the leader and herald of the new humanity, he who dwells in our midst and carries on his work of redemption in the very depths of our being, in the darkness of death and what comes after. Then, I understood that the Christ of moral perfection in justice and love, and the Christ who leads the vanguard of humanity in the search for the attainment of integral perfection is far from the Christ of faith. A Christ thus represented does not require an extraordinary amount of supernatural faith. He could be just another leader of mankind, albeit the most perfect.

"As I spoke with the pupils, my attitude regarding them changed. I found myself obliged to account for my procedure which differed entirely from theirs. I explained my point of view to them honestly and compared it with that of our surroundings. One thing which soon became clear both to them and to me was that this new viewpoint, which we had never discussed before, was, in effect, the very essence of the faith. At first sight, it might appear the last refuge which remained to us, but it was nothing of the sort. It was a purifying process which freed us from the self-deception which had clouded our ideas of Christ. It was like jumping from a springboard almost without human support." [1]

This simple testimony of an Argentinian priest touches the heart of the matter. It unmasks a real danger inherent in the old theology (including that in modern disguise which can always call upon skillful pens) and of the modern theologies (even in their deeper, existential forms, written with dedication and a feeling for mysticism). The "old" theology is too much based on static "essentials" and the "new" often simply concerned with temporal values so that they sometimes almost cease to be theology at all.

However much some may say that the hereafter is a flight from reality and thus "the opium of the people," this cannot alter the fact that Jesus' resurrection is the principal event and the climax of Christianity. The priest we have just quoted goes on to say that, from the time he spoke to the pupils of his true belief, all of them felt Osvaldo in their midst. "Our faith and our confidence in the risen Christ, led us to see that he was a leader, while our imagination drew for us in vague lines a risen Osvaldo before our eyes."

[1] P. Angel Conrero (Córdoba, Argentina) in a work for *I.C.L.A.* (Instituto Catequistico Latino-Americano).

Naturally, the resurrection is not a reality because it is a "nice idea," a solution for the mental anguish of a group of faithful friends. It is a solution because it is a reality. Osvaldo's case cannot be "solved" by deliberation in the classroom, nor my personal case by a sudden intuition. Unamuno, on the one hand, anguished by the dark night of death, and on the other, "incapable of accepting the dogma of the resurrection as presented by the Church," constructed for himself a world in which he did not believe. His feelings were stronger than his intellect, and did not cease from tragically wrestling with the mystery of death and of the afterlife.[2] In the last resort, everything depends upon the fact and the nature of the resurrection.

The study of the resurrection of Christ is thus quite simply a necessity, since it is the only yardstick by which we can judge *our* future. And yet, this is not the reason why we intend to discuss it here, for there is surely another source of interest: love. How can one love a person without inquiring whether he is alive or dead? How could one love a person without wishing to get to know him in every phase of his existence and especially, in the present phase? How can one love Jesus without following his traces to the end, without desiring his presence, or longing for his living touch?

In view of this it is difficult to find an excuse for the scarcity of literature on this subject.[3] It is to be hoped that in judging the following pages the reader will take into account the fact that the ground has been but little smoothed by the dogmatic theologians who tend to rely too much on speculative knowledge. On the other hand, however, whatever ground they have ventured upon they have consolidated.

This consciousness of my own inadequacy and the precarious nature of my task emboldens me to ask something of the reader. Wherever he sees only dead, cold, and theoretical words, let him add himself the memory of loved ones who await the resurrection. Where he laments a lack of depth and inspiration, let him make a special effort, bring to bear all the acuteness of his mind, and lend to all his powers the wings which may in some measure approach the dizzying heights of this mystery. It is possible that these pages will be thought "very vague," or "extremely literary," although they were not written during moments of exaltation or in a romantic mood. Others will seek in vain that religious inspiration which is a real help in establishing living contact with the risen Christ. They are quite right to protest against this lack, unfortunately quite common in many works of this sort which have not succeeded in combining objectivity and the scholarly approach with the luminous, limpid sense of religion which we all desire, since it was for this we were created. There is perhaps a remedy. You can place yourself before the risen Lord in the full clarity of your understanding and read from his face. He will fill in what I omitted in my semi-absence.

Our plan is simple. After a critical examination of the origin of the belief in the resurrection, we consider the risen Lord in his relationship to the Father and to the world. A number of subdivisions in each point give us the following outline:

1. The origin of the belief in the resurrection.
   (a) two simplistic theories.
   (b) probable course of events.
2. The risen Christ in his relationship to the Father:
   (a) the Father approves his life and work.
   (b) the glorification of the Son of God.
   (c) the high priest in his perfect tabernacle.
3. The risen Christ active in the world.
   (a) his dwelling in us.
   (b) manifold "acts" of presence.
   (c) dynamic presence throughout history.

[2] Xavier Iturgaitz, in the introduction to the Spanish edition of the book by his colleague F. X. Durwell on the resurrection (Barcelona, 1962); see No. 3, p. 11.

[3] J. Heiler, *Unser Glauben an den Auferstandenen* (Freiburg, 1937); A. M. Ramsay, *The Resurrection of Christ* (London, 1964); C. Oomen, *Het bijbelgetuigenis over Christus, de levengevengevende Geest* (Bruges, 1946); J. Schnitt, *Jésus ressuscité dans la prédication apostolique* (Paris, 1949); W. Künneth, *Theologie der Auferstehung* (Munich, 1951[4]); K. Adam, "Das Problem der Entmythologisierung und der Auferstehung des Christus," in *Theol. Quart.*, 132 (1952), pp. 385-410; F. X. Durwell, *La résurrection du Christ, mystère du* salut (Le Puy, 1954[2]), Eng. trans: *The Resurrection*, (New York, Sheed and Ward, 1960). R. R. Niebuhr, *Resurrection and Historical Reason* (New York, 1957); "Christus Victor Mortis," special number of *Gregorianum*, 39 (1958), pp. 201-524; J. Comblin, *La résurrection de Jésus Christ* (Brussels, 1958); G. Koch, *Die Auferstehung Jesu Christi* (Tübingen, 1959); A. Descamps, "La Structure des récits de la résurrection," in *Biblica*, 40 (1959), pp. 726-741; C. M. Martini, *Il problemo storico della risurezione negli studi recenti* in *Analecta Gregoriana*, 104 (Rome, 1949); G. D. Arnold, *Risen indeed. Studies in the Lord's Resurrection* (London, 1959); K. H. Rengstorf, *Die Aufer-*

This plan alone is sufficient to show that the mystery of the risen Christ embraces more than the fact of the resurrection, comprising what are usually spoken of as the ascension, the descent of the Holy Spirit, grace, the charismata

The Origin of the Belief in the Resurrection

To the Corinthian Christians, who had their doubts about the fate of their deceased relatives, since a physical resurrection seemed to them impossible, Paul wrote these revealing words: "If there is no resurrection of the dead, then Christ has not been raised." [4] This one sentence illustrates sufficiently to what extent Jesus' resurrection was one of the bulwarks of the Christian faith. Paul could understand a person doubting the continued existence of a grandfather or spouse, but not that of Christ. The same conviction dominates the whole of Christian tradition. All the evangelists speak in their closing chapters of the resurrection of the crucified Christ. In Luke's second book, this fact forms the principal theme of *all* the apostles' speeches, be they called Peter or Paul.[5] It is also generally accepted that the risen Jesus is the basis of the Pauline theology, from the first short epistles to the reflections on his imprisonment, not excluding the Epistle to the Hebrews.[6]

In the face of such widespread and concrete testimony, modern exegetes can do nothing but reject the so-called psychological explanations which seek to dismiss the whole affair as self-deception, hallucination, or collective hysteria. Such theories are absolutely at variance with the structure, nature, and content of the texts. According to these texts the following facts form the basis of a belief in the resurrection:

1. The empty tomb, confirmed by many witnesses.

2. Apparitions made by the risen Christ, particularly to his apostles.

3. Spiritual apparitions during gatherings of Christians. These facts have been handed down to us by various traditions, and our present investigation will thus be chiefly concerned with analyzing and comparing these traditions, their origin, their content, and any eventual contradictions. It is only by way of these traditions that we can attain to the historical facts upon which they are based.

Two Simplistic Theories

To begin with, it seems to me essential to discard two widely held theories which are too simplistic to correspond with reality. Moreover, the second of these theories is often presented in a form which is scarcely acceptable to those who believe in the inspiration of the holy scriptures (at least according to Catholic norms) and is hardly to be reconciled with the Catholic view of the actual resurrection.

1. The widely held Catholic version of events which attempts to fit all the Gospel data into a tight chronological framework seems to me to resemble concordism. The timetable of this theory runs as follows: on Sunday morning the women establish that the tomb is empty; on the same day Jesus himself appears to various people, including the apostles gathered in the Cenacle, with the exception of Thomas. On the following Sunday, more apparitions take place, this time with Thomas. The apostles then depart for Galilee, where Jesus appears again. They then return to Jerusalem where, on the fortieth day after Easter, the last apparition and the ascension take place. Ten days later, at Pentecost, there is the first manifestation of the Holy Spirit, and finally, one last appearance, this time to Paul.

I do not believe that there is one modern exegete of any importance who would accept this sequence of facts, at least not in the strict sense. In actual fact, this timetable, which claims "to combine all the data" is at variance with several of these data and above all, takes little account of the literary genre of the various sources.

On closer examination it does indeed appear that Matthew and Mark (in his first edition, thus only up to 16, 8) foresee only one apparition, or in any case, only one series of apparitions in Galilee: "There you will see him." [7] Matthew describes this apparition during which Jesus grants apostolic powers to the eleven.[8] In what is usually called "the second conclusion of St. Mark," one day of apparitions is mentioned, in Jerusalem. Those favored on this occa-

---

stehung Jesu (Witten, 1960 [4]); L. Vercammen, "De heilswaarde van de verrijzenis," in *Coll. Mechl.*, 45 (1960), pp. 506-518; 605-620; H. Grass, *Ostergeschehen und Oster-berichten* (Göttingen, 1962 [2]).

[4] 1 Cor. 15, 13.

[5] E.g., Acts 2, 24.32; 3, 15.26; 10, 40;

13, 30-37; 17, 31-32.

[6] Cf. 1 Thess. 1, 10; 1 Cor. 15, 25; Phil. 2, 8-11; Rom. 1, 4; Col. 1, 18; Eph. 1, 20-22; 1 Tim. 3, 16; Heb. 1, 3 etc.

[7] Mt. 28, 7; Mk. 16, 7.

[8] Mt. 28, 16-20.

sion are Mary Magdalen, "two, who were walking into the country and the eleven." [9]

In Luke's version, Mary Magdalen is simply one of the women who report that the tomb is empty.[10] The two disciples on the road are identified as Cleopas and his companion, on the way to Emmaus. This same evening Jesus appears to the eleven, still in Judea and specifically in Jerusalem, and commands them *to remain in Jerusalem* "until you are clothed with power from on high." [11] Evidently, it is still on this same Sunday that Jesus goes with them to Bethany, where he ascends to heaven.[12] The apostles then remain in Jerusalem as they had been ordered and become noted for their piety; they were continually praying in the temple.[13]

John for his part mentions the apparitions in Jerusalem,[14] beginning with that to Mary Magdalen (in contrast to Luke) and those in Galilee,[15] but does not speak of the gift of the Spirit there; this occurs in Jerusalem (contrary to Matthew).

In the Acts, this same Luke astonishes us with a radically different timetable, which should be a decisive point in arguing that it was not his intention to compile an accurate chronological table, and speaks of "many" apparitions which took place over a fairly long period ("forty days" is a symbolic figure). He now places the descent of the Spirit on the fiftieth day (contrary to John).[16]

Finally, there is another list derived from St. Paul.[17] This is the earliest and is presented as traditional. He starts with an appearance to Peter—Luke is the only one of the evangelists who alludes to it and then without giving any details [18]—and continues with one to the twelve. Paul also knows of an important apparition seen by five hundred people, of another made to James, and finally of one to himself. Paul makes a distinction between this apparition and later visions, so that we are obliged to assume at least one true resurrection appearance which does not fit into the framework of the forty days.[19] This then does not correspond with the Acts.

2. The difficulties are so real that they have given rise to a theory which is radically divergent from the first. Ignoring those who consider "the contradiction among the evangelists" as sufficient reason for denying them any historical value, let us examine more closely the so-called theory of the double tradition. According to this, there were two versions and two concepts of the resurrection. The first, which may be found in Paul, Mark (without the second ending), and up to a certain point, in Matthew (with the exception of 28, 9-

10) deals only with appearances outside Jerusalem, that is, in Galilee, near Damascus. These are taken to have been, not apparitions in the strict sense, but rather a very spiritual vision, with light phenomena. Nobody was perceived but a spiritually surviving Jesus made his power felt. The second tradition, represented principally by Luke and John, lays increasing stress on the material and the proofs of Jesus' continued physical existence grow stronger and more numerous: Jesus eats; the disciples can place their fingers in his wounds; the tomb is empty, etc.

Although this theory is subscribed to by reputable scholars, including "independent Protestants" like Maurice Goguel, it seems no less simplistic than the other. In the first place, its supporters seem to suffer from a peculiar loss of memory whereby they "forget" that all the evangelists, including Mark up to his first ending, speak of the empty tomb, which shows that they are thinking of a *physical* resurrection. Admittedly Paul does not explicitly mention the empty tomb, but he undoubtedly assumes it, for he stresses the burial (physical element) [20] and speaks of a resurrection *on the third day*.[21] This would have no meaning at all if he were merely referring to a spiritual resurrection. It is for that matter most unlikely that Jews—for this is not Greece—would have been able to imagine a continued existence without the "flesh."

It would seem that Catholic exegesis is approaching a consensus.[22] One of the first data is the repeated assertion that the tomb was empty. Here, two people emerge in the foreground—Mary Magdalen and Peter. For the rest, the different traditions have varying

[9] Mk. 16, 9-18.
[10] Lk. 24, 10.
[11] Lk. 24, 49.
[12] Lk. 24, 50.
[13] Lk. 24, 53.
[14] Jn. 20, 11-31.
[15] Jn. 21.
[16] Acts 1, 2.
[17] 1 Cor. 15, 1-8.
[18] Lk. 24, 34.
[19] Cf. 2 Cor. 12, 1; Acts 18, 9; 23, 11.
[20] 1 Cor. 15, 4; Rom. 6, 4; Col. 2, 12.
[21] 1 Cor. 15, 4.
[22] To give some idea of the more recent articles: W. Nauck, "Die Bedeutung des leeren grabes fur das Glauben an den Auferstandenen," in *Zeitschr. f. Neut. Wiss.*,

47 (1956), pp. 243-267; E. Dahanis, "L'Ensevelissement de Jésus et la visite au tombeau dans l'évangele de saint Marc," in *Gregorianum*, 39 (1958), pp. 367-410; J. Manek, "The Apostle Paul and the Empty Tomb," in *Nov. Test.*, 2, (1958), pp. 276-280; A. Descamps," La structure des récits évangeliques de la Résurrection," in *Biblica*, 40 (1959), pp. 726-741; P. Benoît, "Marie-Madeleine et les disciples au tombeau selon Joh. 20, 1-18," in *Mélanges Joach, Jeremias, Beihefte Z.N.W.*, 29, (1960), pp. 141-152; F. Gils, "Pierre et la foi au Christ resuscité," in *Eph. Theol. Lov.*, 38 (1962), pp. 5-43; J. Schmitt, "La

points of interest, and do not trouble to stipulate the number of women or the time. We are not even informed of the exact number of participating angels.

PROBABLE COURSE OF EVENTS

With this somewhat confused report and the angels' message that they should go to Galilee, the apostles then left for the north. There, most probably on several different occasions, they saw the risen Christ. These apparitions take place in a climate of uncertainty, almost of disbelief. On the other hand, they bear an official character, for Jesus confers upon his disciples the powers which they need for their coming apostolate. Peter's role, for example, is most remarkable, in both Mark and John. It is not clear how long this period lasted, but it must have been quite a time, for not only is there an appearance to a crowd of five hundred people, but there is, also and especially, the one to Paul, which must certainly have occurred a couple of years after Jesus' death.

The appearances to the women are of a different nature. They initiate no official mission but are extremely well-suited to establishing the reality of the resurrection. We are dealing with a recognition"; the women see the same Jesus whom they had formerly known and served. The story of the travellers to Emmaus is in the same category as that of Thomas—in increasing evidence of the tangibleness of the risen Christ. In all these accounts, which have been localized in Jerusalem for editorial reasons, the exhortative and apologetic element predominates. The writers are dealing with real facts, but they are naturally presented in a way which will tend to confirm our conviction. Anyone who sets out to convince must keep to the facts, but can scarcely avoid being a little one-sided. And instead of parading a complicated chronological table, he will try to simplify matters. It is impossible that such narratives could have given rise to a belief in the resurrection; on the contrary, they *presuppose* that belief in the writer and also the reality of the apparitions.

As a result of these contacts with the risen Christ, a remarkable change took place in the apostles, all the more since the coming of Jesus was not confined to a "contemplation" of their master in his new condition, but was accompanied by a phenomenon which touched them more deeply: the descent of his Spirit. Everything seems to indicate that numerous mystical phenomena took place, individual as well as collective. Luke has left us a suggestive group photo of one of these taken at Pentecost, but he omits to give a date.

Thus gradually, the facts proved that the presence of Jesus was powerful enough to start a movement of people whose ardor, intense piety, and humanity were to reach to the ends of the earth. And these were very ordinary people who had lived and still lived in an atmosphere of constant imputation subject to terror, openly disapproved of by the highest authorities of the nation and of their religion. The closed doors which John evokes so realistically [23] will gradually be replaced by the busy caravan routes and soon by the boats which set sail for the West.

THE RISEN CHRIST AND THE FATHER

If we now wish to determine the meaning and purpose of the resurrection, it is difficult to proceed in an orderly manner unless we are prepared to distinguish various aspects. This, of course, leaves us open to the danger of too sharply distinguishing what is in reality indivisible, for instance, the subjective and the objective redemption. With this serious reservation we shall then make a distinction between the significance of the resurrection for Jesus' relationship to the Father, and its influence with regard to the world. In each section we shall distinguish three subsidiary aspects.

1. *The Father Gives His Approval to Jesus' Life and Work*

On reading the Acts of the Apostles, we become convinced that we are witnessing here one of the most radical "revisions" in the history of the human race. Jesus had been condemned and executed by the authorities. His disciples and a large section of the population had never faltered in their opinion that this had been an unjust judgment, but it so often happens that the righteous man remains undefended during his lifetime, while his honor is sullied after his

résurrection du Christ: des formules kérygmatiques aux récits évangéliques," in *Mélanges* J. J. Weber (1962), pp. 93-105; J. Sint, "Die Auferstehung Jesu in der Verkündigung der Urgemeinde," in *Zeitschr. f. kath. Theol.*, 84 (1962), pp. 129-151.

[23] Jn. 20, 19.26.

death. For once, however, things turned out differently; God himself intervened in an amazing, unheard of manner: "This Jesus . . . you crucified and killed by the hands of lawless men. But God raised him up . . ." This is the principal theme of this great revisionist movement within Judaism, which is Christianity.[24]

This Jesus thus, whom they had known, this young man who had been so absolutely holy, who had travelled the roads of their homeland and paused in the squares and in the houses "doing good and healing all that were oppressed by the devil," [25] he who had opposed the Pharisees with prophetic voice and almost incomprehensible self-assurance, and who had not faltered before the high priests, this silent companion of the oppressed and of sinners who fulfilled a transcendent mission and wagered everything for God's kingdom while following his own absolutely unexpected way, this eventual messiah who, though not yet forty, was already in a category by himself, concerning whom no one dared to risk a definite opinion —this man was alive again! Now or never was the moment to inquire: what is God doing?

What is God doing? The poet would say that God is singing, for death is silence, a hard, terrible silence, especially in the case of loved ones or particularly worthwhile people. They die and nothing happens. Everything continues as before. A piece of the world is viewed by two eyes less; there is one person less to appreciate it; a string has snapped. The grave is silent. God is silent. But in Jesus' case, God himself began to sing, loudly, joyfully, and long enough to change the whole world.

We can read what God is doing in Peter's Pentecost address. Through the resurrection all the house of Israel may know that "God has made him both Lord and Christ, this Jesus whom you crucified." [26] Many authors seem to see in these two titles a *new* function which only begins through the resurrection. Oscar Cullman goes even further and regards the title, "Lord," as valid for the actual work of Jesus (i.e. from the resurrection to the parousia, the age in which we live), while the title, "messiah," only comes into its own at the time of the parousia and thus for us too should refer to Jesus' future function.[27] This seems to me somewhat exaggerated. Jesus had already acted as the messiah during his public life.[28] The first Christians did not expect the coming of the messiah; they knew that he had already come, but would return as "the Lord," whom he had become through the resurrection.

It could scarcely be otherwise. The first conclusion to be drawn from the fact of the resurrection must of necessity be linked with the events which were still fresh in everyone's memory. God's finger is nowhere seen more clearly than in the raising of a dead person to life. And if that dead person had only recently been condemned in the name of this same God, or at least with the connivance of those who according to public opinion represented the highest religious authority, it was impossible to view God's gesture as anything but a divine squashing of the human verdict. For those who were closely involved no more solemn intervention was conceivable.

In one stroke, the whole of Jesus' work had been justified. He had had a particular concept of the messiah's task. The authorities had rejected the possibility that a messiah so humble, so poor, without army or prestige and lacking any defense against those who nailed him to the cross, could be the true one. Now, in the light of the resurrection the apostles saw that they had misunderstood the Old Testament, and that the messiah *must* suffer and so enter into his glory.[29] To sum up: the messiah, Jesus, had remained silent, faithful to the image of the Suffering Servant of Yahweh, yet, God had spoken, more clearly than ever.

2. *The Glorification of the Son of God*

One should not conclude from all this that the resurrection was merely a divine judgment in the settlement of a human dispute, an irrefutable testimony with no intrinsic value for salvation. The theological tradition of the last centuries inclined towards this idea in having the "objective salvation" end with Christ's death and considering the resurrection as the necessary "condition" for the "distribution of grace" or "subjective redemption." Such a view lays too much emphasis on the "merits"—for it is true that Jesus could only "merit" up to the moment of his death—and panders to our inclination to think in material terms of even the most spiritual and the most personal things. This is contrary to the New Testament.

According to the whole of the New Testament, the resurrection had an objective result. Paul, for example, in the first lines of the Epistle to the Romans, says that, "he who was descended from

24 Acts 2, 23-24; 3, 15; 4, 10; 5, 30.32; 10, 39-40; 13, 27-30.
25 Acts 10, 38.
26 Acts 2, 36.
27 This is clearly evident in the table of contents of his *Christologie du Noveau Testament.*
28 Cf. pp. 250ff.
29 Acts 3, 18-20; 26-28; 8, 32-35; 13, 32-37; Lk. 24, 25-27, 44-46.

David according to the flesh," was "designated Son of God in power according to the spirit of holiness by his resurrection from the dead." [30] Although Jesus had never ceased to be the Son, the resurrection nonetheless granted him a new power, the nature of which may be deduced from a parallel passage in the same epistle in which the resurrection is linked with the glory of the Father.[31] Certainly, Jesus' earthly life had not remained devoid of glory (a quality exclusive to God, that which makes him great, gives him fullness and light, vitality and supreme power).[32] Yet, his true glory comes from the resurrection. One cannot really know Jesus without comprehending the full extent of his pasch which was a transition from death to glory. It was because of his death that God granted him a name which is above every other, that of Kyrios, the Lord.[33] It is the only fitting name for the Son of God, but he had, as it were, renounced it; he had emptied himself . . .[34]

The distance bridged in this way is enormous. We have only to think of our human littleness, our dullness, our social and inner limitations, the great religious void within us whereby our hunger and thirst increase the closer we come to him who is everything, and which caused such violent, almost biological pain in the noblest of our race comparable to that of a starving man or to the loss of a limb; all this can be transformed into glory. We have our proof and our concrete example in the pitiful suppliant of Gethsemane, the lamentable crucified one, who is now "the Lord of glory." [35]

We find exactly the same in John, where Jesus prays to the Father: "Glorify thou me in thy own presence with the glory which I had with thee before the world was made." [36] Jesus returns from a journey which has not been in vain: In the period between the departure from the Father and the "hour," the work of redeeming the world had been accomplished.[37]

In what did the glorification consist? The synoptics and John, too, in his later chapters give us a somewhat more concrete idea of it, although in doing so they make a series of concessions to the image of the world prevalent at that time. That image is out of date, but their observations contain a considerable theological enrichment, which must be considered as permanent.

In the first place, the accounts of the resurrection indicate a series of enviable qualities—penetrating knowledge, unrivalled mental activity, quickness and sensitivity of the body as contact instrument, ease in overcoming resistance. The fact that the tomb is empty points to a certain continuity between the dead and resurrected body, but the activities embarked upon by the risen Christ are a clear indication of how new his present status is. Nonetheless, it is not advisable to study the stories of the apparitions with the eye of a biologist seeking to detect new "physical qualities." We should also be cautioned by the difference between Paul's contact with Jesus [38] and the impression given by the gospels, where naturally more connection is made with what has gone before and where Jesus even eats again.[39]

To get a better idea of what is meant by glorification we should turn rather to Paul, who indirectly mentions Jesus' resurrection in speaking of our own. The risen body recalls to him the radiance of the celestial bodies such as the sun, moon, and stars.[40] Compared with this, our previous condition was mere transience, smallness, weakness, a natural (physical, very ordinary) body.[41] But the risen man is raised in glory; now he can no longer be called flesh, but spirit, which is stronger, purer, more powerful, all-penetrating. It is even more; it is of itself living and life-giving.[42] If then, this is to be *our* stature, it is even more certain that the second Adam, whose image we shall bear [43] possesses these qualities.

Yet the best known expression for Jesus' glorification, or for its climax, still current today, says that he "is seated at the right hand of the Father." [44] This formula corresponds to Jesus' declaration before the high priest [45] and indicates executive power and intimate unity. When the kings held their supreme council they positioned themselves to the right of the statue of the god, and those who desired a privileged place, begged to be allowed to sit at the right hand.[46]

It is thus an article of faith among the apostles that Jesus possesses

[30] Rom. 1, 4.
[31] Rom. 6, 4.
[32] Cf. pp. 217ff.
[33] Phil. 2, 9-11.
[34] Phil. 2, 7.
[35] 1 Cor. 2, 8.
[36] Jn. 17, 5; cf. v.24.
[37] Cf. Jn. 13, 1; 17, 4.
[38] 1 Cor. 15, 3-8; Gal. 1, 15; Acts 9, 3-8; 22, 6-10; 26, 12-15.
[39] Lk. 24, 30; Acts 10, 41; Jn. 21, 12.

[40] 1 Cor. 15, 40-41.
[41] 1 Cor. 15, 42-44.
[42] *Ibid.*
[43] 1 Cor. 15, 49.
[44] Acts 7, 55 (cf. 2, 33; 5, 31; exalted at the right hand of the Father); Rom. 8, 34; Col. 3, 1, Eph. 1, 20; Heb. 1, 3; 8, 1; 10, 12; 12, 2; 1 Pet. 3, 22.
[45] Mt. 26, 64.
[46] Mt. 20, 21; Mk. 10, 37. 40.

absolute privilege. Mark puts it most incisively: "So then the Lord
Jesus, after he had spoken to them, was taken up into heaven and sat
down at the right hand of God." [47]

Only Luke, in his gospel and in the Acts, has left us a more
graphic picture of this ascension: the apostles stand looking on,
receive the last blessing, and watch as he is lifted up and disappears
from sight behind a cloud.[48] One may argue whether the author
intended to describe an actual event which took place on the Mount
of Olives or whether he who was naturally inclined to see everything in pictures wished to compose a scene with more human appeal in order to proclaim the fundamental Christian thesis. What is
beyond doubt is the deep significance of the "ascension into
heaven," and this remains the same in either case. The cloud is
God's vehicle, the expression of his presence. This was true in the
time of Moses and the Ark [49] and is still true, for example, in the
transfiguration [50] and in Jesus' promise to come again on the clouds
of heaven.[51] Luke's ascension scene finds its complement in a vision
of the Apocalypse, where the author describes Christ *as he is* in
these terms: "Then I looked up, and lo, a white cloud, and seated on
the cloud one like a son of man, with a golden crown on his head and
a sharp sickle in his hand." [52]

Modern man does not feel at ease with such language, but it is no
solution to reduce it to pure symbol, for the question still remains:
where is Jesus now?

3. *The High Priest in His Perfect Tabernacle*

If we wish to carry on with our attempt to "localize" the risen
Christ, the most likely source would seem to be the Epistle to the
Hebrews, with the Book of Revelation as closest competitor. The
setting is—we must say regrettably enough [53]—thoroughly familiar;
the risen Christ has departed for a place high up in the sky, a long,
long way away from us. This is "heaven," where he is seated beside
the throne occupied by the "Ancient of Days." He is now in his
definitive "tabernacle" which is, for the rest, of ample dimensions so
that the angels (and later mankind) have no difficulty in performing
their liturgical ceremonies.[54]

Before examining the question of Christ's function and activity
there, some points need clarification concerning the significance of
this setting. Let us begin by saying that we are dealing here with an
obsolete vocabulary, which, while it may be acceptable in certain

milieux, has a decidedly harmful effect in others. One need think only of the atheistic propaganda based upon the experience of the cosmonauts who "pass through heaven," of the *Life of Galileo* put on by the famous Berthold Brecht for crowded Berlin audiences, and of the thousands of copies of the pamphlet *Der Sputnik und der Liebe Gottes* (1958). All sing the same refrain: "Heaven has been found empty." But if heaven is empty, where is God?

Popular attention has recently been focussed on this problem by the sound exegete and pastorally-minded bishop, Dr. J. A. T. Robinson.[55] His book, which immediately became a best seller, and the sharp television discussions to which it gave rise, pose in a new and much more general manner the problem raised by Rudolf Bultmann and others; namely, the demythologizing of Christianity.

It would be impossible here even to pose the question in its entirety, but it is our duty, from the exegetical point of view too, to ask ourselves what idea we must have of heaven. It is quite clear that the zenith cannot possibly be the same for our brothers from Ireland, Australia, Alaska, and Argentina, and anyone with any idea of astrology must find it incredibly naïve to imagine that Jesus' tabernacle is perhaps situated on one of the planets or somewhere in the Milky Way.

On the other hand, the resurrection has a physical implication; and does not "body" also signify "place"? Undoubtedly, but this does not necessarily mean our actual concept of place. We must on no account seek the risen Jesus in the infantile spaces where traditional representations had relegated God. For we must first and foremost "demythologize" our concept of God. Since God is not a physical being, he cannot be located in a high temple. What then

[47] Mk. 16, 19.

[48] Lk. 24, 50-51; Acts 1, 9-11.

[49] Ex. 14, 20; 16, 10; 19, 9; 1 Kings 8, 10-13; Ps. 18, 12; Is. 1, 9 etc.

[50] Mk. 9, 7.

[51] Mk. 19, 62; Rev. 1, 7.

[52] Rev. 14, 14-16.

[53] This is "unfortunate" in the sense that the dogma often seems reduced to the scenario; on the other hand, the language of the Apocalypse is a thousand times more modern than the many tasteless representations taught from childhood and which stick in the mem-

ory. One must thus not speak too much of heaven; and yet, too little is said of it even when the theme is discussed.

[54] Cf. Heb. 8-10; Rev. 1, 4-5; 7, 14.

[55] There already exists a whole series of commentaries on *Honest to God* (S.C.M. Press Ltd., London, 1963); e.g. *The Honest to God Debate* (S.C.M. Press, London, 1963); E. Schillebeeckx, "Evangelische Zuiverheid en menselijke waarachtigheid," in *Tijdschr. v. Theol.*, 3 (1963), pp. 283-326.

is the meaning of the dogma that a *person* (with soul and body) has ascended to God. Perhaps the following elucidation, which is modern and in keeping with the scriptures, may be of some help. The glory given by the Father to his incarnate and executed Son comprised for his physical state a "new dimension" whereby he was granted an indescribable facility for radiating over the world.

Just as a three-dimensional being infinitely surpasses a two-dimensional being in influential power, since he can move freely on all planes and thus, suddenly appear in the flat plane of the two-dimensional being, move about, and disappear again with no visible explanation from the two-dimensional standpoint, so too, the risen Christ appears to move in a higher dimension, inaccessible and incomprehensible to us, whereby his localization, appearance, presence and disappearance seem to us mysterious and above all the laws of logic.

We shall also discuss the miraculous results of this new condition with regard to ourselves. Concerning the vertical relationship, the New Testament authors see in it the perfect realization of the *priesthood*. Jesus is, as it were, no longer bound to our reality, which is confined to the narrow limits of the senses, but according to the Epistle to the Hebrews, he has solemnly entered into a new tabernacle as high priest, as minister of a more perfect covenant.[56] "But when Christ appeared as a high priest of the good things that have come, then through the greater and more perfect tent (not made with hands, that is, not of this creation), he entered once and for all into the holy place." [57] The earthly temple and its sacrifices were merely prefigurations of this new temple "not made with human hands" through which Jesus "has entered into heaven itself, now to appear in the presence of God on our behalf." [58] For this reason, too, his priesthood is eternal, and he "is able *for all time* to save those who draw near to God through him, since he always lives to make intercession for them." [59]

The Apocalypse, too, stresses this positive, intrinsic aspect of heaven, the intimate and effective priestly contact between Jesus and the Father. Jesus appears before us, robed in white, the high-priestly garment: "One like a son of man, clothed with a long robe and with a golden girdle round his breast"; his eyes are like a flame of fire, his voice like the sound of many waters; from his mouth issues a sharp, two-edged sword, so that the seer falls at his feet as though dead. "But he laid his right hand upon me, saying, 'Fear not,

I am the first and the last, and the living one. I died, and behold I am alive for evermore, and I have the keys of death and hades.' " [60] It is still this risen Jesus whom we have as "advocate" with the Father, if we have sinned.[61]

This is heaven: Jesus erect, that is, not lying down like a slaughtered sheep, but risen up as the lamb that *was* slaughtered, entirely irradiated by the glory of the Father, and acting on our behalf as the great high priest who by definition is close to God. This is the vision of the Apocalypse and of all Christians in those days of savage persecution. This image inspired forgiveness and heroic courage in the wounded breast of Stephen, for on his knees he could pray to "heaven" where he saw "the glory of God, and Jesus standing at the right hand of God." This is what "going to heaven" means for the Christian: to lay down his life in the hands of this priest and this (risen)Lord and say: "Lord Jesus, receive my spirit." [62]

The Risen Lord, Active in the World

If we love Christ, we must rejoice that he has gone to the Father. We must try to realize what this means to him and show interest in his present state. Yet, it is also possible for us to gain some insight into what the resurrection means for ourselves.[63]

1. *He Takes Up His Abode in Us*

Since the resurrection, man's general religious situation has fundamentally altered. The incessant, often quite unconscious guest of humanity has entered new paths, for we who have always sought for happiness, for goodness, for peace, for love, given and received, have longed implicitly for God. This homesickness for God remained hidden or pierced through, but in any case it was there—in conversations, in lonely meditations, songs and dances, in married life, in art and poetry. Above all, there existed throughout the world a mighty movement to seek God in one particular face, to confer on him visible features, to experience his presence, to find the favorable time to invoke and to adore him. All the religions of the world, and

56 Heb. 8, 1-2.6.
57 Heb. 9, 11.
58 Heb. 9, 24.
59 Heb. 7, 25.

60 Rev. 1, 13-19.
61 1 Jn. 2, 1; cf. Jn. 14, 13-14.
62 Acts 7, 55-60.
63 Jn. 16, 5-7.

every form of devotion have their origin in this need for contact with God.

The location for this contact might be a sacred tree, a "high place," a corner of the living room, a sanctuary to which pilgrims flocked. The chosen people had their Ark, their holy city, their temple. They had their appointed hours, their weekly, monthly, or yearly feasts—hours and places for God. But the hour of Jesus sounded and since that moment there is no more question of adoring on the Gerrizim or in Jerusalem: to adore God in spirit and truth is to adore him in and through Jesus.[64] Now we have but one holy place and one auspicious hour: the risen Jesus. Where he is and when he is there we have access to God. This is a tremendous evolution, an inestimable progress in the religious history of mankind. But fundamentally, this is not so much a discovery on our part, a secret taken from God as a free initiative on his part who succeeded in reaching and understanding us and in taking up his abode among us and in the depths of our being.

It would become a different and for the rest, most interesting theme, to see how this life of Christ in us begins, grows, and comes to full maturity. Theologians have written whole treatises on the subject under the titles of grace, the virtues, Christian morality. These are basically commentaries upon a number of enlightening texts of St. Paul which deserve an entire life of admiration, gratitude, and practice, even more than the most detailed exegesis. Through faith and baptism, says St. Paul, "we have put on Christ." [65] Through faith, Christ dwells in our hearts.[66] We are rooted and built up in him.[67] We are his.[68] Although we cannot yet see this risen Jesus, we can behold him and according to the law of transformation, be slowly re-created in *his* glorious likeness.[69] This will one day change into the perfect transformation, at the moment when we *see* him as he is.[70]

This dwelling of Jesus within us brings with it new conditions and a new mentality. First and foremost, it gives us a respect for ourselves formerly unknown. A temple is something sacred. If Christ dwells in us, we are inviolable, holy. Our members are members of Christ; we are one spirit with him and therefore—one must excuse Paul's coarse language—"shall I take the members of Christ and make them members of a prostitute?" [71] The pure practice of Christian marriage, virginity, the dignity of the rough manual worker, feminine beauty and simplicity, the nobility of the martyrs, the deep reverence for the painful, ruined bodies of the sick, Christian burial all proceed from this. John says it in a mystical manner: "If a man loves me, he will keep my word, and my Father will love him and we will come to him and make our home with him." [72] Who would dare ruin such a dwelling?

This same law of respect naturally holds good for our brothers. We shall no longer judge by purely human yardsticks—wealth, talents, fame. The reality which dominates everything is the risen Christ. "From now on, therefore, we regard no one from a human point of view . . . Therefore, if anyone is in Christ, he is a new creation, the old one has passed away; behold, the new has come." [73]

Hence, the vehement outburst against the presidents of the Christian assemblies who flatter the rich and despise the poor: this is nothing less than "blaspheming the honorable name," i.e., Jesus himself.[74] The simple people who belong to Jesus are often defenseless, unprotected, like small creatures in the face of the powerful and influential; but woe to anyone who causes one of them to sin,[75] for these are brothers for whom Christ has died, and anyone who sins against them sins against Christ.[76] In a word the presence of the risen Lord transforms the faithful into "saints"; he elevates them to a higher level . . . Paul indeed employs this word as his customary greeting at the beginning of all his epistles and very often on other occasions, as in these closing words: "Greet every saint in Christ Jesus." [77]

Another striking renewal in the religious attitude brought about by the resurrection concerns the devotional life. A new way of praying developed, the dialogue. Of their very nature people have always adored God, sung his praises, prayed to him in supplication. They have very seldom tried to "speak" to him. They may indeed have spoken with projections of their own egos, but the difference between ourselves and God appeared too great to allow of a conversation. In the Old Testament there is, so to speak, no place for a dialogue.

---

[64] Jn. 4, 21-24.
[65] Gal. 3, 27.
[66] Eph. 3, 17.
[67] Col. 2, 7.
[68] Gal. 3, 29.
[69] 2 Cor. 3, 18; cf. Rom. 8, 29; 1 Cor. 15, 49.
[70] 1 Jn. 3, 2; it is not certain that "him" refers to Jesus; it may also

refer to the Father.
[71] 1 Cor. 6, 15-18.
[72] Jn. 14, 23.
[73] 2 Cor. 5, 16-17.
[74] Jas. 2, 1-7.
[75] Mt. 18, 6; Lk. 17, 1-2.
[76] 1 Cor. 8, 12-13.
[77] Phil. 4, 21.

Yet now, we find that someone who has grown up in the sense of God of the prophets, someone who has an incomparable apprehension of God in every act and event, and whose prayer is, in the last instance, always addressed to God (the Father), someone like Paul has evolved a form of dialogue in his prayer. Paul converses with Jesus. He had a thorn in his flesh which hampered him enormously in his apostolic work, and three times he asked the Lord (Jesus) to remove it. He received his answer too, in a manner which he does not explain but which is different from the Father's method of replying. Jesus made him understand that his weaknesses revealed more clearly the power of his Lord: "And he said to me, 'My grace is sufficient for you, for my power is made perfect in weakness.' " [78]

Since Jesus' resurrection man has become at the same time extraordinarily humble in the tone of his prayer and extraordinarily intimate as regards essentials. Such was Emily Dickinson's conversation with the living Lord:

" 'Unto Me?' I do not know you—
Where may be your House?
'I am Jesus—Late of Judea—
Now—of Paradise'—
Wagons—have you—to convey me?
This is far from Thence—

'Arms of Mine—sufficient Phaeton—
Trust Omnipotence'—
I am spotted—"I am Pardon"—
I am small—"The Least
Is esteemed in Heaven the Chiefest—
Occupy my House."

(*The Complete Poems of Emily Dickinson*, Thomas H. Johnson, ed., Boston, Little, Brown and Company, 1960, p. 451.)

Uncultivated people and others with a high degree of culture, souls that are crystal clear and those who must struggle to attain purity all pray in this manner. For them prayer is a dialogue, and this is truly a *new wave* in the history of prayer. Before this man came to dwell in the little houses of our earth, ate our bread, died our death and prepared our resurrection, God was not yet for us a friend.

2. "Acts" of Presence

Is it because we are dynamic beings requiring repetition and variety in our acts that Jesus was not content to take up his abode with us in a settled manner? Just as two people who love each other and have no doubts at all about their mutual feelings, constantly seek to express their love in new and different ways to keep it from becoming mechanical, so the risen Lord too reveals himself in concrete, well-defined activity. "He who loves me will be loved by my Father, and I will love him and manifest myself to him." [79] It will be a revelation that the world does not see, because the world does not "live," but we live and can recognize the living Lord. [80]

A number of the "forms of presence" are absolutely certain and were even the subject of dogmatic pronouncements on the part of the Church doctrinal authorities. They concern the holy scriptures, the eucharist and the remaining sacraments. These are signs, symbols which have no life of themselves—a book, bread and wine, sacramental rites.

We have already written at some length about the "real presence" of Jesus in the eucharist. [81] It is not difficult either, in the light of Scripture and tradition, to show that the risen Christ is mysteriously, but truly active in the remaining sacraments. For it is clear, to take only one example, that power to forgive sin does not rest with the apostles themselves; [82] only Christ among men has this authority and this effective power, [83] so that in the sacrament of penance it is Jesus himself who is at work. The same is true of the anointing of the sick; it is the Lord who "raises up." [84] Christ, too, is the invisible minister of the sacrament of marriage. For when Paul speaks here of the union between Jesus and the Church, [85] he has more in mind than a simple explanatory comparison. For the ancients, the *exemplary cause* was at the same time the *effective cause*: Christian marriage grants an extra value to that which God unites in all who marry throughout the world, since the risen Christ himself makes them sharers in his own life and especially in his mysterious union with the Church.

In what sense can we speak of a presence of the risen Jesus in the scriptures? This naturally means more than that the entire history

[78] 2 Cor. 12, 7-8.
[79] Jn. 14, 21.
[80] Jn. 14, 19-20.22.
[81] Cf. pp. 194ff.
[82] Mt. 18, 18; Jn. 20, 23.
[83] Mt. 9, 6.
[84] Jas. 5, 15.
[85] Eph. 5, 22-23.

of salvation is orientated towards Christ or that the doctrinal unity of the scriptures is to be found in Christ. We are concerned here with a real presence which can be summed up as follows: Jesus is the exegete of the Old Testament and the Word that speaks particularly through the New Testament message.

We needed an exegete like this. Luke shows us how the risen Jesus granted insight to the disciples so that they realized that everything spoke of him and wondered that their hearts did not catch fire with enthusiasm when he opened the scriptures to them.[86] Paul will tell how Jewish thought stagnated; "for to this day, when they read the old covenant, that same veil remains unlifted, because only through Christ is it taken away . . . but when a man turns to the Lord, the veil is removed." [87] Here we have a real presence of the Lord Jesus in the scriptures; when the veil is pushed aside, we behold with unveiled face the glory of the Lord, and so "are changed into his likeness from one degree of glory to another." [88]

Paul says that this is brought about by the Spirit of the Lord,[89] but we can just as well say that it is Jesus himself, for the *object* of this beholding-through-the-scriptures, and the light operating in the subject (the Spirit) are so intimately one that Paul dares to write: "the Lord who is the Spirit." [90] It is, for that matter, in this same sense that another, more realistic presence of Christ must be spiritually interpreted He who has ascended to the place from whence he came, namely, the risen Jesus, is indeed present in the eucharist, but "it is the Spirit that gives life, the flesh is of no avail." [91]

Concerning the other nonscriptural and nonsacramental "presences" of the risen Jesus, these are in a certain sense more impressive than the others, since we are no longer dealing with material "signs," but with persons. It is all the more regrettable therefore that they should be surrounded by something like a theological vacuum; they are not studied with the known exegetical precision instruments and the required philosophical depth. Yet, they are constantly talked about, perhaps not always relevantly Christ is present where two or three are gathered together in his name; Christ is present in the poor, the downtrodden, those who exercise authority.

What does all this really mean? Is it merely a manner of speaking or is there some metaphysical basis? The impression gained from reading many scholarly commentaries—we shall quote a few of the best and most widely read [92]—is that they do little more than skim the surface and many pious sermons are no better. This is perhaps

• the clearest proof of the practical underestimation of the resurrection during the past centuries, for everything in these texts stands or falls by the answer to the question: where is the risen Jesus? Here, we shall venture onto this almost virgin territory and halt by the principal texts: Matthew 18, 20; 18, 5; 25, 40; 10, 40.

Where two or three are gathered in my name, there am I in the midst of them (Mt. 18, 20).[93]

Most commentators give nothing more than a paraphrase. Lagrange says that Jesus "is evidently not speaking of his actual presence, but of a mystical presence, in the nature of the divine presence" without explaining the difference between an actual, divine, and mystical presence; probably, the "mystical presence" refers to a more or less platonic idea. Another commentary speaks of "a sort of identification between Christ and the faithful" (BL).

We may, in my view, start by postulating that the Christ speaking here is not the earthly Jesus. When he was visible among the apostles, what meaning could be attributed to "union in his name"? Do not all our texts take the "name" of Jesus, i.e., his "lordship" (for this is the name which he received and still bears on the lips of Christians) to be the resurrection? If Christ is in our midst, "speaking on our behalf" (BAC), then he undoubtedly does so as high priest in his glorified body. As three German commentaries rightly point out, the speaker here is none other than "the risen and glorified Lord" (RNT) who "is close to his disciples" by a "presence of grace," by a "personal presence" (BB). "He himself is present in his community" and this, in the opinion of Schniewind (NTD), is so general an affirmation that it could be the title of the entire Gospel.

This, at least, is in the right direction. At the time and in the milieu when a team of editors was working on Matthew—that communal product par excellence, also as regards content—Christian gatherings in the name of the Lord were a reality of the day.

86 Lk. 24, 26-27, 32.44.
87 2 Cor. 3, 14-16.
88 2 Cor. 3, 18.
89 *Ibid.*
90 *Ibid.*, v. 17.
91 Jn. 6, 62-63.
92 Abbreviations of some commentaries on St. Matthew: P. Buzy, *Bible de Lille* (BL); P. Benoit,

Bible de Jérusalem (BJ); P. Dausch *Bonner Bibel* (BB); J. Schmid, *Regensburger Neues Testament* (RNT); J. Schniewind, *Das Neue Testament Deutsch* (NTD); J. Leal, *Biblioteca de Autores Christianos* (BAC); also Lagrange and Plummer.
93 Cf. J. Hamer, "La Présence du

All the sources inform us of the existence of mystical phenomena, in the sense of *experimental* experiences of God in Christ. Paul expressly mentions the problem of these charismatic phenomena, and we even possess some of the hymns, devices, and ardent cries which resulted from them, such as "Jesus the Lord" and "Come, Lord!" [94] If it is thus an established fact that an experience of Jesus existed in the primitive Christian gatherings, it needs but a short step to arrive at the insight that this same risen Lord was present even for those who were not themselves inspired at that moment, and even during moments when the mystical transports did not occur. For my part, I would not find it difficult to see the concept of the Matthean communities in connection with Matthew 18, 20, reflected in the "testimony" of a seminarian from Santiago in 1963:

"In the *población* (large working class district amounting to a small city which may number up to a hundred thousand inhabitants) where I work, there is a young man of twenty-four who had sunk terribly low; he is a drunkard, a thief, and an adulterer (he has relations with a married woman and indeed with any woman he meets). This young man falls in love with a girl from our Christian community. She brings him along to our group meetings where the Gospel is regularly discussed. The young man makes friends with two of our group, well trained militants. Very soon this twenty-four-year-old feels himself gripped by God; he wants to be converted, to begin to lead a better life, no longer to drink or steal.

"A few days ago he came to me almost in tears and said that he wanted to be a Christian but that this would require so much of him that he thought it practically impossible. I gave him a book of Michel Quoist's and the gospels, in which I had underlined certain important passages for him. In addition, I advised him to attend all the meetings of our Christian community. Now I ask myself this: where did that young man meet Christ? For I do not doubt for a moment that it was a meeting with Christ that changed him so radically. He did not meet Christ in the eucharist which, so to speak, he does not know. Nor did he meet him in prayer, for he says that he cannot pray and has never prayed. I dare to assert *that his meeting with Christ took place in the community*. Where two or three are gathered in his name, there is he in the midst of them.

"This presence is real, like the presence of Christ in the eucharist, although it is not substantial. *This man met Christ in the community because he was really present there* . . . There is no eucharist reserved in the chapel of our *población*, but the red lamp beside the altar could be lit whenever the community meets there, for Christ is *truly* present there in our midst. We can all go there to adore him. For anyone estranged from religion, this presence is there for the grasping. Such a meeting with Christ purifies, elevates, Christianizes, sanctifies."

The presence of Christ among the needy and the "little ones" of the community (Mt. 18, 5; 25, 50) is often interpreted without any relief, except in the sense that Jesus is hereby expressing a heavy moral obligation. A number of commentaries speak simply of a certain "identification" (BB, BAC); the weak among us represent Christ (Plummer) and "he regards everything as though done to himself" (BAC). Very many authors employ this same term (*as, as though*) in order to indicate whom one must see in the sick, the hungry. The unfortunate "are considered as his brothers" (BJ, BAC), whose cause he makes his own (BJ).

It is beyond dispute that the moral interpretation is the most obvious: Jesus employs this locution to indicate the importance of brotherly love and the reward associated with it. But must we not go further? Lagrange speaks of a "mystical truth" (reality): "Is this not exaggeration, sheer imagination, poetry? No, the circumstances are too solemn to allow of an extravagant use of words . . . The terms are not exaggerated and the formula is correct." (BL). Certain authors specify that the reference is to a presence of the son of man in the poor (BB, RNT). Plummer sees here the "reverse" of the mysterious bond between the messiah and humanity; he can suffer for mankind, and mankind can receive his presence. A number of Catholic authors allude to the doctrine of the mystical body, but they themselves admit that this application is not entirely accurate, since we are concerned here not exclusively with Christians but with all sorts of people in need (BAC, BL). On the other hand, Schniewind rightly observes that the union of Christ and the community does not consist of an absorption of the Christian in Christ (NTD).

Christ (Mt. 18, 20)," in *Evangéliser*, 95 (1962), pp. 443-454.

[94] 1 Cor. 12, 3; 2 Cor. 15, 22; Rev. 22, 20.

In order to form an opinion, we must first and foremost take into account the very special character of these passages in the evangelical tradition. Jesus, who was always so careful when it came to messianic titles and power, here quite plainly represents himself as the ultimate judge. The titles, "Lord" and "shepherd," [95] lead us to assume that we are here concerned with the *risen* Christ, thus not as in the parable of the hundred sheep in which the *Father* is the shepherd,[96] but as in the parable of St. John in which *Jesus* can be the good shepherd because he has died and can grant his life to all.[97] The natural *Sitz im Leben* of both texts under discussion is thus the life of the first Christian groups with their inner difficulties and the attitude which they ought to adopt towards the oppressed and persecuted. This brings us automatically to the period after Jesus' death, so that the person who here asserts that he is with the poor and the little ones, is the risen Jesus.

A second observation concerns the number of people who are said to enjoy the special presence of Christ. It goes without saying that the list—the little ones, the hungry, the naked, the imprisoned—is not exhaustive. May we express this idea more generally: Jesus is present with all the needy. And can we make a distinction between those who are in need and those who are not? Is the reference to material need or is spiritual need included? The answer is clear: *everybody* is included in this concept. But this would mean that Jesus is present in everyone? Is this not a little exaggerated?

Not necessarily. In the first place it solves very little to reduce the "poor" to a strict minimum of the most necessitous, for even then at the present time, one soon reaches the billion mark, which might just as well be four. Then, it is natural for the risen Jesus to possess an unlimited possibility of mutual contact. We shall not have to await our short monthly audience, but will *always* be with him.[98] It is therefore not all that fantastic to assume that he who invited all those who were troubled to come to him [99] truly assists all men now that his spiritualized body makes this possible. We may assume that he, more than the angels, accompanies the little ones." [100] He can say, in the realistic meaning of the word, that anyone who persecutes Christians persecutes him.[101] Nor is the author of the Apocalypse merely speaking metaphorically when he has Jesus say: "Behold, I stand at the door and knock; if anyone hears my voice and opens the door, I will come in to him and eat with him and he with me." [102]

Finally, it is important not to allow ourselves to be mislead by our imagination. The risen bodies are not present in the same way as the purely material. There are degrees of presence. We would probably do as well not to speak too much of presence "in" the poor. This could lead us to a wrong concept of the mystical body, as though there were one great body, composed of the personal Jesus (the head) and the Christians (the trunk as far as the neck) with which one would come into contact or conflict in doing good to or persecuting Christians. There is no such superbeing.[103]

At the same time, by the discreet use or omission of the little word, "in," we combat a failing of which we are, perhaps somewhat exaggeratedly, accused; that in the needy we see only Jesus (in order to gain a reward from him) and do not love the person himself. It goes without saying that no presence of Jesus can banish the person, and that it is false to imagine him, as it were, hidden under a human disguise.

Perhaps, another image can help us combat this false idea. Recently, a friend was telling me enthusiastically of the latest invention in the area of film of the International Industries Fair in New York. You are led into a big round hall of which the walls form one large screen. A scene is shown—for example, a man walking along the street. The novelty consists in the fact that in one place you see him in front of you, a little further along in profile, elsewhere from behind, here in close-up, then again at a long range. Every section of the wall is brought into play, and the result is astounding. One sees the same man, at the same moment, from every possible angle. The picture imposes itself with irresistible force; one finds oneself beginning to identify completely with that man; his reaction impinges upon one's own feelings . . . In the same way, we cannot say of the risen Jesus that he stands to the left or right of people, above or below them, in front of them or behind them. He possesses a different dimension whereby he can encompass us completely, with varying degrees of intimacy, with his own rhythm. When, therefore, we give something to a simple child of man, he stands there, the risen Jesus, with his large, open eyes, with his love which is so much greater than that of a mother gazing down upon her child when it receives a gift.

[95] Mt. 25, 32. 37. 44.
[96] Mt. 18, 12-14; Lk. 15, 4-7.
[97] Jn. 10, 11.
[98] 1 Thess. 4, 18.
[99] Mt. 11, 28.
[100] Mt. 18, 10; cf. v. 11.
[101] Acts 9, 4.

He who receives you, receives me (Mt. 10, 40).

Can there be said to be a special presence of Christ in the apostles and, since then, perhaps rather less intensely, in the hierarchy of the Church? The majority of exegetes regard the text quoted above as merely a figure of style, stressing the importance of "receiving," especially inwardly, the evangelical missionaries and their message. One must welcome the preachers *as though* one were receiving Christ himself (BB, RNT, Lagrange). On the other hand, Plummer detects here the beginning of a "mystical union" between Christ and the Christians, which will be further developed in Matthew 25, 31-45, while Schniewind thinks expressly of the risen Christ who decides everything in the community. He adds, however, that the reference is not only to the apostles but to every Christian who proclaims the Word of God (NTD). Buzy goes even further. In his opinion, the phrase was intended to cause a "mystical shock," for it means nothing less than a "mysterious interaction which seems to progress to a sort of identification between Christ and the apostles" (BL).

Regarding the presence of Christ in the hierarchy, one may object that a bishop can make a mistake. Can Jesus make a mistake? This argument does not hold water, however, for "he who hears you, hears me" must not be taken completely literally even in the moral interpretation. For that matter, not even the presence of grace is irrevocable or unconditional. Nor is it a decisive objection to say that all precepts and commandments are considered justified in the name of this principle condemning the faithful to passive silence or oppression or even in the case of doctrinal error on the part of the authorities, to serious moral conflict. These objections apply as much to the purely moral as to the "realistic" or mystical interpretation.

The question is this: how did the apostles themselves interpret this phrase? And here again we must be on our guard against a purely legalistic interpretation. They claimed that they spoke "in the name of Jesus." Was this not something more than "on the authority of," "in place of"? For the Semite the name is identical with the person; to baptize "in the name of" is to bring into communion with the person (or persons) himself. Anyone who can speak "in the name of Jesus" possesses something more than a passport conferring the necessary authority.

We know the name of that "something more": it is the Holy Spirit. When Jesus granted them that Spirit, he did not do so in the manner of one conferring an academic degree or qualifications. He breathed on them [104] as God did when creating man. The apostles, thus, will possess the gift of the Spirit permanently, just as Adam permanently possessed the spirit of life. Paul claims that he possesses the Spirit of Jesus,[105] and this is perhaps why he can "assemble" with the Corinthians "in the name of the Lord Jesus" and command "with the power of our Lord Jesus." [106] The apostles even dare to use the expression: "it has seemed good to the Holy Spirit and to us . . ." [107]

Perhaps even more realistic is John, when he says that there are three sorts of witnesses, actually three sources of Christ-experience: the water of baptism, the blood of the eucharist, and finally, the people who are moved by the Spirit.[108] Through these three comes Jesus Christ, and these three are inseparable. The witnesses of the Spirit whom John refers to here are not exclusively members of the hierarchy, although it may be deduced from the text that bearing witness presumes a realistic presence of the Spirit. And together with the Spirit, as the reverse of the same reality, stands the presence of the risen Christ.

It is therefore completely logical, one and the same thing, to say that the apostles are the bearers of the first gifts of the Spirit [109] and those who have seen the risen Christ.[110] This again is not so much a legal condition, laid down more or less by chance in order to maintain a norm. Anyone who did not posssess in heart and soul the certainty and presence of the risen Jesus, would by that very fact have ceased to be an apostle.

Let us listen to the voice of a veteran in the study of St. Paul, someone who proceeds with the utmost caution when approaching the mystical. L. Cerfaux thinks that with Paul we must accept a *conscious* contact with God, a contact *immediately* perceived even in his actual apostolic activity. This presupposes, too, "a permanent relationship to *Christ*." His thought has been illumined and altered

---

[102] Rev. 3, 20.

[103] See the pertinent remarks of L. Cerfaux, *Le chrétien dans la théologie paulinienne* (Paris, 1962); pp. 324-342 (Communion avec le Christ. Art. 5: "La mystique paulinienne").

[104] Jn. 20, 22-23.

[105] 1 Cor. 7, 40.

[106] 1 Cor. 5, 4.

[107] Acts 15, 28.

[108] 1 Jn. 5, 6-8.

[109] Eph. 4, 11-12; 1 Cor. 12, 28.

[110] Acts 1, 22; 1 Cor. 9, 1.

by Christ; it is now light and glory of Christ. We are not deceived
in taking seriously the formulas which Paul employs in this connection and in not considering them purely as figures of speech . . . If
the apostolate means an intimate contact with God and with Christ,
then this contact must be passed on to the Christians. The apostle
was enlightened by God in order that he might grant to the Christians that same light which is Christ.[111]

One would then need to examine further the modalities acquired
by all this as the apostles are succeeded by the "college of bishops."
May it suffice here to have made a plea for a thorough study of the
presence of Christ in the hierarchy, taking the resurrection as a
starting point.

3. Dynamic Presence throughout History

"Lo, I am with you always, to the close of the age." [112] These are
the closing words of St. Matthew's gospel. Despite the feverish
atmosphere of the first Christian assembly and their intense expectation of a parousia which they thought to be close at hand, the
apostles have nonetheless left us valuable indications regarding the
activity of the risen Jesus throughout human history. Christianity as
a whole and each individual Christian must be inspired by the idea
of progress, in and with the risen Jesus. The fact that history has
reached a climax, urges us on to greater speed: "You know what
hour it is, how it is full time now for you to wake from sleep. For
salvation is nearer to us now than when we first believed. The night
is far gone and day is at hand." [113] "God, who has begun a good
work in us (by granting us the risen Lord) will bring it to completion at the day of Jesus Christ." [114]

The first thing that strikes us about this dynamic action of the
risen Jesus through the ages is precisely this tension, this forward
urge. This is no passive waiting but truly a longing, a passionate
expectation of the perfect revelation of the glorified one. We are
more "en route" in the Lord's absence than enjoying his presence,
for our age is that of faith, not of sight.[115] Every Christian must
imitate Paul: he was "touched" by the risen Jesus, and now presses
on in order to "touch" him.[116] The entire Church must grow "until
we all attain to the unity of the faith, and of the knowledge of the
Son of God, to mature manhood, to the measure of the stature of
the fullness of Christ." [117]

This forward striving can be so intense that it leads to radical and even hazardous anticipation, expressed in the advocation of virginity. This cannot be explained on the basis of what are now called "apostolic motives," nor justified as asceticism. It is the result—at least this was the intention—of such a consistent faith in the risen Jesus that they thought, even affectively, that "they had enough in him alone," as will be the case in the resurrection, "where they neither marry, nor are given in marriage." [118] This longing on the part of the Christian "hastens the coming of the day," [119] so that "the Church is the arbiter of how long this world will last" (Durwell). This explains why this same world, in bitter self-defense, feels towards her an almost instinctive hate.[120]

Turning now to the concrete content of that dynamism of Christ in the course of history, we cannot even attempt to outline it here. Any such attempt would develop into a treatise on the Church and even more than that. We shall merely touch upon two aspects which are directly linked with the influence of the risen Jesus: the gifts and the re-creation of the cosmos.

At the close of St. Mark's gospel we read:"And these signs will accompany those who believe: in my name they will cast out demons; they will speak in new tongues; they will pick up serpents and if they drink any deadly thing, it will not hurt them; they will lay their hands on the sick; and they will recover." [121] These popular and perhaps not very spiritual sounding sentences serve to conclude a gospel! [122] And they are nothing more than the truth. When Luke sketches us a number of scenes from the life of the early Church, he gives us a clear idea of the impression made by the miracles worked in the name of Jesus.[123]

Yet, why should this surprise us? The miracles are normal. Not of course if we regard them as corrections made in a divine plan that is less than perfect, or as a means of capturing our attention or proving some religious thesis. The miracles, so characteristic of Christi-

111 Cf. L. Cerfaux, *op. cit.*, pp. 338-339.
112 Mt. 28, 20.
113 Rom. 13, 11-12.
114 Phil. 1, 6.
115 2 Cor. 5, 4-8.
116 Phil. 3, 12-16.
117 Eph. 4, 13.
118 Cf. Mt. 22, 30.
119 Acts 3, 19, 2 Peter 3, 11-12.

120 Cf. Jn. 15, 19.
121 Mk. 16, 17-18.
122 V. 20 sounds a little more spiritual.
123 From the quotation from Joel 2, 28-32 in Acts 2, 17-20, and the miracle of the lame man, cured in the Name of Jesus, (Acts 3, 6) to the miracles of the journey to Rome.

anity, are not meant primarily as witnesses to an "invisible world." Theoretically, of course, they could be just that, as they are implicitly in actual fact, but in the first place, and directly, they are signs of a *risen* world.

In Jesus, the coming glory has already reached its climax, and since he is in such intimate contact with us, it is to be expected that influence and a mingling of the one world upon and with the other will occur from time to time. Paul, witness and theologian of these "heavenly gifts," links them with the risen Christ who has taken our prison chains with him.[124] He himself attaches great importance to the institutional charisma of the apostolic office, which comes first on the list, and among the other gifts, his preference is for prophecy —an inspired speaking in the name of God—and above all, love.[125] John says more than once that the risen Christ will perform greater miracles through the Christians than when he himself was active in Palestine.[126] Therefore, it was better that he should go away.

Is the miracle an exception, or is there something more general in progress in the whole of creation? We know for certain that the whole of the created world is still sighing and groaning in travail as it waits with eager longing for the redemption, for it too must share in the glorious liberty of the children of God and is thus at one with the resurrection of Christ.[128] Is this redemption in progress or will everything happen at once, at the end, through the unprepared intervention of God who will suddenly and totally change the face of all things?

The texts say that it will be a gift of God, that God will accomplish it. This is only right and to be expected, for God does everything always and everywhere. The question is whether the re-creation is already in progress, being accomplished through social, economic, artistic, and other "temporal" values and initiatives. The apostles give us no explicit answer to this question; we can only state that they for their part, like people newly in love, thought not so much of the implications and consequences of their love as of the loved one. If one asks a man in love what he is thinking of, he will tell you of whom he thinks. Speak to him of the best methods of educating his descendants, and he will listen politely while thinking of the quickest way to reach his beloved. For the first Christians, "time" was entirely dominated by the sign of the risen Jesus.

The Apocalypse undoubtedly contains the most impressive global picture of the activity of the risen Christ in time. Here the churches can read their present situation, their position in the hands of the living Lord, and the flaming message that he sends them.[129] For belief in Christ is not a sort of higher *Weltanschauung*, a sublimating of the earthly in a more exalted and more complete "vision." It is a reality because the risen Jesus lives and intervenes in the world. He can punish the cities.[130] In this sense, he has already "come again" and has already passed a "judgment," for example, through the destruction of Jerusalem.[131] This we find in the synoptics who are thus in complete agreement with John when he indicates—either by the silence in the sky or by the signs which succeed each other there with dizzying rapidity—that human history is dominated by the erect lamb, the risen Christ.

These few reflections, imperfect as they are, may perhaps have given some idea of the new element introduced by the fact of the resurrection into the answer to the three eternal questions of human existence: Where do I come from? Why do I exist? Where am I going?

[124] Eph. 4, 9.
[125] Eph. 4, 11-12; 1 Cor. 12, 28-13, 1.
[126] Jn. 1, 50-51; 13, 12.
[127] Jn. 15, 7.
[128] Rom. 8, 19-25.
[129] Rev. 2, 3.
[130] Rev. 2, 5.16.
[131] Mt. 10, 23 (according to many authors); Lk. 17, 22-37 (according to A. Feuillet, in DBS 6, K 1359); 21, 22-24 etc.

VI
Christ Present

"Do you desire to die on a particular feast
day? I need no feast day in order to die.
The day of my death will be the greatest
feast of all."

(Thérèse of Lisieux)

The attitude of certain Christians towards death, not only in
the pious journals or written meditations of novices in the spiritual life, but in reality, has often astounded the world. The desire to
die can certainly be a sickly thing; it can arise from a wish to avoid
real problems, or even from an act of capitulation. And yet, it is
scarcely conceivable that sheer naïveté has led the Church to celebrate the death of her best sons throughout the centuries. There
must be something great about death. The accepted ecclesiastical
term is *transitus*, a transition. Even in our day one can recall "condemned" resistance leaders grooming themselves before the final
meeting, their rooms adorned by flowers requested by themselves.
Imitators of the priest who asked that the Easter bells should be
rung at the moment he was pronounced dead are not all that rare.
When, even in the middle of the twentieth century, we read aloud
Ignatius' letter to the Romans, we feel a thrill of respect and happiness linking us with Antioch across a bridge of eighteen centuries.
This bishop, who desired a grave in the jaws of wild animals so that
he might be pure bread of Christ is intimately related to the Christian of today. From time to time the same desire grips us "to be
always with the Lord." [1]

Little is said of the "four last things" and what is said is usually
expressed from an anthropocentric standpoint. We think of *our* last
moments and this naturally gives rise to fear, disquiet, revulsion, or

forced optimism. Let us then try to see all this *as a mystery of Christ*. After the birth, the hidden life, the message, death, and resurrection, we come to the parousia of Christ. Parousia means the presence or coming of Christ.[2] The parousia is the mystery of Christ present among us once again or, to put it more accurately, in a newer, fuller, more definitive manner.

A fuller analysis of the important points of the parousia would run into a very long treatise, even leaving aside the critical problem of the so-called deferred parousia.[3] We shall concern ourselves only with those aspects which throw some light upon the manner in which Jesus reveals himself therein. In this respect, it is difficult to accept the attitude of authors who treat this point as a corollary or closing page of the resurrection. In reality, it is indeed a new phase, of which we as yet know little, but which has an incomparable bearing on what we have called "the existence of Christ." We shall study this mystery in its initial moment and in its nature or duration. This gives us two sections:

1. The last intervention of Christ; in biblical language, the day of the Lord. This comprises the return of the Lord, judgment, resurrection of all mankind.

2. Christ as light of the re-created universe. Here, we derive our terms from John (the light)[4] and from Matthew and Paul (all will be re-created).[5] This perhaps says more to us than John's magnificent metaphorical image of the new Jerusalem. We are interested in discovering the nature of this light, and of that life in the new Jerusalem, at least as regards the relationship to Christ.

---

[1] Cf. 1 Thess. 4, 18.

[2] Presence or coming; the term, "parousia," occurs in the New Testament: Mt. 24, 3.27; 1 Cor. 15, 23; 1 Thess. 2, 19; 3, 13 etc. Jas. 5, 7; 2 Pet. 1.16; 3, 4.12; 1 Jn. 2, 28.

[3] Along with the bibliographical data in connection with the kingdom cf. p. 41 and the resurrection cf. pp. 303ff. cf. O. Cullmann, *Le retour du Christ. Esperance de l'Eglise selon le N.T.* (Neuchâtel, 1945 [2]); Y. Congar, "Le purgatoire," in *Le mystère de la mort et sa célébration* (Lex Orandi, Paris, 1951, pp. 279-336); J. Dupont, *Sun Christo. L'union avec le Christ*

suivant saint Paul. 1. Avec le Christ dans la vie future (Bruges, 1952); "La fin du monde estelle pour démain," in *Lumière et Vie*, 11 (Paris, 1953); A. Feuillet, "Le royaume céleste et la destinée des chrétiens (2 *Cor. 5, 1-10*)," in *Rech. Sc. rel.*, 44 (1956), pp. 360-402; J. Daniélou, "Christologie et eschatologie," in *Das Konzil von Chalcedon*, III, (1954), pp. 269-286; L. Cerfaux, *Le chrétien dans la théologie paulinienne* (Paris, 1962), pp. 143-215.

[4] Jn. 1 *passim*.

[5] Mt. 19, 28; Eph. 1, 10; Rom. 8, 21.

CHRIST'S LAST INTERVENTION

The risen Jesus never rests, nor does he need any relaxation. He develops an enormous activity of love in deep happiness, making countless others happy, as we have outlined in the previous chapter. But, there comes a moment of extraordinary concentration in his activity; the day of the parousia, called simply, since Paul's first epistle, "the day of the Lord." [6]

Jesus will return. This has been an article of faith for all Christians of every century. The "eschatological speech" describes this event as a collapse of the universe: "The sun will be darkened and the moon will not give its light; the stars will be falling from heaven and the powers in the heavens will be shaken." [7] This is the usual jargon of all apocalypses and, for that matter, a literal quotation from Isaiah.[8] It means simply that a formidable intervention by God will take place. "Then they will see the son of man coming in clouds with great power and glory," the text goes on.[9] This, too, is a quotation to indicate that this will indeed be a manifestation of the *glorified* Christ. The cloud is a symbol of the divine glory into which Jesus was received. Not unnaturally, the popular imagination has found a more precise locality for this great event of Jesus' return: the valley of Jehoshaphat,[10] which was originally none other than the valley of "Yahweh—Judges" and which was later identified with part of the Cedron valley, near Jerusalem, i.e., the center of the earth.

Logically speaking, we imagine that Jesus will first return and only afterwards pronounce judgment. In any case, it is solemnly and repeatedly affirmed that he will come "to judge the living and the dead," [11] that is, all who are alive at that moment and all those who have ever lived. "For this we declare to you by the word of the Lord," clarifies Paul, "that we who are alive, who are left until the coming of the Lord, shall not precede those who have fallen asleep." [12] This same Paul, although more sober with regard to apocalyptics, nonetheless has recourse to popular metaphorical language: the voice of the archangel, the trumpet, the descent of the cloud. The artists have combined all this with Matthew 25 and arrived at a picture which even today clings to everyone's memory: an immense public tribunal, two masses of people, the judge. This spectacular exhibition does us perhaps more harm than good! There is no valley in the world which could fulfill the necessary requirements.

Concerning the course of the entire event we must beware of giving too much rein to our imaginations. "When, in the drama of the last judgment we have set aside all that corresponds to the traditional apocalyptic framework, we retain as established elements the appearance of the Lord, the separation of good and bad, the laying bare of consciences, the reckoning. All these elements are immediately realized in the resurrection, whether to glory or to perdition. A judgment pronounced when the fate of everyone has already been decided would be pure exhibitionism, a luxury article tacked on to the judgment already passed, and thus something very different from the last judgment of which the prophets, Christ and the apostles spoke: an enormous menace and an enormous hope, the fire of wrath and a glorious salvation . . . The three elements, therefore—parousia, resurrection, and judgment—are not three successive scenes from the last act of the redemption, but its only and greatest scene." [13]

One thing, however, of which we are positive, is that Jesus will be the great actor of this production; it is he who returns, he who grants the life of resurrection,[14] he who possesses the authority to pronounce judgment because he is the son of man.[15] During our lifetime he was, deep within us, like a living force, and above all as vindicating life: he who receives his Word has already passed from death to life.[16] At the moment of death our situation is, as it were, definitively established. Then, after an intervening period, difficult to define and of a different tempo from our present world, which may perhaps last for thousands of centuries, whereas everything passes extremely quickly [17] for the soul in the intermediate phase, comes the "last judgment," the *public,* communal revelation of our redemption,[18] of our dependence on Jesus, of our gratitude, of our physical state, re-created in magnificent splendor and radiant glory. All this we owe entirely and consciously to Jesus. What shall

[6] 1 Thess. 5, 2; cf. 2 Thess. 2, 2; Phil. 1, 6.10; 2, 16.

[7] Mk. 13, 24-25.

[8] Cf. Is. 13, 10; 34, 4; a little further Zech. 2, 10 (6).

[9] Mk. 13, 26; cf. Dan. 7, 13; 1 Thess. 4, 16.

[10] Joel 3, 2.12; cf. v. 14 = "Valley of Decision."

[11] Acts 10, 42; 2 Tim. 4, 1; 1 Pet. 4, 5.

[12] 1 Thess. 4, 15.

[13] F. X. Durwell, *The Resurrection* (New York, Sheed and Ward, 1960).

[14] Jn. 5, 21-26.

[15] Jn. 6, 39-44.54.

[16] Jn. 5, 21-22; cf. 2 Cor. 5, 10; Mt. 25, 31.

[17] Cf. Y. Congar, "Le purgatoire," n.3.

[18] In Paul the communal character is revealed chiefly in a joyful entry procession (1 Thess. 4, 14-17).

we do not only to master the emotions of that moment, but to withstand the reality of that experience? Theologians speak of the "light of glory" (*lumen gloriae*) which we shall need if our faculties are to comprehend all these sights and experiences. This is another way of saying the same thing as the heaven-shocking apocalypse of the synoptics, namely, that it is ineffable, for it is something that "no eye has seen, nor ear heard, nor the heart of man conceived".[19]

If we wish to understand properly Jesus' activity at that moment, we must, however, consider especially the vertical dimension. The crowd, many billions strong, viewed horizontally perhaps makes more impression, but the qualitative event touches more essential roots. According to a modern interpretation of one of John's piercing phrases, we shall see Jesus *as he is* and therefore become similar to him.[20] This is thus a re-creative contemplation. Perhaps the assembled philosophers and theologians will one day decide how a glance can change a person's being. For the present I regard a passage from the account of Thérèsa's death as the best commentary on our text.

In a style which is painfully accurate, but may not be to everyone's taste, her sister Agnes has given us an account of the long illness and the terrible last two hours.[21] It was a quite "normal" death, normal, that is, for her merciless disease—swollen face, purple hands, ice-cold feet, uncontrollable trembling of the body. Then, her eyes fixed on the crucifix, came her last words: "Oh, I love him . . . My God, I love you." A short time after this declaration of love for the Lord Jesus—called simply "God" after the custom of the time—came the great surprise.

"Scarcely had she pronounced these words than, to our great surprise, she suddenly sank back, her head turned towards the right. We thought that all was over and our mother hastily had the bell of the sickroom rung in order to summon back the community. Suddenly she rose up, as though called by a mysterious voice, opened her eyes and fixed them, radiant with heavenly joy and unspeakable happiness, upon a spot a little above the statue of Our Lady. The sisters were back in time to kneel down by the bed and witness the ecstasy of the last moment. The face of our saint had regained its natural, healthy, lily color; her eyes gazed upwards, radiant and expressing a happiness which exceeded all her expectations. She made movements with her head, as though being repeatedly wounded in a divine manner by a dart of love. Soeur Marie de l'Eucharistie held a burning candle close to her eyes in order to see this exalted gaze closely in the light of the candle; her eyelids did not flicker. Immediately after this ecstasy, which lasted for the space of a Credo, she closed her eyes and breathed her last sigh. It was about twenty minutes past seven."

Another of her sisters, Geneviève, notes:

"Afterwards I have often tried to analyse her deathbed ecstasy, to comprehend the intensity of that look, which was much more than a look of bliss, for it expressed at the same time a great *wonder* . . . On the one hand, she was, as the Gospel says, found worthy to stand before the son of man (Lk. 21, 36), and on the other, she saw that the overwhelming nature of her joy far exceeded her immeasurable longings, for this expression of unspeakable wonder was accompanied by a shuddering of her entire being; she seemed incapable of bearing the force of so much love, like someone exposed to repeated attack who in his weakness remains joyfully unconquered. It was too much for her; she closed her eyes and breathed her last sigh."

It is no small thing to see Jesus, and in a certain sense, this is but the first step, for by his presence he has accomplished a great work: the kingdom is now complete. What will he do with it? He will, as it were, embrace in one gesture all those whom he ransomed with his blood, and turn towards him whom he loves: the Father. "Then comes the end, when he delivers the kingdom to God the Father." [22] Then "the righteous will shine like the sun in the kingdom of their Father." [23] A number of authors interpret this "transfer" so literally that they think that Jesus will then disappear from the scene for good. This is impossible; Jesus will be the light of the universe for all eternity. Let us now ponder on this for a while.

[19] Cf. 1 Cor. 2, 9.
[20] Another interpretation translates "him" by God (the Father). In any case the sight of the Father is essential (cf. 1 Cor. 13, 12).
[21] Cf. The famous "Twelfth Chapter" of the *Story of a Soul.*
[22] 1 Cor. 15, 24.
[23] Mt. 13, 43.

The Light of the Re-Created Universe

Could it be possible that Jesus' role is played out with the last judgment? Can someone who has been our only mediator throughout the centuries disappear from our eyes and hearts when God becomes "everything" to everyone? [24] If so, we should be forced to conclude that all ties of family and friendship, all the contacts we had on earth, even the human community itself, will be nonexistent in "heaven." Can there be such a great difference between "this world" and the "next"?

No, the fact that Jesus "transfers" the kingdom to God must be understood in a biblical sense. When God acts, he does not eliminate the earthly causes and freedoms. When Christ builds his Church upon the rock, Peter, this in no way prevents him from remaining himself the cornerstone.[25] The apostles are shepherds, but this does not detract from Jesus' position as the only shepherd.[26] Similarly, the fact that *God the Father* is the deliberate, uninterrupted culminating point of all heavenly experience tends rather to suggest that the entire atmosphere of eternity will be pervaded with Christ.

What form will this "Christ-atmosphere" take? One of the first indications may be found in what might be called the physical nature of the framework. Admittedly, the New Testament texts do not always give the same impression. The Second Epistle of Peter, for example, strongly emphasizes the difference between our world now and "the new heaven and the new earth," which will only be brought about by a complete dissolution of our present world.[27] On the other hand, there is the generally recognized fact that our resurrection will be physical. Paul and John lay greatest stress on the fact that our resurrection must be conceived after the model of Jesus' own; "He is the firstborn from the dead, that in everything he might be preeminent." [28] The Apocalypse, too, employs the title, "firstborn of the dead," [29] but much stronger still is the statement: "I am the resurrection and the life." [30]

This Christ-reflection through an identical resurrection extends to cover the whole of creation, for all that has been created waits with eager longing to share in the glorious liberty of the sons of God.[31] Here, we have a more positive or, more accurately speaking, a more progressively continuous appreciation of the material. All the achievements of mind and will, race and people, art and beauty, the mysteries of number and of form, of the atom and the galaxies, will be revealed and glorified, and through man who has risen again in Christ,[32] will bear the stamp of the Son of God.

This same truth is revealed in the Apocalypse in an entirely different manner. We shall dwell in a gigantic city called new Jerusalem; it has come down from heaven and occupies a surface of about 3 million sq. miles, roughly the size of the earth as it was known then, and thus of the universe.[33] It is a city of Christ, for the river which is the source of life for the trees which yield fruit each month and of which the leaves are for the healing of the nations, flows from the throne of God and of the lamb.[34] Indeed, Christ's name [35] is on everyone's forehead. The city gates, shining jewels set in walls of precious stones, must never be closed. Peace reigns there, the peace preached and brought about by Jesus.[36] In short, the source and the goal of the beauty and happiness of this eternal city is Jesus; the new Jerusalem is a bride adorned for her husband.[37]

Another, more qualitative aspect, is the fullness of life. Paul and the Apocalypse express it in terms of war. Jesus defeats and destroys death, "the last enemy." [38] The fruit which ripens every month on the tree is, of course, nothing but the feeling of immortality mentioned in the story of paradise; and the sap comes from the lamb.[39] There is perfect peace, total safety in Christ, clearly demonstrated in the resurrection of the adult, Lazarus, and expressed more generally at the beginning of St. John's gospel: "In him is life." [40] Immortality, absence of darkness or fear are negative concepts to convey this superabundance of life, but it is a fullness derived from Christ.[41] He is glorified in his saints [42] just as the condition of being "condemned to eternal perdition" expressed in Christological terms is an "exclusion from the presence of the Lord," being separated from him.[43]

[24] 1 Cor. 15, 28.
[25] Eph. 2, 20; cf. 1 Pet. 2, 6-7.
[26] Cf. 1 Pet. 2, 25 with 5, 1-4.
[27] 2 Pet. 3, 10-14.
[28] Col. 1, 18; cf. Rom. 8, 29; 1 Cor. 15, 20.
[29] Rev. 1, 5.
[30] Jn. 11, 25.
[31] Rom. 8, 18, 25.
[32] Rom. 8, 11.
[33] Rev. 21, 16.

[34] Rev. 22, 1.
[35] 2 Pet. 3, 10-14.
[36] Rev. 21, 25.
[37] Rev. 21, 2.
[38] 1 Cor. 15, 24-26 54-56; Rev. 20, 14.
[39] Gen. 2, 9; 3, 22; Rev. 22, 1-2.
[40] Jn. 1, 14.
[41] Col. 1, 19-20.
[42] 2 Thess. 1, 10.
[43] 2 Thess. 1, 9; Mt. 25, 41.

Finally and above all, this re-created universe is the place where God and man can meet and live together. Yet here too, Jesus has an essential part to play. He has called this being-together a feast. The Father is the host and ultimately the focal point of every life and heart. But no one can forget that it is a *marriage feast*,[44] for the son being married is Jesus, and the bride who, her whole life long, inspired by the Spirit, has longed for this moment is the Church. No longer need she say, "Jesus, come." [45]

The essence of this "eternal life" [46] is defined almost abstractly by Matthew as being "in the joy of the Lord." [47] Paul says that we will understand God as we are now understood by him.[48] These definitions are profound, for our comprehension and our joy comprise our entire being. Neither mentions Jesus by name, but John resolves all doubts. Eternal life is to know the Father and Jesus Christ who was sent by the Father.[49] If it is indeed the Father's house to which we are admitted, it is Jesus who returns to take us with him, so that we may be with him forever.[50]

This is why the joyful songs of praise of the Apocalypse are addressed alternately to the Father and the lamb.[51] The most striking point of all is that the two symbols of religious experience and of human existence—the temple and light—are always applied to both in indissoluble unity: John admits that he has seen no temple in the new Jerusalem, "for its temple is the Lord God the almighty *and the lamb*. And the city has no need of sun or moon to shine upon it, for the glory of God is its light and its lamp is the lamb." [52]

In that new universe, therefore, the most exalted intuitions and religious emotions of the sanctuaries of all religions throughout human history will fade. The words of the best of the Christian mystics will be as the prattling of children. Every emotion aroused by love in human hearts, from joyful surprise and grateful admiration, to the most sacred loyalty and perpetual union, will suddenly find its deepest explanation in the mystery which it so poorly prefigured. Everyone at last will be able to love on both the horizontal and the vertical plane, to be active and receptive, deeply personal

---

44 Mt. 22, 1-2; 25, 1-12; cf. 9, 15; Jn. 3, 29.

45 Rev. 22, 17.20.

46 We find this expression particularly in 2 Cor. 4, a result of Paul's "dialogue" with the Greek world.

47 Mt. 25, 31; "Lord" refers here to God the Father.

48 1 Cor. 13, 12.

49 Jn. 17, 3.

50 Jn. 14, 2-3; cf. 17, 24.

51 Cf. Rev. 4-7.

52 Rev. 21, 22-23.

and intimately bound up with the community. Happiness will no longer be based on naïveté, and the clear-seeing will abandon their skepticism. And in that new universe, where there will be no more darkness, the Father will be all in all and Jesus "the true light that enlightens every man." [53]

[53] Jn. 1, 9.

Epilogue

PARABLE OF THE CIRCUS

One day, a circus came to the village. The people in the fields raised their heads and watched the wagons solemnly rolling towards the village square. The women came out of their houses and stared wide-eyed at the colorful acrobats and clowns. A whole troup of children, wild with excitement, ran shouting alongside the travelling cages with their monkeys, leopards, and lions and surreptitiously stroked the stiff legs of the elephants which cheerfully waved their trunks.

With bated breath, they waited while the tents and stands were put up with all possible speed. Then, the circus manager appeared with a notice board: "Entry—One price only: 50¢." The children's faces dropped. They were disappointed. But just then a car drove up; a handsome, simply dressed man stepped out, looked at the children and ordered the chauffeur to drive away. "Why are you all looking so sad?" he asked the children.

"Because we have no money for the circus."

"I'll see about that," he said, and went up to the ticket office.

There were about a hundred children waiting, and the gentleman asked for a reduction because there were so many of them. The ticket seller consulted the manager, but he stood his ground and insisted that all tickets were the same price. Then the gentleman looked at the children again and took out $50. Then he said to the children, "Here are the tickets, but on one condition: before we all go in, your must wash your hands and faces. You may also invite all the children you know to come in with us."

Then, there as an indescribable bustle of activity, one great rush to wash, with brush and soap all for the communal purification inspired by the desire to be at the big treat which was so near. The unknown gentleman himself had tied on an apron, bent, and knelt down in order to help the children who had hardly ever washed in

340

their lives. Enthusiastically, he set off at the head of a group to bring the news to the outlying districts. "Come, the circus has arrived. Wash your face and your hands, and we'll go to the circus." And three hundred children came to join them.

There was one very dirty child who came and stood at the entrance. The gentleman would not allow him in, but asked, "Why won't you wash yourself?"

"My face is my own," he snapped, "I don't take orders from anyone."

"But that was the condition. You can't go in like that, you can't just make fun of us."

But although the three hundred children came outside again with water and soap, and begged and beseeched him, he still refused. The door was shut and he remained outside.

The trumpets blared and the performance began—and went on. Just before the last act, when the children seemed to be getting a little lively because the show was almost over, the circus manager appeared. The orchestra fell silent. "Dear children," said the ringmaster, "the moment has come to let you in on a secret. The gentleman who paid for your seats and took his place among you was no stranger to the manager of the circus. He is my son. He is also our principal actor." And amid deafening cheers and applause, the man stepped forward, brilliant as the music and radiant in the full glare of the spotlights.

But it was the son himself who gave them the greatest surprise, when he had finished his exceptional number and everyone was already standing up to leave the stands. "Brothers," he said, "I am coming back. This is our last tour and soon we will return. Then our circus will settle here for good, and we will change the face of the village. Every day, we will put on a different program. You yourselves will have to join in. Ask for information at the offices of Peter Peace and Company, and do not forget to give a special greeting to our social assistant, Mary Hope. She is my mother. Good-bye, friends, I'll come back soon."

It would certainly be superfluous to elaborate on how this parable sums up the content of this book in symbolical form. The gospels outline Jesus' message for us: "Come, the kingdom is at hand." They give us an idea of his attractive personality. They introduce us to his mystery, beginning with his humble arrival in our midst and ending with the cross, where he paid the price for us, his glory and his second coming.

"The Circus" is a translation, a small attempt to render the eternal Gospel comprehensible for the people of today, while retaining all its newness. It is not a very original translation, for it owes much of its inspiration to the mission sermons of a remarkable bishop of South Chile, Bernardino Pinera.

But, more than a translation, it is perhaps a declaration of impotence. The Gospel is *too little* translated. A true translation must succeed in really bringing alive the message of Christ. The message itself is there; it is perfect and need not be invented or improved. But is it really translated? Is it accessible to the masses—the workers, the farmers, clerks, and businessmen, university graduates and ordinary newspaper readers? Has it penetrated the world of men and the women's household round?

When Jesus tells us to "go and preach the Gospel to all mankind," we can immediately define the Church as a gigantic translation undertaking. She must be constantly renewing and thus be always new herself. This is why the best Gospel translation is one's own life. We must not—and this applies first and foremost to ourselves—allow Jesus' words, which are a mountain stream of crystal clear and singing water, to be covered over by the dust of our routine preoccupations or covered under our failings. But we must also translate *together*, speak the language of all men, arrive at a dialogue.

Perhaps this children's circus expresses a more personal view: at the end of this volume of introduction and of these years of Christological study and meditation, I should like to make myself very small. I desire this: that I may one day enter the kingdom.[1] HE must increase, I must decrease.[2]

[1] Mt. 18, 3.   [2] Jn. 3, 30.